WILLIAM
MORRIS
LIBRARY

THOEMMES

JOURNALISM

CONTRIBUTIONS TO *COMMONWEAL* 1885–1890

William Morris

EDITED AND INTRODUCED BY
NICHOLAS SALMON

THOEMMES PRESS

This edition first published by Thoemmes Press, 1996

Thoemmes Press
11 Great George Street
Bristol BS1 5RR
United Kingdom

ISBN 1 85506 459 6 : Paperback

The William Morris Library Second Series
Six-volume set : Hardback : ISBN 1 85506 456 1

CONTENTS

INTRODUCTION

William Morris's achievement as a serious political commen-
tator and journalist remains largely unappreciated. The main
reason for this is that May Morris, when she edited her
father's *Collected Works* (1910–15), omitted almost all the
articles he contributed to the socialist journals *Justice* and
Commonweal. R. Page Arnot has claimed, probably with
some justification, that this was due to the publishers
discouraged the inclusion of Morris's political writings on the
grounds that they did not enhance his overall reputation.[1]
Even when May Morris published two further volumes of her
father's writings – as *William Morris: Artist, Writer, Socialist*
(1936) – she passed over his articles in favour of reprinting
more of his lectures. Subsequent collections of Morris's work
compiled by Asa Briggs, G. D. H. Cole, Holbrook Jackson,
and A. L. Morton have adopted the same approach.

   The intention of this volume, along with the *Political
Writings* which appeared in the Thoemmes Press William
Morris Library in 1994, is to rectify this situation by making
available for the first time all the important articles Morris
contributed to *Justice* and *Commonweal*. Each volume
provides the reader with a comprehensive chronological
selection of this work. The *Political Writings* contains all the
important essays he contributed to the two papers, along
with *Socialism from the Root Up* which he jointly wrote
with Ernest Belfort Bax between 1886 and 1888. The
present volume, meanwhile, reprints the numerous columns
of contemporary political comment he published in
Commonweal as 'Notes', 'Notes on Passing Events' and
'Notes on News'. The latter were written during the period

---

[1] R. Page Arnot, *William Morris: The Man and the Myth* (Lawrence &
Wishart, 1964), p. 109.

of his active involvement in the Socialist League of which the *Commonweal* was the official journal. Taken together these articles throw new light on the development of Morris's mature political vision, as well as offering unique insights into his views on contemporary issues as diverse as the Channel Tunnel, Jack the Ripper and the Irish Question. The importance of Morris's work in this field must not be underestimated. When he founded *Commonweal* it was one of only a handful of journals pioneering revolutionary socialism. Prior to 1884 proto-radical newspapers such as the *Daily News* (1846), *Reynolds News* (1850) and the *Pall Mall Gazette* (1865) had generally supported the Liberal cause. Others had advocated specific programmes of social reform like Feargus O'Connor's *Northern Star* (1837) which supported the Chartist movement. It was only when the Democratic Federation – later renamed the Social Democratic Federation after its Fourth Annual Conference on 4 August 1884 – launched its paper *Justice* on 19 January 1884 that the modern British socialist press can be said to have begun. *Justice* was joined in the same month by a monthly socialist review called *To-day*, edited by J. L. Joynes and E. Belfort Bax. Along with *Commonweal* these two papers remained, with a few lesser publications like the Norwich *Daylight* and the *Christian Socialist*, the only socialist journals of any importance until the arrival of the *Labour Elector* (1888), Annie Besant's *The Link* (1888) and Keir Hardie's weekly *Labour Leader* (1894). The Labour Party remained without a daily newspaper until the launch of the *Daily Herald* and *Daily Citizen* in 1912.[2]

The first edition of the eight-page monthly *Commonweal* appeared in February 1885 with Morris as editor and Edward Aveling as sub-editor (the latter was subsequently replaced by E. Belfort Bax and then H. H. Sparling). From the April 1885 edition the paper was extended briefly to twelve pages by the addition of a four-page supplement. These supplements were included with all the editions up until September 1885, after which the paper reverted to its

---

[2]   Stephen Koss, *The Rise and Fall of the Political Press in Britain* (Fontana, 1990), p. 500.

original format. It became an eight-page weekly on 1 May 1886. Morris served as editor of the paper until the Sixth Annual Conference of the League in May 1890 when he was replaced by David Nicoll. Shortly after this the paper returned to being a monthly publication.

Some of Morris's contemporaries felt that he would have preferred to have delegated the editorial responsibilities of *Commonweal* to someone else in the League. John Bruce Glasier recalled, in his book *William Morris and the Early Days of the Socialist Movement* (1921), that 'Morris undertook the editorship of the *Commonweal* with great reluctance, and only because there was no one else who had the time or capacity for the work who could be entrusted with it'.[3] He went on to add that in making his decision Morris was also obliged to take into account practical considerations: 'as he knew that he would have to be financially responsible for the paper, it was, of course, rather important, in view of the laws of sedition and libel that he should have control of its contents.'[4]

Nevertheless, under Morris's editorship the paper justifiably took its place as one of the foremost socialist journals. E. P. Thompson, in *William Morris: Romantic to Revolutionary*, described it as 'a remarkable paper' and added that it 'would rank among the best of [the] socialist journals at least until 1888 or 1889'.[5] This view was shared by many of Morris's comrades in the League. John Bruce Glasier, in an article entitled 'Humours of Propaganda' published in *Commonweal* on 28 October 1888, recalled how one street-seller in Glasgow advertised it as the best 'Socialist paper in the country. Edited by William Morris, the greatest poet, painter, designer, and art critic of the age.'

Such was Morris's reputation in the movement that he was able to attract contributions from many of the most

---

[3] John Bruce Glasier, *William Morris and the Early Days of the Socialist Movement* (Longmans, 1921), p. 177. This book has now been reprinted with a new introduction by Peter Faulkner as volume 7 in the Thoemmes Press *William Morris Library*.

[4] *William Morris and the Early Days of the Socialist Movement*, p. 177.

[5] E. P. Thompson, *William Morris: Romantic to Revolutionary* (Pantheon, 1977), pp. 392–3.

Introduction

important socialist theorists. Amongst those who wrote articles for the paper during its first year were Edward Aveling, E. Belfort Bax, E. T. Craig, Frederick Engels, Laurence Grönlund, Frank Kitz, Paul Lafargue, Joseph Lane, Eleanor Marx, Andreas Scheu, George Bernard Shaw and Sergius Stepniak. Morris was particularly keen to encourage the accurate dissemination of Marxist theory. Edward Aveling's contribution to the early editions of *Commonweal*, for example, was a series of articles entitled 'Lessons in Socialism' which were described as 'the first attempt to put the ideas of Marx...before the English people in their own language'.[6] These articles were supplemented by a series of lectures on *Das Kapital* that Morris organized on behalf of the Socialist League at the South Place Institute. Later he was to publish an article by Engels – entitled 'How Not To Translate Marx' – which attacked the imprecise nature of the first installment of an English translation of *Das Kapital* which had appeared in *To-day* in October 1885. This trans-lation, which was advertised as by 'John Broadhouse', was in fact the work of H. M. Hyndman.[7]

The first issue of *Commonweal* – which went to a second edition – sold 5,000 copies. According to the Socialist League's *Minutes* the circulation then stabilized at between 2,000 and 3,000 copies during its most successful period between 1886 and 1888. The circulation subsequently went into decline as a result of the increasing divisions within the League and competition from rival papers such as H. H. Champion's *Labour Elector* (1888) and the *Yorkshire Factory Times* (1889). The circulation would undoubtedly have been far higher if the League had possessed an efficient national distribution system. As it was, sales depended on the efforts of the various provincial branches and the co-operation of local newsagents. Many of the latter were far from sympathetic to the socialist cause and refused to stock the paper. The fact that sales remained so high was largely due to the efforts of Morris who personally coordinated the

---

[6] *Commonweal*, April 1885, p. 21.

[7] Hal Draper, *The Marx-Engels Chronicle* (Schocken, 1985), p. 240.

distribution of the paper from London. His correspondence with Glasier, Glasse and Mahon reveals him constantly devising schemes to raise funds for the paper and urging the branches to increase its circulation.

A difference of opinion exists over the quality of Morris's contributions to the paper. Glasier, writing in the 1920s, felt that Morris's journalistic writings were 'often laboriously censorious' as 'he was expected to write, week after week, about the tiresome ... incidents and controversies of Gladstone-Salisbury politics – a task into which he could put no heart'.[8] George Bernard Shaw made much the same point. In his essay 'Morris as I Knew Him' he claimed it was a 'grievous task for him ... to keep *The Commonweal*, the weekly paper of the League, going from number to number with topical paragraphs. Some of the stuff thus produced went to the rock bottom truth of the situation; but it did not come easily or happily.'[9]

Understandably, Morris's daughter May was more impressed with her father's achievement. In *William Morris: Artist, Writer, Socialist* she claimed his articles for *Commonweal* showed 'him trying every movement, every scheme, every foreign war of annexation, by the light of his own directness of principle, and expressing in the plainest language his distrust of opportunism that involves giving way in principle'.[10] E. Belfort Bax, who served for a time at sub-editor of *Commonweal*, certainly agreed with this assessment. In his autobiographical *Reminiscences and Reflexions* (1918) he deplored the fact that Morris's journalism had been ignored and suggested that a 'selection of his political articles ... might be worth republishing in book-form, as likely to be interesting to his many admirers'.[11]

---

[8] *William Morris and the Early Days of the Socialist Movement, op. cit.*, p. 178.

[9] May Morris, *William Morris: Artist, Writer, Socialist* (Blackwell, 1936), vol. 2, p. xxxix.

[10] *ibid.*, vol. 2, p. 288.

[11] E. Belfort Bax, *Reminiscences and Reflexions of a Mid and Late Victorian* (George Allen & Unwin, 1918), p. 82.

What is beyond doubt is that Morris's articles in *Commonweal* constitute one of the most powerful and sustained attacks ever made on the nineteenth-century capitalist system. They were inspired by his implacable belief that socialists should abstain from all forms of electioneering and 'treat Parliament as a representative of the enemy'.[12] His central aim in his weekly 'Notes on News' column was to attract new recruits to the socialist cause by showing how the bourgeois executive, irrespective of which party was in power, always governed in its own class interests. He also hoped to dissuade socialists from ignoring the existence of the class war and attempting to bring about the social revolution by parliamentary methods.

It was for this reason that Morris seized every opportunity in *Commonweal* to discredit measures that were promoted by politicians and philanthropists as benefiting the working classes. One of the most popular of these was a scheme to provide rural labourers with allotments so they could supplement their wages by growing their own food. This gained widespread support on both sides of the house and was promoted in the bourgeois press as a 'socialistic' measure. In fact both parties supported the scheme for their own political reasons. The Liberals hoped that the purchase of the land required for the allotments would help break-up the old aristocratic estates and hasten the demise of landlordism. The Conservatives, on the other hand, were keen to halt the drift of the rural labourers to the towns. They hoped that allotments and smallholdings would restore the attractions of agricultural labouring, encourage thrift and reduce rural crimes like poaching. It was Salisbury's Conservative government who finally introduced an Allotment Bill in 1887.

Many radicals actively supported this Bill on the grounds that it sought to improve the living standards of the rural labourers at the expense of their landlords. Morris, on the other hand, argued that far from being progressive the

---

[12]   *The Collected Letters of William Morris*, ed. Norman Kelvin (Princeton University Press, 1987), vol. 2, p. 656.

measure was essentially reactionary: 'J. S. Mill said all that was necessary when he said it was simply allowing the labourers to work to pay their own poor-rates. The bill is really in the interests of the employing farmers and the rank-renting landlords.'[13] He went on to suggest that it should be viewed as part of a conspiracy by the bourgeoisie to disguise the widening gap in wealth between the middle and working classes by encouraging a process of embourgeoisement. As he wrote, 'this allotment swindle...is a part of the regular plan of holding down discontent which specially characterises this second half of the nineteenth century.... Briefly it means the plan of raising the condition of a part of the working class at the expense of the whole class; it would create an aristocracy of labour.'[14] The chief function of this 'aristocracy of labour', he argued, would be to act as a buffer between the degraded proletariat and the bourgeoisie, thus hindering the potential growth of class consciousness.

Another popular measure Morris frequently attacked in the columns of *Commonweal* was emigration. Inspired by J. R. Seeley's *The Expansion of England* (1883), which advocated emigration to Britain's English-speaking colonies, a whole series of emigration proposals were put forward with great success in the 1880s. Indeed, the number of people from Great Britain and Ireland who emigrated during the decade was phenomenal. Between 1881 and 1890 no less than 3,259,000 people – 9.3 per cent of the population – left the country to begin new lives in the United States, Canada and Australia. Emigration was a particularly attractive policy for the government as it not only contributed to the efficient administration of Britain's colonial empire but also offered a practical means of relieving the problems of unemployment and poverty at home.

The socialists were well aware that emigration was an extremely effective counter-revolutionary ploy. It was often the most discontented workers who were attracted by the idea of starting a new life in the colonies. Morris recognized

[13] *Commonweal*, 20 August 1887, p. 265.

[14] *ibid.*, February 1886, p. 12.

this, and warned the readers of *Commonweal* that if 'those who are most keenly stung by the evils of class domination, and at the same time have energy to resist them, leave the country which is the very forge of class domination, their desertion will surely put off the Revolution'.[15] He urged his readers to see emigration as a convenient means for the bourgeoisie to absolve themselves from the worst consequences of capitalistic exploitation: 'when our "State" nurses emigration, and when private capitalists suggest the nursing and egg on poor men to emigrate, their intention is only to get rid temporarily of *their* responsibility and trouble over people thrown out of work by the system of artificial famine...which they are determined to uphold.'[16] When the National Association for the Promotion of State Colonisation – or, as Morris dubbed it sarcastically, the Society for the Punishment of Poverty by Transportation – held its annual conference in 1888 he pointed out the hypocrisy of its leaders who claimed to be working on behalf of the poor, while, as he put it, really being motivated by a desire 'to get rid of all elements of discontent, that is to say, those whom they and their idleness have made poor and helpless'.[17]

Morris also had nothing but contempt for well-meaning philanthropists who advocated the creation of model communities *within* the existing capitalist system as a means of eradicating poverty and unemployment. In 1887 Herbert Mills, inspired by a study of the 'beggar colonies' that had been established in Holland and Germany, devised a more humane system based on the same lines which he euphemistically termed 'Home Colonisation'. He proposed that a fund should be set up to purchase cheap land in England on which to settle poor families and individuals chosen by the Charity Organization Society. Life on these 'communities' was to be strictly regulated, with all the colonists working three hours each day in return for a subsistence existence which would be supplemented by the cultivation of a small plot of land. Each

---

[15] *Commonweal*, May 1885, p. 35.

[16] *ibid.*, 5 June 1886, p. 73.

[17] *ibid.*, 7 July 1888, p. 209.

community would be entirely self-sufficient and would only sell the surplus it produced.

On the face of it Mills' communities appeared to be based on ideas borrowed from utopian socialists like Fourier and Owen. However, in reality, Mills was not advocating cooperation amongst equals but a vigorous form of social control administered along evangelical lines. As Morris pointed out in *Commonweal*, a similar scheme in Berlin had been no rural idyll but had involved 'people by dint of working eleven hours a-day and a strong dose of church to boot, all under strict discipline, ... to earn a splendid livelihood of 61/2d. per diem'.[18] Morris went on to dismiss Mills' proposals – in the same way as he had those of Fourier and Owen – on the grounds that the social revolution could only be accomplished by destroying the whole capitalist system: 'if Mr Mills' scheme is taken up, it will be as an evasion of the demand of the Socialists that monopoly in the means of production should cease. And it is quite as certain, as has been said over and over again, in these columns, that this demand will only be yielded on compulsion. A proprietary class neither will nor can yield its privileges voluntarily.'[19]

One scheme that did reach fruition was the building of the Beaumont Hall, or People's Palace as it was pompously referred to, in the East End of London. This was designed to bring art and culture to one of the most deprived areas of the capital. The bourgeois press promoted the People's Palace as an example of middle-class philanthropic paternalism. As the leader writer in *The Times* put in on 14 May 1887, the day that Queen Victoria officiated at its opening, it was an example of 'practical Socialism which works by co-operation and kindness, and not by envy and antagonism'. The writer conveniently omitted to mention that the Queen was continually jeered and hooted at as she made her way through the East End streets. Morris dismissed the whole scheme as hypocrisy of the most blatant kind: 'All this People's Palace

[18] *Commonweal*, 3 December 1887, p. 385.

[19] *ibid.*, 31 December 1887, p. 417.

business means is that "the people" are perforce such strangers to orderliness, cleanliness and decency, let alone art and beauty, in their own dwellings, that the upper classes, who force them into this life of degradation, do now and then bethink them if they cannot provide them with a place where they can play at being comfortable, so long as they behave like good children, between the spells of their stupid hopeless weary work and their miserable and hideous "homes".[20]

The only significant progressive reform to be passed during the period of Morris's editorship of *Commonweal* was the Local Government Act of 1888. This established the County Councils who assumed control of local services such as the highways, justice and sanitation which had previously been administered by ad hoc bodies dominated by the local gentry. The measure was greeted with approval by radicals and parliamentary socialists who hoped it would finally destroy the landlords' control over local affairs. The Local Government Act was particularly welcomed by the Fabians, who believed that the first step towards State Socialism was the creation of an efficient administrative structure at a local level. As George Bernard Shaw put it in the *Fabian Essays*, 'without efficient local machinery the replacing of private enterprise by State enterprise is out of the question'.[21]

Given Morris's anti-parliamentary stance it is hardly surprising that he opposed the measure on the grounds that it was another bourgeois ploy aimed at distracting the socialists from their primary task of educating the workers in revolutionary socialism. He also argued that the composition of the new County Councils was unlikely to make them progressive bodies: 'it must be a very sanguine Socialist indeed who can really believe that they will have any inclination to go beyond the well understood lines of very moderate "reform", which will make no monopolist in the least in the world anxious about the safety of his heart – *i.e.* his purse.'[22] In the context of the late 1880s there was some

---

[20] *Commonweal*, 13 November 1886, p. 257.

[21] Quoted in *A Hundred Years Ago: Britain in the 1880s,* by Colin Ford and Brian Harrison (Allen Page/Penguin, 1983), p. 204.

[22] *Commonweal*, 26 January 1889, p. 25.

justification for this criticism. The County Councils that were elected in the rural south and west of England continued to be dominated by the local gentry and their representatives. Indeed, only half of the 3,240 electoral divisions in England was contested at the elections held in 1889.

In the towns and cities, however, the elections were to prove a boost to the radicals and parliamentary socialists. This was most obvious in the new London County Council where a coalition of Lib-Lab 'progressives' was able to introduce a number of reforms based on those pioneered by northern authorities. These measures included the building of new housing for the poor and an increase in the wages of staff employed by the local authority. The Lib-Lab's progressive policy did a great deal to raise the profile of the Fabians and other parliamentary socialists. Morris ignored these achievements in *Commonweal*. On the few occasions he did refer to the London County Council it was to dismiss it as a trivial body. He gave prominence to any of its actions which could be construed as reactionary. Amongst these he referred to its decision to ban the public from its committee meetings and its consideration of a report by its Licensing Committee suggesting that Music Hall songs should be censored. These comments are amongst the least impressive of Morris's writings for *Commonweal* and reflect his growing isolation in the movement over the issue.

Morris was most effective as a journalist when analysing government policies which could be interpreted as repressive or indicative of the imminent break-up of capitalism. In this respect he was often aided by the actions of the authorities. One of the socialists' best means of making contact with the workers was to hold regular outdoor meetings in the East End of London. Morris was a frequent speaker at these meetings and could be found most Sundays at the pitches organized by the Hammersmith Branch of the League at Walham Green, Weltje Road and at the end of Hammersmith Bridge. For a time these meetings were tolerated by the authorities. However, this attitude changed in May 1885 when the police broke into the International Socialist Working Men's Club in Stephen's Mews, Tottenham Court

Road, and arrested over fifty of its members. Soon after this the police disrupted the open-air meetings of the Social Democratic Federation in Dod Street and arrested several speakers for obstruction. Jack Williams, who refused to pay his fine, was sentenced to a month's hard labour. Thereafter, hardly a week went by without further arrests for 'obstruction'. Even Morris was summoned on 18 July 1886 for 'wilfully obstruct[ing] the free passage on the public footway and Highway at Bell Street, Marylebone, by placing himself upon a stand for the purpose of delivering an address'.[23] This campaign of intimidation was to culminate on 13 November 1887 when the police attacked a massive demonstration in favour of free speech held in Trafalgar Square. 'Bloody Sunday', as it subsequently became known, resulted in two deaths and 200 injuries.

The free speech campaign won a great deal of popular support for the socialists. It was evident to most observers that their meetings were being attacked by the police as part of a concerted attempt to suppress their political activities. As Morris wrote in *Commonweal*: 'It ought to be quite obvious to those who, though not Socialists, are prepared to defend freedom of speech in England, that this is mere persecution for opinion.'[24] He also claimed that the actions of the police were aiding the socialists by undermining many workers' faith in the forces of law and order and engendering class hatred. This was probably true as the radical press reported numerous incidents of police brutality and of prisoners being beaten in their cells after their arrest. For a time Morris even believed that the government's persistent suppression of free speech could 'become so unbearable that it will *force* the revolution to break all bounds and sweep it away'.[25]

Despite the importance of the free speech campaign, the government's use of coercion was most obvious in Ireland. Throughout the early 1880s the Irish nationalists had

[23] Fiona MacCarthy reproduces this summons as illustration 8 in her book *William Morris: A Life for Our Time* (Faber & Faber, 1994).

[24] *Commonweal*, 8 September 1888, p. 281.

[25] *ibid.*, 3 December 1887, p. 385.

pursued an effective campaign in support of their demand for Home Rule. Eventually Gladstone had been converted to their cause and in April 1886 had introduced an Irish Home Rule Bill in parliament designed to give self-government to the province. After one of the most acrimonious debates in British political history this Bill was defeated on its second reading on 7 June 1886 by a combination of Conservative and Liberal MPs who supported the Union. Following this defeat the Liberals resigned and were replaced by a new Conservative administration led by Salisbury.

The defeat of the Bill led to an upsurge of violence in Ireland. Serious riots broke out in Belfast which lasted throughout the summer of 1886. In November, further civil disobedience was encouraged by O'Brien and Dillon when they drew up their 'Plan of Campaign' with the aim of organizing the Irish tenants in opposition to the landlords. The government responded by arresting the leaders of the Plan of Campaign and putting them on trial in Dublin in February 1887. The authorities were greatly embarrassed when the jury failed to reach a verdict. Faced with a rapidly deteriorating situation, Salisbury appointed A. J. Balfour as Chief Secretary for Ireland on 5 March. Balfour's first act was to introduce a Crimes Bill for Ireland which gave the police greatly increased powers to arrest and detain suspected terrorists. The police also began to use force when breaking-up peaceful demonstrations. One of the first examples of this occurred at Mitchelstown in Cork on 9 September 1887 when they fired on a crowd killing one man and wounding many others. Two other men died later from their wounds.

Morris followed the government's policy of coercion in Ireland closely in his 'Notes on News' column in *Commonweal*. He presented the government as defending middle class interests at the expense of the rights of the workers: 'the Coercion Bill...is an impudent attack on the most elementary liberties of the country. The Parliamentary sham-fight of compromise and expediency has once more served the purpose it is sustained for, that is keeping the people down.'[26] He also pointed out to his readers the

[26] *Commonweal*, 28 May 1887, p. 172.

hypocrisy of the Liberal Party condemning the Crimes Bill when they had passed a similar measure following the Phoenix Park murders in 1882. As he put it in *Commonweal* in May 1888, these 'very same men, when *they* were opposed by the Irish people, acted much in the same way as those whom they now condemn, and would do so again if occasion served'.[27]

On the other hand he was impressed by the Irish people's determination to pursue their demand for full independence from Britain. He took every opportunity in *Commonweal* to encourage the agitation for Irish Home Rule on the grounds that if it were granted it would threaten the integrity of the British Empire on which the whole capitalist system depended. He also felt that the agitation offered encouragement to the socialists' own propaganda campaign by proving that the workers could be successfully organized in opposition to the bourgeois executive.

Morris linked the free speech campaign in Britain and coercion in Ireland to a wider international trend towards repression. In support of this claim he cited the anti-socialist laws in Germany, the threat to political asylum in Switzerland and proposed curbs on immigration into the United States. However, for the socialists the most obvious example of foreign repression was the case of the Chicago Anarchists. On 4 May 1886 anarchist leaders had called a meeting in Chicago's Haymarket Square to protest at the killing of four strikers by the police outside the McCormick Harvester Works. When a detachment of 180 police attempted to disperse the crowd at this meeting a bomb was thrown that killed seven police officers. The police responded by firing into the crowd killing several innocent people. The authorities subsequently arrested eight prominent Chicago Anarchist leaders despite the fact that only one of them had been present at the time the bomb was thrown and he had been addressing the crowd. After a protracted legal battle four of the men were hanged in October 1887 and three others given long jail sentences. The eighth committed suicide in his cell.

[27] *Commonweal*, 26 May 1888, p. 161.

The severity of the sentences passed on the Chicago Anarchists had a profound effect on the British socialist movement. While the socialists were well aware of the petty perjuries and injustices that took place in the English courts, their own speakers were rarely sentenced to more than a few months' imprisonment. The fact that the anarchists had been prosecuted for their ideas rather than their actions immediately elevated them to the status of martyrs. As Morris wrote in an article published in *Commonweal* to commemorate the first anniversary of their death: 'There was *no* real evidence offered or required for the condemnation of our comrades: their guilt was clear enough – they were the friends and fellow-agitators of the workmen on strike; that was enough.'[28] Elsewhere he was to add that 'these men who have dared to speak of freedom to the republican people of America [have been]... sacrificed to that spirit of cold cruelty, heartless and careless at once, which is one of the most notable characteristics of American commercialism'.[29] Engels even thought that the episode had finally destroyed the illusion 'that America stood *above* class antagonisms and struggles'.[30] Ironically, as far as Morris was concerned, the incident encouraged many of his close colleagues to abandon socialism in favour of anarchism and thus contributed to the collapse of the Socialist League.

Although most of Morris's articles in *Commonweal* were aimed at discrediting the workings of the constitutional system he also took great satisfaction in ridiculing prominent Liberal politicians, radicals and working-class leaders. One of those he most often attacked was the American economist Henry George. Morris's attitude to George underwent a profound change during the mid-1880s. In 1882 he had read with enthusiasm George's *Progress and Poverty*; a book which Marx described as 'significant because it is a first, if unsuccessful attempt at emancipation from the orthodox political economy'.[31] George's demands for a single tax and

---

[28] *Commonweal*, 10 November 1888, p. 356.

[29] *ibid*., 24 September 1887, p. 305.

[30] *The Marx-Engels Chronicle, op. cit.*, p. 244.

[31] *William Morris: Romantic to Revolutionary, op. cit.*, p. 291.

land nationalization proved extremely popular amongst intellectuals and advanced radicals, and, according to E. P. Thompson, 100,000 copies of the book were sold in England between 1881 and 1883. At first Morris was impressed by George's efforts as a pioneering socialist. In an article published in *Justice* in 1884, following the latter's second lecture tour of Britain, he had praised George's socialistic aspirations and oratorical skills and ended 'we English Socialists therefore give a hearty farewell to our friend and noble fellow-worker the American Henry George'.[32]

However, it was not long before Morris began to criticize George on ideological grounds. Amongst theoretical socialists George's primitive ideas about land nationalization and tax reform were rapidly superseded by Marxism with its emphasis on the class war. At the same time George was further discredited when establishment figures like John Morley, Herbert Spencer and Joseph Chamberlain seized on his outdated ideas as the acceptable face of socialism. Morris lost what little faith he had in George when the latter stood for election as the Mayor of New York on a programme promoted as socialistic but in reality no more than a series of radical reforms. By the time George returned to England on a third lecture tour in 1888 Morris no longer had any delusions: 'Mr Henry George has come to England once more with his old pretensions to Socialism abandoned, but clinging obstinately to his old economical heresies, with which in past days he used to weave a veil of vague socialistic aspiration and eloquence.'[33] He went on to add: 'To be a forward politician; to make a great agitation, clamouring for a great change which would change nothing in the life of the toiling people; but which happily cannot by itself be attempted even. This seems now Mr George's career, after all his big words.'[34]

Other popular working-class leaders and radicals to be regularly attacked by Morris in the columns of *Commonweal*

---

[32] *Justice*, 5 April 1884, p. 4.

[33] *Commonweal*, 1 December 1888, p. 380.

[34] *ibid.*, 1 December 1888, p. 380.

included Joseph Arch the veteran agricultural unionist, Charles Bradlaugh ('the doughty champion of the rights of monopoly') and the aged Liberal, John Bright.[35] Without doubt Bright received the roughest treatment. Morris had first-hand knowledge of Bright's popularity as he had been present as part of the SDF's contingent at the great franchise demonstration sponsored by the London Trades Council at Hyde Park on 23 July 1884. At this meeting John Burns had made the mistake of abusing Bright, with the result that the crowd had rushed the SDF's speakers and nearly succeeded in dumping Burns in the Serpentine. Thereafter, Morris did everything he could to discredit Bright in *Commonweal*, describing him as 'one of those persons who roar out for sweeping reforms as long as there is no chance of their being realised, and draw back in terror as soon as they seem likely to come about'.[36] Even when Bright died in 1889 Morris showed little sympathy, characterizing him as 'so essentially blood, bone and soul a middle-class person, that he could not escape from the conventionalities of that class, *i.e.* from its innate hypocrisy'.[37]

Morris occasionally extended these attacks to prominent literary and intellectual figures like Matthew Arnold, Henry James and Alfred Lord Tennyson. In each case he attempted to discredit their perceived liberalism by presenting them as hangers-on of the establishment. In May 1886, for example, he launched an attack on Matthew Arnold who had just published a paper in the *Nineteenth Century* outlining his views on the Irish Question. Morris had lost what little respect he had for Arnold when the latter had accepted a Civil List pension of £250 in August 1883. Not surprisingly he dismissed Arnold's essay as 'a piece of Whig commonplace, such as may be seen in any Whig organ by the dozen, but helped out somewhat (not much) by adroitness and neatness of style'.[38] He concluded sarcastically: 'it is sad that

[35] *Commonweal*, 9 July 1887, p. 217.

[36] *ibid.*, 11 December 1886, p. 297.

[37] *ibid.*, 6 April 1889, p. 105.

[38] *ibid.*, 8 May 1886, p. 41.

a man who once had a genuine, not copious poetic gift, should narrow himself to the limits of such a poor world of pedantry and hypocrisy as the cultured middle-class is; that culture should greatly ignore the struggles and aspirations of the greater part of humanity, and elect at last to live and die in a flunkey's coat.'[39]

Of particular interest are Morris's comments on two of the literary controversies of the period. The first of these was the prosecution and conviction of Henry Vizetelly in 1888 for offending public morals by publishing English translations of Zola's novels. It has generally been argued that Morris, like Kropotkin and Engels, dismissed contemporary realist fiction out of hand as bourgeois and anti-proletarian. One would have assumed, therefore, that Morris would have had little sympathy with Zola's naturalistic fiction. This was not the case. In fact Morris expressed guarded praise for works such as *Germinal* for presenting 'a true picture of the life which our civilisation forces on labouring men'.[40] Although he had little sympathy with the plight of Vizetelly, whom he dismissed as 'a mere capitalist publisher', he defended Zola against the charge that his works were in bad taste: 'What is good enough to be done is good enough to be told of; and I think it is but fair to assume (since the books are undoubtedly powerful) that he is not merely wanton in writing them, but wishes to show modern Society what a foul beast it is. On these grounds he may claim at least the pardon accorded to the hearty good-humoured grossnesses of Shakespeare and Chaucer.'[41]

Morris made much the same point when he considered the mixed response to Ibsen's play *A Doll's House* which opened at the Novelty Theatre on 7 June 1889. Many respectable critics professed themselves shocked, and argued that Nora – the central character in the play – was 'a young woman of criminal proclivities'. The socialists, on the other hand, were delighted with the play which they saw as aiding their own

[39] *Commonweal*, 8 May 1886, p. 41.

[40] *ibid.*, 25 August 1888, p. 265.

[41] *ibid.*, 10 November 1888, p. 356.

Introduction xxv

propaganda programme. Morris attributed this difference in
critical perception to the play's realism: 'it is a piece of the
truth about modern society clearly and forcibly put.
Therefore clearly it doesn't suit the critics, who are parasites
of the band of robbers called modern society.'[42] He also
praised Ibsen's optimistic qualities: 'the representation of the
corruption of society carries with it in Ibsen's works
aspiration for a better state of affairs.'[43]

Despite the implacable anti-parliamentary stance Morris
adopted in *Commonweal*, he did not confine himself to
attacking the constitutional system and its supporters. He
was also quick to praise genuine attempts by the workers to
organize themselves in effective opposition to the capitalists.
He was particularly impressed by the rise of the new
unionism in the late 1880s. Between 1888 and 1892 the
number of adult working-class men who belonged to a union
more than doubled from just under 10 per cent to around 20
per cent. The spread of unionism amongst unskilled workers
was quite phenomenal. When Will Thorne, Eleanor Aveling,
John Burns and Tom Mann succeeded in organizing the
gasworkers in 1889 they managed to recruit 20,000 members
in four months. This new union was so effective that the men
were able to obtain concessions from their employers without
even resorting to a strike.

Prior to the arrival of the new unionism, Morris, in
common with many other socialists, had regarded the unions
as essentially reactionary bodies which merely served as
adjuncts to capital. This hostility to the trades unions was
partly historical in origin. Trade unions on the continent had
developed alongside the spread of Marxist theory whereas in
Britain they had been established before Marxist ideas had
taken hold. The result was that British trade unions had
tended to develop as respectable liberal organizations.
Morris made this point when writing about the International
Trades Union Congress of 1888 which he described as 'a
contest between the reactionary trades unionism of the

---

[42] *Commonweal*, 22 June 1889, p. 193.

[43] *ibid.*, 22 June 1889, p. 193.

ordinary English workmen and the Socialism more or less pronounced of their Continental brethren'.[44] He was particularly scathing of British trade union officials who he claimed had only one function: '*i.e.* the spreading of the idea that the English workman has no conception of the class struggle, but admits his dependence on his master.'[45] Nevertheless, he was confident that such attitudes would change: 'The trades' unions *will* develop, even if in doing so they have to change their old form and be no longer recognisable by their once enemies, now their anxious allies, the Whig politicians.'[46]

The first indication of a change in Morris's attitude to the unions occurred in the summer of 1887 when he wrote an article in *Commonweal* following the defeat of the miners' strike. In this he noted with satisfaction that at the miners' annual gala held on 31 July 1887 a number of the men had expressed their disgust at the weakness of their leaders during the strike. Morris interpreted this as the first sign of 'a gathering determination for real union founded on a complete sense of the fact that the interests of all workers are the same, and that workers' organisations cannot stop short at merely fighting a matter of wages in the passing day; but must aim at the one thing worth aiming at, a condition of things in which the workers should control their own affairs, and not as now pay the heavy price of slavery to the employers for managing matters for them.'[47]

He was also impressed by the solidarity shown by the 672 women match workers in their dispute with Messrs Bryant & May which began on 5 July 1888. Their strike was important as it was one of the first to be successfully organized by the socialists. Annie Besant and Herbert Burrows, who jointly edited the weekly socialist paper *The Link*, were both prominent in supporting the agitation and worked tirelessly to get the girls' case taken up by the London Trades Council. The success of the strike was an early

[44] *Commonweal*, 17 November 1888, p. 361.

[45] *ibid.*, 17 November 1888, p. 361.

[46] *ibid.*, 17 September 1887, p. 297.

[47] *ibid.*, 13 August 1887, p. 257.

indication that even ordinary unskilled workers could be organized effectively in opposition to the capitalists. On 28 July 1888, shortly after the girls had gained their increase in wages, Morris wrote an article in *Commonweal* in which he assessed the significance of the strike. While he was not impressed by the concessions the girls had won, he praised the agitators and concluded 'it quite sickens one to have to call such a result of hard work for the girls and of courage on the part of the girls themselves, a victory; and yet it is one'.[48]

Morris also sensed a change in attitude within the older trade unions. At the Trades Union Congress of 1889 the TUC secretary and Liberal MP Henry Broadhurst was given a rough time by Keir Hardie. In his autobiography Broadhurst complained that 'my simplest words and actions were misconstrued and placed in a false light'.[49] Although Broadhurst was re-elected secretary on this occasion he resigned the following year. Morris interpreted the skilled workers' hostility to Broadhurst as indicative of a growing schism between the TUC's leaders and its ordinary membership: 'Mr Broadhurst's triumph and the solidifying of the Whig element in the official trades-unions does nothing but widen the gap (always a pretty wide one) between him and the workmen of the country.'[50]

The event which did most to change Morris's attitude to the unions was undoubtedly the dock strike of 1889. Backed by a gift of £30,000 donated by fellow trades unionists in Australia, the dockers were on strike for a month during the summer for their 'tanner' (6d) an hour. Once again socialists like John Burns, Tom Mann and Ben Tillett were prominent in organizing the strike. Under their leadership marches were held, literature was sold and strike pay effectively distributed to the men. The success of this strike, along with those of other workers like the building labourers and gas-workers, had a profound effect on the socialist movement. For the first time many activists began to see the organization of the

[48] *Commonweal*, 28 July 1888, p. 233.

[49] H. Broadhurst, *The Story of My Life*, (1901), p. 218.

[50] *Commonweal*, 14 September 1889, p. 289.

trade unions from *within* as a viable means of furthering the revolutionary cause. Engels even claimed in 1890 that the strikes indicated a revival of class consciousness amongst the workers and claimed that 'the *English proletariat*, newly awakened from its forty years' winter sleep, [had] *again entered the movement of its class*'.[51]

Morris also viewed the strikes as an encouraging sign of the growth of class consciousness amongst the workers. In one of his 'Notes on News' columns published in *Commonweal* on 29 August 1889 he argued that the strikes were important because they enlightened 'the workers on their real relation to the masters, and...show them that the position of antagonism between the two taken up at a time of strike, is not an accident to the system of capital and labour, but an essential of it; that the masters as a body, and whatever may be the good will of any individual, are at enmity to the men, and that that enmity must take an obvious and practical form as soon as any group of the workers attempt to be anything more than mere passive tools in the hands of the employers.'[52] Later he returned to the issue arguing that the strikes showed 'that the workers are gradually becoming conscious that their existence as workers means that they are engaged in a class war'.[53]

Where Morris differed from an increasing number of his colleagues in the Socialist League was on how best to exploit the strikes. While he welcomed them as an encouraging sign that a new stage had been reached in the class war, he did not consider them to be of sufficient importance to change the official policy of the League. Indeed, on 12 October 1889 the Executive Council issued a statement in *Commonweal* in which it urged that members of the League should 'not in any way compromise their principles by taking part in strikes [or]...to let the revolutionary propaganda suffer thereby'.[54]

---

[51] *Karl Marx and Frederick Engels: Selected Writings* (Lawrence and Wishart, 1968), p. 198.

[52] *Commonweal*, 24 August 1889, p. 265.

[53] *ibid.*, 14 December 1889, p. 393.

[54] *William Morris: Romantic to Revolutionary, op. cit.*, p. 531.

Morris continued to argue that the Socialist League should remain an independent organization educating the workers in socialism. As he wrote after the dockers had gained their victory: 'it is our business to make them understand that they never can be anything less than slaves till they have swept away class domination and privilege.... When they have learned that, their combination will both be infinitely improved as an instrument, and they will also be compelled to use it for its one real use, the realization of Socialism, to which undoubtedly this strike has been a step, as part of the labour struggle, as part of the attack on our enemy – Capitalism.'[55]

Differences of opinion on this issue contributed to the ultimate disintegration of the League. Some of the most effective activists like Tom Maguire and Alf Mattison were firmly of the opinion that the League should follow the example of Eleanor Aveling, John Burns and Tom Mann and help organize the unskilled workers from within the unions. Their success in pursuing this policy in the north revitalized the Leagues' branches in Leeds and Bradford at the expense of isolating Morris and his comrades in London. The anarchists, on the other hand, took the view that the outbreak of strikes indicated that the workers were on the brink of precipitating the revolution. They consequently set about bombarding the strikers with inflammatory literature which urged violence and insurrection. They also succeeded in gaining control of the Executive Council at the sixth annual conference of the League held on 25 May 1890. One of their first actions was to oust Morris from the editorship of *Commonweal* and replace him with David Nicoll. Henceforth the paper became an unequivocally anarchist organ. Morris was eventually forced to resign from the League, and founded the Hammersmith Socialist Society in November 1890.

The loss of control of *Commonweal* was a great disappointment for Morris, but he was sanguine about his experience with the paper. As he wrote to Bruce Glasier on

[55] *Commonweal*, 21 September 1889, p. 297.

16 December 1890: 'we have after a very long experiment found out that a sectional paper cannot be run.'[56] However, in the same letter he suggested to Glasier that if it was decided to publish a new journal it should either be 'a penny monthly, merely as a means of communication' or 'a *general* Socialist paper...to include all sections'. Despite this he remained loyal to *Commonweal* and ended his letter by saying he would not start a rival paper 'as long as a monthly *Commonweal* exists; I would rather support that if I could'. In fact the Hammersmith Socialist Society did continue to sell *Commonweal* at its meetings for a time. But as the paper became more overtly anarchist in orientation it was abandoned in favour of Keir Hardie's *Labour Leader* and Burgess's *Workman's Times*. Following the successful launch of Robert Blatchford's *Clarion* in Manchester on 2 December 1891 – the first edition of which sold 40,000 copies – the Society also sold it at its meetings.

Morris's plans for a 'general' socialist paper were never to materialize. When he did return to journalism it was as an occasional contributor to a four-page monthly journal called the *Hammersmith Socialist Record*. This modest publication, which was edited by Sam Bullock but financed by Morris, first appeared in October 1891 and was intended more for the information of the members of the Hammersmith Socialist Society than for a wider audience. One page each month was devoted to a list of forthcoming lectures, and from the March 1892 edition a map was also included showing the location of Kelmscott House and the Society's open-air pitch at the end of Hammersmith Bridge. Glasier described the journal as 'the smallest and most homely Socialist publication in the country'.[57] As none of the contributions were signed until the March 1892 edition it is impossible to assess Morris's personal contribution to the *Hammersmith Socialist Record*. We do know that he drafted 'The Statement of Principles' that appeared in the first two

---

[56] *The Letters of William Morris to his Family and Friends*, ed. Philip Henderson (Longmans, 1950), p. 331.

[57] *William Morris and the Early Days of the Socialist Movement*, op. cit., p. 136.

editions of the journal as this had been approved by the Society in January 1891. In addition seven of the articles bear his initials 'W. M.'. Internal evidence suggests he may well have also written some of the earlier unsigned articles. The subsequent history of *Commonweal*, after Morris was rejected from its editorship in 1890, is more complicated than has often been realized. The paper continued in the anarchists' hands until 4 September 1892 when it ceased publication following the arrest and imprisonment of Nicoll for incitement to violence following the Walsall Anarchist case. However, volume 1, number 1 of a 'New Series' of the paper appeared less than a year later on 1 May 1893. Published by H. B. Samuels from 6 Windmill Street, Tottenham Court Road, London, the four-page paper had the same format as that adopted by Morris during his period as editor. It is possible that Samuels hoped to boost the initial sales of the paper by giving his readers the impression that Morris was still involved in its production. Early editions of the paper reprinted part of one of Morris's 'Notes on News' columns from an 1889 edition of *Commonweal* and his poem 'No Master'.

If this was the case the deception was soon abandoned. Samuels was in reality a hardline anarchist whose brother-in-law, Henri Bourdin, was subsequently to die in an attempt to blow up the Greenwich Observatory on 15 February 1894; an incident which provided the inspiration for Joseph Conrad's novel *The Secret Agent*. His attitude to Morris was therefore extremely unfavourable. This became clear in 1893 when he used an editorial to attack *The Manifesto of the English Socialists* which Morris had co-written with George Bernard Shaw and H. M. Hyndman. Later he went on to dismiss Morris's view on anarchism, as expressed in an interview which appeared in *Justice* on 27 January 1894, in a sarcastic article entitled 'With William Morris on the Bridge of Sighs'. However, Samuels' opportunity for political comment was short-lived as his version of the paper ceased publication on 12 May 1894.

Meanwhile Nicoll, on his release from prison, had been appalled to discover that *Commonweal* had been appropriated by Samuels. According to E. P. Thompson he immediately 'engaged in a bitter polemic with his old comrades, who would not permit him to resume the editorship of the paper'.[58] Instead, Nicoll founded the *Anarchist* in Sheffield on 18 March 1894. This continued to appear until 18 April 1896. At the back of the final issue of the paper Nicoll declared that it was his 'intention to revive the past glories of [*Commonweal*] the oldest revolutionary paper in England'. In what was obviously a rebuff to his erstwhile colleagues he dated the demise of the paper to 4 September 1892, thereby ignoring the existence of the version edited by Samuels. This particular 'revival' of the paper was a sorry affair that lasted for just two issues. Printed on inferior paper the journal was barely a quarter the size of the original *Commonweal*. The first edition, which was dated 6 May 1896, was dominated by a long description of 'The Raid on the Commonweal' in April 1892 in which Nicoll occupied centre stage. The second edition, dated June 1896, had a similarly long piece on 'The Walsall Amnesty Meeting' in London.

Even this was not the end of *Commonweal*. Nicoll launched yet another 'New Series' of the paper on 20 June 1897. Once more reverting to the size of the original *Commonweal* this revamped four-page version of the paper was published at 82 Randall Street, Sheffield. The first edition, which appeared at the time when Victoria was celebrating sixty years as Queen, was ironically subtitled a 'Grand Jubilee Number'. The paper, which appeared irregularly, later moved back to London where it was again published from the premises at 6 Windmill Street. In a truncated form it limped into the new century: the last edition bearing the date of November 1900. Although this marked the end of the original paper, the title was resurrected in January 1914 when Annie Besant launched a new *Commonweal* which aimed 'to be the voice of the dumb, the defender of the oppressed, the reformer of evil, the upholder

---

[58] *William Morris: Romantic to Revolutionary, op. cit.*, p. 595.

of righteousness'.[59]   Morris would no doubt have endorsed these sentiments, although he would probably have deplored the paper's name being associated with Besant's pro-parliamentary politics.

In the end anyone who reads Morris's journalism must be struck above all by his consistent opposition to the socialists becoming involved in the constitutional process. The reason for this opposition was his belief that parliament and other elected bodies existed to safeguard the class interests of the bourgeoisie, and that any efforts by the socialists to gain concessions from within the system could only be achieved by abandoning their revolutionary principles. His refusal to compromise on this point has often been cited by critics as proof that he was out of touch with the contemporary socialist movement. Even in the 1890s, when he came to accept that the labour movement was being inexorably drawn into experimenting with parliamentary methods, he warned that it was essential that an extra-parliamentary body committed to revolutionary socialist principles should be retained to lead the struggle once the experiment failed. With the advantage of hindsight it is clear that his worst fears have come true. After one hundred years of parliamentary representation we are no nearer the social revolution and, more significantly, the Labour Party now openly defends the system it was originally intended to destroy. Just as Morris predicted, the working classes are now leaderless as there is no effective extra-parliamentary body from which to continue the class struggle. Surely it is time we reassessed his political writings and considered their implications for our own age.

Nick Salmon
Buckinghamshire, 1996

---

[59] Arthur H. Nethercot, *The First Five Lives of Annie Besant* (London, 1961), p. 218.

CHRONOLOGY: 1885-1890

2 January 1885: A Fenian bomb on the London underground injured a number of people.

7 January 1885: The Hammersmith Branch of the Social Democratic Federation (SDF) joined the Socialist League (SL).

24 January 1885: Fenian bombs exploded at the Tower of London and Houses of Parliament causing several injuries.

26 January 1885: Khartoum was captured by the Mahdi and General Gordon killed.

February 1885: The first edition of the monthly *Commonweal* was published with articles by Bax, Stepniak, Shaw, Kitz, Engels and the Avelings.

5 February 1885: News of the fall of Khartoum reached England.

7 February 1885: Morris spoke at a public meeting held at the South Place Institute, Finsbury, to introduce Edward Aveling's series of lectures on Karl Marx's *Das Kapital*.

10 February 1885: News of the death of General Gordon at Khartoum reached England.

12 February 1885: Edward Aveling gave the first of his series of lectures on *Das Kapital*.

16 February 1885: A demonstration of between 3,000 to 4,000 unemployed workers assembled on the Embankment and then marched to Westminster to demand that the Local Government Board institute public works.

25 February 1885: Morris spoke at a meeting sponsored by the Oxford Socialist Society at the Music Room, Holywell,

Oxford. The meeting ended in chaos when one of the students let off a stink bomb.

2 March 1885: The SL issued its *Manifesto on the Sudan War*.

4 March 1885: A meeting of the Peace Society was held to protest against the Sudan War.

11 March 1885: Morris testified before the Parliamentary Committee on the Restoration of Westminster Hall.

30 March 1885: Russian forces attacked and defeated the Afghans. The defeat of the Afghans was interpreted as a threat against British interests in India and for a time war seemed likely between Britain and Russia.

2 April 1885: Morris moved a socialist rider to an anti-war resolution referring to the Sudan at a meeting at St James's Hall, London.

9 May 1885: The police broke up a socialist meeting near the International Socialist Working Men's Club in Stephen's Mews, Tottenham Court Road.

June 1885: The SL acquired new headquarters at 13 Farringdon Road, London.

9 June 1885: Gladstone's government resigned.

13 June 1885: Lord Salisbury formed a Conservative government.

5 July 1885: Morris acted as chairman at the first annual conference of the SL at Farringdon Hall, London. At the time national membership of the SL stood at around 230.

6 July 1885: The first of W. T. Stead's articles on child prostitution in London appeared in the *Pall Mall Gazette*.

22 August 1885: A mass meeting took place in Hyde Park to protest against the exploitation of young women in London. Morris spoke at this meeting. His wife, Jane, was also present.

20 September 1885: A socialist meeting held in Dod Street, London, was charged by the police. Eight members of the crowd were arrested for 'obstruction' or resisting the police.

21 September 1885: Those accused of 'obstruction' were brought up before a magistrate at the Arbour Square Police Court. On hearing the verdict Morris shouted out 'shame' and was promptly set upon by the police. Two hours later he was brought before the magistrate for assaulting a policeman but was acquitted.

27 September 1885: A crowd of between 30,000 and 50,000 defied the police and held a meeting in Dod Street.

November 1885: It was revealed that two candidates sponsored by the SDF in the first election under the new Reform Act had been backed by 'Tory Gold'. This caused a rift between the SDF and the SL.

21 November 1885: Parnell issued a *Manifesto* which urged the Irish Nationalists to vote Conservative.

18 December 1885: The general election ended with 334 Liberals, 250 Conservatives and 86 Irish Nationalists.

1 January 1886: Upper Burma was annexed by Britain.

21 January 1886: Queen Victoria opened Parliament and made clear her opposition to Irish Home Rule.

26 January 1886: The new Conservative government announced that it would resume coercion in Ireland.

27 January 1886: The Conservative government was defeated in the House of Commons by 329 votes to 250.

29 January 1886: Gladstone became Prime Minister.

8 February 1886: 'Black Monday'. A demonstration by the unemployed in Trafalgar Square was hijacked by the SDF. The crowd then marched down Pall Mall and through Piccadilly to Hyde Park. As they passed the Reform Club they were jeered by the members and smashed windows in retaliation. A number of shops were also looted. Hyndman, Burns and Williams were subsequently arrested for sedition.

21 February 1886: A large demonstration organized by the SDF in Hyde Park was brutally dispersed by the police.

22 February 1886: At a meeting of London members of the SL it was decided to turn the *Commonweal* into a weekly.

18 March 1886: *A Short Account of the Commune of Paris* – written by Morris, Bax and Victor Dave – was published to coincide with a meeting held to commemorate the Paris Commune.

27 March 1886: Chamberlain and Trevelyan resigned from the Cabinet in protest at Gladstone's Home Rule scheme. Charles Warren replaced Sir Edmund Henderson as Chief Commissioner of the Metropolitan Police.

8 April 1886: Gladstone introduced his Home Rule Bill. The trial of Hyndman, Burns and Williams for their part in 'Black Monday' began.

12 April 1886: Hyndman, Burns and Williams were acquitted.

1 May 1886: *Commonweal* became a weekly.

4 May 1886: Queen Victoria opened the Imperial and Colonial Exhibition in London.

15 May 1886: Morris published the first chapter of 'Socialism from the Root Up' in *Commonweal*.

30 May 1886: Wardle and nine others were arrested at Grove Street, Stratford, for obstruction.

7 June 1886: Gladstone's Home Rule Bill was defeated on its second reading by 341 votes to 311.

12 June 1886: Mowbray and Lane were arrested for speaking in Grove Street, Stratford.

30 June 1886: The general election campaign began.

11 July 1886: Sam Mainwaring and Jack Williams were arrested for obstruction while addressing a large crowd in Bell Street.

17 July 1886: The general election ended with 191 Liberals, 317 Conservatives, 85 Irish Nationalists and 77 Liberal Unionists.

18 July 1886: Morris addressed an open-air meeting at Bell Street sponsored by the Marylebone Branch of the SL. It was at this meeting that his name was taken by Chief-Inspector Shepherd.

24 July 1886: Morris appeared before Mr Cooke the magistrate at Marylebone Police Court charged with obstruction. He was fined 1s.

25 July 1886: Salisbury took office as Prime Minister of the new Conservative government.

13 August 1886: Williams and Mainwaring were sentenced to pay £20 each or to serve two months in prison. Mainwaring paid the fine but Williams went to prison.

29 August 1886: A large meeting was organized by the SDF in Trafalgar Square to mark Jack Williams' release from prison.

9 November 1886: The SDF organized a demonstration of the unemployed to coincide with the Lord Mayor's Show.

13 November 1886: The serialization of *A Dream of John Ball* began in *Commonweal*.

20 November 1886: O'Brien and Dillon drew up their 'Plan of Campaign' to organize the Irish tenants.

23 December 1886: Churchill resigned as Chancellor of the Exchequer. He was replaced by Goshen.

4 January 1887: At a meeting of the unemployed in Norwich a deputation tried unsuccessfully to see the Mayor. Some of the crowd then rioted in the centre of the city and looted a number of shops. Mowbray and

Henderson, who represented the SL, were among four people arrested.

7 January 1887: The socialists seriously disrupted Brabazon's emigration meeting at Clerkenwell.

22 January 1887: Mowbray and Henderson were sentenced respectively to nine months and four months in prison.

25 January 1887: Morris started his short-lived *Socialist Diary*.

4 February 1887: Morris took part in a debate on the class war, held at the Chiswick Club.

24 February 1887: The jury failed to agree at the trial of the Plan of Campaign leaders in Dublin.

27 February 1887: The SDF disrupted a service at St Paul's Cathedral.

5 March 1887: Balfour was appointed Chief Secretary for Ireland.

28 March 1887: Balfour introduced his Criminal Law Amendment (Ireland) Bill. This proposed the abolition of trials by jury for crimes where the sentence would be less than six months.

4 April 1887: The first Colonial Conference was held.

11 April 1887: Morris travelled to Northumberland to address the striking miners. At an open-air meeting held in a field at Horton he gave a speech to a crowd of nearly 10,000 people.

18 April 1887: The *Times* published forged documents that suggested that Parnell was implicated in the Phoenix Park murders.

25 April 1887: Morris ended his *Socialist Diary*.

3 May 1887: A meeting of strikers in Chicago was fired on by the police. A number of strikers were killed and many others injured.

4 May 1887: A mass meeting was held in Chicago to protest at the actions of the police the previous day. At this meeting a bomb was thrown which killed seven policemen.

14 May 1887: Queen Victoria opened a 'People's Palace' in the East End of London.

21 June 1887: Queen Victoria's Jubilee Service was held at Westminster Abbey.

19 July 1887: The Irish Coercion Bill became law.

9 September 1887: William O'Brien and John Mandeville were summoned for calling a meeting on 9 August to encourage resistance to the government's policy of coercion in Ireland. A preliminary hearing was held at Mitchelstown – although neither men were present – at which a scuffle broke out. The police fired on the crowd killing two people and wounding several others.

24 September 1887: William O'Brien was sentenced to prison.

12 October 1887: A coroner's jury in Ireland returned a verdict of wilful murder against the police who had fired on the crowd at Mitchelstown. Despite this no action was taken against those responsible.

14 October 1887 : Morris gave a speech at a meeting at the South Place Institute to protest at the impending execution of the Chicago Anarchists.

15 October 1887: The first performance of Morris's socialist interlude *The Tables Turned; or, Nupkins Awakened* was held at the SL Hall, Farringdon Road. Morris played the part of the Archbishop of Canterbury.

17–19 October 1887: Meetings of the unemployed in Trafalgar Square were repeatedly cleared by mounted police.

29 October 1887: The SL issued a *Manifesto* stating its views on the renewal of the unemployment agitation.

3 November 1887: The *New York Times* reported that the United States Supreme Court had rejected an appeal for writ of error in the case of the Chicago Anarchists.

7 November 1887: The *Pall Mall Gazette* published a letter from Morris in which he condemned the 'judicial murder' of the Chicago Anarchists.

8 November 1887: Sir Charles Warren banned all further meetings in Trafalgar Square on the pretext that it was Crown property.

11 November 1887: Four of the Chicago Anarchists were hanged.

13 November 1887: A meeting called by the Radicals and Irish at Trafalgar Square to protest at the imprisonment of William O'Brien and affirm the right of assembly led to what became known as 'Bloody Sunday'. The police broke up the demonstration with considerable violence and arrested Burns and Cunninghame Graham. Three people were killed including a prominent Deptford Radical called William Curner.

17 November 1887: Around 6,000 special constables were enrolled to curb future riots.

18 November 1887: The Law and Liberty League was formed at a meeting at the Memorial Hall, Farringdon Street, with the aim of raising bail for those arrested as a result of the fight for free speech.

20 November 1887: A large demonstration was held in Hyde Park to protest at the action of the police on 'Bloody Sunday'. Alfred Linnell, a Radical law-writer, was ridden down by the police in Northumberland Avenue and later died of the injuries he received.

18 December 1887: A crowd of 10,000 attended the funeral of Alfred Linnell. Morris acted as one of the pall-bearers.

7 January 1888: William Curner, who had been killed on 'Bloody Sunday', was buried. Morris's 'Death Song' closed the proceedings.

18 January 1888: Burns and Cunninghame Graham were imprisoned for a month.

2 March 1888: Sir Charles Russell moved that Parliament inquire into the legality of holding open-air meetings in Trafalgar Square as it was not within the jurisdiction of the Royal Parks Act of 1872 as Sir Charles Warren had claimed. Charles Bradlaugh also moved that an inquiry was launched into the conduct of the police on 'Bloody Sunday'.

3 March 1888: Russell and Bradlaugh's motions were defeated in the House of Commons.

27 April 1888: Keir Hardie stood as a member of the Scottish Labour Party in the Mid-Lanark by-election. He was defeated but did poll 617 votes.

20 May 1888: At the annual conference of the SL a number of anarchists were elected to the Council.

28 May 1888: The SL suspended its pro-parliamentary Bloomsbury branch.

5 July 1888: The Bryant & May match girl strike began.

August 1888: The Jack the Ripper murders commenced in the East End of London.

11 August 1888: Parnell brought an action against the *Times* claiming £100,000 damages. The action was eventually successful and the *Times* paid £5,000 in damages on 3 February 1890.

25 August 1888: The inaugural conference of the Scottish Labour Party was held.

17 September 1888: A Royal Commission was set up to investigate the *Times* articles attacking Parnell.

31 October 1888: Vizetelly was fined for publishing English translations of the works of Zola.

10 November 1888: Morris gave a speech welcoming Mrs Albert Parsons, widow of one of the executed Chicago Anarchists, at a meeting held at St Paul's Cafe.

21 December 1888: The British defeated – or massacred – the Dervishes at Suakin.

23 January 1889: The first meetings of the new County Councils took place.

27 March 1889: John Bright died.

May 1889: Morris read Edward Bellamy's *Looking Backward*. He wrote: 'I wouldn't care to live in such a cockney paradise as he imagines.'

June 1889: The circulation of the *Commonweal* fell to around 2,300 copies.

7 June 1889: Charles Charrington and Janey Achurch's production of Ibsen's *A Doll's House* opened at the Novelty Theatre. The play aroused a great deal of controversy.

28 December 1889: Captain O'Shea filed a petition for divorce citing Parnell's adultery with his wife.

11 January 1890: Morris began the serialization of *News from Nowhere* in *Commonweal*.

12 May 1890: Morris appeared in the one-act play *The Duchess of Bayswater & Co* which was performed in aid of *Commonweal* at a hall in Tottenham Court Road. Shaw was also in the cast.

25 May 1890: At the sixth annual conference of the SL the anarchists took control of the Council leaving Morris isolated. He and Sparling were ejected from the editorship of *Commonweal* and replaced by Nicoll and Kitz.

3 August 1890: A 'Revolutionary Conference' was organized by the new Executive of the SL and held at the

Autonomic Club. Here anarchist doctrines were preached openly.

4 October 1890: The serialization of *News from Nowhere* was concluded in *Commonweal*.

1 November 1890: Morris delivered an open-air speech at a meeting called by a number of socialist and anarchist groups in London to protest against 'the persecution of Jews in Russia'.

8 November 1890: Morris contributed his last article – 'Where Are We Now?' – to *Commonweal*.

21 November 1890: Morris and the Hammersmith branch of the SL withdrew from the organization.

28 November 1890: The Hammersmith branch of the SL was reconstituted as the Hammersmith Socialist Society with Morris as treasurer.

CONTRIBUTIONS TO
COMMONWEAL

1885

THE MANIFESTO OF THE
SOCIALIST LEAGUE

Fellow Citizens,

We come before you as a body advocating the principles of Revolutionary International Socialism; that is, we seek a change in the basis of Society – a change which would destroy the distinctions of classes and nationalities.

As the civilised world is at present constituted, there are two classes of Society – the one possessing wealth and the instruments of its production, the other producing wealth by means of those instruments but only by the leave and for the use of the possessing classes.

These two classes are necessarily in antagonism to one another. The possessing class, or non-producers, can only live as a class on the unpaid labour of the producers – the more unpaid labour they can wring out of them, the richer they will be; therefore the producing class – the workers – are driven to strive to better themselves at the expense of the possessing class, and the conflict between the two is ceaseless. Sometimes it takes the form of open rebellion, sometimes of strikes, sometimes of mere widespread mendicancy and crime; but it is always going on in one form or other, though it may not always be obvious to the thoughtless looker-on.

We have spoken of unpaid labour: it is necessary to explain what that means. The sole possession of the producing class is the power of labour inherent in their bodies; but since, as we have already said, the richer classes possess all the instruments of labour, that is, the land, capital, and machinery, the producers or workers are forced to sell their sole possession, the power of labour, on such terms as the possessing class will grant them.

These terms are, that after they have produced enough to keep them in working order, and enable them to beget children to take their places when they are worn out, the surplus of their products shall belong to the possessors of property, which bargain is based on the fact that every man working in a civilised community can produce more than he needs for his own sustenance.

This relation of the possessing class to the working class is the essential basis of the system of producing for a profit, on which our modern Society is founded. The way in which it works is as follows. The manufacturer produces to sell at a profit to the broker or factor, who in his turn makes a profit out of his dealings with the merchant, who again sells for a profit to the retailer, who must make his profit out of the general public, aided by various degrees of fraud and adulteration and the ignorance of the value and quality of goods to which this system has reduced the consumer.

The profit-grinding system is maintained by competition, or veiled war, not only between the conflicting classes, but also within the classes themselves: there is always war among the workers for bare subsistence, and among their masters, the employers and middle-men, for the share of the profit wrung out of the workers; lastly, there is competition always, and sometimes open war, among the nations of the civilised world for their share of the world-market. For now, indeed, all the rivalries of nations have been reduced to this one -a degraded struggle for their share of the spoils of barbarous countries to be used at home for the purpose of increasing the riches of the rich and the poverty of the poor.

For, owing to the fact that goods are made primarily to sell, and only secondarily for use, labour is wasted on all hands; since the pursuit of profit compels the manufacturer competing with his fellows to force his wares on the markets by means of their cheapness, whether there is any real demand for them or not. In the words of the Communist Manifesto of 1847:–

> Cheap goods are the artillery for battering down Chinese walls and for overcoming the obstinate hatred entertained

against foreigners by semi-civilised nations: under penalty of ruin the Bourgeoisie compel by competition the universal adoption of their system of production; they force all nations to accept what is called civilisation – to become Bourgeois – and thus the middle-class shapes the world after its own image.

Moreover, the whole method of distribution under this system is full of waste; for it employs whole armies of clerks, travellers, shopmen, advertisers, and what not, merely for the sake of shifting money from one person's pocket to another's; and this waste in production and waste in distribution, added to the maintenance of the useless lives of the possessing and non-producing class, must all be paid for out of the products of the workers, and is a ceaseless burden on their lives.

Therefore the necessary results of this so-called civilisation are only too obvious in the lives of its slaves, the working-class – in the anxiety and want of leisure amidst which they toil, in the squalor and wretchedness of those parts of our great towns where they dwell; in the degradation of their bodies, their wretched health, and the shortness of their lives; in the terrible brutality so common among them, and which is indeed but the reflection of the cynical selfishness found among the well-to-do classes, a brutality as hideous as the other; and lastly, in the crowd of criminals who are as much manufactures of our commercial system as the cheap and nasty wares which are made at once for the consumption and the enslavement of the poor.

What remedy, then, do we propose for this failure of our civilisation, which is now admitted by almost all thoughtful people?

We have already shown that the workers, although they produce all the wealth of society, have no control over its production or distribution: the *people*, who are the only really organic part of society, are treated as a mere appendage to capital – as a part of its machinery. This must be altered from the foundation: the land, the capital, the machinery, factories, workshops, stores, means of transit, mines, banking, all means of production and distribution of wealth, must be declared and treated as the common property of all. Every man will then receive the full value of his labour, without deduction for the profit of a master, and as all will have to work, and the waste now incurred by the pursuit of profit will be at an end, the amount of labour necessary for every individual to perform in order to carry on the essential work of the world will be reduced to something like two or three hours daily; so that every one will have abundant leisure for following intellectual or other pursuits congenial to his nature.

This change in the method of production and distribution would enable every one to live decently, and free from the sordid anxieties for daily livelihood which at present weigh so heavily on the greatest part of mankind.

But, moreover, men's social and moral relations would be seriously modified by this gain of economical freedom, and by the collapse of the superstitions, moral and other, which necessarily accompany a state of economical slavery: the test of duty would now rest on the fulfilment of clear and well-defined obligations to the community rather than on the moulding of the individual character and actions to some preconceived standard outside social responsibilities.

Our modern bourgeois property – marriage, maintained as it is by its necessary complement, universal venal prostitution, would give place to kindly and human relations between the sexes.

Education freed from the trammels of commercialism on the one hand and superstition on the other, would become a reasonable drawing out of men's varied faculties in order to fit them for a life of social intercourse and happiness; for mere work would no longer be proposed as the end of life, but happiness for each and all.

Only be such fundamental changes in the life of man, only by the transformation of Civilisation into Socialism, can those miseries of the world before mentioned be amended.

As to mere politics, Absolutism, Constitutionalism, Republicanism, have all been tried in our day and under our present social system, and all have alike failed in dealing with the real evils of life.

Nor, on the other hand, will certain incomplete schemes of social reform now before the public solve the question.

Co-operation so-called – that is, competitive co-operation for profit – would merely increase the number of small joint-stock capitalists, under the mask of creating an aristocracy of labour, while it would intensify the severity of labour by its temptations to overwork.

Nationalisation of the land alone, which many earnest and sincere persons are now preaching, would be useless so long as labour was subject to the fleecing of surplus value inevitable under the Capitalist system.

No better solution would be that of State Socialism, by whatever name it may be called, whose aim it would be to make concessions to the working class while leaving the present system of capital and wages still in operation: no number of merely administrative changes, until the workers are in possession of all political power, would make any real approach to Socialism.

The Socialist League therefore aims at the realisation of complete Revolutionary Socialism, and well knows that this can never happen in any one country without the help of the workers of all civilisation. For us neither geographical boundaries, political history, race, nor creed makes rivals or enemies; for us there are no nations, but only varied masses of workers and friends, whose mutual sympathies are checked or perverted by groups of masters and fleecers whose interest it is to stir up rivalries and hatreds between the dwellers in different lands.

It is clear that for all these oppressed and cheated masses of workers and their masters a great change is preparing: the dominant classes are uneasy, anxious, touched in conscience even, as to the condition of those they govern; the markets of the world are being competed for with an eagerness never before known; everything points to the fact that the great commercial system is becoming unmanageable, and is slipping from the grasp of its present rulers.

The one change possible out of all this is Socialism. As chattel-slavery passed into serfdom, and serfdom into the so-called free-labour system, so most surely will this latter pass into social order.

To the realisation of this change the Socialist League addresses itself with all earnestness. As a means thereto it will do all in its power towards the education of the people in the principles of this great cause, and will strive to organise those who will accept this education, so that when the crisis comes, which the march of events is preparing, there may be a body of men ready to step into their due places and deal with and direct the irresistible movement.

Close fellowship with each other, and steady purpose for the advancement of the Cause, will naturally bring about the organisation and discipline amongst ourselves absolutely necessary to success; but we shall look to it that there shall be no distinctions of rank or dignity amongst us to give opportunities for the selfish ambition of leadership which has so often injured the cause of the workers. We are working *for* equality and brotherhood for all the world, and it is only *through* equality and brotherhood that we can make our work effective.

Let us all strive, then, towards this end of realising the change towards social order, the only cause worthy the attention of the workers of all that are proffered to them: let us work in that cause patiently, yet hopefully, and not shrink from making sacrifices to it. Industry in learning its principles, industry in teaching them, are most necessary to our progress; but to these we must add, if we wish to avoid speedy failure, frankness and fraternal trust in each other, and single-hearted devotion to the religion of Socialism, the only religion which the Socialist League professes.

Commonweal, Volume 1, Number 1,
February 1885, pp. 1–2.

SIGNS OF THE TIMES

In the *Daily News*, March 17th, there is a long detailed report from a Geneva correspondent (of course anonymous) of an interview with a terrorist. We ask the *Daily News* for evidence of the genuineness of this report, which on the face of it looks doubtful. Even the general public which knows perhaps, no more of police tricks than it has gathered from M. Andrioux' recent revelations are bound to join us in this demand.

The first number of the *Anarchist* has appeared, with articles by Elisée Reclus, G. B. Shaw and Henry Appleton. Of course the honesty and enthusiasm of the writers are beyond all question; but we cannot think that they make their position quite clear. In any case we welcome the temperate discussion of differences between various Socialist schools, in the hope that the obvious necessity for revolutionising society will force us all to study the question so diligently that the path may at last become plain to us. The *Anarchist* is published by the International Publishing Company, 35 Newington Green Road, N.

Commonweal, Volume 1, Number 3,
April 1885, p. 22.

REVIEWS AND NOTICES

Socialist Rhymes. By J. L. JOYNES. Modern Press, 13 and
14 Paternoster Row. – We heartily recommend these rhymes
to our readers; the verse is nearly everywhere brilliant and
spirited, and in some of the pieces the depth of feeling raises
them into the rank of poetry of no mean order. Sincerity and
enthusiasm are obvious throughout the whole of them, and
must make some impression on those who read them, even if
they are not wholly on our side. John Ruskin once wrote
that 'A cause which cannot be sung of is not worth
following.' We have to thank Mr. Joynes for his share in
demonstrating that Socialism cannot fall under this condemnation at all events.

Commonweal, Volume 1, Number 3,
April 1885, p. 23.

SIGNS OF THE TIMES

In declaring for Socialism another member of the 'respectable' class has fallen out of the ranks, and denounces the competitive system roundly. Says Mr. Charles Rowley, jun., of Manchester, in his *Social Politics*: 'Let us each decide what is just in the matter, and then give ourselves no rest until we achieve, or help to achieve, a better state. Our supineness on most of these vital social questions is simply incredible. Why do we sleep in our beds when we know that there are shipowners who send ships and men to sea for the sole purpose of being lost? The facts are incontrovertible, and yet we never hang a ship-owner, or a stink maker, or an air poisoner, or a polluter of rivers, or a mill owner who fattens on a high death-rate among children. We hang a few poor and wicked wretches who are born so and who are made so by our vicious arrangements. The real criminals escape, and yet we know them and know their guilt.' So we do, Mr. Rowley, and *yet they escape*. But be of good cheer! The time is evidently coming when we shall 'suit the word to the action and the action to the word.' Then a thief will be called a thief and treated accordingly. This 'better state' we hope and think you will help us to achieve.

Commonweal, Volume 1, Number 4,
May 1885, p. 35.

[REVIEW OF *SOCIAL POLITICS* BY CHARLES ROWLEY]

Social Politics. By CHARLES ROWLEY, Jun. John Heywood, Manchester. – There is an allusion in the 'Signs of the Times' to this pamphlet, which is undoubtedly a sign of the times, and a cheering one. Mr. Rowley is by no means mealy-mouthed, and the two sentences printed on the inside of the cover show that he has grasped the essential fact of the class struggle, and knows that the worker's lot cannot really be bettered except at the expense of the exploiters. It is a pity, since this is the case, that he should have taken the word 'expansion of England' into his mouth except to condemn it, and that he favours emigration *as a remedy for class evils*, if he really means this. If those who are most keenly stung by the evils of class domination, and at the same time have energy to resist them, leave the country which is the very forge of class domination, their desertion will surely put off the Revolution which Mr. Rowley desires, and make it more disorderly when it comes, as it must come. 'The expansion of England' means the expansion of capital; that is to say, the spreading to other countries and the perpetuation in our own of these horrors, of that death in life, which Mr. Rowley so forcibly and sincerely attacks. Of course the expanded England of Professor Seeley is by no means the England which Mr. Rowley hopes for, and which will be certainly attained at some time, but by no road that goes roundabout to avoid the entire abolition of classes.

Commonweal, Volume 1, Number 4, May 1885, p. 35.

[REPORT ON AN ANTI-WAR MEETING]

The Socialist League determined to move a rider to the first
resolution at the meeting against the Soudan War held in St
James's Hall on April 2nd. Comrades Morris and Mowbray
were told off to move and second the rider, which ran thus:–

> And that this meeting believes that the invasion of the
> Soudan has been prompted solely by the desire to exploit
> the country in the interests of capitalists and stock-jobbers;
> and warns the working classes that such wars will always
> take place until they (the workers) unite throughout the
> civilised world, and take their own affairs into their own
> hands.

The audience was attentive and moderately enthusiastic
against the war – any reference to the cause of which was
carefully avoided in the resolution. Mr. Bradlaugh from the
chair opened the meeting, and was followed by Prof. Beesley,
Mr. Storey, Prof. Thorold Rogers, and Mr. N. L. Ghose. In
spite of the inspiriting subject, the speaking was on the whole
below the average: Mr. Storey's speech was the stupidest,
and Mr. Bradlaugh's the most conventional; Mr. Thorold
Rogers alone made a vigorous and pointed speech, justly
throwing the onus of the war on the sluggishness of the
whole British people who have permitted it to be undertaken
and continued. He also, using partly the words of our
Manifesto, pointed out the large share which Gordon's
treacherous conduct had in bringing about the invasion, and
his remarks on this point were received with applause by the
greater part of the audience. At the close of Mr. Ghose's
somewhat dreary speech, the Chairman announced, without
reading out, our rider, and said that he would allow the
mover and seconder five minutes each. This promise he
broke by calling Morris to time after he had spoken a few

sentences, which were reported verbatim by the *Daily News* next day, and can only be spun out to something less than two minutes. There was no excuse for this unfairness on the Chairman's part, as the audience was quite prepared to give a fair hearing to our speakers; the reading of the rider was interrupted by widespread applause, the mention of the Socialist League was well received, and so were the few words spoken by Morris. The mover, protesting against the Chairman's unfairness, Mr. Bradlaugh offered to let him speak through the seconder's time if the latter would give it up. This he (very reasonably) declined to do, and Morris was compelled to retire. Mowbray was then allowed to speak for his allotted time, after which the chairman rose and announced that '*we* cannot accept the rider' thus dictating to what was supposed to be a free public meeting. He then called on Mrs. Besant to oppose the rider. This lady, called on to answer arguments which Mr. Bradlaugh had forbidden the meeting to listen to, made but a poor job of it, and would scarcely have had a cheer till the close of her speech if she had not quoted the last sentence of the rider, which was received with loud applause. After she had concluded, she of course received the applause that politeness usually awards to a lady. Though Morris asked the chairman to allow a brief answer to Mrs. Besant, and John Burns (S.D.F.) attempted to reach the platform and speak, this slight indulgence to freedom of discussion before a good tempered and more or less sympathetic audience was refused by the chairman, who then put the rider (again without reading it). As [a] matter of course, after such treatment, it was rejected. The only other remarkable event of the meeting was the uproarious applause which greeted Mr. Labouchere's rising to move the second resolution, compared with which Mr. Bradlaugh's reception was cool. This seemed to indicate a large contingent of Northampton voters, which makes the reception by the audience of our speakers the more encouraging. A considerable number of the *Commonweal* was sold at the hall doors, and the Soudan War Manifesto was widely distributed. – In considering their delegates' report of the meeting, the following resolution was unanimously passed:-

*This meeting of the Provisional Council of the Socialist
League considers the action of Mr. Bradlaugh as Chairman
of the St James's Hall meeting of 2nd April to have been a
flagrant breach of faith towards a delegate of the League,
and in future resolves to treat Mr. Bradlaugh in accordance
with this consideration of his conduct on that occasion.*

Commonweal, Volume 1, Number 4,
May 1885, p. 36.

[UNTITLED PARAGRAPHS]

A friend writes deprecating a forcible revolution; it would be better, he says, to obtain justice without violence, lest we should have violence without justice. True; yet surely, whatever may be in the future, we have not far to seek to find violence without justice in the present. Do men *choose* a miserable life, or are they *forced* into it? No one wants violence if a decent life for everyone can be obtained without it. But it is to be feared that the natural sequence of enforced misery will be violent revolution. We ask our friend, is that the fault of the wretched or of the system which has made them wretched?

Our friend also regrets that the *Commonweal* shows a tendency towards Communism, and appears to be departing from Lassalle's position, that to everybody should be secured the fruits of his industry. We ask, in turn, how can you measure the fruits of a man's industry as an *individual*? It is as *a social being*, helping and helped by all others that he can claim anything; and surely nothing but Communism can satisfy this claim, by taking his deeds, giving his needs.

Commonweal, Volume 1, Number 5,
June 1885, p. 52.

NOTES ON THE POLITICAL CRISIS

The past fortnight has been fertile in surprises. By something as sudden as the stroke of Harlequin's wand, the Gladstone Ministry found itself resigning as the consequence of a defeat which was the result of 'accident,' say the Liberal leaders, with so much solemnity that it would be uncivil to doubt them. Yet when one considers that they were pledged to bring in a Coercion bill, which the Radical wing were pledged to oppose (though, indeed, they would pretty certainly have broken that pledge), one can't help thinking that if it was not an accident carefully provided for, it was an accident that resulted from a sudden flash of inspiration on the part of the leaders, who saw on the night of the debate what could be made of the turn which things were taking. By such inspirations do great generals win battles, and usually they are not so modest as to call them accidents afterwards.

The trap, though thus laid in the sight of the bird, was entered with apparent willingness. But then comes another surprise. The Tory leaders, who surely might have taken it for granted that they would have to be at least as kind to their enemies as to their friends, seemed to think it worth trying whether they could not have a Session without any enemies at all; or, perhaps, as their heads cleared from the intoxication of their triumph, they began to see that they might, in turn, put their opponents in a more or less awkward position, which would tend to discredit them before the new electorate. Hence has resulted a curious game of some interest to those who are fond of watching the domestic game of 'Patience'; of no interest otherwise, except so far as it may discredit both parties before all sensible people.

But where are the 'sensible people'? Scattered thinly, I fear, among the general population. Yet, if they would only unite, they would move the world.

Meanwhile Mr. Gladstone, having threatened more than once to retire altogether, has had his hand forced by the offer of the gilded shelf of an earldom, and has declined it, to the great jubilation of the semi-radical Liberals, who, probably with reason, see in his refusal a token of his sticking to his post of leader, even when this 'crisis' is over.

Sir Stafford Northcote, on the other hand, has been shoved on to the shelf willy nilly – an incident of little significance even in the insignificant game of politics.

Except that it betokens that, whatever other results the 'Political Crisis' may have, it will at any rate have put Lord Randolph Churchill in the place he has been playing for – the virtual leadership of the Tory party. Time will show what he will do there. It may turn out that his cleverness is only that of the ordinary Parliamentary trickster, and that he will simply kick down the ladder by which he has mounted, according to the rule in such cases; or he may show the higher qualities of the gamester, and be original enough to stick to his text of Tory Democracy, in which case he may lead his party into some queer places, out of which it is possible that the worker may win some advantage.

Nervousness about the consequences of action on the results of the General Election seems to have weighed much on the possible office-holders. For instance – a small instance: Sir M. Hicks Beach, tackled by temperance societies as to his utterance in the Budget debate championing the licensed victuallers by favouring a tax on tea and sugar rather than spirits and beer, is driven to a reply which recalls Mrs. Wilfer to us; for he says, in fact, that when he advocated the said taxes, he did so with the reservation that he didn't mean it in any sense whatever.

Again, as to the coercion for Ireland. At first it was asserted (or assumed) that Lord Salisbury would only take office on the understanding that the Liberal leaders would pledge themselves and their party to help in passing that aid to 'the reign of order' in Ireland. But again, the *Standard* indignantly proclaims that there is no foundation for this assertion. Indeed, the Tory Ministry would be in a tight place here; for surely their passing a Coercion Bill would mean their giving up all hope at the general election.

The imaginative man is almost driven to suppose that this surrender and acceptance of office is a sham battle on *both sides* – a tacit plot of Whig, Tory, Liberal, Radical, in view of the general election, to let coercion slide with a certain amount of dignity. If so, it is a curious illustration of the proverb – When rogues fall out honest men prosper.

Mr. Chamberlain seems inclined to pronounce in favour of Home Rule, and condemns the Castle Government unsparingly, whatever his opinion once was. After all, we are getting on, along some lines at least. Or will there be a fresh reaction after the general election, when it turns out that the new Parliament is composed of much the same elements as the old?

The *Times* calls on Lord Salisbury to make alliance with the moderate Whigs rather than with the Tory democrats. A writer in the *Pall Mall* follows suit, and has a vision of a 'patriotic' party of the future. It is clearly quite impossible for Lord Salisbury to follow this advice at present; but perhaps such a coalition will one day take place, and will produce a party not only reactionary, but of such portentous priggishness and stupidity, that it will be of great service to the cause of the people.

———————

And now at last the crisis *is* over, and Lord Randolph Churchill and his cloak, Lord Salisbury, are 'masters' of the parliamentary hubbub. Nor need anybody sleep the worse for it to-night, not even the editor of the *Pall Mall*, although he threatens dreadful things, the Russian ambassador, for instance, leaving London unless he gets an explanation of the language used by Lord Salisbury and Lord Randolph. Well, well, he will have the explanations, I suppose, and will stay.

———————

And Mr. Chamberlain and Sir Charles Dilke, longer sighted than some, are going to Ireland to get used to the atmosphere of Nationalism – or to try and outflank Mr. Parnell. Who would have thought it four years ago? Not I, who heard a Radical meeting yelling with joy at the announcement of the arrest of Mr. Parnell by the Government of which the two allies were members. So the world moves.

———————

If in the foregoing notes the subject of this crisis seems to be treated with levity, I can only say that it is almost impossible to speak seriously about such contemptible trifling, which is unparalleled by anything save the Court changes in the worst periods of the Byzantine Empire. If only people could see how contemptible it is, and so duly estimate the worth of Parliament.

———————

One thing, of course, it points to – the break-up and confusion of all the old parties. There is hope in that, at any rate. Futile as the new Parliamentary parties will certainly be, they will not be so long-lived as the old, consolidated as these have been by tradition, and long habits of attack and defence. Doubt, irresolution, and waiting to see which way the cat jumps will be for a long time the characteristics of the new parties, under which, contemned by all 'respectabilities,' the revolution will form, and at last, when it gets strong enough, will drive all parties which are not of it to consolidate into one party of open conscious reaction. May we all live to see the day which will bring that about!

Commonweal, Volume 1, Number 6,
July 1885, pp. 53–4.

REPORT OF EDITORS OF COMMONWEAL

Our report is really before you in the six numbers of the *Commonweal* issued. Following out the principles of the League, the journal has been as much as possible educational and organising. With eight pages for the first and second numbers, the supplement from No. 3 onwards has made each issue one of twelve pages. The earlier numbers bore witness to the fact that the leading Socialists of Europe were in sympathy with the League.

The first number, necessarily a hurried production, was hardly to be, and we believe never was, taken as typical. But it contained the Manifesto.

As to the chief articles and their writers, you are in a better position to judge than even we are. But, although thanks are out of place in an organisation where all work is a free-will offering, we are constrained to mention the earnest help given by many working men.

The Reports, the most important part of the paper, have been fairly full. They can be yet fuller if all Branch Secretaries will make a point of forwarding, if possible week by week, notices of the doings of their branches.

The help, not only of secretaries and officials generally, is asked. Every individual member can aid by forwarding extracts from newspapers, paragraphs and quotations bearing upon the movement and Socialism generally. These should be sent week by week, and even day by day. Nothing that is to go into the *Commonweal* of a particular month should reach the Editors later than the first post on the 23rd of the preceding month.

An Inquiry Column has been started in the July number. The success and usefulness of this depends on the energy with which members of the League propound and answer questions and encourage the friends and enemies of the Cause to ask questions.

We are quite conscious that the *Commonweal* has not been a newspaper. As a monthly journal it could not assume this character. In discussing, as you will, the question of keeping the paper as a monthly or making it a weekly, we feel sure that you will bear in mind the relative expense and amount of literary work involved in the two cases.

Commonweal, Volume 1, Number 7,
August 1885, p. 66.

SIGNS OF THE TIMES

As a consequence of the crisis, the shower of 'Court holy-water' has been falling pretty heavily, and has even reached artistic circles in the form of baronetcies for Mr. Millais and Mr. C. F. Watts. Mr. Watts has declined the 'honour' however, a fact which artists must rejoice over, as Mr. Watts, in spite of his being a member of 'Society,' has always show real enthusiasm for his art. Mr. Millais, once a great painter, now a great picture-dealer, seems to have accepted. His acceptance does not disgrace his *second* calling.

Commonweal, Volume 1, Number 7, August 1885, p. 72.

MR. CHAMBERLAIN AT HULL

Mr. Chamberlain may be said on the whole to stick to the road he has taken; perhaps even his Hull speech shows a slight advance. He may be said to have preached from a text furnished by an agricultural labourer in these words: 'Neighbours and friends, you have known me for forty years; I have lived and worked amongst you. I am not a drunkard; I am a steady man; I am an industrious man; I am not a spending man. I have worked and laboured for forty years; it has been a weary task, and I ain't any forwarder now than I was when I began.' 'What,' said Mr. Chamberlain, 'is the remedy?'

I think it at least possible that Mr. Chamberlain knows what the remedy is; but he is 'a politician,' and the exercise of courage and good faith, to say nothing of logic, is forbidden to all 'politicians;' therefore Mr. Chamberlain could only show his audience as much of the remedy as he thought they were prepared to receive, which in fact consisted of free education, graduated taxation, and a queer muddle of land reform, in which free trade in land, fair rent for the farmer and allotments for the labourer, were mingled with the restitution of charitable trusts and stolen commons.

Although Mr. Chamberlain admitted that no prescription should limit restitution, he was careful to disclaim 'confiscation,' which will not reassure those who understand that word as it is understood by the privileged classes; even a writer commenting on this speech in the *Pall Mall Gazette* is able to see this, though otherwise he is a person of quite peculiar stupidity.

He (the specimen of stupidity), though rejoicing in Mr. Chamberlain's adhesion to the 'eighth commandment,' with charming simplicity quotes Macaulay to show that no property would be safe unless there were a strict limitation to the application of the ancient Hebrew law, 'Thou shalt not steal.'

Mr. Chamberlain's attack on common-stealing will, however, tend to make him popular with the general public, and it certainly is something that he is willing to apply the 'eighth commandment' so far. Will it be possible to educate him to apply it to those who steal people's labour from them generally, and not only by making them pay for the use of land which is their own – certainly a gross form of stealing?

For if Mr. Chamberlain comes to think of it (if politicians ever do think, which is doubtful), he cannot fail to see that all his reforms together will not get his labourer much 'forwarder.' He will still have no time to accept education, however 'free' it may be. No magic, no shuffling of the cards, will get taxation in the long run out of anything save labour; the labourer must pay it. And as for the disgorging of the land-thieves, Mr. Chamberlain will find it little use asking for 'restitution' without an army at his back, which army, as it will be composed of workmen, will ask for something more than the restitution of the commons: it will claim for the labourer the right to a full share in all the wealth to the production of which he is necessary. That is the only way in which he can 'get forwarder.'

Commonweal, Volume 1, Number 8, September 1885, p. 77.

[MEETING ON THE RECENT EXPOSURES]
[*Held on 5 August at Farringdon Hall*]
[*Includes this quote attributed to Morris*]

WILLIAM MORRIS: Two things are to be noticed. First, that the children of the poor are always the victims. Second, the terrible and miserable unhappiness of the whole affair. There is much talk of immorality. Whatever is unhappy is immoral. It is unhappiness that must be got rid of. We have nothing to do with the mere immorality. We have to do with the causes that have *compelled* this unhappy way of living; the causes that drive girls and women into the streets, to sell their love, not to give it. These causes are the same that make a man degrade himself by over-hours and competition. There is the closest of relations between the prostitution of the body in the streets and of the body in the workshops. Women's wages are not even subsistence wages. They are intended to cheapen labour for the manufacturers. The first thing that is necessary, is that all women should be freed from the compulsion of living in this degraded way. We aim at the real liberty of every human creature, not the liberty to starve or to sell oneself or one's child. Society to-day is like a wrecked ship where people eat one another. The real Minotaur is Capital – not one man, but the whole system is guilty. To get rid of this system is our serious business. We desire that all should be free to earn their livelihood – with that freedom will come an end of these monstrosities, and true love between man and woman throughout society.

Commonweal, Volume 1, Number 8,
September 1885, p. 78.

SIGNS OF THE TIMES

The great Whig champion, Lord Hartington, has spoken; his speech was eagerly expected by the gamesters in the political game. But when it came it was a matter of many words and nothing said; and the Liberal Party is still without a cry for the coming elections. Inane as it was, however, it has been taken as a manifesto against the Radicalism budding into demi-semi-Socialist Democracy which Mr. Chamberlain represents.

Mr. Chamberlain's Radicalism resents this and 'pronounces' in its turn. Mr. Chamberlain's Radicalism, I say; for Lord Hartington's program of 'nothing to be done but unite to defeat Irish Nationalism,' will content ordinary Radicals well enough.

The 'advanced Radicals,' therefore, must prepare themselves to be left out in the cold. What can they do? Though drifting in the direction of Socialism, they are in the habit of using rather hard words against us, so I abstain from advising them to turn Socialists at once, especially as they will have to do so sooner or later, unless they are sucked into the great Moderate Party which is clearly beginning to form. Perhaps the best education for them would be for them to go in heartily for supporting the Irish Nationalists; that would at any rate cut them off from the worship of the Great Jingo, which the Moderate Party will certainly cultivate – moderately.

Curious to see, meanwhile, how anxious Liberal-Whig politicians are to assure us that they and the Tories are implacably opposed to each other; as witness Lord Cowper in the *Nineteenth Century*. A worthy parson has been trying to get the leading men on each side to tell him what *is* the difference between them. How glad they would have been to tell him in this electioneering season! But they could not; who can? The *Pall Mall* might offer a prize.

Mr. Chamberlain at Warrington pronounced against Mr. Parnell and so probably sealed the doom of the Radical party for the present; all the more as he also pronounced against the 'Moderate Liberals,' whoever they may comprise. In spite of the conventional party twaddle of the beginning of his speech, his challenge to the Moderates towards its close was unmistakable to any one except a party optimist.

It was noteworthy that the social part of his speech was specially well received, and that the name of Socialism warmed the audience somewhat, however little they might know about its principles in detail. It is clear that everywhere the word means hope, whereas the names of the old parties, including Radicalism, mean – nothing.

Commonweal, Volume 1, Number 9,
October 1885, p. 91.

INQUIRY COLUMN.
ANSWERS

W. Cabell. – Part of W. Cabell's inquiries will be answered in the Notes to the Manifesto of the Socialist League by Bax and Morris, which are going through the press. 'Will the social family,' says W. Cabell, 'take the place of the present private family?' I ask in turn, 'What is the present private family?' It is surely not always entirely composed of people akin to one another; only the present distinction of classes has crept into it. It is surely clear that Socialism could never assent that a family should be confined to blood-relations; for the rest there would be no hard and fast line as to what a family should be; it would be what people might choose, what they might find convenient according to the circumstances.

Commonweal, Volume 1, Number 9,
October 1885, p. 92.

MOVES IN THE GAME POLITICAL

Mr. Chamberlain in making his declaration of independence at Lambeth, took a step which was both more important to the Liberal Party than its organs chose to admit, and also very important, it would seem, to his own career. The curious person who occasionally writes – what shall I call it? – Gladstonian Toryism – in the *Pall Mall Gazette*, was indeed much perturbed by what he at least perceived to be something like revolt on Mr. Chamberlain's part; but all the other Liberal and Radical papers assumed, naturally enough, that he only intended to stick to his declaration if he found it convenient to do so; according to the custom of politicians of this epoch.

There will, however, probably be no occasion for Mr. Chamberlain to withdraw from his position. Mr. Gladstone, who was called upon to find a cry and a programme for the Liberal Party which should differentiate it from the Tories, found the task too much for him, and put forth a manifesto which was enough to make the boldest (Liberal) tremble. Verbosity is a mild word to apply to its style, evasion feebly characterises its matter. The result is that if the great moderate or reasonably reactionary party is formed soon enough for Mr. Gladstone to take a part in it, he may be its figure-head; otherwise he is at present the leader's cloak of the Liberal Party, Mr. Chamberlain being the leader, though under perilous conditions.

It is clear that is so, for in all the speeches of the great men of the Liberal Party which have followed the Lambeth declaration, when we get away from the nightmare of apologies for filibustering, thinly-veiled admissions of failure, and somewhat ignominious party attacks on the enemy, we find one thing clear, that they dare not face Mr. Chamberlain with a repudiation of his three 'advanced' propositions; the Liberal Party is practically committed to them – such as they are.

The stout Gladstonian, Lord Roseberry, indeed, turned round on Mr. Chamberlain in a way not quite new with our territorial rulers, and showed that he thought the manufacturing interest also might be made to tremble at the word 'ransom,' by declaring for a legal limitation of the working day. I will not insult his lordship's intelligence by supposing that he thinks it possible to carry out this bold threat so long as Capitalism exists; so that his threat was a safe one to make; yet that he made it, is another straw which shows which way the wind is blowing.

The fact is, I suppose, that after the first surprise at Mr. Chamberlain's declarations, the Liberal leaders set to work to look at his propositions, and found them after all not so desperately Socialistic; the taxation business might be made to mean anything or nothing; the land-allotment scheme would not work, would be a dead letter if carried; and as to Free Education, why it is not a great strain on the intellect to admit the uselessness of trying to skin a cat twice over.

Mr. Chamberlain has surely won his terrible Socialist reputation rather cheaply. He enunciated certain maxims that caught the ear of the people, who were almost touchingly moved by them, so anxious are they now getting to hear of something more hopeful than the worn-out Liberal catchwords. Compelled to suggest something immediate and practical, he has been able to set nothing before the public but schemes which are insignificant or likely to be hampered into impracticability by the very party for whose benefit he has concocted them.

There remains this residuum of significance in the reception of Mr. Chamberlain's plans of 'reform.' They are *thought* to be progressive or even Socialistic, and it is because they are so thought of that Mr. Chamberlain is so heartily cheered by the rank and file of the Radical Party, and so heartily cursed by the Tories and Moderates – when these latter dare. This certainly is a hopeful sign.

Lord Salisbury has also had his say, and he also has had little success in his attempt at a Tory platform. He won a cheap victory, indeed, in criticising Mr. Chamberlain's feeble outburst towards peasant proprietorship; and finally put his foot down on Disestablishment. Doubtless he is sincere in this, as he like Mr. Gladstone, belongs to the unsavoury type of ecclesiastical layman hard to find out of England. Doubtless, also, he believes that the Liberal party will be divided over this small matter; which is certain, and one might hope points to the waning power of the Protestant Nonconformists, the great bulwark of the bourgeoisie in England.

If one may judge of Lord R. Churchill from his recent election manifesto, it would seem that his Tory Democracy had run off him like water off a duck's back, and left him a clean-washed Tory. I should feel inclined to praise him for this if I could think it would last longer than the next convenient opportunity for getting on his Tory-Democratic skin again. Anyhow he is more likely to be a success if he sticks to his Toryism till the great Moderate Party is formed.

It is significant of the necessity felt for the formation of the said Moderate Party, that Mr. Goschen's carefully measured and clever clap-trap at Edinburgh was received with such applause by the Liberal Press. Mr. Goschen is the very type of that moderatism, and I should think would be its founder, though not its leader.

———————————

Mr. John Bright has actually chanted one more song of triumph over the abolition of the Corn-laws. Surely this must be 'positively the last time,' as the theatres have it.

———————————

There – it sickens one to have to wade through this grimy sea of opportunism. What a spectacle of shuffling, lies, vacillation and imbecility does this Game Political offer to us? I cannot conclude without an earnest appeal to those Socialists, of whatever section, who may be drawn towards the vortex of Parliamentarism, to think better of it while there is yet time. If we ally ourselves to any of the presen[t] parties they will only use us as a cat's-paw; and on the other hand, if by any chance a Socialist candidate slips through into Parliament, he will only do so at the expense of leaving his principles behind him; he will certainly not be returned as a Socialist, but as something else: what else it is hard to say. As I have written before in these columns, Parliament is going just the way we would have it go. Our *masters* are feeling very uncomfortable under the awkward burden of GOVERNMENT, and do not know what to do, since their sole aim is to govern from above. Do not let us help them by taking part in their game. Whatever concessions may be necessary to the progress of Revolution can be wrung out of them at least as easily by extra-Parliamentary pressure, which can be exercised without losing one particle of those principles which are the treasure and the hope of Revolutionary Socialists.

Commonweal, Volume 1, Number 10,
November 1885, p. 93.

FREE SPEECH AND THE POLICE

On Sunday, September 27, the Socialists and Radicals gained a complete victory over the police. Rejecting all offers of compromise they carried out literally that which they had said they would do, and that which the authorities had said they should not do. A procession of some thirty thousand marched from the East London United Radical Club to Stepney Green, and thence to Dod Street. There and thereabouts some fifty thousand others were assembled. A few policemen were present helping to keep a way for the procession. But the immense crowd was its own police. The procession marched into Dod Street. There John Mathias (E.L.U.R.C.) as chairman, Edward Aveling (S.L.) as having pledged himself to speak in Dod Street that day, despite the threats of Mr. Saunders, the police magistrate, and Benjamin Ellis (Peckham Radical Club) spoke. Then, as the victory had been won, as many thousands could not get into the historic street, as the traffic in Burdett Road was obstructed, and as Socialists and Radicals alike wished to avoid such obstruction, an adjournment was made to the open space in front of the West India Dock-gates, a place also interdicted by the police. There speeches were delivered by the Rev. Stewart Headlam, a Christian Socialist (English Land Restoration League), Vanderhout (Tower Hamlets Radical Club), Rose (E.L.U.R.C.), John Burns (S.D.F.), G. B. Shaw (Fabian Society), and H. M. Hyndman (S.D.F.). The resolution passed apparently unanimously by the vast crowd was—

> That this meeting of the Workers of London protests against the arbitrary action of the police in endeavouring to suppress the right of open-air speaking in public places, where no actual obstruction is caused; that this meeting is

of opinion that the power of deciding the legality or illegality of such meetings should not be vested in the hands of irresponsible police constables; and further, this meeting demands that the same right should be accorded to speakers of all shades of opinions, no distinction whatever being made; also that steps be taken to prosecute the police as soon as possible for their gross perjury in the cases of Samuel King, Waters, Hunter Watts, Morris, and Lyons, and that the attention of the Home Secretary be called to the misconduct of Mr Saunders, the magistrate at the Thames Police court.

The thousands of people dispersed perfectly quietly and in order.

At a subsequent meeting of the Vigilance Committee, it was decided that as the Social Democratic Federation had initiated this struggle, and as by the combined aid of that organisation and other bodies the victory was won, to the S.D.F. should now be left all further conduct of affairs in Dod Street. The societies that had fought with the S.D.F. pledged themselves, in the event of any further attack, to renew the contest.

On the Sunday following, 10,000 people welcomed in Victoria Park, John Williams, who had been sent to prison for one month by Mr. Saunders. The proceedings were most enthusiastic, and the following resolution was passed:–

That this meeting of the workers of London proclaims its strong sympathy with John Williams in his unjust and cruel imprisonment for no offence, congratulates him upon the universal admiration which his courageous self-sacrifice for the right of free-speech has called forth, and pledges itself to support the right for which he has suffered against any further attack by the governing classes of this country.

After such a battle and such a result that any personal questions should have arisen is pitiable. This journal is, however, compelled by the conduct of Mr. H. M. Hyndman, to publish the following extracts and documents, on which no comment is necessary:–

'Social Democrats have proved that they are on excellent terms with the members of other Socialist bodies, and particularly with those of the Socialist League. It is necessary, however, to state here, for the information of our comrades in London and the country, that the breach of faith committed on Sunday last by Edward Aveling will render it impossible for those who are cognisant of the facts ever again to have confidence in any arrangement entered into by him.'– *Justice*, October 3.

Resolution of the Council of Socialist League, Oct. 5.– 'That Wade, Lane, and Aveling be sent to the Vigilance Committee with instructions to report their opinion of affairs, and to assure them of our confidence in our delegate's integrity.'

Resolution of the Vigilance Committee. – 'That this meeting of delegates considers paragraph 5, col. 2, page 1, in *Justice*, Oct. 3, 1885, contains a false and cowardly attack upon Dr. Aveling, and it calls upon the editor of *Justice* to publicly withdraw and apologise for it.' The German *Communistische Verein* have passed the same resolution.

Resolution of the Council of Socialist League, Oct. 12. – 'That an official letter be written to the Council of the S.D.F., calling their attention to the paragraph in *Justice*, enclosing resolution passed by Vigilance Committee, and offering them opportunity to repudiate the accusation made against our delegate.'

Letter from the Secretary of the Social-Democratic Federation, Oct. 16. – 'To the Council of the Socialist League. – Comrades, I am instructed by the Executive Council of the Social-Democratic Federation to acknowledge the receipt of your letter with regard to the charges made against your delegate, Dr. Aveling, in *Justice*, and to state, that after having discussed and considered the matter, they beg to refer you to the editor of *Justice*. – Yours fraternally, H. H. CHAMPION.'

Mr. H. M. Hyndman, after the receipt of communications from Dr. Aveling for insertion in *Justice*, burked the whole of those communications. When, under compulsion, he inserted in his journal of Oct. 17 the resolution of the Vigilance Committee, he appended to it the following:–

> We the undersigned delegates of the Social-Democratic Federation distinctly remember that an agreement was entered into by all the Socialist speakers at the meeting of the Free Speech Vigilance Committee at the East London United Radical Club on the Friday evening preceding the Demonstration of Sunday 27th September in Dod Street not to speak at Dod Street or elsewhere until after the Radical speakers appointed by the Committee had addressed the people. This arrangement was never altered by the Committee. – Signed by G. Bateman, Herbert Burrows, H. H. Champion, J. Fielding, C. L. Fitzgerald, H. M. Hyndman, J. Oliver.

To this statement of seven members of one organisation, the Social-Democratic Federation, the following statement from 31 members of 10 organisations is the reply:–

> We the undersigned delegates of various Radical Clubs and other organisations to the Vigilance Committee in connexion with the Dod Street difficulties, having had our attention called to a statement in *Justice* of Oct. 17, signed by seven members of the Social-Democratic Federation, feel bound to declare that no agreement whatever was entered into by the Socialists or by any other speakers that the Socialists should not speak in Dod Street or elsewhere until after the Radical speakers appointed by the Committee had addressed the people. This 'arrangement' was never altered by the Committee because it was never made. Dr. Aveling for the same reason could not have changed an 'arrangement' never entered into. No breach of faith whatever was committed by Dr. Aveling on Sunday, September 27.' – Signed by John M. Mathias, Chairman of the meeting in Dod Street; Thos. Humphrey, secretary of the East London U.R.C., and secretary of the Vigilance Committee; Percy C. Wilkin, Minutes' secretary of the Vigilance Committee; Stewart D. Headlam, E.L.R.L.; Annie Besant and George Bernard Shaw, Fabian Society; A.

D. Holliday, Rad. Assoc.; Benjamin Ellis, Sydney Robeson, and John W. Samwell, Peckham and Dulwich R.C.; W. Charles Wade and Joseph Lane, Socialist League; William March, Progressive Club; J. Vanderhout, Tower Hamlets R.C.; J. D. Nieass, Eleusis Club; Lewis Lyons (sentenced to imprisonment for two months by Mr. Saunders); Thos. Grady, Daniel Paterson, Joseph Gardner, Wm. Pearce, J. Abrahams, D. Abrahams, J. Middleton, H. Rosenblatt, joint treasurer, J. Rosenblatt, Saml. W. Alderton, W. A. Rose, T. Ivatts, and J. Cain, members of the East London U.R.C.; G. Kahan and H. Backaukamp, International Working Men's Club.

Resolution of the Council of Socialist League, Oct. 19. – 'That in the opinion of this meeting of the Socialist League Council, Mr. Hyndman, by continuing to attack the League delegate to the Vigilance Committee in connexion with the Dod Street Demonstration, after his accusation has been proved to be false, has shown himself a discredit to his party; and further, that this Council expresses its sincere pity for those who by their action have proved themselves to be Mr Hyndman's tools.'

The right of open-air meeting has for the present been vindicated by the energetic efforts of those who had most to lose by its suppression – the Socialists and the Radicals. It is to be hoped that all friends of freedom of speech will note that we should have been suppressed if the authorities had not been made to feel that they *could not* do otherwise than yield. It is not likely that this will be the last attempt at suppression of 'dangerous doctrines,' and we must be prepared to do as well in the future as we have in the past.

The imprisonment of our Comrade J. E. Williams has a lesson of its own quite apart from the fact that he was punished for nothing at all. There is even something more to be said than the expression of disgust and indignation that a person convicted of a technical crime should receive just the same treatment as a felon.   It is clear that the idea of our English Prisons is to inflict torture on the prisoners: a man in for a month is treated worse than one in for two, and he again worse than if his sentence were six months: the meaning of which is that the shorter-termed prisoners can bear more torture than the longer, and therefore shall have it. Thus does Society revenge itself on the degraded whom it has degraded, on the criminals whom it has made criminal.

Commonweal, Volume 1, Number 10,
November 1885, pp. 99–100.

TO OUR READERS

The *Commonweal* has now been in existence for eleven months and the editors think that at the end of this first volume they have some reason to congratulate the Socialist League on the support which its organ has received, and on the progress which it has made in the teeth of more diffi- culties than usually beset a young paper.

The editors with, they believe, the general assent of the League, have done their best to keep up the literary and educational quality of the journal, but within those lines have always been anxious to get as much variety as possible. They are glad to think that it is attracting young writers, and hope that this will go on growing, especially as all available talent will be needed when the paper takes its weekly form.

The editors appeal to those outside the Socialist party to subscribe to and read a paper which is the recognised organ of a school of thought and politics which they have no right to be indifferent to if they have any claim to be interested in the progress of humanity or the expression of free opinion; however small our beginning may be, they may be assured that it is the cloud no bigger than a man's hand which is destined to spread over the whole sky.

This number concludes Vol. I of the *Commonweal*. It is thought best to make our first volume of 11 numbers, that subsequent volumes may run with the year. An Index for 1885 will be given away with each number of the January 1886 issue. Covers for binding the 1885 *Commonweal* can be obtained at the office, price 2s.

Commonweal, Volume 1, Number 11,
December 1885, p. 104.

CONTRIBUTIONS TO
COMMONWEAL

1886

THE MORROW OF THE ELECTIONS

The results of the elections so far are curious and instructive, although apart from the Irish question, surely no voting contest has ever been held on such apparently trivial issues. In spite of which fact it must be said that the elections have gone in a way satisfactory to revolutionists. For in the first place they have been a humiliation to both the two nominal parties that govern the State; nay, they certainly tend to make parliamentary government ridiculous and impossible under those two parties. Only by intensifying the party hypocrisy to a degree which will make it obviously monstrous, can the Liberals and Tories continue the pretence of their existence as separate and opposing forces. The formation of the Moderate or Anti-revolutionary Party is going on much more quickly than one dared to hope it would a few months ago.

The Tories have been forced from one entrenchment after another of their untenable position of sham feudal reaction, and have been forced to become Whigs. The Whigs on the other hand have had, and still have, groundwork of reality for their position, namely the resistance of Capitalistic society, at present so powerful, to any and every change which will further the emancipation of labour. Therefore they have not budged an inch, and neither will nor can do so until Revolution sweeps them away. Here are two parties then, with absolutely no difference in their policy, who have been struggling desperately for office at the poll, and striving to discover differences between them which might warrant their contention in the eyes of the electors.

It would have been quite impossible to sustain this appearance of difference but for the fiction of the Great United Liberal Party including in itself the advanced opinions of the Radicals. Mr. Chamberlain has been worth his weight – in votes – to both Tories and Whigs in the past elections; first by giving a cry to the Tories against the Liberals, which drew a great many 'Liberal' voters into the Tory-Whig ranks, and next when the Whigs were in process of being soundly beaten, coming to their rescue with the field-labourers and other genuine Radicals who saw (never having been taught anything better) in the vague hints and meagre programme of the Radical leader hopes of progress or even revolution, and thought that he might at some time or other (date not given) be able to impress his opinions on his Whig colleagues.

This is a farce which is not likely to be played again; indeed Mr. Chamberlain in his speech at Leicester as good as promised that he would not be a party to it. So that we are on the eve of the declaration of a distinct Radical Party which will force the so-called Liberals into alliance with the Tories, although that coalition is not likely to come about so bluntly and frankly as the Tories seem to imagine it will; though it is natural to them, since they are now beaten into nonentity, to call on the Whigs, who rarely agree with them, to declare their agreement at once with no more palaver.

But the Radicals deceive themselves if they think they are likely to form a strong party in Parliament. For if they are progressive they must become revolutionary, as I believe many of them are disposed to be; and as events open before them and they declare themselves, section after section will fall off from them. When the Nonconformists find that the disestablishment of the Church will not further their form of superstition they will become Whigs; when the lower middle-class find that democracy will not keep the rates down they will become Whigs. And so the game will go on till we have Whigs on one side, and on the other those who are against privilege of all kinds, that is to say who are striving for the abolition of all classes: such people are now called *Socialists*, whatever they may be called in the future.

In short Parliament is not kept together for such a 'residuum'; the powerful party in it, now that the strife *for* the people and *against* them is declaring itself, will always be the party that sees in all progress demands to be resisted or evaded as time and circumstance may serve. This party may change its name and may within the next few years even be called the Radical party, but it will not include in it a vast number of those who for want of the knowledge of a really popular creed are now proud to be called Radicals, and who will then oppose it (though I hope not in Parliament) as they have just been opposing the Tories, and in a few months it is to be hoped will be opposing the Whigs.

One word of warning meantime to such men as these. The Radical Party, at least through its leaders, has declared against the right of the Irish to govern themselves; it has now at any rate become impossible for anyone to deny that the Irish nation is determined that their government shall be Irish and not English; the Radicals, therefore, had best ask themselves what right a party has to be considered progressive that denies their right to this. The question is a serious one, for it means no less than this: Is England prepared to grant the demands of the Irish people in this matter, or to govern them by court martial? There is no third course open in the matter, even to Mr. Gladstone. The members of the Radical Party who cannot see their way straight in this question will soon find themselves Whigs and declared reactionaries.

Finally, it may seem a small matter to many Socialists that the field-labourers have generally voted Liberal; but it must be remembered what their circumstances are, and how strong the influences brought to bear upon them have necessarily been, and then I think it will be acknowledged that the fact is encouraging, although, of course, their 'representatives' that were all they had to choose from, will betray them. For they have at least voted against their masters, and generally shown much spirit in so doing. It is our business now to show them what their masters are, and why they are their masters, and when we do this I cannot think that they will be slow to learn that there is something more helpful for them than Parliamentary Radicalism, to wit the combination of themselves with their other brethren of the Residuum for the doing away with the master-class altogether.

Commonweal, Volume 2, Number 12,
January 1886, p. 1.

NOTES

Mr. Gladstone has got the difficult task before him of propounding a scheme of Home Rule which the Parnellites *can* accept and which the Whigs *will* accept; but perhaps, after all it is not so difficult as it looks; for at present the Whigs seem prepared to swallow anything, absolutely *anything*, if they can only get into office and keep there. They *have* made their wry faces over the Home Rule pill; that is a thing of the past now; memory has no sorrow for them. Of course the Tories would have done the same thing if they had had the chance; nor can we hide the fact that the Radicals have cried out just as loudly against the dose. It is a good thing that they do not see where this Irish affair is leading. They think it a mere matter of party politics; fortunately it means – revolution.

There is Arab war again in Egypt, and there are plenty of signs that it will not be the fault of those whose business it is to fish in troubled waters if we do not have another Soudan affair. In spite of all disclaimers, we seem to be in danger of getting into the stream let loose by the exploiters and of drifting in it once more. In excited articles the *Pall Mall Gazette* cries out against the folly of conquering Dongola – meaning clearly Dongola only without the rest. This has a suspicious resemblance to the 'Don't drag him through the horse-pond!' of the old election candidate. Mr. Wilfrid Blunt did not get into Parliament, which is scarcely to be regretted, as he would have been an honest and intelligent man thrown away there; but it is to be hoped he will remember that there are extra-parliamentary means of agitation.

Commonweal, Volume 2, Number 12, January 1886, p. 4.

'THE HUSKS THAT THE SWINE DO EAT'

'At the Aldershot police court, on Thursday, Henry Smith, labourer, was charged with stealing refuse food, value 3d., the property of William Newland. George Squires, provost corporal of the Medical Staff Corps, stated that he saw the prisoner taking food off the men's dishes as they were taking it to swill tubs for the contractor. In cross-examination the witness said that no soldier had any right to give any portion of his food away, whether he paid for it or not, as all broken food was sold to the contractor. Smith, for his defence, stated that he was hungry, and that a soldier asked him to take a little food off his dish. The accused was sentenced to a month's hard labour.' – *Daily Telegraph*, Dec. 12th, 1885.

The Prodigal Son is starved out, then; 'the husks that the swine do eat' are to have their full share in the apotheosis of property; they are become holy things, which no unprivileged person must touch. Ghost of William Cobbett, here is another 'vast improvement' for you on the Scandinavian law that decreed a thousand years ago that he who stole from necessity of hunger was to go scot free. The whole case seems like a cruel practical joke, and it may be hoped that the Home Secretary will at least carry the jest on by *pardoning* Henry Smith for the crime of eating when he was hungry.

But when Henry Smith comes out with his prospects brightened by his having been in jail, if he has any leisure to think amidst the pangs of hunger, he might ponder on the meaning of the words *free, freedom, enfranchisement*, as they are used in political language to-day. He may have the leisure, if it be true that at one period in the process of death by starvation it is possible to think, or at least to dream.

Apart from the question of what punishment was given to a Roman slave at the worst period, or a plantation nigger for 'stealing' 3d. worth of hogswash, I feel a curiosity on the following questions: How much hogswash Henry Smith ate? How it agreed with his digestion? What is in scientific accuracy the amount of nourishment (to a man, not a hog) in 3d. worth of hogswash? What weight of hogswash one can buy for 3d?

It seems, though, this matter of hogswash for men is becoming a burning question; for I have noticed in the papers charitable suggestions that collections of that article shall be made and sold to our 'poorer brethren'; sold, if you please, not given, lest pauperisation should result.

Two more questions yet: How much worse – or better – is Aldershot hogswash than the ordinary food of Henry Smith and of the many thousands that he represents? And lastly, How long is it to be borne?

Commonweal, Volume 2, Number 12,
January 1886, p. 7.

NOTES

Since our last issue politics have practically come to a dead stand before the Irish question. On that point there has been some talk and boundless speculation, but nothing else, till quite lately a man with eyes in his head could at last begin to see whither it was all tending. Mr. Gladstone has apparently let a Home-Rule scheme be put forward in his name, which was officially repudiated after it had played its part of drawing out various opinion, some of it, the reactionary part, emphatic enough. Lord Salisbury's scheme of ignoring the Irish question by means of a Local Government Bill for both the islands, including Scotland and Wales, has also been given us in hints obviously official. Mr. Labouchere has propounded a definite Home Rule constitution, very pretty – on paper; Fitzjames Stephens has dealt with the subject in his usual coldly truculent manner; and at last comes the scheme from 'Economist' in the *Statist* – a very pretty scheme indeed – for the Irish landowner; for it arranges to buy his land out and out and to give him a bonus in reward for his past oppression on the one hand, and on the other burdens the taxpayers both English and Irish in the long run, for the sake of sustaining rent and eviction in Ireland. If this scheme could be well and thoroughly carried out, speculation in eviction would become a special and lucrative profession – if the game could only last.

The shouts of delight with which this notable suggestion has been received by the capitalist press, point to the real intentions of our legislators, in which they will be backed by the whole of the Bourgeoisie, little and big. They mean to yield, as far as they are forced, in the direction of giving 'such a measure of Home Rule' as will muzzle the Parnellite party in

Parliament by its appearance of liberality to the Radicals; while at the same time they will so cumber the gift as to safeguard the scared rights of rack-rent and eviction. If they can do this they do not care much about names: County-boards or Irish Parliament, either will do so long as the landlords are the masters of the situation. It is not to be supposed that Irishmen will be amused into inaction by this disgusting farce; but English advanced Radicals may be; and that is the reason why I call attention to it, and beg leave to point out to them that if they share in the plot they will be giving themselves up a prey to the Whigs. They have some ideas, vague enough as yet, that something should be done with the land in Great Britain beyond 'freeing' it for the direct advantage of the capitalist: let them be sure that the Irish peasant is fighting their battle as well as his own (I am thinking of the working-men Radicals of course) and that they will bitterly repent it if they let themselves be nose-led by their *Representatives*, who are so eager for the honour of the eighth commandment in its Bourgeois development, as given us by A. H. Clough:

Thou shalt not steal: an empty feat
When it's so lucrative to cheat!

About this Irish business Mr. Chamberlain has pretty much effaced himself, which I must say seems to me both cowardly and impolitic; but he has given us a long speech at the meeting of the Allotments and Small Holdings Association, of which there is little to be said except that he does not seem to be moving from his old plan of following up vigorous denunciations of the land-owners with the proposal of absurdly insignificant 'practical' suggestions. The logical outcome of his oratorical attack on the Duke of Richmond's 300,000 acres, if it was sincere, would certainly be that the Duke should no longer 'own' them. Mr. Chamberlain's proposal is that he *might* be compelled to sell a few of them to the state at a fair market price. This *is* a small mouse to creep forth from the birth throes of the mountain.

As to the Allotments business, I think it is time that this swindle should be exposed; the accompanying quotation from the *Standard's* leader on Mr. Chamberlain's speech will help us to see what it means; it is good to learn from the enemy:

> We yield to no one in our appreciation of the good effects of the allotment system. It gives the labourer a new interest in life, and an additional motive for sobriety, frugality, and industry. It helps him to keep his pig and to pay his rent, without interfering in the slightest degree with the work which earns his weekly wage.

So much for the enemy; now for a friend, our staunch old comrade, E. T. Craig:

> If an agricultural labourer hold, say two acres of land at £2 per acre, he will have to seek employment at the hands of a farmer, and till his small allotment at his leisure. This would doom the man to an endless, increasing life of toil. Real leisure for social enjoyment he would never possess. These small individual allotments are most sordid agencies for the development of selfishness, ignorance, egoism, and superstition.

You see the two agree; only the veteran co-operator knows only too well what 'sobriety, frugality(!) and industry' mean, in a condition of abject poverty, unenlightened by the manly hope inspired by communal good fellowship.

On the surface, then, this allotment swindle means the keeping down of wages by means of over-work; but it does not concern the field-labourer only, but the whole labour-class. It is a part of the regular plan of holding down [the] discontent which specially characterises this second half of the nineteenth century; and which, but for the sickness of the commercial system in general, would be more dangerous than all the bayonets of absolutist monarchs. Briefly it means the plan of raising the condition of a part of the working class at the expense of the whole class; it would create an aristocracy of labour in whom, as our comrade puts it, 'selfishness, ignorance, egoism and superstition' would be indeed developed. Those on the one hand, and on the other would be the real proletariat, the lower class indeed, doomed to life-long torment and degradation in the workshop, the street, the workhouse and the prison; these and their discontent it would be the function of the aristocracy of labour to keep down.

Words are but weak to express one's horror at this scheme for the last and worst, because most hopeless, oppression of the people; but I can at least call on the better-off of the workers to think what they will sink to if they lend themselves to it; what base flunkies of the upper classes they will become. And the only way to escape from complicity in this plot is to remember that the wretched fringe of labour the tramp, the prostitute and the thief, are what they are because of the conditions under which they have been born and bred; modern society would have them so, and will keep them so (not in the least knowing what to do with them save, if it can, to forget their existence) until you decent working men understand that they also are part of the Brotherhood of Labour and *must* be raised out of their misery as that rises. Not at the expense of these miserable men, but at the expense of the system of slavery of which they are now the foundation must come the bettering of the condition of the working classes.

There is no great need to swell the chorus against Mr. Lusk since it has been taken up so strongly by the press in general; but we may remind the public in general that even when he is extinguished (and he will survive the present attack) the law which he administers will exist. The same may be said of Mr. Hadden: it is not that special fool who is the important thing; nay scarcely even the workhouse system itself, but the society which is forced to support such monstrosities.

The people of Bedfordshire are very naturally and properly crying out for help against Lord Brownlow who is setting about robbing them of some of the open ground on the beautiful chalk headlands of the Chiltern Hills regardless all the while of any obliteration of the historical records which may hinder his 'doing what he likes with his own.' The outcry against all this clearly comes mostly from cultivated people; they will of course be quite helpless against 'the rights of property,' and their defeat might teach them, if they could only learn, that there will be some gain even to well-to-do persons in a change in society which would prevent a man destroying other people's pleasure in beauty and history for his own gain of L.S.D.; a change which would only admit the right to possession when the owner could personally use the wealth possessed. Lord Brownlow has as much right to walk about the downs as anybody else – not a bit more. When the good people of south Bedfordshire have learned this lesson thoroughly they will be able to enjoy their chalk hills freely. Meantime, if they think the law will help them – why then who can help them?

There has been a great deal of talk about intimidation at the late elections. Our comrades will not be surprised to hear that Socialists have had their share in this; for instance, a comrade at Oldham, a good workman and an earnest Socialist, has been dismissed from his employment on account of his principles, and is now out of work. His case is a hard one as he and his wife and children are in great distress.

Commonweal, Volume 2, Number 13,
February 1886, p. 12.

NOTES ON MATTERS PARLIAMENTARY

Big as the passing days are with hopes of events to come, hard as the times are now, and troublous as the outlook is, there has seldom passed a month in which there is so little to say about the proceedings of that 'representative' body called Parliament, which according to the views of some worthy persons is the only instrument by means of which the reconstruction of Society can be carried out. It has as usual manifested its mingled tyranny and impotency, and for the rest has been doing nothing but trying hard to sit on two stools at once, with apparently little fear of the consequences, which however duly follow in the shape of a more peremptory dismissal than the ordinary 'dissolution' – a final one, to wit.

Its impotency was well shown in the matter of the £50,000 lopped off the estimates by Mr. Labouchere's *successful* resolution. The august assembly was gravely told that though it was its undoubted duty to watch the out-goings of the national purse, it must exercise that duty reasonably – *i.e.*, not at all. Then presently the Government uttered its official 'can't be done,' and relegated Mr. Labouchere to the making of a funny speech on the subject next year, and every year as long as the farce of Parliamentary Government lasts. This incident is a good measure of the real power of the Radicals in Parliament, and if tney (*sic*) are encouraged by its results, they are sanguine men indeed.

While we are on these small matters, we may note the petty piece of tyranny exercised by our *popular* House in forbidding the people to use the national property on a

Sunday. The House of Lords has just discovered that the
world would not come to an end if the museums and picture
galleries paid for by the people could be seen by the people.
When it is attempted to endorse this opinion in the
Commons, the attempt will probably be defeated by an
opposition led by the pious Broadhurst and the still more
pious Arch. Perhaps after all, then, the Primrose Habitation
of Buccleuch, who petitioned the House of Lords to abolish
the Commons' House, were democrats in disguise, who
wished to get rid of the Hereditary House by beginning first
on its only support, the House of Commons.

For indeed Society need not tremble at Mr. Labouchere
[h]aving nearly achieved a second success. The second or
third generation of money-bags elevated to seats in an upper
house by means of various cajolery and bribery exercised on
servility, will be quite 'hereditary' enough to be *safe* men,
especially when helped by a good cohort of successful
bamboozlers and muddlers up of facts, under the name of
lawyers.

One thing has happened in Parliament of some importance to
the party faction-fight, though of little otherwise: Mr.
Bradlaugh has practically declared his adherence to the
Whigs. I congratulate the Whig Party on their gain of a
really able man, and Mr. Bradlaugh on having at last reached
his level. He now stands on firm ground after much floun-
dering through sham democratic mud.

To come to matters of more importance. There is Mr.
Chamberlain's circular to the Boards of Guardians, which is
as complete an exemplification of the helplessness of our
present governmental system as could be. We may fairly
assume his wish to do all that can be done under the present
circumstances. Considering his position, he may be said to
admit the existence of hard times to the full, and to be

anxious not to say anything offensive to the feelings of the working-men. But, after all, phrases will not feed folk, and it seems to me he gives them little else. I should like to ask Mr. Chamberlain if he really thinks that useful work (and he clearly aims at that) can be given to the unemployed 'without competing with that of other labourers now employed'? And also how long such hybrid work as he proposes can go on if the present distress goes on, or only betters a little? It is after all only playing at finding productive or serviceable work for the unemployed. Surely Mr. Chamberlain knows this. Is he thinking nothing more exalted than, 'After me the Deluge'?

Well, at least he is resigning his place, and his motives for doing so are being much canvassed. One can easily imagine them. Perhaps he thinks Mr. Gladstone will not carry his Irish measure, as he probably will not. Perhaps he is not very anxious to see the Irish landlords rather more than compensated for their land, which pleasure Mr. Gladstone's bill will probably do for them. Perhaps also he sees that, the arrangements made, the Irish peasants will decline to pay this 'compensation' to the landlord, unseen, indeed, but still existing; and that the English taxpayer will have to pay it; and Mr. Chamberlain may well dread the English taxpayer.

But perhaps, again, he sees that Mr. Gladstone's scheme means separation simply, in the long run, and that when this is found out, the 'great heart of the English people,' of which we sometimes hear, will be ready to burst with rather undignified rage, and will serve out those politicians who brought matters to this pass, and Mr. Chamberlain naturally does not want to be served out. Yet it would scarcely answer his purpose to find himself the representative of the stupid prejudice of Englishmen against Irishmen, which is quite as strong among Liberals and Radicals as it is with the other side.

But of course he has a good opportunity for sitting on two stools. If the democratic side and Home Rule win he can say, 'How could I consent to buying out the landlords on their own terms, with all the dangers obviously appertaining thereto?' If the Whig-Radical integrity of the empire wins, he can say, 'How could I consent to the injury done to the great Anglo-Saxon race and its future – by admitting that a nation of Celts don't belong to that race?' The temptation towards shuffling is great; but it might be better not to yield to it. For after all, the question for *England* really is, 'Shall Ireland separate with civil war or without it?' And for *Ireland*: 'Shall we be allowed to deal with the land as we think good?'

Commonweal, Volume 2, Number 15,
April 1886, p. 28.

[RAILWAY MONOPOLY]

Sir Michael Hicks Beach the other day said that he was anxious that the railways should not be so dealt with as to 'deprive the public of the benefits of competition.' Perhaps something might be said on the other side as to competition; but in the meantime Sir M. H. Beach was in point only using language to conceal thought when he used the word. What he meant was *monopoly*, not competition; and the benefits of monopoly can be studied by us Londoners very satisfactorily in the beastly sewers through which run stink-traps under the name of carriages – the whole of which arrangement is dignified by the name of the Metropolitan and District Railways. This monopoly we may be sure the railways wont give up until they are *forced* to by more comprehensive measures than Mr Mundella's Bill.

Commonweal, Volume 2, Number 17,
8 May 1886, p. 45.

NOTES ON PASSING EVENTS

The kind of news which we have lately received from Chicago could be a surprise to no one who has watched the course of events in America even through the medium of the bourgeois press. On the one hand the vast number of men out of work, 'at least a million,' says the *Daily News*; on the other the struggle of the Knights of Labour for the eight hours' day (elsewhere told of in this number of the *Commonweal*) which means really the claim for a rise of wages: on the one hand dislocation of the labour-market and want of 'employment,' on the other claims for a greater share of the waning profits of the 'employers.' Such a condition of things is just the one to bring about collision between two parties obviously irreconcilable – the employers, brutal, domineering, short-sighted, seeing nothing but immediate gain or loss of money; the employed, no sheep to be shorn with pleasure and thanks for the removal of a burden. The lightening (*sic*) was bound to flash from two such dark clouds as this drawing near to each other.

As for the immediate events, the fight of May 4th, was one of those pieces of bloodshed which are the natural results of driving oppressed men into a corner: it must have been clear to those taking part in the meeting that the police would take the first opportunity for attacking them, and that even their dispersal would scarcely have saved them from a volley of shot. Men assembled in a great mass under such conditions are not likely to imitate the sham chivalry of the eighteenth century drilled hirelings, and request their enemy to fire first: it was a fight between people prepared to fight.

CONCERNING THE 'COMMONWEAL'

A comrade writes to us, on the naming of the *Commonweal* the 'official' organ of the League, a letter which he himself summarises thus:

1. While agreeing with most that appears in the *Commonweal*, I (and I doubt not many others) absolutely decline to be held responsible or to be expected to agree with all that appears in that paper.
2. The public invariably hold the whole League responsible for all that appears in their official organ.
3. It is impossible for any man to be responsible for the utterances of another, unless he has previously *fully* instructed him, which is clearly impossible in the present case.
4. Therefore, the title should be changed somewhat in this fashion: 'The *Commonweal*, an exponent of Socialism and organ of the Socialist League.'

The propositions 1, 2, 3, would, I think, meet with general assent from the members of the League. I beg to remind our correspondent that all articles are signed, and therefore those that write them are the only persons fully responsible for the opinions in them, but the Editors are responsible for their appearance in the paper. The *Commonweal* is called the 'official' organ of the League, because the Editors are responsible to it for the whole conduct of the paper, are appointed by the League, who have the power of making them amend or repudiate in the name of the League anything that seems to mitigate against our principles. Undoubtedly the Editors would not insert any matter with the opinions of which they did not agree in the main, without making some sign of their disagreement. I must add that it seems to me that the difference between 'the organ of the League' and 'official organ', is one of words only.

Commonweal, Volume 2, Number 16,
1 May 1886, p. 38.

[MR CHAMBERLAIN AND IRELAND]

Mr. Chamberlain was much exercised at the anti-democratic nature of the Home Rule Bill at Birmingham the other evening. Nor are we Socialists at all concerned to defend its details, as is said elsewhere in this paper; but when he said that it was ridiculous to suppose that the Irish people would accept it, it is really strange that he was not met by a shout of laughter even in the halls of the Caucus, and the fact seems to show that the Birmingham Radicals are deficient in a sense of humour, and Mr. Chamberlain has the same right to be displeased with them as the teller of a Joe Miller has when one of his audience requests a reasonable explanation of the joke. Mr. Chamberlain knows perfectly well that the Irish people have accepted the Bill, because they understand that whatever shortcomings or follies there may be in it, it is intended to give them the management of their own affairs. Mr. Chamberlain's constituents ought to know, and do know unless they are fools, that this is the very reason why Mr. Chamberlain opposes it.

Commonweal, Volume 2, Number 16,
1 May 1886, p. 38.

NOTES ON PASSING EVENTS

In ordinary political matters there are at present but two subjects wherein any one pretends to take any interest in this country – the Irish question and the Greek. The general English public know next to nothing about the first, and nothing about the second. Yet it is not uncommon to find people more interested (even though quite ignorant) in the Greek question than the Irish, probably because they expect, or have expected, the dramatic entertainment of a war for which they will not have to pay. As to the Irish question, the so-called educated classes stick with great fidelity to the opinions of their favourite newspapers, and by this time have learned to conduct an 'argument' on the subject by those means – the whole operation being called the 'formation of public opinion.'

Meantime that opinion seems to be setting somewhat in favour of Mr Gladstone's Bill, in spite of the shrill and almost triumphant cry of the parliamentary people and their hacks that it was doomed. One is fain to hope that the reason for this is that another and more genuine opinion, or instinct rather, is acting on the leader-made 'public opinion,' and that a real undercurrent of popular feeling is at work, and is teaching the people to see through the elaborately-woven veil of pretences to wisdom, foresight, and statesmanship that is hiding a mere lust for conquest and greed of exploitation in the great mass of our 'respectable' classes about this Irish business. If this is so it is well, because, as I pointed out last week, it is not the details of Gladstone's Bill that we need note, but whether the Irish people see their independence in it; and the cheerful acceptance of that independence by the English working-class (the opinions of no other class are of any importance to *us*) would mean a great blow to Jingoism, which is one of the great foes of the Revolution, and which has already been sorely shaken by the disgraces of recent piratical wars waged by the Gladstone as well as by the Tory governments.

One cannot, however, ignore the fact that there is one thing which makes it probable that the democratic side of Liberalism will accept Irish independence – to wit, worship of Mr. Gladstone. The enthronement of a temporary and most powerful king, to which (strange irony of history!) democracy, as opposed to Socialism, tends, is certainly all too obvious in this case. Nay, it is not to be thought that the burst of hero-worship which the Irish themselves have expressed towards this G.O.M. is hypocritical: they are clearly touched at so great a man condescending to befriend their contemned race. Who can wonder at this? Individually we are weak, poor, ignorant; as democrats we have not learned to understand the power of combination inspired by principle and a high ideal, or how it can transform the man whom it draws out of the slough of grovelling individualism: therefore we naturally feel grateful to a man on whom all eyes are fixed, if from his pedestal of greatness he will condescend to half-adopt, and half-spoil in adopting, the very ideas which we have forced him to express for us. Democracy while it lasts will never be free from this hero-worship, and all the traps which the heroes (poor devils!) wittingly and unwittingly lead their worshippers into. Socialism alone will give us manly independence of thought, which, again, can alone lead to harmonious action, instead of machine-made policy.

Meantime, all the hints at alternative measures to Home Rule mean nothing more nor less than the retention of our English Poland, whether they are put forward by Conservatives, Liberals, or Radicals. Provincial councils *we*, at least, should not find fault with, if they were intended to be genuine and independent; in that case they would educate people towards the condition of the free federation of free communes, which is the only solution of politics. But these 'light and leading' provincial councils are just meant to choke off the demand for practical independence, which naturally is the only thing which the Irish demand. They are not meant to deal with anything on principle; they are, in fact, to be enlarged *vestries*.

Of course this means a desperate attempt to shunt the land question – which cannot be shunted. We may well believe Mr. Wilfrid Blunt when he says that it cannot be put off for even six months; matters, he says, are growing so desperate that the landlords are hard at work evicting, as if with the consciousness that their time is drawing near; and they are using their power even though its exercise rather damages than forwards their money interests. In short, it is high time that Mr. Chamberlain should leave his dreams of a possible Radical Ireland, and that the Liberal Associations should leave off babbling pedantry about representation and taxation and the 'expulsion' of the Irish members (expulsion of a man from prison!), and find out what form the Irish will accept in order to look to their own affairs.

As to the Land Purchase Bill, it provides a monstrous compensation for the Robbers of Ireland; and one would think that landlords would break their necks almost in their hurry to run to meet it; but it does not seem that they will. Perhaps they feel it as such a joke that they should be compensated for the glorious times that they have had at other people's expense, that they cannot help thinking there is something else behind it, and can scarcely believe in the reality of the English money with which Mr. Gladstone is bribing them to take themselves off from Ireland. To us all this matters little so long as in England and elsewhere landlords sit awaiting the compensation which Democracy may one day offer them; while capitalists compensate themselves by the daily and hourly robbery of labour. That the Irish accept in any way this Bill, shows probably that they consider it a mere futile and temporary experiment, which will not interfere with their dealing with the matter in their own way.

Mr. Matthew Arnold's paper in the *Nineteenth Century* is noteworthy, though not for its own sweet sake; for it is not worthy of the author's reputation as a clever essayist with an occasional gleam of insight. It is in fact a piece of Whig commonplace, such as may be seen in any Whig organ by the dozen, but helped out somewhat (not much) by adroitness and neatness of style. But as showing wither-ward 'Sweetness and light' are drifting, it is of interest, since it is Mr. Arnold's manner of doing what Professor Huxley has recently done more emphatically, to wit, declaring formally for Reaction, as perhaps a pensioner is bound to do in the long run.

If any of our friends may happen to think Arnold's views on the Irish question are original and valuable, they had better refer to the passages in which he openly advocates the suppression of the rights of public meeting, or note his newborn admiration for the King of Pettifoggers, Bismarck. Though perhaps he is not wrong in elevating that 'buffoon,' as one of our comrades called him in the *Commonweal* last week, into the rank of the statesmen, when one considers the history of those pests of the human race. Well, it is what was to be expected. Since Mr. Arnold has sorely developed the prig in him since his early days, it is natural that he should at last distinctly put forward the Prig Government: and yet it is sad that a man who once had a genuine, though not copious poetic gift, should narrow himself to the limits of such a poor world of pedantry and hypocrisy as the cultured middle-class is; that culture should greatly ignore the struggles and aspirations of the greater part of humanity, and elect at last to live and die in a flunkey's coat.

As to Greece, it was clear from the first that she was to be coerced into peace if it suited the robber powers of Eastern Europe who use England as a cat's paw. It is not worth while even to think about the dark and tortuous intrigues which have been at work in the matter, further than noting them as part of the general ignominy of European 'statemanship' to which we are forced to submit. The robber powers nearest to these weak Eastern European peoples will of course take any advantage that they can, amidst their first business of keeping down their own populations, of the development of the energies of those peoples. It is to be hoped that intrigue will fail in stimulating them into artificial outbreaks founded on unhappy race prejudices. The true opportunity for the development of Eastern Europe will be found when that war begins which will lead to Revolution: a war which is bound to be the outcome of the blatant scoundrelism of the robbers aforesaid.

Says Mr. Gladstone in his latest address to his constituents: *'The adverse host then consists of class and the dependents of class'*. This might serve as a motto for us, only we should mean something by it that Mr. Gladstone does not; he still imagines a compact Tory party and a compact Liberal one in the main, though the latter may suffer from occasional secessions. He does not see that the march of events towards real freedom is forcing men to declare themselves, that they are being frightened out of their hypocrisy. Yet his sentence is true, and coming from a bourgeois Prime Minister has even a prophetic ring about it. We accept it, but in its literal meaning, which probably is not quite Mr. Gladstone's.

Commonweal, Volume 2, Number 17,
8 May 1886, p. 41.

[THE SOCIALIST TRIAL]

The government were badly beaten in the Socialist trial, and in fact it is difficult to understand why they persisted in it after their breakdown in Bow Street. Some attempt there was in the bourgeois press to make as little as possible of the defeat, but most people with memories will connect it with the police defeat of Dod Street last summer. The result shows that the general public are not prepared as yet to attack mere opinion, however *dangerous* it may seem, and should encourage all Socialists to speak plainly to the people; though it must be admitted that those who are fairly enlisted in the cause do not want much encouragement on that side. On the other hand, if our bourgeois have not the heart to resist such very plain attacks it shows how bad their conscience must be.

Commonweal, Volume 2, Number 16,
1 May 1886, p. 36.

[THE PIT-BROW WOMEN]

One of the saddest things in the terrible struggle for life at the present day is the eagerness with which any 'employment' however miserable, ie (*sic*) clutched at; so that when the Bourgeois conscience awakes to the fact that some occupation or other is so disgracefully carried on that something must be done to amend it, the victims of the abuse themselves are often among the first to cry out against the interference. The case of the pit-brow women is an example of this: they are prepared to fight tooth and nail in defence of their wretched work, and are being helped in their battle by philanthropists and fine ladies whose imaginations are not strong enough to master the picture of their daughters or themselves working day in day out on such terms. When will the workers at least come to understand the meaning of employing women and children to do work which men can do better, which is simply the reduction of the wages paid to the adult male at tne (*sic*) expense of the over-work and degradation of the weaker members of the household; a price not too high to pay for cheap labour, thinks the capitalist, since I don't pay it.

Commonweal, Volume 2, Number 16,
1 May 1886, p. 37.

Meantime, we may note what was the nature of the speech of Samuel Fielden as told of in our bourgeois press, and the report of which brought out the 'body of 400 police armed with staves and muskets...in extended platoon, which occupied the entire width of the street from house to house.' It was just such a speech as is made by any of our speakers at street corners in London on Sundays. It was to guard against dispersal and arrest at the least, and probably also against immediate musket-shot that the revolutionists came armed on this occasion. They were driven into a corner, and they fought, as men of mettle are apt to do when in such a plight.

In short, it seems clear that the dominant class was determined in its fear of revolutionary action, to put down revolutionary opinion with a high hand; nor can it be denied that Tuesday's fight has given them a good occasion to do so, and they are probably rejoicing even amidst their terror at the outbreak, because of its affording them their opportunity, whether they deliberately provoked it or not. A white terror is certainly setting in, which is likely to be specially ferocious, since in America the tyranny of middle-class democracy is not hampered by any of the sentiment which, half real and half hypocritical, still clings to it in England – till the middle-class shall become quite awakened by fear.

The American press is even suggesting the repression of immigration as a remedy for the spread of Socialism. If they are really in earnest, and succeed in carrying out such a measure, the great uprising will not be long delayed. That such a thing should be even spoken of, shows how swift has been the advance of Socialism. Once the two great Commercial Democratic Countries of the world prided themselves on being an asylum for political refugees: that was in the days when the refugees seemed no danger to commercial tyranny; which, therefore, was not sorry to hold in its bosom a half-hidden threat, for which it was not responsible, against absolutism, its own special enemy. Now, on the contrary, any spurt of fear sufficiently felt may at any time arouse the White Terror, either in England or America; nor will either Democracy, and, as aforesaid, especially the latter, be a whit behind the old Absolutisms in vigour of repression when it is really touched by fear.

The thoughtful middle-class man – the master – sees two prospects before him – the first baleful, the second fortunate. The first is the practical break up of the system which makes him master, and his place void in a society in which the rich and the poor have alike melted into equality. He sees himself no longer what he was – the stern director of healthy compulsion, or the condescending distributor of unpauperising rewards – but a man like other men, working for his own livelihood, winning his own pleasures, all chance of his keeping a thousand men poor for his pleasure denied to him. This is a dreadful prospect to him; therefore, looking round on the power which he and those like him wield, he comforts himself with another possible prospect. He sees his class, wise in time, suppressing all opinion determinedly, though as slyly as possible; he sees part of the working-classes bribed into being his supporters, and the rest, the true have-nots, rigidly kept down. The old tyranny of the Roman empire is the model of his ideal: the jarring of families and tribes over now; the slaves reduced to sullen silence; the people kept quiet with bread and dog-fights; the rich free – free each man to hunt out his pleasure amidst the form of corruption which best suits his own sordid soul. This is the ideal of our masters of to-day, expressed with more or less hypocrisy, more or less timidity, but always returned to as a solid comfort amidst the fears engendered by the obvious decay of their system.

Well, these two prospects are visible to us as well as to the masters; but there is another which they do not seem to see, though it is more likely to be realised than either of the others. It involves, however, the partial realisation of their ideal. This second *Pax Romana* (peace of the empire) brought about, no corner of the civilised world in which a man can openly proclaim the wrongs of the have-nots; any spoken word which may break the peace of corruption, a crime, a wickedness; for the proletariat the civilised world one vast prison, in short, and no escape from it save death; and then – the upheaval. Since nothing but death will deliver us, there will be men who will choose a death which may bring about at least something. The word which may not be spoken will be whispered, and the whisper will be a gathering sign.

It is the course which will bring about this that the American middle-classes seem to be taking. Already the air is stifling with the sense of repression, and heavy with boasts of the violence of the well-to-do, who see success before them, especially since they hope to detach the mass of their own workmen from the revolutionary camp. And they probably will succeed in this at least, in showing the starved-out proletarians of Europe that they no longer have a city of refuge in America, but will meet there exactly the same oppression which they are used to in Europe. Once more, it is impossible that this should not hasten the coming Revolution all over the world.

Nor it must be said are the ruling classes quite ignorant of the fact that they will at least have rough times to pass through before they can attain to the peace of perpetual universal slavery, the hope of which they so vainly hug. It is a sign of the times that the Tory *Standard* should have an article on the Chicago riots which fairly admits, as it does, the facts of the genuine evolution of Socialism, and which sees that the outbreak is no mere accident to a peculiar form of our present system, but a consequence of the spread of enlightenment, and the results of steady propaganda. In the face of such admissions we need not combat the usual fallacies which the same article puts forward, since although the writer says, 'That in the long run the forces of order will prevail in America and in Europe, we do not for a moment doubt;' it is clear from the rest of his article that he does very much doubt it.

Grand Court ceremonies have varied the budget of terrible and doubtful news to hand during the last few days; the same morning which gave the papers the happy chance of describing the hard won police victory at Chicago, gave them the opportunity of a long account of the glories of the costumes of the Drawing Room. In other words, the loads of idiotcy (*sic*) with which the Court ladies try to set off their somewhat doubtful charms. One almost wonders that even such empty fools as these are, are not ashamed to play such a farce in the midst of all these tragedies.

Or that farce of all farces, the Queen opening the Colonial Exhibition with a Court ceremonial, crowned by the degra- dation of a man of genius! It fairly sickens one to think that the man who wrote 'Rispah,' with all its passion and deep sympathy for the wrongs of the poor, should have been driven by mere yielding to convention, to allow such flunkey doggrel (*sic*) as this Jingo 'Ode' to appear with his name tacked on to it. That the Press, including the *Pall Mall*, should puff it is proper and natural, of course; they know that this Exhibition is just a piece of commercial adver- tisement (who gets the money realised by it, by the way?) and with their tongues in their cheeks proceed to praise the exemplification it offers of the hopes of the perpetual unity of the empire; and even poor Home Rule must be lugged in to point the moral.

Examples of the last remains of the art of India which our commercialism has destroyed, have been made to do duty as a kind of gilding for the sordidness of the rest of the show,

and are a sorry sight indeed to one who knows anything of
what the art of the East has been. But let that pass. There
are, perhaps, certain exhibits of examples of the glory of the
Empire which have been, I think, forgotten. We might begin
at the entrance with two pyramids, *à la Timour*, of the skulls
of Zulus, Arabs, Burmese, New Zealanders, etc., etc., slain in
wicked resistence (*sic*) to the benevolence of British
commerce. A specimen of the wire whips used for softening
the minds of rebellious Jamacia (*sic*) negroes under the
paternal sway of Governor Eyre might be shown, together
with a selection of other such historical mementoes, from
the blankets infected with small-pox sent to unfriendly tribes
of Red-Skins in the latter eighteenth century down to the
rope with which Louis Riel was hanged last year, for resisting
a particularly gross form of land-stealing. The daily rations
of an Indigo ryot and of his master under one glass case,
with a certificate of the amount of nourishment in each,
furnished by Professor Huxley. The glory of the British arms
gained in various successful battles against barbarians and
savages, the same enclosed in the right eye of a louse. The
mercy of Colonists towards native populations; a strong
magnifying-glass to see the same by. An allegorical picture of
the emigrant's hope *(a)* on leaving England; *(b)*, after six
months in the Colonies. A pair of crimson plush breeches
with my Lord Tennyson's 'Ode' on the opening of the
Exhibition, embroidered in gold, on the seat thereof. A great
many other exhibits of a similar nature could be found
suitable to the exposition of the Honour, Glory, and
Usefulness of the British Empire.

Rebellion, it seems, will soon be the fashion. Lord Wolseley
disdains to deny the apparently preposterous brag of the
Orange Chieftain; so it may be supposed there is at least
some truth in it. We Socialists are not, of course, going to cry
horror on rebellion; but the complacency with which the
idea is received forms a curious comment on the outcry made
by respectable people against other forms of rebellion.

Bourgeois moralists will discover that everything is fair and even beautiful in defence of the sacred rights of property, when they are once seriously attacked.

Commonweal, Volume 2, Number 18,
15 May 1886, pp. 49–50.

[FOOT-NOTE TO BAX'S ARTICLE THE COMMERCIAL HEARTH]

I think that whatever damage Ruskin may have done to his influence by his strange bursts of fantastic perversity, he has shown much insight even into economical matters, and I am sure he has made many Socialists; his feeling against Commercialism is absolutely genuine, and his expression of it most valuable.

Commonweal, Volume 2, Number 18,
15 May 1886, p. 50.

NOTES ON PASSING EVENTS

The Home Rule question is much where it was last week; the
beginning of an outrageously dull debate in which the slain
are slaughtered over and over again, has only shown what
was obvious before, that Mr. Gladstone and Mr.
Chamberlain can no longer row in the same boat, and that
Mr. Chamberlain in spite of all his fervid would-be Socialistic
sentiment of last year, is quite as ready as other politicians to
sacrifice the welfare of a people to his career of leadership.

The Bill, say politicians, will certainly be thrown out: in
which case it is probable that a Tory Government will pass a
Home Rule measure stronger than the present one, though
perhaps with one or two pieces of sham precaution added.
Meantime one noteworthy feature of the present hocus-pocus
is the extreme eagerness of so many of the Radical members
to label themselves Whigs, from Mr. Chamberlain
downwards, even in the teeth of the fact that the Radical
party outside Parliament is mostly Gladstonian. This is
accounted for on the face of things by their conscious hope
(not without foundation) of their being able to humbug their
constituents; but there is a deeper cause than that for the
enthusiasm of their ratting, the resistless march of events
towards the formation of the Great Moderate Party. These
quasi-Radicals fear their constituents much, but they fear the
advance of revolution more, and they are but acting naturally
and after their kind.

The official disclaimer made for Lord Wolseley in Parliament
was a sufficiently farcical incident in the great farce of the
hypothetical Orange Rebellion. Nobody doubts that Lord

Wolseley and the other barrack-room fools have been bragging in the usual swash-buckler style as to what they would do if only the circumstances were to hand: they again are but 'doing after kind.' But it is a little remarkable that the whole Tory press from the sober *Standard* to the romantic *St. James's Gazette*, have taken the matter so seriously, and with one consent have joined to egg on the Orangemen – if that were needed so long as the rebellion is only hypothetical. Has the result of the Socialist trial encouraged our Law-and-Order contemporaries? Anyhow, again we are shown how obvious it really is to all men's minds that physical force is the basis of our Society.

———————

The Bourgeois, both directly through their Governments, and by their joint-stock associations artificially supported by the said Governments, are prepared to act steadily by open force more than ever. Bismarck in Berlin forbids all public meetings; while from Chicago comes this piece of news, showing that the triumphant capitalists are going to make their most out of the present situation and their recent police victory: 'The wholesale Clothing Association in this city has resolved upon a lock out against their employés; by this step twenty-seven thousand hands will be thrown out of employment.'

———————

The American capitalist is certainly a bold, even a reckless man, and deserves to succeed in a 'survival of the fittest' world. But even brutality may be carried too far, and we hereby tender our thanks to the Chicago sweaters, who, if the above piece of news is true, are determined to show the American non-Socialist workers that their cause is one with the revolutionists, whom they are now denouncing under the influence of very natural fear inspired by the White Terror. A few more such brutal attacks on the lives of the workers as this of the Wholesale Clothing Association, and the whole mass of workers in America will see the hopelessness of incomplete and isolated attacks on monopoly by means of strikes and boycotts, and will be *forced* to set themselves to the one necessary work, the abolition of the classes of privilege.

In this age of fads there is a curious fad labelled by its supporters 'Imperial Federation.' Now, as we Socialists have learned to suspect all qualifications, even the most simple of us will be likely to smell out the 'Imperial' qualification of that good thing Federation. Yet a word or two on the subject may not be untimely in these days of enthusiasm over the huge Commercial Puff at Kensington, besung by Court poets and dry-nursed by the boundless ignorance of Sir Philip Cunliffe Owen.

The point is that while the aim of Federation is the extinction of pational (*sic*) rivalries, that of Imperial Federation is their artificial supnort (*sic*). Imperial Federation means the bolstering up of the decaying supremacy of England in the world-market with the help of a worthless sentiment called patriotism; which, however, has done rather successful work as regards the leaders in this movement themselves, who can see nothing but through its mist. *E.g.*, the *Pall Mall Gazette* has been compelled by it to join the Hartington-Chamberlain Whigs, and is prepared to dragoon Ireland if she fails to see the beauty of neglecting her own business of making her people happy by allowing them the use of their own land, for the sake of nursing the trade in English shoddy wares all over the world.

The attempt, however, like that of other artificial revivals now current, is not very dangerous, because it is artificial. In point of fact that humbugging phantom, 'the marvellous energy of the Anglo-Saxon race,' covers at least the average amount of incompetence and laziness common to commercial mankind. The material of which 'England' is composed, is doubtless good, since it includes contributions from so many races assimilated at so many periods; but it is not miraculous, nor capable, most happily, of forming a great prominent Empire.

———————

In fact, the matter of the English markets is becoming serious enough to shake our 'patriotic' hypocrisy; and some frank admissions of the truth are oozing out. The *Times*, *e.g.*, publishes, and the romantic *St. James's Gazette* reprints what amounts to an attack on our traders for their insolent stupidity, which is not quite the same thing as their stupid insolence, and does not serve their turn quite as well as that has done when war-ships and bayonets accompanied it. The text which this gentleman preaches upon, with a vigour which really inspires confidence, is as follows: 'The universal complaint against them, from Auckland to Montreal, from Tokio to Smyrna, is that they are impervious to new ideas, and they act on the principle that it is the business of their customers to adapt themselves to their manufactures.'

———————

Yes, and it is the business of our Imperial Federation wisemen to *force* 'our customers to adapt themselves to our manufactures;' and, in fact, we always play that game, Federation or no Federation, when we find it safe to do so.

———————

Well, the *Daily News* also follows suit in a leader on the Consular reports: 'Manufacturers are not so quick as they once were in adapting their products to the wants or prejudices of their customers.' The truth will out. How long ago was it since the whole bourgeois Press was busily denying the depression in trade? Says the *Daily News* in its leader: 'The first thing which strikes every reader of the Reports for the year 1885, is the universality of the depression from which trade and agriculture are suffering.' This time last year I caught the following sentence in one bourgeois paper (I admit that it was the *Spectator*): 'It is yet to be shown that there is any depression of trade.'

Good news all this, good news! The obvious obstacle to the spread of Socialism is the commercial prosperity of England. That is now past praying for. Yet, if the centre of commerce only shifted, it would not help us much. That will not happen, England will not crush other countries as she hoped, as the insane fanatics of Imperial Federation still hope, but she will not be utterly crushed either. There will be no centre; the field will be left free for limitless cut-throat competition between the nations, which will lead the Depression of Trade out at the *other end* – Revolution.

Good people of Britain! when in times to come you are become modest about yourselves, and neighbourly to all the world (which *may* take place according to the proverb: '*Only the unexpected happens*'), when in those times some flattering visitor praises you, as guests in their kindness are wont to do, and extols the 'famous men and fathers that begat you,' for their cleverness and enterprise past all other people, will not truth compel you to exclaim: 'Sir, and dear guest, you are somewhat mistaken; it was not we who were so clever, *but our coals!*'

Commonweal, Volume 2, Number 19, 22 May 1886, p. 57.

[UNTITLED NOTES]

'Count Samuel Teleky is organising an expedition for the exploration of Central Africa. The fitting out will be completed by the end of May, and one hundred well-armed men will reach Zanzibar in the course of June. Captain Hähnel, of the Austrian navy, will take part in the expedition, and two boats will be taken out in pieces. It is believed here that the expedition will not confine itself to scientific explorations only.'

The last sentence is really almost superfluous: 'scientific explorations' is only 'markets writ large.'

'The collar manufacturers at Troy, New York State, have ordered a lock-out owing to the demands of their employés. Eight thousand persons are consequently thrown out of employment.'

'Væ victis!' – Woe to the vanquished! – is a saying that holds good still. American workers, hold your tongues and bear it all – if you can do nothing else.

Commonweal, Volume 2, Number 20,
29 May 1886, p. 68.

BRANCH REPORTS.
BIRMINGHAM

For the information of comrades, I have to state that besides the lecture at Baskerville Hall at Birmingham, noticed in last week's *Commonweal*, I lectured there in the evening of the same day on Socialism, and had a full audience, many, or most of which, as usual, seemed to agree with the indictment against our Sham Society; the questioning was of the usual kind. On the Monday evening (17th), I lectured on 'The Political Outlook,' at the Exchange Buildings, under the auspices of our Branch. Although it was a wretchedly wet night, and there was a counter attraction in the building in the form of the Performing Fleas, the attendance was good. Mr. Walker, the leading Land Nationaliser in Birmingham, was in the chair, and opened with a liberal-minded and sympathetic speech. The audience was very attentive, and a large part of it again appeared to agree with me, though I found it impossible to avoid the chance of shocking some sensibilities on the subject of the immediate crisis. Birmingham is a difficult place to deal with. Open-air speaking is not allowed in the borough, though the Board Schools can always be had for a meeting at a moderate rate, and there is much intolerance of advanced thought outside the cut-and-dried party. Still, one must suppose that there are intelligent men there not drilled into nonentity by the party caucus, and our comrades have only to go on and attack vigorously and persistently in order to gain these.

Commonweal, Volume 2, Number 20,
29 May 1886, p. 72.

NOTES ON PASSING EVENTS

Mr. Gladstone, in hopes of passing a resolution in favour of the principle of his Bill, did last week almost climb down from the heights of that principle, and at first it was thought that the Chamberlain Radicals would accept the compromise to the extent of remaining neutral in the division; but these hopes have been overthrown, the Chamberlainites decided to vote against the Bill, and on Tuesday night their leader made his manifesto in the House of Commons. So, in all probability, the Bill will be finally thrown out. Will there be a dissolution then? is the question which the Press generally is answering in the affirmative; and yet, strange to say, it does not seem quite certain. As things have gone it would be a piece of imbecility to avoid it, which would brand all Mr. Gladstone's proceedings in this matter with the same mark. There would in any case have had to be a dissolution in the autumn had the autumn Session come off; and also in any case the two opposed camps of the once Liberal party would have had to meet face to face. Mr. Gladstone's attempt at compromise will give him an advantage in the struggle, because he can now say truly that what the Chamberlainites object to is real Home Rule.

Mr. Chamberlain's speech makes that clear: the independence of Ireland is what he is fighting against; and he was not ashamed to emphasise this fact by an outburst of Jingo platitude in the midst of his speech. His disclaimer of stirring up religious animosity between the two sections of Irishmen is futile; for whether he wills it or not, his line of conduct is certainly helping to excite this animosity. Mr. Chamberlain must know, one would think, what the Ulster opposition means at bottom, that if civil war has to be in Ireland, though the excuse may be the supremacy of Catholic or Protestant, the real cause will be Landlordism, for and against. If Mr. Chamberlain does not know that, the Tories who cheered him, the Tory press which (surely to his grief) praises his 'manliness' and his patriotism, know it well enough.

Mr. Auberon Herbert has, amongst others, written his manifesto on the Irish Question. To the politicians playing the above-mentioned game, for and against, he will be quite insignificant; but he is a straightforward and honest man according to his lights, and wields a somewhat sharp pen. It may be worth while, therefore, to call attention to one or two points in his late letter to the *Pall Mall*, for the advantage of those who may be impressed by his quite genuine contempt of the 'circular dodgers' of Parliamentary life, and may be inclined to follow him accordingly. His anxiety for the Irish minority of Ulster is no doubt genuine; nor perhaps is he disturbed by the obvious question of how to deal with the minority in Ulster when you have settled the matter of the minority in Ireland. He is perhaps prepared with some scheme which does not go as far as free and federated communes, to the consideration of which the difficulty leads us. But after all it is clear that his defence of the Irish minority is based on his assumption of the eternal and indefeasible rights of private property – that is, of class robbery.

His 'view of justice and great human rights' does not embrace the freedom of all men to live naturally and without artificial restraints: freedom to fleece and be fleeced is all the freedom he admits. Ireland, he says practically, may be free – nay, *should* be free – if she will but pay for her own land. To whom, we ask, and what for? The answer is clear: 'To the rich; so that the rich may still be rich and the poor poor.' If Irish independence can mean that – if Ireland means it – she is striking strokes in the water indeed. It is only in the hope that through that independence she is groping her way to

Freedom that to us Irish independance (*sic*) is worth thinking
about.

So goes on merrily the political disruption of our present
system. Far more grim than this bad joke of Parliament and
representation is the process of its economical break up. All
over the country an attempt is being made to stimulate trade
by the huge advertisements called exhibitions; and royalty is
playing its due part in a commercial country be opening
these, and so killing, if possible, two birds with one stone –
exciting loyalty on one hand, and trying to get it to spend
money on the other. The success on the commercial side is
not yet great, and trade is still 'dull' – a word which covers
something of the same suffering as the conventional phrases
used in describing a battle do. 'The enemy annoyed our
advance much:' we all know, if we choose to think, the kind
of misery that such phrases cover, and in our commercial war
it is, I repeat, much the same.

Here are a few sentences taken from a letter to the
Manchester Guardian: 'In the meantime they have no food
and no furniture or clothing left to sell or pawn.' 'Man,
wife, and six children: husband steady and hard-working,
but very little work for a long time; wife recently confined; no
fire; no food in the house; no clothing left.' 'Widow and two
little children; when in work earns 9s. a-week; one of the
children ill with inflammation of the lungs.' '*This man can
now get work, but through prolonged starving is too weak
for it.*' 'The people are growing more feeble and spiritless,
because, though we keep them from starving to death, *we
cannot pay their rent.*' 'Some men who were specimens of
manly vigour a few months ago are almost like skeletons, and
I know several whose prolonged suffering under the Poor
Law has, I believe, made them insane.'

These are a few phrases taken from one letter as to Manchester. Multiply them by thinking of other great centres such as Glasgow, where the distress is terrifying the authorities even, and then consider what 'dull trade' means - a thing which is one of the ordinary incidents of our commercial system, since the introduction of the 'great industries.' Only remember that though the phrases above quoted are an amplification of 'dull trade,' they are still conventional: no language can express the sufferings brought on by our artificial famine. And every one of these men – nay, the women also – could earn a comfortable living if he or she were only allowed to do so.

The writer of the letter in the *Manchester Guardian* says 'something must be done with these men: you must either feed them or shoot them.' There is a third alternative, as the rich men of this generation will probably find out if they persist in their present course; but let that pass. 'You' *cannot* feed them; they can only feed themselves. The writer dimly feels this, and as a remedy suggests emigration, with help from the State of various kinds. The 'bones of one's mind' fairly ache at the thought of the number of times this 'remedy' has been met and disposed of. When will well-intentioned men like this writer understand that when our 'State' nurses emigration, and when private capitalists suggest the nursing and egg on poor men to emigrate, their intention is only to get rid temporarily of *their* responsibility and trouble over the people thrown out of work by the system of artificial famine – which they are determined to uphold – so that it may work the smoother? Men are expatriated, so that fresh men may be bred for compulsory expatriation. Let us think of organised emigration when we shall be able to find freedom before us and leave freedom behind us; not till then.

Commonweal, Volume 2, Number 21, 5 June 1886, p. 73.

NOTES ON PASSING EVENTS

Mr. Chamberlain gained last Monday one of those curious
reactionary victories which mark the progress of ideas almost
as clearly as reactionary defeats do; because they draw the
limits of the camps of reaction and progress, and force men
to declare themselves for what they really are. Mr. Gladstone
might well say that his side on the division was on the
flowing and the other on the ebbing tide, and he did well to
renew his appeal to the heart of the people which his
Midlothian manifesto contained. It is to be hoped that he
will have the courage not to draw back from his words. At
present, though beaten, he has the glory of the contest, and
Chamberlain the victorious has its shame; but if Mr
Gladstone now shrinks from a dissolution, or if he has the
chance of bringing in a new Bill after the dissolution and
makes any compromise in it, then Mr Chamberlain will have
the laugh on his side. Meanwhile, what is to become of the
Liberal party? Where will it be after this next election?
Victorious Whiggery exults now, and probably it will now
for some time to come appear to be the sole party that has
any power; it is now only the unseen or utterly despised
growth of the instinct towards real freedom which will be
formidable to it. Vain-glorious inflation and sudden collapse
are what await it now.

'A meeting was held at Lady Maxwell's, 15 Ennismore
Gardens, on Tuesday last, to consider the interesting question
of the prevention of pauperism by national insurance. The
Earl of Derby, while passing over as by no means insuperable
many of the commonly alleged objections to the proposal,
indicated as stronger ones the difficulty of collecting the
contributions from some wage-earners,' etc., etc. Really, in

common with Baillie Nicoll Jarvie, one finds some 'glimmerings of sense in the creature' – which, however, were not strong enough to keep him away from Canon Blackley's meeting. Yet we ought to be rather thankful to the worthy canon for the resolution he displays in his *reductio ad absurdum* of the wages-system, and his exposition of the blessings of the 'iron law.' I have heard that some people have an inborn incapacity for seeing proportion between things; I *know* that some people are incapable of seeing a joke. The canon doubtless shares these incapacities, and hence his usefulness to Socialists.

The following is a curious example of another kind of philanthropy from Canon Blackley's – though like his it wants to take something from nothing – and is suggested, apparently, by a joker as unconscious of his humour as the canon is; it really is too quaint to be missed:-

> Sir, – A gentleman has offered to give £20 for a picture to measure about seven feet by five feet, and to be painted by a young artist for the pleasure of the working-classes; this picture to be then held in trust for them by the Kyrle Society. The donor's object is twofold – to enrich, so far, the lives of the poor, and to enable a struggling young painter to produce a high-class picture. The £20 will be sufficient to pay his expenses of materials and of models, and he will then be enabled to paint a thoroughly good picture, without lowering his conception to please the paying public.

'From those that have not shall be taken even that they have' must be rubbed very deeply into this 'gentleman's' mind. My good sir, this is a job for baronet artists; *they* surely won't refuse it.

It is announced that an office is to be established for providing authentic information for emigrants; and the *Daily*

News is righteously sarcastic on the circumlocution which has been so long making up its mind to this step at the moderate expense of £500 a-year. But working-men had better look to it that the remedy does not prove worse than the disease – that the office does not get into the hands of emigration agents and other sharks of a similar character. The following paragraph, among many of a similar character, may serve as a warning to them:-

> Sir John Rose, Bart., presiding to-day at the fiftieth Annual Meeting of the South Australian Company, said although the colony was passing through a period of temporary depression, he did not think they need be under any apprehension as to its future. The Company owns 80,522 acres of land; its property is of the estimated value of £1,135,650; and a dividend of 10 per cent., with a bonus of 4 per cent., payable half-yearly was declared.

Indeed, one sees every day how hard our rulers are at work to give us information on subjects which concern the workers, as well as their keen insight into the nature of things and their freedom from class prejudice! As an example, the Commission which has been enquiring into the depression of trade has finally come to the conclusion that it is all due to 'the appreciation of gold and the depreciation of silver.' Useful creatures! To drop irony, such stupidity fairly sickens one.

Meantime we might ask those who have a lingering idea that the present system of the distribution of wealth is a good one, or even a tolerable one, to take note that according to its supporters the welfare of hugh populations, their very life or death, are dependent on the relative scarcity of two of the more useless metals. It is their opinion that the accumulated intelligence of the human race, having brought us after so many ages of ingenuity into this pass, will be contented henceforth and for ever to play such a hugh game of hazard as this, in which circumstances play against us always with loaded dice.

Again, as to the depression in trade. I have thought it not unlikely that there are many whose faith in the stability of our capitalist society is shaken, but who are holding back from the acceptance of Socialism till they see whether after all the present condition of trade (which has been going on more or less for some seven years) will not mend, and things be on the upward road again. To these we may say it is not improbable that there will be a partial recovery, which will set the monied classes on their legs for a while once more, and will confer some temporary benefit on the upper part of the working-classes, and if that happens Socialism will be discredited for the time; but remember, that the causes which have produced the present depression will still be at work. Cut-throat competition, which is the real cause of the present depression, will be stimulated to fresh excesses by the relief from the burden which it now feels, and will produce new and increasing armies of lack-alls against the new evil day, when it will not know what to do with them save send them out of the country, or to try, perhaps, under a new Canon Blackley, to take something from their nothing. Those waverers may be assured that the first hour that the clock struck of evolutionary Socialism tolled the knell of capital and wage-labour, and was the tocsin of Revolution; the people was sure thenceforth of becoming conscious of the wrong it had so long blindly resisted.

'It is understood that in the majority of cases the Liberal candidates defeated at the last General Election are declining, when appealed to by the local Associations, to stand at the next election as supporters of Mr. Gladstone. The despondent view which the Ministerialists now take of the situation is to a great extent due to this fact, which adds seriously to the difficulty of finding Government candidates of wealth and local influence.' – *Standard.* A fine tribute this to the beauties of our representative system, and a curious commentary it makes on Mr. Gladstone's appeal against class influence in his last Midlothian manifesto! Wealth and local influence are, after all, but a roundabout application of the straightforward bribery of Walpole's days.

The American funny paper, *Puck*, amidst a farrago of ferocious and brutal insults against those who fail to see the beauty of a tame life under the rule of Jay Gould, has the following kind of Balaam's prophecy on the subject of the emancipation of labour: 'Wherever one brave man, or a handful of brave men, stands boldly up and insists on every man's natural right to make his own price for his labour, or to sell it for what he chooses to sell it for, a blow will be struck in the cause of the labouring man's independence. And it rests with the labouring man to work out his own salvation.' *Puck* will not see these lines, but some half-converted American worker may, so for his benefit I ask the following questions: Can any working-man *choose* to sell his labour for less than it is worth? Is not every working-man in America, as well as other 'civilised' countries, *compelled* to do so? If that is not the case, how did Jay Gould and his kind make their fortunes?

The same journal has a cartoon in which it uses the wife-and-child sentiment for the labour-thief's benefit. A workman is inclined to join that 'handful of brave men,' and 'stand boldly up to insist on every man's right to sell his labour for what he chooses to sell it for.' His wife, her infant in arms, and child with her, are saying to him: 'Husband, don't waste your time here. What will become of *us* while you are neglecting your work?' The factory is seen through an open door; that factory in which both wife and child are *compelled* to work to reduce the husband's wages. Is this sort of thing the work of ignorance or malice? Well, well, probably of Journalism!

Commonweal, Volume 2, Number 22,
12 June 1886, p. 81.

[UNTITLED PARAGRAPH]

The fact is, as individualism suppresses individuality, so nationalism suppresses all that is worth keeping in the special elements which go to make up a real and not an artificial nation. The sham community of the present – the nation – is formed for purposes of rivalry only, and consequently suppresses all minor differences that do not help it to supremacy over other nations. The true community of the future will be formed for livelihood and the development of all human capacities, and consequently would avail itself of the varieties of temperament caused by differences of surrounding which differentiate the races and families of mankind.

Commonweal, Volume 2, Number 22,
12 June 1886, p. 83.

NOTES ON PASSING EVENTS

The dissolution is to be, then. The announcement has already cleared the air: the Hartingtonians and the Chamberlainites are no longer to be separated as favouring different lines of policy – they are a solid phalanx against Home Rule. Nobody takes the trouble to split hairs on this point. The old pretences which hung about the Chamberlainite opposition to the Bill: 'Would vote for it if such and such were altered,' 'as much a Home Ruler as anyone,' and so forth, have all vanished, and the Tories are chuckling, very naturally, at getting their work done by Radicals; no wonder they are pleased to find that dreadful leader who threw out the ominous hint about 'ransom' now leading an auxiliary band to the defence of property, because after all that is what the whole thing means.

Mr. Chamberlain has issued his manifesto also, so that we may be in no sort of doubt on the matter. It is in the main a mere Jingo document, a little coloured by the remains of ideas on the land subject which last year made Mr. Chamberlain so terrible to many people; and also by hints at measures of local self-government, foreshadowing some scheme which certainly in itself might have something to recommend it, but which is now to be used as a bait for attracting Radicals to the Radical reaction which Mr. Chamberlain leads. In this remarkable document Irish Independence is attacked unsparingly; appeals to English prejudice against Ireland are made, though cautiously; the loyalty of the Orangemen is lauded, although they have distinctly declared that it is not Parliament but the sovereign that they owe allegiance to; and although everyone knows that it is supremacy and landlordism that they have been

swaggering for.   Clearly Mr. Chamberlain thinks that any
stick is good enough to beat a Gladstonian dog with, and so
to make all safe with his Whig and Tory allies he writes
himself down Jingo – as he is.

As a favourer of Socialism no one need regret him much, as
the following sentence will show: 'There is a consensus of
opinion that it is desirable to increase the number of owners
of land in Ireland; and I believe that this object, Conservative
in the best sense of the word, etc., etc.' There is no need to
qualify; peasant proprietorship is Conservative in all senses of
the word, as the poor Irish people are, I fear, likely to find
out before they become really free.

Mr. Gladstone's manifesto is this time very simple and quite
judicious.   The whole tactics of the Chamberlainites have
enabled him to put the matter to the public cleared of all
pretence and intrigue.   The real question is, 'Shall the Irish
have a real opportunity of managing their own affairs?' Mr.
Chamberlain says 'No' in his manifesto, at some length, but
will no lack of distinctness.   Lord Salisbury is of the same
opinion, only he is partly prepared to accept the consequences, which are simply unlimited coercion.   Mr.
Gladstone, therefore, is right in saying that the wager of
battle is between himself and Lord Salisbury.   Mr.
Chamberlain is only an ally of the latter: the extravagant
praise which he is receiving from the Tory party should teach
him that.

The Belfast riots and the slaughter which took place in them
are sufficiently miserable; especially in view of the wretched
tweedledum and tweedledee of Catholicism and
Protestantism which was the occasion for them, whatever or
whoever was at the bottom of them.   But whatever caused
the rioting, it was the police that caused the slaughter; if they
had not appeared as the lords of law and order, the men,

women and children that they shot, at the moment it may be granted in defence of their lives, would now be alive.

Also, to compare great things with small, we may well think the crowd that received the conquered and conquering politicians at Westminster after the great division, could have kept order for themselves, at least as well as the police kept it for them. We Socialists shall lose a feather out of our cap if this goes on: we were thinking that it was Socialists who were specially doomed to be hustled by the police, but now it seems it is the whole public who are their enemies. Anyhow it is not a bad thing that 'respectable' people engaged in satisfying their curiosity or loyalty in an obviously legal way should understand by experience what it is that we complain of.

The patching-up of Humpty-Dumpty is exercising the minds of the Liberals a good deal. Says the *Daily News*, à propos of the elections: 'Opposition to Mr. Bright we should regard as a sort of petty treason, unless, indeed, any Liberal should be foolish enough to put himself up against Mr. Gladstone in Midlothian.' Once a leader always a leader, then, even when the led have got to be a mile in advance of the leader. What doleful nonsense the exigencies of the parliamentary party struggle does give birth to.

Commonweal, Volume 2, Number 23,
19 June 1886, p. 89.

NOTES ON THE ELECTIONS

The elections have gone against the Gladstonites so far, – which, indeed, was only to be expected. Every constituency which returned a Tory at the last elections would return one with a bigger majority this time, and most of those that returned a Liberal by a narrow minority would now return a Tory, – in either case supposing there was no Irish vote to neutralise the Whig vote. Then all respectability, right down to the lowest ranks of the lower middle-class, will vote jingo: the clerks, grooms, gardeners, and general hangers-on of villadom, will of course vote on the same side. Traditional national spite and 'rampant-lionism' will follow suit; and the obedient followers of big names, such as Bright and Chamberlain, will – perhaps sometimes with a sigh – put the cross against the name of the Jingo candidate. All this makes a very formidable reactionary phalanx. Against it is arrayed the personal following of Mr. Gladstone, which probably will not make so good an appearance at the polling-booths as it would in the streets; and lastly – much lastly, it is to be feared – the body of people who are convinced, either by study of the facts or instinctively, that it is neither creditable nor convenient for England to stagger along dragging a second Poland after her.

To investigate the chances of the elections in detail is rather the business of an election-agent than a human being. But, without being eager to risk a prophecy which next week may give the lie to, it does seem most probable that the new parliament will give us much the same party cohorts as the last; only of course the Whigs and Jingo Radicals will go to Westminster pledged to a kind of loose alliance with the Tory Rump, from which will result wrigglings exceedingly amusing and refreshing to the cynical onlooker. Meantime a lesson will be given to the devotee of parliamentary agitation and the believer in the perfection of 'representation,' if he will only use his senses and learn it. He may see, if he will, that the body of professional politicians formed by M.P.s, candidates, and wire-pullers, is far more powerful than a reasonable man would expect it to be, judging from the very low average of the talent in that body. The constituencies do certainly allow themselves to be led, or rather driven, by the group of shuffling and intriguing self-seekers whom they have elevated to rule over them, and at the best consider that when they have voted for the candidate provided for them they have fulfilled all the duties of citizenship. In short, as a rule the voters expect everything to be done for them; and what the representatives really represent is unreasoning habit formed by implicit trust in the magical powers of the word 'Representation.'

It is humiliating indeed to think of the shouts of applause with which working men have greeted John Bright's last feat of digging himself up from the political grave, in which he has lain all these years, to oppose his galvanised corpse to the march of events. And yet it is more humiliating still to think that Home Rulers would have been to-day but a powerless faction if Gladstone had not at last make up his mind to take them up.

As it is, 'His Leadership' has undoubtedly pushed forward the cause of Revolution; nor can it be denied that he would never have attempted to do so unless there had been some growing instinct in its favour. Nor if he is beaten in the elections will his defeat much check the growth of that instinct. As has been said before in these columns, the Tories and Jingoes have been driven to see the impossibility of mere coercion. What are they to do, then, when they find themselves apparently masters of the situation? They *must* bring forward their Home Rule measure, which will of course be framed in such a way as to give the Irish the shadow without the substance of independence – the 'tub-to-the-whale policy' is the only one possible to them. They will hope partly to tire out the Irish party and partly to divide them into moderates and irreconcilables: in the latter attempt they may succeed beyond their expectations, and beyond what is good for the health of their own party. The Irish may, and probably will, accept the compromise offered them – accept it as a compromise, that is, without leaving off the agitation for complete independence. In a short time it will no more be a question of some Gladstonian Bill, with its safeguards and constitutional provisions, but of something far more revolutionary. The Irish will be divided indeed, like the familiar demon in the old fable, cut by his unhappy employer into two unmanageable devils; and the more unmanageable will not be asking for a mere Dublin parliament, but will be claiming his right to do something with the country of Ireland itself, which will make it a fit dwelling-place for reasonable and happy people.

In short a triumph for the great Whig Rump or Moderate Party seems at hand, which will undoubtedly strengthen it very much in Parliament, and will overawe the parliamentary and constitutional opposition to its dull and eyeless tyranny; but may it not be hoped that its very success, and the woodenness with which it stands in the way of the progress which it was once supposed to further, may open the eyes of ingenious people not wedded to mere party names? It seems to me a fair hope, and that many driven back on themselves and compelled to turn away their hopes from the parliamentary squabble, will begin to bethink them of what the true end of politics is, and that a new party will begin to form outside Parliament, a party of the People prepared to help themselves, by education first, consultation next, and at last, when the happy day comes, by action. It seems to me that the defeat of the present attempt to give Home Rule to Ireland which is founded on a genuine popular instinct, will be a blessing in the form of a curse if it helps to purge people's minds of this waiting on parliamentary providence, which is such a heavy weight on our over-patient democracy.

On the other hand, if the Gladstonites manage to snatch a victory from the hands of the Whig-Tory-Jingo coalition, they will still find that the battle is to be fought over again: compromise, hesitation, evasion, and all the many forms of lawyer-like delay which so-called statesmanship has had such long practice in, will whittle their triumph away to nothing; and those of them who have been in earnest in championing freedom and its hopes, will find out before long that the day which will make them parliamentary outcasts is only deferred and not got rid of. The Great Whig Rump will die hard, and even the first days of obvious Revolution will find it still there, still supposing itself the only real political party, still fulfilling its real function as the battle-flag, the car-borne standard of respectable legalised robbery.

Commonweal, Volume 2, Number 26,
10 July 1886, p. 113.

NOTES

The Liberty and Property Defence League, *i.e.*, the League that defends the liberty of robbery and the property of the privileged in other people's labour, have been having a field-day; they have seen the necessity of doing something towards internationalism, since it is clear that their principles cannot be bounded by narrow geographico-political limits. So M. Léon Say has been holding forth to them; and a very proper person he is to do so, considering that he is one of the directors of the Decazeville mines, in whose liberty and property he is so seriously interested. He admitted and lamented the spread of Socialism from France to England, and spoke of it as taking two forms, centralising and municipal Socialism, which he spoke of as already affecting the liberty to live at other people's expense. But if M. Léon Say lives, he will see what real Socialism means, something very different from the first nibblings at crude State Socialism that he has got into his head as being the enemy. He expressed a sort of after-dinner hope of crushing out Socialism in France, which aspiration of a true defender of Liberty no doubt he will do his best to realise. Just so sailors, who find there is an irretrievable leak in their boat, try to keep out the limitless ocean with whatever of rags or oakum happens to lie handy; not because they really hope to succeed, but because they must needs satisfy their consciences by hoping against hope.

Bad news from Burmah – or good, if you be not a confirmed Jingo. The Dacoits are giving trouble indeed, and are as eager for other people's goods as the veriest Englishman would have them to be; this is always on the assumption that they are Dacoits, *i.e.*, robbers; as, of course, all people are who resist the progress of our commercial body-guard. And yet, if the history could be written by the vanquished, their resistance would seem uncommonly like that defence of hearth and home that has been so besung amongst us, though we have had so little to do with the practice of it, except as affording occasion for it. Indeed, as regards our dealings with barbarous foreigners, we English are like the poor in the capitalist morality, whose function it is to afford occasion to the virtues of charity and benevolence. If the Burmese, therefore, are troubled to account for such unaccountable evils as English invaders, they had better conclude that they were made to give them an occasion for practising hopeless courage first, and fortitude under injury secondly. They are hardly like to find a better solution of the problem.

By the way, the Indian mutiny is an old story now; but it is worth while to quote a line or two from the very frank author of 'Life on Board the Alabama' in the *Century* magazine, who says in passing as a matter not worth much attention, 'I must say that the "pandies" were not a whit more brutal and savage than the English civilians and soldiers.' He saw Gordon afterwards in China, and found him 'a very common-place gentleman,' with a great talent for swearing. General Ward, the ['Jex-Yankee clipper-mate,' he admired far more as 'bold, bloody, and resolute.' The poor devils of Taipings probably found out the meaning of those words, which give one a kind of shudder, as of Captain Teach or Blackbeard come back again. Truly our soldiers of fortune are a fine present for us to give to the 'outer barbarians.'

Commonweal, Volume 2, Number 26, 10 July 1886, p. 116.

REVIEW

MODERN SOCIALISM by Annie Besant

Mrs. Besant has written a useful pamphlet under this name, all the more useful as with her name on the title-page it will reach some groups of advanced political thinkers who would otherwise have been frightened off the subject. It is clearly and pleasantly written, with as little technicality as may be, and in the main steers clear of subjects that are in controversy among Socialists. The arrangement is good. After a brief notice of the utopian Socialism of Robert Owen and the communities which resulted from it, it takes up the question of production for profit, with the consequent antagonism of classes; then deals with competition, and points out its evils and the remedies for it; then points out what capital is, and deals with the objections to a society producing without profit. The opening sentence of the chapter on Land which follows, is somewhat sanguine: 'It is hardly necessary to argue at this time of day that land – *i.e.*, natural agents – ought not to be the private property of individuals'; but that there *is* a public to whom such words can be addressed is true, and is a hopeful truth indeed. The concluding chapters deal with Education, Justice, and Amusement, and the Conclusion takes up some of the more ordinary objections which anti-Socialists make who have pretence to economical knowledge.

Perhaps the American communities are dwelt on rather disproportionately to the length of the pamphlet. Although these communities were experiments in association, from one point of view they were anti-Socialistic, as they withdrew themselves from general society – from political society – and let it take care of itself. They were rather modern and more extended forms of monasticism, and were distinctly exclusive, – hence their failure. To me, in common with other Communists I should suppose, Mrs. Besant's definition of Socialism and Communism seems incorrect: 'Socialism merely implies that the raw material of the soil and the means of production,' says Mrs. Besant, 'shall not be the private property of individuals, but shall be under the control of the community.' But I ask is not the part of wealth which can be called 'the means of production' that part which individuals do not use for satisfying their personal needs? And that part which they are so using no Communist would meddle with. What each takes from the common store for his personal needs he will use as he pleases, so long as he does not turn it into an instrument of compulsion for the exploitation of others. The Socialism which Mrs. Besant and others sometimes distinguish from Communism, is only an initial and imperfect form of it. The abolition of private property in 'the raw material of the soil and the means of production' *must* lead to Communism, as the present monopolists will instinctively perceive, and they will in consequence resist the initial stage by any and every means in their power.

In a future edition Mrs. Besant might put back the commencement of the Industrial Period to a date before the Great Machine Industry. Adam Smith belongs to the Division of Labour Period, what Marx calls the 'Periode Manufacturiére,' during which the workman was himself the part of a machine, the *group*, which was the unit of industrial production. This system was at work early in the seventeenth century, and under it exploitation of labour went on merrily, though of course the old individualist system of production survived partly amidst it, just as the division-of-labour system still survives amidst our machine-industry. A sentence or two on this point need not interfere with the clearness of Mrs. Besant's exposition of profit-mongering.

I may add that Mrs. Besant has had a testimonial to the usefulness of her pamphlet in the eagerness, or indeed the brutality, with which it has been attacked by some of the members of the party with which she has hitherto been identified.

Commonweal, Volume 2, Number 26,
10 July 1886, p. 117.

THE WHIG-JINGO VICTORY

Mr. Gladstone's appeal to the country has resulted in a complete defeat for the Home Rulers; nay more, in what must be called under the circumstances, a triumph for the actual Tories; under the circumstances that is to say, the extinction of the Tory party of principle and its melting into the Whig party of utilitarian reaction. The present Tory triumph is as good an exemplification of the disappearance of the old Tory party as may be; they are delirious with joy over it; but what does it come to as a mere party victory? They will probably come back to Westminster with at most a very small majority over the so-called Liberals of all shades and Parnellites united, which means that they will rule by the leave of the Whigs.

───────────

And they will need the support of their definitely Whig allies, because the Jingo-Radicals are by no means wholly to be counted on, except for the oppression of Ireland; and even in that case they will wish the oppression to be carried out by sly and underhanded methods, while in other matters they will be anxious to prove what good Radicals they are in everything else except the allowing people to govern themselves. Though, perhaps, we can hardly expect Mr. Chamberlain to revert to his hints of demi-semi-Socialism for the next few months.

───────────

For the Whigs, however, the triumph is complete. It is true that the seats gained for Gladstone are mostly in the possession of Tories; but the Tories are now mere employés of the Whigs, kept from doing their dirty work. On the other hand the Whigs have once more got the rope firmly round the neck of the Radicals, who a short while ago seemed in danger of breaking away. They may if they choose help in the triumphal march of the Constitutional party to nowhere; but if they do not they can be done without, and if they are restive can be easily throttled out of the way. The Whigs are now in a truly majestic position, which could hardly be bettered by lifting lazy mediocrity in the shape of Lord Hartington into the premiership.

As to what they will do in the present juncture, the completeness of their victory somewhat changes the aspect of things from what it was a week or two ago. This is clear from the tone of Mr. Chamberlain's last speeches, in which he has utterly dropped the mask, and stands forward as the champion of mere oppression à la Poland. It is not improbable that coercion, which the very Tories dropped before the elections, may now be picked up again. The victorious coalitionists cannot do absolutely nothing, however much they may be inclined to; some beneficent measure will be prepared, and the question will then be in what way it shall be crammed down the Irish throat. Shall the resistance to it be met by a challenge to civil war? That is the question which Lord Salisbury will presently have to answer.

Meanwhile the reactionist press, including the perfidious *Pall Mall Gazette*, which hardly takes the trouble to veil its exultation at the Jingo victory, is busy twitting Gladstone with his phrase about the 'classes and the masses,' asserting that the masses have declared against Home Rule. It is possible (or if you please, probable) that even supposing the 'masses' had the vote, they would have voted for the retention of Poland-Ireland, as the last twenty years have shown us how even universal suffrage can be manipulated as long as there are rich people in the country; but to assert that this election could be a test of opinion is sheer impudence, since the most innocent can compare the number of votes cast with that of the population. The vote is a property vote

– a vote of bricks-and-mortar, and not men. A working-man friend says that in London you do not meet one man in five who has a vote. The present writer has *seven*, although but a professional man, a hanger-on of the privileged class. In short, the vote, like other boons to the 'lower classes,' is simply thrown to them to amuse them with the semblance of power, lest they should bethink them and claim the reality of it.

To thinking-people, indeed, these elections should show the powerlessness of the working-classes under our present industrial system, of which our constitutional government is an adjunct and a servant. It *is* true that the Independence of Ireland is a class question under the present circumstances, since the settlement of it *must* force people to deal with the question of the subsistence of the Irish workers, and so by implication with that of the workers in England and all other countries. In fact, the question is as simple as this: 'Shall the Irish people be an appanage, a convenience, to the landlords and capitalists of the British Empire?' On this question it is clear that the 'masses' would have the 'classes' against them; and it should have been equally clear that, as the electorate is arranged, like everything else in our society, to give all the real power to the classes, the masses would be beaten. The classes have answered the question as they were bound to: 'Yes, it is right and proper that Ireland (in common with all the world) should be enthralled for our benefit.'

One sees nonsense in the papers about the 'New Democracy,' the 'Two Democracies,' and so forth; but, in fact, there is no Democracy or Rule of the People in Great Britain. There is a monstrous bourgeoisie or exploiting class, all the more powerful as it embraces everybody who lives even partially by exploitation, and thus is very numerous, and in the average grossly ignorant. There is also a genuine working class or proletariat, which under the present system has no power, except so far as it can make the danger of its existence felt by the bourgeoisie: nor will it have any power until it makes up its mind, or rather is driven by the march of events, to take to itself *all* power. Outside these two classes there is nothing but a fantastic accidental fringe, which must drift in the long-run into one or the other of the two great classes; though it must be admitted that the members of it have a tendency to 'run with the hare and hunt with the hounds,' until some great crisis like the present finds them out.

Commonweal, Volume 2, Number 27,
17 July 1886, p. 121.

'AN EMPTY POCKET IS
THE WORST OF CRIMES'

The poor lad who set out from Fulham to find work, and found it at Eastbourne in the form of oakum-picking rewarded by bread-and-water, will have leisure to consider the enormity of his crime in daring to be born and to require sleep and shelter. But after all, though the Eastbourne magistrates might have tempered their logic with mercy, and though all persons of a kindly nature would be glad to lend a hand to their tarring and feathering, their view of the property in an empty boat, looked on as a potential lodging-house, is in strict logical accordance with the bourgeois view of property in general. 'This is mine, and whether I can use it or not, nobody else shall,' is the watch-word of property; and Queen, Lords and Commons, Army and Navy, Judge, Magistrate, Lawyer, and Policeman are kept in their places and paid (handsomely too) by Society in order to carry out this watchword to its legitimate consequences, that is, the semi-starvation and complete degradation of the majority of the people.

Commonweal, Volume 2, Number 27,
17 July 1886, p. 123.

REVIEW.
CASHEL BYRON'S PROFESSION

A mere novel bearing on the face of it no controversial opinion, might not seem a suitable subject for review in these columns, but even apart from the author's well-known views and his power as a Socialist lecturer, a Socialist will find much in 'Cashel Byron's Profession' to interest him as a Socialist. Everything that Mr. Shaw writes must bear with it an indictment against our sham society, and it would be harder to find more incisive criticism of its follies than in this book. Perhaps, to a reader not a Socialist, and therefore not in the secret, it would seem to be nothing more serious than a fantastic piece written on pessimistic lines, as all clever modern novels are, and with no further aim in it; but anyone must be forced to admit that it fulfils the first function of a novel by amusing the reader. As in all literary works of art, one is bound to accept its special atmosphere, which doubtless at first might rather confuse the ordinary reader, since the plot which one has to accept as possible consists of the development of the love at first sight of a very rich and refined young lady for a prize-fighter. The said heroine is not very much alive, is rather the embodiment of the author's view of life than a real personage; but the hero is most carefully studied and very successful, and every one of the minor characters is highly finished and natural. Indeed, Mr. Shaw gives very good penn'orths in the matter of invention of incident, and is almost reckless in the care which he bestows on his scenes, as witness the sparring-match before the 'African King' in the Agricultural Hall, or the burst of confused excitement on studious solitude after Byron's great fight with Paradise. Mr. Shaw sees his scenes clearly and accurately; indeed more after the manner of a painter than a

dramatic writer. This is a quality which is much rarer than is
generally supposed in these days of word-painting. It is
probably a defect which naturally goes with it that the scenes
are, as far as their artistic effect goes, isolated and lacking in
the power that accumulation gives: the whole story rather
leaves off than comes to an end, also. However, this is a
defect which it shares with all novels of this generation that
have any pretence to naturalism. As Mr. Shaw is quite
successful in establishing his claim to keen observation and
vivid representation, one must not quarrel with him for not
attaining to what is mostly beyond the aim of a modern
novel, but which both Scott and Dickens now and then
touched – the unity and completeness of a great drama.
Whatever is attempted in 'Cashel Byron' is done conscientiously and artistically.

Commonweal, Volume 2, Number 27,
17 July 1886, p. 126.

POLITICAL NOTES

The Tories in office again and dividing the spoils won by their recent victory – such as it is. A purely Tory Ministry, with the assurance of the 'benevolent neutrality' of the Whigs: that is to say, their complicity without responsibility in the game of reaction which the new Parliament is pledged to play. What are their chances in the game? In the first place it is only the Irish question which need be taken into consideration; on all others points the Tory Government will do pretty much the same as a Liberal one would; so we need only consider how they will deal with their Irish kettle of fish.

There are signs even in the more moderate of the Tory prints that they are expected to make *some* move in the direction of coercion; to take advantage of any opportunity the Irish may give them by riding rusty under their defeat. But after all, the Tory rank and file has to put up with as many disappointments at the hands of its leaders as the Radical rank and file has, and it is likely that this will be one of them. Lord Salisbury will do nothing at all as long as he can; and will at least try what he can do in the way of saying 'Yes' and 'No' at once to the Home Rule claim. He will bring in some 'gas and sewage' Home Rule Bill, which the Irish need not fight against, but which of course will not choke their agitation; nay, many Irishmen think and have thought for some time, that any Bill for Local Government would be of use to them; that they would use the bodies so constituted to organise their agitation still further and more completely. Perhaps they are sanguine in this; but, at least, the most revolutionary Irishman need not be afraid that Lord Salisbury will offer Ireland so much or put what he does offer in such a dramatic manner that it will injure the sentiment for Home Rule among the people.

Of course, what the Tories would do if they could would be to offer such a 'concession' as would irritate the Irish into open resistance, while it would seem a fair offer to outsiders. Happily this is scarcely possible after the frank and almost too effusive way in which Ireland received Mr. Gladstone's incomplete and unsatisfactory measure. Indeed Lord Salisbury is much more likely to spoil his game by acting like a timid whist-player and being stingy with his trumps. So we may wait without excitement for the Tory Home Rule Bill.

Meanwhile how great is the relief from a sense of danger, which all Tories and Whigs are now feeling is shown obviously enough not only by the ordinary jubilations after a successful electoral contest in the party papers, but also in more grotesque and downright fashion. The prospectus of the Loyalist League of Great Britain (printed in true-blue) which has found itself at the Socialist League office, is a fair example of this terror calmed for the present. After stating in fairly plain terms that one of their objects was to further civil war if they could not have *all* their own way, they appeal for help 'to resist to the utmost the disloyal and Socialistic associations in their persistent efforts to disintegrate society and weaken the empire.' Well, some people may laugh at their big words and their premature terror; but after all their instinct has not misled them. Home Rule doesn't aim specially even at the weakening of the empire, still less at the disintegration of society, yet it is a sign that both these movements are going on. Friend 'Loyalists,' it can't be helped! An empire which is the empire of cheating and hypocritical traders cannot last for ever; 'society' which is but a band of thieves has a tendency to disintegrate, you need not doubt that!

As to the 'Cabinet-making' which has been going on lately, no one scarcely pretends to take any interest in it except so far as concerns the position of Lord Randolph Churchill. But we Socialists need not trouble our heads about that either; the fact that such a man could be considered of any importance in Parliament does but give us a measure of the weight and depth of the others. It is scarcely worth while to say that he has all the faults of a reactionary demagogue, and not much else, since the man himself scarcely professes to be more than a machine, whose design has been taken from a much more exquisite piece of machinery, the late Lord Beaconsfield, to wit. One thing we may be pretty sure of, that the new Parliament will play a considerable part in sickening people of the whole business of Parliamentary Party Government, and help still further to discredit the knot of wire-pullers, landlords, money-lenders, lawyers, and professional politicians, who profess to represent the people of these islands.

––––––––––––––––

While on the one hand the instruments of bourgeois domination are visibly wearing out, on the other there is a feverish activity arising against Socialism. In America, the determination, whatever may happen, to have some victims to middle-class revenge for the Anarchist outbreak at Chicago, and the suppression of freedom of speech generally; in Belgium the vindictive sentences against the rioters, in Holland the sentence against Domela Newenhuis, and the arrest of Fortuin and Vanderstadt at Amsterdam; the obstinate deadlock in Denmark; in France as the latest item, the approaching trial of Louis Michel and Jules Guesde for 'inciting to murder and plunder;' and finally, with us, the attack treated in the English, or petty and hypocritical style, by setting the police at us as street nuisances, and pretending that opinion has nothing to do with it, and that they do not notice our utterances, though the police make elaborate notes of them. All this does specially and above all things show fear on the part of our rulers, a sense of insecurity, the origin of which is not so much the open Socialist agitation (that is an effect rather than a cause), as the crumbing away of the basis on which 'Society' is built, to wit, the safe and continuous expansion of the exploitation of Labour by Capital.

Commonweal, Volume 2, Number 30, 7 August 1886, p. 141.

[UNTITLED PARAGRAPHS]

WORKMEN AND HORSES. – Nothing is more instructive from a Socialist standpoint than the way the Paris 'Company of Omnibuses and Tramways' treats its men and its horses. The men don't cost the Company a farthing, they are to be found in all places ready to fight one another for the privilege of working for the Company, but the directors don't find horses running about the streets anxious to be harnessed. They have to be bought at a cost of from £48 to £60, and hence they are treated in a different manner from the men. From the accounts of the Company the cost of food, stabling, and grooming is 3s. 9d. a day per horse; the average wages of the drivers, conductors, and employés of all kinds is 3s. 2d. a day. It will be seen that the Company gets the service of a man for 7d. a day less than a horse, and in addition it is to be noted that the men work three and in some cases four times as many hours as the horses. The horses work four hours a day, the men from twelve to sixteen hours. When the horse is ill he is carefully attended to in the stable, and sent to the country to recover his health; if the employé is ill, for all the company cares he can go to the d— if he likes. – Paris *Le Socialiste*.

An article in the *Daily News* the other day, called 'School in Prison,' is well worth attention. The ordinary middle-class person, who is not likely to see the inside of a prison except as a visitor when he is sitting on a grand jury, is not more sure of anything than of the perfection of our prison system; he regards it as the culmination of all reason, and is absolutely convinced that if there are still any criminals in existence in England it must be on account of their inherent wickedness, since the last twenty years of our prison system, with its mingled fimness (*sic*), mildness, and forethought, must have converted all those who were so ill-judged as to become inmates of a prison. 'School in Prison' should be rather startling to this optimism. Although it only draws up a very small corner of the curtain, it shows a picture of petty tyranny and torture, almost the more hopeless because it is the result not of malice, but of hopeless imbecility and dishonesty. The truth is, that in this matter of prison life, as with work-a-day life, the society of to-day has become hopeless of any real progress, though habit will not allow it to confess as much. It is almost becoming conscious that it is but waiting till the Revolution shall sweep it away, and that meantime it is not worth while to try to do anything. Apply the official rules, since they are ready to hand, and will ease us of all responsibility; let them take the place of hope, desire, emulation, and sense of duty – of life in short.

Commonweal, Volume 2, Number 30,
7 August 1886, p. 147.

NOTES ON PASSING EVENTS

On Wednesday appeared an abstract of the report of the Commission on the Depression in Trade, which, however, was repudiated the next day. In fact the report according to the account given was so grotesque, that it did look as if it might have been drawn up by a Socialist joker; yet it is by no means so sure that it did not contain the gist of the genuine report somewhat denuded of its raiment of verbiage. After all there would be nothing wonderful in the Commissioners being at the bottom of the joke, as such people take great care never to study economy except from the point of view of the most worn-out bourgeois theories; ignorance is an essential of their position as Commissioners. Also as they obviously can *do* nothing they may think it matters little what they *say*. Yet for one item I wonder what this solemn farce costs the country?

It has been suggested that the Liberal members shall revenge themselves on Lord Randolph Churchill for his truculent address to the electors of Paddington, by rising and leaving the house in a body as soon as he begins to speak for the first time. This is not a bad idea, but such protests might be organised in a more complete manner, each one, for instance, of these protesting members might be brought back in turn, and a similar protest made against him for *his* special delinquency, ratting, fighting shy, lying, or what not; which would make a lively time of it in the house. Perhaps the very best organi-sation would result in each member so protesting against himself, walking out of the house and not coming back again. There would be many dry eyes at these departures.

Commonweal, Volume 2, Number 31, 14 August 1886, p. 156.

NOTES ON PASSING EVENTS

It is worthy of remark that while there are some brief notices in the Tory evening prints of the trial of our comrades, those papers that were most open-mouthed in support of the freedom of speech in the Dod Street affair, have not one word to say on this much more important case; if we except the *Weekly Dispatch*, which condemns the action of the police and the prosecution generally, though strangely enough it considers £20 a 'small fine'; and still more *Reynolds*, who condemns the conduct of the authorities without qualification. One cause of this poltroonery is clear enough. Sir Charles Warren calls himself a Liberal or Radical, and is also, it is said, a Salvationist. No doubt he reckons on being able to let his friends of that 'religion' have a good deal of their own way; but is he so sure that he will be able to do so?

As to the Tory papers, of course one does not go to them for support of freedom of speech, and their hard words do not break our bones. The *Globe* is as befits its 'pinkness', philistine, dull and moderate. The *Evening News* has a joke not so bad as to the possibility of a Socialist behaving well for a whole year. Our romantic friend the *St. James's Gazette*, follows its kind; the report tells the obvious lie that Mainwaring's speech was almost a repetition of Mr. Thompson's. The budding genius who has written the leaderette says they were 'ordered to enter into recognizances of £20 each and to find sureties for their good behaviour.' The rest of this novelist's romance is not worth quoting; but really the editor should keep an eye on the cheap boys who do the inferior (?) work for him.

A friend writing from Bedford says that the working-men thereabout call the first morning train that brings down the newspapers, the Liar Train. There must be glimmerings of sense in the creatures, as Baillie Nicoll Jarvie says of the highlander.

The platitudinous speech of Lord Salisbury delivered at the Mansion House banquet contained nothing in it except a taunt against the working-classes of England for not having or not using the vote, and a sort of veiled intimidation which there was no need to give, veiled or otherwise, that the Irish question was to be shelved as long as possible, and that the present Government would go as far in the way of coercion as they durst. But is was no wonder that the tone of the speech should be self-gratulatory as far as the party is concerned, as there is little likelihood that he will be disturbed by the 'Liberal Party,' wherever *that* is to be found.

I owe an apology to Mr. Cook, of Birmingham, for assuming last week that he was likely to be successful in his attempt to get himself returned for East Birmingham. But it did appear that he had made up his mind to win, and it is clear that he could only win by ratting just so far as would please the Jingoes of that borough. It is satisfactory that he has refused to do so; but meantime it seems to be growing clearer that if the 'Liberal Party' ever unite once more it must be under the leadership of Lord Hartington, and his humble follower Mr. Joseph Chamberlain; which would be a bad look-out indeed if the 'Liberal Party' were what it gives itself out to be, to wit, the bearer of the torch of progress into the dark places of the earth. Fortunately there is something behind all that, which did indeed push the Liberal Party into its late position, and which is preparing to take its place. Lord Hartington and Mr. Chamberlain and their Whigs may shut the shutters, but that will not prevent the sun from rising.

We have not yet had the pleasure of meeting our French comrades in labour who have come over to England to study the differences between our slavery and theirs. We can at least assure them of our sympathy; and we shall believe that if any of them have any doubts of the necessity of Revolutionary Socialism as the only remedy for the misery of the workers, they will have those doubts removed by what they see here – our commercial successes on the one hand, our social failures on the other.

Sentence of seven years' penal servitude was passed on a man (a Russian) the other day for having in his possession a block for printing Russian bank notes. Of course we all know that commerce safeguards itself by the most ferocious punishments as compared to those meted out to offenders against the person of their fellow-citizens; but apart from this, what was the crime for which this man is being punished! The wrappings of conventionality being stripped from the case, we perceive it to be that he designed *to live without producing.* It must be admitted that this is a heavy offence, because it entails infinite misery on the world if it is widely committed, and especially if those who commit it manage to acquire large fortunes, as they often do, and along with them the respect and admiration of the greater part of mankind. Heavens! what a cost we shall be at for new prisons, jailers, and so forth, when all these criminals are under lock and key, from the highest aristocracy down to the lowest pettifogging lawyer or unjust judge! Here, as with other criminals, turning them into honest men working for their livelihood is the cheaper and cleaner remedy. A remedy which, alas! these foolish persons will resist tooth and nail, invoking the ten commandments to protect their special robbery all the while; so that it is to be feared that they must be compelled to be honest, since argument does not touch them.

Commonweal, Volume 2, Number 32, 21 August 1886, p. 164.

NOTES ON PASSING EVENTS

Michael Schwab, Samuel Fielden, Albert Parsons, Adolph
Fischer, George Engel, and Louis Lingg have been
condemned to death, and Oscar Neebe (probably more
unfortunate than the others) to imprisonment for fifteen
years. If they had anything to do with throwing the bomb,
Society will not attempt to justify itself for slaying these men,
but will consider that it has done well. But, as was said in
these columns when the news of the conflict first came,
whatever had taken place before the meeting, at that meeting
itself it was a matter of battle, and the men were defending
their lives as all soldiers must; and truly revolutionary
soldiers do always fight with a rope round their necks. For
the rest no thoughtful and honest man, whether he be
Socialist or not, who has ever considered the nature of a
'White Terror,' the shopkeeper in terror for his shop, will
doubt that it was impossible that these men should have a
fair trial. We do not need the evidence of Wm. Holmes's very
interesting and useful letters as given in our last and present
issues, to show us that victims were needed, and would be
found whatever the evidence might be. To American
respectability all Socialists are Anarchists, and all Anarchists
are bomb-throwers to be so treated whenever the opportunity shall occur.

The following paragraph is sufficiently significant of what is
going on in America in this matter: 'It is understood that the
Chicago authorities contemplate the immediate arrest of all
persons even indirectly connected with the May riot on the
charge of conspiracy.' 'Indirectly connected' may stretch
widely enough to include any one who has said a word
against the system of robbery on which 'Society' rests in

America, as elsewhere; or who, if it must be so, and when the assent of the real Society, the Society of the producers, becomes general, is prepared to use what force may be necessary; though he may lament isolated outbreaks like the Chicago affair; for such outbreaks irritate 'Society' without shaking it, and are aimless as long as the mass of the workers have not learned to understand their true position.

Some of the correspondents of the bourgeois papers state the verdict and sentence against the Anarchists was received with cheers. It is to be hoped for the credit of human nature that this is a journalist's lie, founded on the bitterness of capitalist society against those who have attacked it openly. It would be difficult to find words to express one's disgust at the baseness of people who live at ease on the labour of others, exulting over the condemnation of their fellow-men to an ignominious death.

'A fair trial' quotha! Well, I mean a *legally* fair trial. After having been an ear-and-eye witness of our own small experience in trials (a comedy, or rather farce, as set beside the Chicago tragedy), I must conclude that under the law of a Society founded on robbery sustained by violence, as ours is, a fair trial is impossible. The maxim, apparently uncontradicted, that the event which is being judged must be isolated as to both time and place from all surrounding circumstances makes the whole thing absurd. So acting, you set out from the first with the determination of not getting at the real facts of the case. All you *can* know about it on such terms are certain formal facts, illumined perhaps by a word or two which has dropped from an eager witness before the judge has had time to stop him; and which the judge takes care to tell the jury they must not consider as evidence, as though they could possibly help doing so when they have once heard it.

Take for example our own case, The Queen *v.* Williams and Mainwaring. In the minds of all people who have interested themselves in the street-corner preaching the chief point was and is whether the police had made an unfair difference between the Socialists and the religious and other bodies. If it could be shown that they had been doing so, then, apart from the duties which the 'Religion of Socialism' imposes on us as Socialists, in the eyes of all ordinary persons of any good will the defendants would have been public-spirited persons resisting the injurious misapplication of a very stretchable law. If on the contrary it could have been shown (as it couldn't) that the police had made no difference between the Socialists and other bodies, then to the general public the defendants were acting as rebels against a law presumably made for ensuring the convenience of the whole pubic, and the case would have been on quite a different footing. But any evidence that tended towards showing the facts on this point was rigidly excluded by the judge; and we have to appeal from a so-called 'court of justice' to the press or other extra-judicial means of publicity.

Parliament has met again to give the Ministry an opportunity of declaring their policy, and to transact a little 'business.' The 'policy' is just what might have been expected – an attempt to live by doing nothing. Lord Randolph Churchill put down his foot on any concession being made in the eviction war, as he was bound to do. 'Her Majesty's troops' are to act as they have acted, as bum-bailiffs – an occupation entirely suitable to them, but somewhat expensive to the tax-payers at home; who, however, deserve a great deal more than they will get for their behaviour in the late elections. Meantime the evictions now going on in Galway are a suffi-cient commentary on the speech of this champion of the landlords and Tory Democracy.

However, the little game now being played in Bulgaria, news of which is lately to hand, will no doubt afford the Ministry a welcome opportunity for a diversion from the home matters which press upon them, since they will be able to get up another Russian scare, not without some foundation. This will be easy to them, but it will not be easy to carry on a war with a great European power, if they should drift into that. Doubtless this consideration does not trouble them.

'A good deal is heard about gambling on the Stock Exchange, but there is reason to believe that the amount of gambling which goes on under the guise of legitimate trade is often more wild and excessive still. The public do not follow so closely the dealings in produce, iron, etc., as in securities, and therefore, on the principle *omne ignotum pro miribile*, ordinary observers are apt to believe that dealings in Mark Lane, Mincing Lane, and the Baltic, are of a superior tone and morality to those which go on in the Stock Exchange. The following incident, however, rather disturbs this complaisant view of the state of British trade. In the Baltic this afternoon it was stated that wheat and linseed for shipment from Calcutta in April to June next year have been already sold; and as these articles are hardly yet even sown – if, indeed, either buyer or seller concerns himself in the least about their existence, present or future – the operation may be stigmatised as gambling of the most shameless description.' – *Daily News*, August 21.
No comment is needed on the above.

'POLICE AND OPEN-AIR PREACHING. – Dear Sir, – The police have been trying to put down our Saturday evening open-air services, and have now given notice of their intention to summon us. We conduct the services on our own property, fronting the main thoroughfare in the parish. The prosecution is to be under some old statute which they say they have discovered. Amongst your many readers there may be legal gentlemen skilled in this question, who would be only too glad to help us in our struggle to preach the gospel of Christ, as our Master did, in the open air. The question is an important one, for if the police were successful it would give them a decision which might prove a dangerous precedent in all future evangelistic effort.- Yours truly, Wm. Adamson, vicar. The Vicarage, Old Ford, E.'

The above letter, addressed to the *Christian*, shows that the police are trying to put a good face on their difficulty by attacking other bodies besides the Socialists; and they will doubtless try to convince the public that they have always done so. Comrades should all the more make careful notes as to such meetings and the amount of complaisance with which they are treated by the police.

Commonweal, Volume 2, Number 33,
28 August 1886, p. 169.

NOTES ON PASSING EVENTS

It cannot be said that the Irish question is much furthered by
the recent speeches in Parliament. Mr. Parnell's speech was
able, and so was Mr. Chamberlain's. The real gist of the
former was a kind of mild persistence in the original claim for
a Dublin Parliament, stated in language so moderate as to
give the impression of yielding perhaps to those who do not
understand the man and the claims which he represents. Yet,
undoubtedly, to Mr. Parnell nothing is worth thinking about
except the said Irish Parliament in Dublin. 'Give us that, and
do what else you like' is practically what he is saying.

As to Mr. Chamberlain, clever and effective as his speech
was, it was little else than a piece of Parliamentary fireworks;
because at this date we scarcely need to be told that he is a
bitter opponent of the establishment of an Irish Parliament at
Dublin, and that really was almost all he had to say that
bore directly on the question. Mr. Sexton again made several
points at Mr. Chamberlain's expense, notably when he
'solemnly asked the House which looked most like a foreign
country – the country which Lord Aberdeen left the other
day, or the country to which Sir Redvers Buller went
yesterday.' Also his little piece of history of the Donegal
peasants was as touching as it was unanswerable. But, after
all, what is there in all this? On one side the expression, not
at all veiled, of the determination to stand by the land thieves
to the last, even if the purse of the British taxpayer has to be
dipped into for their solace; and on the other, a covert threat
of refusal to pay rent.

By the way, it did always seem pretty certain that the Tories
would support a Land Purchase Bill, or measure for safe-

guarding the landlords against their loss of other people's property, if only it could dissociate such a piece of consolation from the company of Home Rule; which Mr. Gladstone vainly tried to make respectable by that association.

Mr. Chamberlain in his speech, took occasion to pronounce very decidedly in favour of peasant proprietorship, and alluded to his own proposal of last year as a basis for it. Such twaddle is rather sickening. Thus the ball is kept up in the air between the Tories and the Liberals; the former sedulous to do nothing, the latter to do something which shall amount to not much more than nothing. And all the while both parties must surely know that the real question is whether the Irish *people* shall have their own land to use for their own livelihood. Neither party wants that to come about; the Tories are quite satisfied with things as they are, if only some one else could be got to insure the landlords' rent; the Liberals would like to see one group of exploiters give place to another; and at that point, it seems, they stick hopelessly.

Socialists will not fail to note that Mr. Chamberlain justified his refusal to relieve the Irish peasants who could not pay tribute to their exploiters by pointing out that others were as badly off as they are. He said: 'We might address Her Majesty and say that we fear during the coming winter that the depression of trade which has continued so long will lead to a lack of employment, and be productive of much suffering, and that it will endanger social order. *That would be perfectly true*, and my only objection to an addition of that kind to the Address would be that it would be useless and improper to do so, unless the House were determined to deal with the subject-matter, and find a full, complete, and satisfactory remedy.' (Ministerial cheers).

Did the Ministerial members know what they were cheering? Surely if words mean anything (and certainly that is rather more than doubtful in a Parliamentary speech), this paragraph means either an incitement to revolution, or a confession of helplessness, which should force the speaker of it into private life as a self-admitted imbecile, or at least a member of a class and a legislative body necessarily imbecile under the circumstances. Mr. Chamberlain assumes the impossibility of the House of Commons finding a remedy for wide-spread destitution among the people. Most certainly he is right in doing so, but it is a curious admission for one to make who is not a confessed Socialist.

For torturing a little boy of eight years old a ship's clerk the other day was punished with a month's imprisonment. It is true that it was done so ingeniously that the doctor said that the boy 'was in no danger or his health permanently impaired.' True also that the culprit was the father of the boy, so that the holiness of the family somewhat excuses him in the eyes of that 'society' of which he is an ornament. Yet certainly the amusement was cheap, compared with street-preaching.

Mr. Burnett at the Workman's Conference in Paris took upon himself to defend Mr. Broadhurst against the attack made by Grimpe. Judging from the report of it, the defence was mostly of the official and conventional kind usual amongst us on such occasions; but it is worthy of note that he thought it necessary to defend the English trades' unions against the imputation of being hostile to Socialism – a significant symptom enough of the progress of our doctrines.

Mrs. Besant returns to the charge in *Our Corner* in an article called 'Why I am a Socialist.' It is very brightly and clearly written, and will no doubt have a considerable effect on the as yet unconverted readers of *Our Corner*. Some exception might be taken to the passage in which she points out the instances of State interference apparently on behalf of the workers. But though a centralised State Socialism is not the goal that we aim at, it is true that these approaches to it, forced as they have been on the dominant classes, are tokens of the decrepitude of the present system of wage-slavery. They are a necessary consequence of the upholding of our false 'free contract' in an age of increasing democracy. The people must be robbed, but the robbers dare not reduce them to extremity, therefore some of the plunder must be given back to them, and especially to some of the more respectable and helpful of them, so as if possible to gain a body of adherents for the robbers amongst the robbed themselves. This device, conscious or not, is a cunning one, but will fail before coming economical changes, which will bear with them commercial ruin under our present system and consequent Revolution. I should like to say how heartily I agree with Mrs. Besant on the failure of our civilisation. That lies at the bottom of our war with the present and our hope for the future, for those of us who have eyes to see and hearts to understand.

Commonweal, Volume 2, Number 34,
4 September 1886, p. 177.

NOTES ON PASSING EVENTS

It is difficult, or rather impossible, to get at the real facts of
the farce enacting in Bulgaria at present. The ultimate
meaning of it is of course that Russia wants to get Bulgaria
into due condition for being eaten – to beat it tender, as
French cooks do with a beefsteak. As to when or how she
will eat her Bulgarian morsel it is little use speculating.
Meanwhile the Prince Alexander, who a few days ago was
such a hero to the English bourgeois, turns out to be a 'hero'
of quite a modern type. He will now doubtless find plenty of
people to give him the very disagreeable names which his
present conduct seems to call for. I think it will be enough
for us to sum them all up in one word – perhaps the most
opprobrious that can be cast at a man – and say that he has
acted like 'a gentleman.'

For the disappointment of the Bulgarian people one does
really feel a pang of genuine grief; that they should be made
the playthings of these scoundrels! Yet one must keep in
mind that even if their dream of independence had been
realised they would have been after all landed amidst the
sordid realities of a backward country undergoing the process
of being opened up to modern commerce. Nothing worse
will happen to them under Russian rule – because nothing
worse could happen to them. Massacre, war, pestilence,
pinching times – all these are incidents to a rough condition
of life; but they come and go, and leave hope behind them.
But the pitiless grasp of commerce, continuous, unrelaxing, is
a robbery of the weak by the strong from which there is no
appeal. All these blessings of civilisation the Bulgarians
would have had to accept as the dark lining to the glittering
robe of their independence. Dependence on Russia can give

them nothing worse, and may make them more discontented, more ready to throw off at once the tyranny of absolutism and the tyranny of the money-bag.

It is at least to be hoped that they will have no illusions as to the help they are likely to get from this country. 'Our best wishes' they can have as much of as they please – a kind of gift-money which several other nationalities have had opportunities of appreciating at its true value – nothing. If they are so rash as to attempt to resist the Czar in arms, and get themselves killed and maimed by the thousand in consequence, they will at least have the further consolation that their sufferings will afford a pleasure equal to the reading of a realistic novel at the breakfast-tables of English middle-class families. But on the whole they had better trust to the paternal promises of the Czar than to the sentiment of the ruling classes of England: there is not a pin to cho[o]se between the good faith of the two.

In the debate on Dr. Clarke's amendment on the Crofter question there was plenty to show how in questions affecting the immediate welfare of the working classes it is hopeless to expect to get anything out of Parliament. 'Non possumus,' how *can* we? was the clear-cut answer to the Crofters' story; and will be the answer always given to any attempt at dealing with the one thing necessary to be dealt with – the exploitation of the workers at the hands of the land and capital grabbers. The occasion was made good use of by those who were anxious to set forth the virtues of the 'Macullum More,' that great chief (of rack-renters and land-agents) known in London as the Duke of Argyll, and to sing the praises of landlords generally.

It was no bad commentary, also, on the curious delusion that Parliament is a good platform for revolutionary propaganda that Dr. Clarke's speech was contracted into three lines of print by the great Liberal paper, the *Daily News*.

The unemployed men who 'demonstrated' in Liverpool on the 3rd ult. met with a similar 'How *can* we?' from the mayor of that city; though the answer was not given so unhesitatingly as in Parliament, and to judge by the report in the *Liverpool Courier* the mayor seemed somewhat uncomfortable, probably because he could not fail to know what an amount of distress there exists close to his own municipal door. One workman asked the mayor if the corporation could not take in hand their work themselves, instead of giving it out to contractors, who would employ less men. The mayor naturally said in answer that he could not say anything on the matter, and pointed out that competition among the contractors prevented any excessive profit. He did not further point out that that profit came out of the wages of the workman, for if he had heard that fact he of course would have tried hard not to believe it, and probably would have succeeded. Neither, it seems, did the workman retort on him that the competition praised by the mayor was the reason why the unemployed were there asking for what in fact amounted to parish relief in a different form.

The workman (poor fellow!) had had no opportunity of learning that 'relief works,' in crises like the present, mean just digging a hole and filling it up again – a make-believe of real work, in short – and that the temporary palliation of employing out-of-work men on non-productive labour must be very temporary indeed, and react on those men who are 'in employment' – *i.e.*, who are working not for their own livelihood, but the profits of a master. Let us hope that he and his fellows are learning in various ways that there is but one remedy for their trouble – employing themselves; living on the wares which they themselves have made, using the machinery and hoarded wealth which they themselves have made to go on producing necessary and pleasant wares for their own use. It is dismal to think what a heavy price they are paying meanwhile for their ignorance of this. Let the thought stir up all Socialists to extra exertions.

Commonweal, Volume 2, Number 35,
11 September 1886, p. 185.

NOTES ON PASSING EVENTS

Mr. Parnell must have been in some anxiety lest his Bill, cut down so fine as it was, should be accepted by the Tory Government. But the master of the Government, Lord Hartington, has a sort of wooden Whig courage, and was not likely to allow them to revolt, and the so-called Unionist-Liberals were still less able to give him trouble; so that Mr. Parnell's victory in the form of a defeat was pretty safe from the first. He has shown his sympathy with the Irish peasant, he has re-established his party in its position of being worth dealing with, even by a government so strong as this one of the Whig in the Tory's skin; nay, it may even come to a matter of necessity with them to deal with him; and finally he will be able to say, 'You see how moderate my Bill was, so much so that the very Tories were almost ready to accept it, and here is my Lord Hartington and Mr. Chamberlain who wouldn't let them.' Not a bad arrangement on his part, certainly; but then the risk of it! Suppose the Bill had passed, what *would* he have done then?

Parliamentary leaders must get used to be[ing] dragged through the dung-hill of lies and intrigue, or they will be of little service to their party; and clearly Mr. Parnell has a quite philosophical indifference to such trifles. If he can keep it up to the end he will deserve canonisation as a Parliamentary saint; and in sober earnest such toughness and steadiness of purpose are worthy of commendation, even if there is little else in the man. But a pity it is that the end aimed at is just a parliament in Dublin, where all will have to begin again – with Mr. Parnell on which side, the right or the wrong?

All this while, does it ever strike the many progressive politicians who are so anxious about the welfare of the Irish peasants (as they certainly should be) that their interest in the sufferings of people who are turned out of house and home because they cannot pay their rents should not be limited to the other side of St. George's Channel or to 'interesting' people like the Highlanders of the west and the islemen? Might not suspension of evictions become an English, nay, a London question, before long? I invite gentlemen who think these matters can have nothing to do with 'prosperous England' to stand before some broker's shop in a poor neighbourhood, and see if their imaginations will carry them far enough to fit some tale of sordid misery to a few of the wretched wares that are hung up there for sale.

There have been some useful articles in the *Pall Mall Gazette* lately. The doughty champion of the Ten Commandments (whoever he may be) appears to be taking a holiday just now, and the semi-Socialist writers on the staff are taking advantage of that fact. The article on the Scotch miners will probably be laid aside rather hastily by the optimist bourgeois if he comes across it, for the facts given in it have a very threatening look even to the most short-sighted. It is true that its writer deplores that the worst features of the Socialistic faith are finding acceptance among the workmen there, with their noble earnings of 12s. 6d. a-week for the privilege of working in a slice of hell; but he does not seem astonished at that fact, but rather looks upon it as a matter of course that when men are much ground down they should be inclined to turn towards Socialism as their hope. So curiously have the times changed since Socialism was, as we used to be told, a very few years ago, quite unknown among the British working classes.

'A Month in Search of Work' will be another discomfort to our optimist bourgeois friend, if he should stumble on it, especially if he has read any article that hints at the number of men out of work even now before the winter comes on, and exercises the multiplication-table a little. Mr. Hyndman and Mr. Champion, also, have both been allowed a run in the columns of the *Pall Mall*; and there has been a paragraph on the street-speaking question which is not without intelligence, though the writer perhaps looks through religious spectacles on the subject.

Our readers will have noticed several letters amongst our correspondence on the subject of Vegetarianism, one or two of which were written in a somewhat aggrieved tone, apropos of attacks by Socialists on that doctrine, if one may call it so, though several comrades and friends of ours are vegetarians. It seems to me that there is no need either to attack a vegetarian or to confer a vote of thanks on him, so long as he is one because he chooses to be so on any grounds that please himself, whether he makes it a matter of health, or economy, or sentiment. But a man can hardly be a sound Socialist who puts forward vegetarianism as a solution of the difficulties between labour and capital, as some people do, and as one may think very severe capitalists would like to do, if the régimen were not applied to themselves; and again, there are people who are vegetarians on ascetic grounds, and who would be as tyrannical as other ascetics if they had the chance of being so. I do not mean to say that Socialist vegetarians are likely to fall into these traps; they only make themselves liable to the sneer of an anti-Socialist acquaintance of mine, who said to me one day 'All you Socialists have each of you another fad besides Socialism.'

The first number of *Freedom* has appeared, published by the English Anarchist-Socialists, and is to appear monthly. In spite of its small size, it is well worth a penny, as the matter is very well written and thoughtful, and must interest all Socialists, whatever their opinions may be.

NOTES ON PASSING EVENTS

Parliament having 'dried up,' and a complete languor having
followed on the excitement of having a real live Tory
Government in office, the bourgeois press was beginning to
reconcile itself to a dull season in politics, when Lord
Randolph Churchill broke the dulness by his speech at
Dartford. That speech comes on people as something like a
surprise, after the stolid 'How can we?' with which the Tories
received Mr. Parnell's measure (no doubt much to his satisfaction). But a little consideration will show them that Lord
Randolph has not been so extra bold as he has been thought,
that he has not made such a very dangerous excursion into
the realms of Tory Democracy. Some, indeed, see him in the
light of the butcher who has just put his knife into the Tory
ox; but that is scarcely the way to look on his position,
because that noble beast was dead before the stroke, and can
barely be made a marketable carcase (*sic*) now.

On the other hand, it is perhaps a question whether he is not
striking a stroke for freedom from the Whig domination,
especially if it be true that his vague hints about local
government in Ireland are to be redeemed by a Home Rule
Bill which will seem somewhat advanced to the ordinary
Liberal mind, but which the Irish party will not and cannot
accept. Perhaps even his extravagant flattery of the Unionist
Liberals (*i.e.*, Whigs), or it may be said his gross servility to
them in words, really conceal this revolt. Certainly if he is
determined to revolt they will have to give way if, also, his
own party follow him, as it is to be supposed they must, and
if he still sticks to the quasi-democratic part of his
programme, or makes a fair show of doing so. And if the
Whigs do let him pull them a step or two out of their beaten

path, they will find after all that when it is done they will not be so much worse off: there will still be room for Whiggery when all that he has promised or threatened has happened.

The three acres and a cow, duly reduced to a very humdrum allotment scheme, will not bring about a very great revolution, and the older Whigs must put up with seeing Mr. Jesse Collings pleased and Mr. Chamberlain somewhat rehabilitated. Local self-government may mean something considerably short of free communes. The threat to the railway interests can be easily explained away – nay, that explanation is already prepared for in the disclaimer of any intention of attacking their *rights* of private property – while the hint about free education means anything or nothing, according to circumstances.

At any rate, whatever he is going to yield to 'Democracy,' he is not going to give, but sell; and the fact that this is clear ought to be enough to keep the Whigs quiet, especially as the gain he proposes to himself concerns their darling institution, the House of Commons. For after all, probably the only serious intention he has is to attempt to muzzle the Opposition, whose feebleness he taunted, not without reason, if we except the Irish party. The Whigs will be bound to help him in this, in spite of all that has come and gone, and the rest of his programme sounds very like a bid for the support of whatever professes to be Radical or progressive in Parliament. 'Will you allow a factious minority to stand in the way of the generous and even sweeping reforms which I am prepared to lead my party into?' is what he practically says. 'Let us make the House of Commons a really good machine for expressing the will of – property.'

In this enterprise he is not unlikely to succeed; and some of us will not be very sorely grieved at his success. The House of Commons will always represent property as long as there is property to be represented, whether that property be aggregated in the possession of the owner of half a county, or divided among sham peasant proprietors and £3-a-week savings-bank-and-building-society examples of 'thrift and steady industry,' who may consider that they belong to a Radical party, but who are really ex-Radicals turned Whigs by the force of the said property. It is far better, then, that the iron exclusiveness of Parliament should be made obvious by Government muzzling of obstruction, than that it should be able to pose as a body that has tendencies towards looking after the interests of the people, which may be developed into something approaching to revolution. If Lord Randolph can rehabilitate the House of Commons and show it clearly to every one as an august and orderly assembly barring the way to revolution by means of constitutional reforms, he will do good service to the cause of Socialism.

Certainly this will scarcely be Toryism, but it will be very good Whiggery; and it is most important to us that the growing elements of discontent shall come to recognise the solid truth that the Whigs will always rule the roast (*sic*) and have the executive in their power till the day when the people are determined to help themselves.

Lord Randolph called on his hearers to be encouraged by the fact that the depression of trade was showing signs of yielding to better times. It may be true, as is commonly said, that we are on the eve of a temporary recovery, although the tokens of it are not very obvious. If it should take place there may be an appearance of retrogression in our propaganda, as it will make a portion of the working class in this country 'contented' once more, who are now inclined to listen to our doctrines. But if that does happen it ought not to discourage us; there must be more general understanding of the grounds of Socialism before the waning night points towards the dawn of action, and it may be that quieter times will not be altogether unfavourable to revolutionary education. 'The poor ye shall have always with you,' while our present system lasts; and during the time of the recovery, which will certainly be short-lived enough, we may still make abundant progress amongst those whom no 'recovery' will advantage, and to whom at all times we must address ourselves most directly.

Lord Randolph Churchill sang the Jingo song at Dartford about as small as it could be sung. In point of fact, he changed Lord Salisbury's 'The Austrian sentinel is on the ramparts' to 'We hope to see the Austrian paw on the hot chestnuts.'

Mr. Norton, the Australian labour delegate, has pretty much knocked the bottom out of the emigration humbug. His letter to the *Daily News* of October 9, about the serious matter of Chinese labour in Australasia, must interest everybody who thinks of the labour question; but he does not quite seem to see the bearings of it. That American or Australian or English workmen should be shouldered out of the labour market by Chinese or any other workmen who can live cheaper than they can is the necessary outcome of the competitive system – of the system which aims at producing profits for the employer and not goods for people to live on. By hook or by crook the employer will have his cheap labour, because he must, and because he *can* as long as the wages system lasts – that is, as long as the workmen must needs pay some one to 'employ' them instead of employing themselves in making what they want and living happily.

Commonweal, Volume 2, Number 40,
16 October 1886, p. 225.

NOTES ON PASSING EVENTS

Lord Randolph Churchill's declaration of policy has been received by the Tory party on the whole as they must receive anything from those of their party who have any capacity, as something, namely, which they must support, though they may not either understand it or agree with it.   There are some signs of restiveness.   Mr. Chaplin, for instance, has found out that all that talk meant little beyond muzzling the Irish members, and is a little uncomfortable; since he thinks that the turn of the wheel may one day put the Tories in the position of their Irish foes.   He threatens opposition, but will probably have to give way; all the more since as a matter of party tactics he is wrong and Lord Randolph is right.   The Tories, indeed, are not likely to have a majority by themselves, but in alliance with the Whigs they are likely to be in a perpetual majority; the Liberal-Radical party only exists as a criticising minority.

The rest of the press has been very rough on the *Daily News* for its announcement of a Government Home Rule scheme. The *Pall Mall*, especially, has exceeded in scorn. Naturally; since the latter journal has had such success in mares'-nesting, that it may well feel that it should be privileged in that occupation.   But after all is it not likely enough that a Tory communication *was* made to the *Daily News*? It would not be a bad move to play: to feel the pulse of the political world by means of a hint to an adverse journal, to go on if the public seemed to approve, and if not to repudiate the hint and thereby to damage the said adverse journal, would really be a good stroke of business in that Art of Lying in which English statesmen are past-masters.

It is pretty clear that the Austrian revolutionary story was an excuse for the arrest of 'dangerous' persons. The press now says that the matter has been much exaggerated, that the saltpetre bottles were, in fact, dummies, and so forth. It is rather weak of the authorities to let this sort of thing leak out after the concoction of such a vigorous romance. On the whole the matter is of bad augury for European peace, and looks as if the Austrian Government were anxious to have as many as possible of its 'dangerous' subjects under lock and key before it takes the field.

A case of white-lead poisoning reported in the press this week is worth a little notice by workmen generally. Stripped of verbiage it amounts to this, that a man was killed by being compelled to work in a place where white-lead was flying about, and that no precautions were taken to prevent his dying speedily. A shilling a-week extra was the handsome sum given to the poor man thus murdered in compensation for his being killed. It is quite impossible that the man's employers did not know the risk he ran of this speedier death, and the certainty of his being poisoned sooner or later, and yet all that the jury durst say about the matter was 'to express a hope that Mr. Lakeman (the factory inspector) would be able to make representations to the Home Office with reference to the case, to show the necessity for some extra precaution being taken for people working in mixing factories.'

Yet further, this is only an exaggerated example of the way in which the lives of working-people are played with. Under present conditions, almost the whole labour imposed by civilisation on the 'lower classes' is unwholesome; that is to say that people's lives are shortened by it; and yet because we don't see people's throats cut before our eyes we think nothing of it. After all, probably Tamerlane was a blessing to the world compared with the factory system.

Commonweal, Volume 2, Number 41, 23 October 1886, p. 233.

NOTES ON PASSING EVENTS

The democratic side of the new Tory Democracy will be severely tried by the new development of the land-war in Ireland, of which the 'battle' of Clonakilty was a dramatic incident. Whether the plan of campaign given in *United Ireland* be carried out or not, we may be at least sure that the resistance to rent will take some definite and organised shape. Under these circumstances the Government will doubtless find the Closure a necessity to them, and Lord Randolph Churchill may well bid a high price for it, and Tories and Whigs of all shades must put up with it.

Or is his lordship really going further on the democratic path? If so here is an opportunity for him. Let him bid the Home Secretary to release the lately imprisoned crofters, and administer a good snub to the judge for his vindictive and cruel sentence; some of us might be shaken in our views of him then, and suppose him capable of something else than the most barefaced chicanery.

'The quality of mercy is not strained,' says Shakespeare, apparently thinking of the jelly-bag. But on this occasion the judge must have strained it very fine indeed, since the jury recommended the convicts to mercy, and the judge admitted that those who had the lighter sentence were little more than lookers-on. Perhaps taught by this judicial champion of common-sense, they will remember a familiar proverb next time, and do something more than look on.

According to the story given of an incident in the Czar's life those who are engaged in defending him run almost as great a risk from his Majesty's hand as those who are plotting his death. This story, though it has been denied, may be true in spite of that, but true or not, it was clearly not thought an impossibility; and even that fact gives us a curious indication of the joys of a tyrant's life, still more curiously emphasised by Mr. Ralston's apology, that it was a true story of the *late* Czar.

The war cloud meanwhile seems to be gathering and darkening. It may well be that with Russia in such a condition the Czar may think it the best chance of prolonging his dastard's life to stir up Russian Jingoism to the utmost, and that the risk, fearful though it is, must be borne. Whatever may happen, the advance of Socialism is not likely to be retarded. Nay, it is difficult to conceive but that a war must inflict a terrible wound, and probably a fatal one, on one or other of the great reactionary powers. Nevertheless, from the point of view which is presented to us English Socialists, a war is to be deprecated for other reasons than the natural human horror at causeless slaughter and misery. It is rather the miseries of bourgeois peace than those of war which will force on the workers perception of the fact that our commercial system is rotting into a chaos which, but for the steady advance of Socialism, would mean a return to a savagery a thousand-fold worse than that from which mankind has slowly and painfully emerged.

For if Europe were to be at war again many worthy persons would point out that all our misfortunes were due to it, and that peace obtained once more all would be well again. Moreover, the pleasurable excitement of reading every morning stirring news of the hopes and fears of the contest, while we sat safe at home, would arouse our latent Jingoism, and would take people's attention off the really important social matters which they are now forced to consider, and the pressing nature of which is now educating the people surely if slowly.

But that is not all, nor the most important side of the matter. It is a frightful thing to have to say, but a true one, that a war would at first benefit those of the workers who were not immediately concerned in it: it would 'give employment' by destroying before they were used some of the commodities made by the workers, not for their own livelihood, but as counters for 'making money.' The miseries of war would not really be felt till peace came again, the sham peace of our class society, bringing with it once more lack of employment, over-production, over-population, and the rest of it, till men at last, unable to bear the consequences of their own folly any longer, would rise in a body and accept the social revolution, thrusting aside the turnip-lantern bogy (*sic*) of fear so sedulously held up to them by interested fools, scoundrels, and cowards. When they do that they will find no tremendous difficulty in making what they want for their own use, and using it.

But all that they might come to without the intervention of war and slaughter, and probably the sooner, since, as aforesaid, they will feel the pinch more speedily, and see the only remedy more clearly.

Meanwhile, it is a favourite amusement with the middle-classes to try to prove to the workers that they do not suffer, or that if they do, yet things are getting better in spite of the depression of trade. Lord Derby (who, though an earl, is mentally as complete a specimen of the bourgeois as could be wished) is the latest player in this game. He professes, however, that he is perplexed at the figures that show that our prosperity is increasing while our trade-profits are falling off. It might be suggested to him as a solution of his 'perplexity' that the ever-increasing productivity of labour, or, if you please, the increasing cheapness in the processes of manufacture, is telling more and more in favour of the 'haves' and against the 'have-nots'; that the tendency is for the middle-class, now that it has embraced the aristocracy and made them all traders, to extend downwards, and so to widen the basis of class-robbery or property; so that at first sight Lord Derby has some reason to be reassured as to the stability of the Robber Association, miscalled Society, which it is his sole business to uphold.

Nevertheless, this very process of the extension of the class to which his lordship (mentally) belongs, tends also to consolidate the genuine working-class by levelling them; and his lordship increases his perplexity, it may be said in passing, by confusing some of the working with the middle-class. But the great difficulty is now arising for the middle-class, which would increase Lord Derby's perplexity if he could turn his attention to it. The middle-class exists only as an employing class, and their success in cheapening the processes of labour is making it difficult for them to employ their – slaves. And unless they can get over that difficulty the days of class-robbery of our modern sham Society are numbered. Nor *can* they get over it; because competition will force them to go on cheapening manufacture in the teeth of an ever-increasing 'reserve army of labour,' which will at last (and surely before long) be *forced* to employ itself – and where will the middle-class and its economical earls be then?

Will Lord Derby explain a thing which one would think might perplex many people? Optimist economists are apt to show with great glee the advantages of our present working population in the cheapness of living, on account of the low prices of necessities and small luxuries; but the very same persons are no less gleeful, and deduce the same lesson of the general rise in the comfort of the people when they are able to show that the prices of commodities are *rising*. Lord Randolph Churchill, for instance, clearly felt that he was on

safe ground at last when he encouraged the Kentish lunatics
(beg pardon, Tories) with the good news of the rise in pepper
and quicksilver; and a writer in the *Daily News* gets really
quite jolly (there is no other word) in recounting the fact
that Cheshire cheese is rising beyond all manner of doubt.
What *does* it all mean? Is it good that prices should rise, or
that they should fall, or that they should both rise and fall?
Here is perplexity for you, surely worthy of Colney Hatch –
or Kent!

The Lord Mayor's Show is to change its character somewhat
this year; there will be the usual sheriffs' and aldermen's
carriages, and the usual company banners and the usual
circus show, and no doubt the usual amount of spectators, or
perhaps more; but in addition there is to be a show,
organised by the Social Democratic Federation, of the
unemployed of London, which is likely to be a curious part of
the pageant. Whatever differences of opinion there may be
about the general tactics of the Federation as to this matter of
the unemployed (and I for one do not agree with them), the
demonstration will no doubt show the dominant classes the
'difficulty' above mentioned in an impressive manner.
Indeed, the mere announcement of the intention to organise
the procession has set the whole of bourgeoisdom in a
twitter, and has drawn from its press various objurgatory
articles which betoken a bad conscience at least; the general
tone of them, stripped of their verbiage is really 'Can't you let
it alone?' The bourgeois is hard to convince that what is on
the whole a pleasant world to him is not as good for those
whose misery makes his ease; and his peevish anger at any
one trying to lift a corner of the curtain for him knows no
bounds, unless it is done in a merely dramatic manner, with
no hint of ulterior consequences.

Colonel Fraser's letter to the Council of the Federation is
not a satisfactory piece; it seems at least possible to read
between its lines a threat of letting loose the indifferent rough

on the procession. Anyhow, since it is clear that the Federation will do their utmost to make the demonstration go off in an orderly manner, there will be no difficulty in the way of the police ensuring that result if they are in earnest in wanting to do so.

Meantime, the commercial classes are so nervous about the affair, that one gentleman has written to the *Daily News* proposing to withdraw the show this year, which a leader-writer in the same paper, with a strange appreciation of the value of words, calls a *bold* proposal. The truth is that the war of Commerce is getting so fierce, and so many people suffer from it, that the rich and well-to-do must expect to have their follies and pleasures interfered with by the necessities of those sufferers, just as they would be in a time of mere open war, and once more it is a good thing to reach their feelings through the tough hide of use and wont, by any means that will do so without doing damage to the Cause in other ways.

Commonweal, Volume 2, Number 42,
30 October 1886, pp. 241–2.

NOTES ON PASSING EVENTS

Lord Randolph Churchill's speeches at Bradford were perhaps principally important because he said nothing very new in them. As at Dartford, he thought it necessary to wave the Jingo flag, while warning people against supposing that its waving meant anything at all; and if a Tory audience ever takes the trouble to think, the hearts of some of his hearers must have sunk with forebodings of dull times in foreign politics as far as the Tory government is concerned. As to home politics, he began the course of explaining away his threat of three acres and a cow, which clearly lies before him. As to that notable scheme, indeed, he spoke more truth than he intended to speak when he claimed it as a Tory measure – which indeed it would be if it could be passed and enforced. He tried to reinforce his hopes of a revival of trade, based at Dartford on those two articles (not *very* filling at the price) pepper and quicksilver, by a conversation with a railway official. All this, however, was but half-hearted, and, as at Dartford, it was quite clear that the part of the political game which he was really interested in was the Irish question.

Of course he felt, first, that neither the Tory Government nor any other could really deal with the economical condition of Britain; and next, that the less they dealt with it the better he would be pleased; and thirdly, that he had done quite enough to give the Whig-Liberal-Radicals an excuse for supporting him; while on the other hand that, as far as Parliament is concerned, it is possible for the Government to block the way to Home Rule and the beginnings of expropriation in Ireland. Accordingly he hinted at the possibility of a new Coercion Bill, and entirely repudiated anything like concession to Home Rule, poking great fun at the *Daily News*, which he or some of his party has hocussed with much success; and finally he waxed eloquent and eager over his intention of clapping the muzzle on the Home Rulers; showing by his reservation on this subject to the last that it was the one matter of real importance that he had to deal with.

He showed with much frankness how he had changed his opinion on this point; that he had resisted the application of the muzzle as unconstitutional when Mr. Gladstone proposed it, only because the then small Irish party had to be dealt with; but that as he saw that the Home Rule party was growing strong, and formed at least a respectable minority, he began to be concerned, and at last saw the necessity for silencing arbitrarily an opponent who was listened to by the people at large. In short, this latter part of Lord Randolph's speech, which has not been so much noticed as it deserved to be, is a model of impudence and brutality, and implies probably a fair appreciation on the speaker's part of the qualities of the audience whom he was addressing. It was no insult to them; but it would have been a dire insult to any other audience than the rump of a ridiculous party, with no chance of sustaining their worn-out theories in practice.

And yet, cynically as Lord Randolph put his proposals, his firm resolve to carry them out shows that he has grasped the true idea of Constitutionalism face to face with Revolution; for in spite of Mr. Parnell's respectable Parliamentary methods the Irish claim is revolutionary, and will be dealt with accordingly; Constitutionalism will not put up with Revolution in its midst, and will not find it difficult to lay hand on some weapon old or new in its armoury to put it down. In all probability Lord Randolph will find himself well supported in his attack on the Home Rulers in Parliament. What will the Home Rulers outside Parliament do?

Russia seems, having counted the cost, to have made up her mind to lay hands on Bulgaria, on the grounds that no great harm can come of it, since England has now with many big words declared that the quarrel is none of hers. The stroke once struck, the 'conscience of Europe' will not be very uneasy at the robbery; nor as far as any of the respectable powers go can they afford to be very sensitive, as each of the said powers would do as Russia is going to do, if opportunity served it. Certainly England with her pockets crammed with stolen goods, would cut but a poor figure as the defender of injured innocence – at any rate if she were beaten.

The three great Absolutist powers, unless they are forced to fall out, seem on the surface as strong as ever; the true development of nations, the harmonious and free development of their varied qualities, still awaits the time when 'national life' in the sense in which we now use the words has come to an end, and the setting up a standard of rivalry, striving after an approach to the monopoly of a market under the name of patriotism, will have come to be looked upon as a monstrous folly, remembered only to be ridiculed.

Commonweal, Volume 2, Number 43,
6 November 1886, p. 249.

NOTES ON PASSING EVENTS

The great rally of the Caucus at Leeds was no doubt of some importance to whatever party quality may be left in the remains of Liberalism, and also it was of importance that this body, formidable enough in the welter of broken principles, halting opinions, and intrigue, should declare definitely its adhesion to Gladstonian Home Rule. But if one had any lingering hopes in the Liberal Party – as who has? – it would be discouraging to note that what really roused the enthusiasm of the audience at Leeds was not the hope of the coming change in Ireland; not the joy of England discarding some part of its long tyranny and injustice to a people whom we call our fellow-countrymen, and will not allow to be anything else; it was not really these reasonable revolutionary aspirations which moved people, but Mr. Gladstone's name as party leader. It is only too likely that the question of justice to Ireland was looked upon by this meeting of would-be progressive leaders, great and small, and their adherents, as an adjunct of Mr. Gladstone's personality; a whim of his to be indulged, and which we, the party, can at least imagine we sympathise with, though we don't in the least sympathise with the results which are sure to follow, or indeed guess what they are.

That the assembled Liberals did not think of or wish for the results of the political freedom of Ireland is not a matter of guess, but is proved by the barrenness of the programme put forward by them – a programme about as valuable as a proposal for the re-enactment of Magna Charta, and which, it must be said, seems to have excited no more enthusiasm than that would have done.

Mr. Morley, in a sentence likely to become famous, mentioned his fears of our being in for a period of 'degraded politics.' This was of course meant for a hit at Mr. Chamberlain, which doubtless he deserves; but there is more in it than that, whether Mr. Morley meant it or not. This 'degradation,' this slough of despond of personalities, intrigues, and trickeries, is the necessary outcome of parties walking about and pretending to be alive when the brains are knocked out of them. With the single exception of the Irish question the Liberal Party is now shutting its eyes resolutely to all the real questions of the day. The last six years of 'crisis' it is determined to look upon as non-existent; it has now come to recognise finality in politics with as little misgiving as the old Tories. Doubtless it thinks itself very progressive as to the matters of Ireland, but the next stage of these will find it out, and 'Liberal' will have the same meaning as reactionary.

As far as mere passing party politics go, this meeting has of course a very simple meaning – no surrender to the Unionist Liberals. They are going, when Lord Hartington can make it convenient to come amongst them, to have a field-day in their turn, which will have less interest than even the Leeds meeting to those who look upon the real politics of life and not the sham politics of Parliament. As far as concerns the game played therein, the result of all this means a quiet innings for the Tory Government, which by means of a few threats of 'dishing,' and a sham attempt to carry them out, can always paralyse the Liberal Party, both sections or either. 'These be thy gods, O Israel!' Surely as mean a set of shufflers and blinkards as ever walked the earth.

Mr. Henry George has belied the confident predictions of the bourgeois press both at home and in America by gaining a substantial vote for the mayoralty of New York. Mr. George is not a Socialist, or was not when last heard of; his programme as candidate could not be considered a Socialist one in any sense. Nevertheless the Bourgeois are determined to consider him the Socialist candidate, and a dangerous one at that, and have done their best in a tremulous manner to belittle his success. We must conclude, therefore, that the robber society of New York feels itself beaten, and is anxious and unhappy under its beating. At the least its obvious terror, reflected by our own press, at what would seem to an onlooker a small matter, is a sign of a very bad conscience. In spite of all the bluster and conventional congratulation on the stability and progress of modern civilisation, it seems easily shaken after all.

The meeting at the Mansion House about the Beaumont Hall, or People's Palace as it is pompously called, was such a queer exhibition of stupidity that Guy Fawkes day seemed an appropriate date for it. The obstinacy of the 'saints' who want to teetotal and sabbatarianise Beaumont Hall (when they get it), the nervous anxiety of the Lord Mayor to muddle up the question till the money was got, and the empty conventional resolutions passed made a pretty kettle of fish of it. As a human being one is really irritated at such simplicity of stupidity as Mr. Charrington and Mr. Wookey showed in mixing up teetotalism and sabbatarianism. Surely if ever they want a job done which none but an incompetent person can do, they need not advertise for one in the papers. Yet we owe them thanks, nevertheless, for showing us what the saints' rule upon earth would be if we suffered it; and also for punching a hole in this patronage of the working classes by the thieves who have robbed them.

All this People's Palace business means is that 'the people' are perforce such strangers to orderliness, cleanliness and decency, let alone art and beauty, in their own dwellings, that the upper classes, who force them into this life of degra-dation, do now and then bethink them if they cannot provide them with a place where they can play at being comfortable, so long as they behave like good children, between the spells of their stupid hopeless weary work and their miserable and hideous 'homes.' Time enough to think about People's Palaces when the workers and the people are one, and no artificial authority stands between them and their human wishes.

Commonweal, Volume 2, Number 44,
13 November 1886, p. 257.

NOTES ON PASSING EVENTS

Mr. Labouchere speaking at Manchester on a Gladstonian-Liberal resolution in favour of Home Rule, had naturally not much opportunity of speaking of the general Radical policy: what he did say showed how feeble he really thought the Radicals and their changes. His amendment of the programme of the Leeds Conference comprised pretty much the Radical platform as it used to be: this platform would now be on the point of being established if it were not that the opinion of the people is now not so much passing beyond these measures as getting on to another line. The end once proposed by Radicalism was the utmost development of the system falsely called that of free contract, that is absolute freedom of the fleecing of labour by money. That end is now seen by everyone to be worthless or unattainable, and the result is that the means necessary to its attainment are no longer interesting, and that the Radical party as a party is 'unemployed'; and even such a brisk politician as Mr. Labouchere, has to put forward its programme speaking from the teeth out. There is no longer any heart in it, and no life, and it has to compete for attention with other lifeless things such as Protection, Paternal Government, the honour of the British Empire, and the rest. Therefore honest Radicals think there is reaction, which is a very great mistake. All that has happened is that the Radical ideal is worn out and has to take its place with other worn-out ideals and be a plaything for those who have nothing to do with practical politics, to use those much abused words in their right sense. Such things are fit subjects for debate in the House of Commons, which means that they are done with everywhere else.

What Mr. Labouchere said about Ireland is out of date since the new adventure of the Government into coercion. As Lord Salisbury promised us at the Mansion House the other day, the Tory Government has announced its sole function to be that of acting as bumbailiff to the Irish landlords. It must be said that in so doing it has shown a much keener appreciation of the meaning of Irish agitation than the Radicals have. To defend property at all hazards and in spite of any suffering that may be caused to innocent people – that is the function of Constitutional Government. The Irish agitation attacks property, *ergo*, it must be put down at any cost.

Commonweal, Volume 2, Number 47,
4 December 1886, p. 281.

NOTES ON PASSING EVENTS

Mr. John Bright fairly tires out one's attempts to understand how a once vigorous and combative man can fall so far behind the times he lives in, and his friends ought to put pen, ink, and paper out of his way. It is absurd enough that he should use Milton as a stalking-horse for his attack on the classic poets, since Milton had not the least sympathy for anything that was not classical; but except as showing Mr. Bright's inaccessibility to facts, and the narrow and conventional turn of his mind, that is of no great importance, since it is only a question of a slight alteration in the education dealt out to the middle-classes at modern Oxford; and whatever alteration is made in that education, it can for the present be nothing more than a cramming of middle-class persons to fit them for their competition for places in the hanger-on group of the well-to-do; a commercial education in the full sense of the word.

But his letter on depressed trade and high wages! Trades' unionism and Protection are still the enemies to him; and a fall in wages is the hope which he holds out to the British workman as a remedy for depression of trade! Nor does he seem to have considered how far the fall of wages is to go, nor how much the 'concessions' of the Nottingham workmen may influence the livelihood of their brethren elsewhere; he can see nothing but a group of manufacturers competing against the world and 'employing' labour as long as it is convenient for them to do so, and no remedy for the workmen, but always making it convenient for the manufacturers, at the cost of any amount of suffering to themselves – the Quaker's peace!

Mr. Bright is not likely to read these lines, nor would he heed them if he did; but for the benefit of any one of our readers who may have some lingering confidence, not in Mr. Bright, but in the middle-class democracy of which he was once a demi-god, one may say this, that when the British trades' unions understand the necessity of trades' unionism being international, they will find some better remedy for depression of trade than that the wealth-producers should quietly starve for the benefit of the non-producers.

Commonweal, Volume 2, Number 48,
11 December 1886, p. 289.

NOTES ON PASSING EVENTS

The 'Dissentient Liberals' have had their field-day; and at first sight the thing which would strike the observer most would be the extreme shabbiness of their purpose. These lords and gentlemen – these superior persons – were met together really for the purpose of enforcing their legal right to take the last penny out of the pockets of a few poor people on the verge of pauperism. Stripped of a very thin veil of pretence to patriotism, fair dealing, ten commandments, and the like, this is the only explanation of their conduct. And one must say that the sweating of the Jews by King John was a generous and almost ideal proceeding compared with this dull, blank shabbiness; for at all events the Jew had something worth taking, and his 'portable property' might well captivate the imagination of a hard-up mediæval king.

Their desperate earnestness in their purpose was also striking. 'The manly straightforwardness' of Lord Hartington – which an enemy might perhaps call grovelling stupidity – the old-womanish spite of Mr. Bright's much be-cheered letter, Mr. Chamberlain's quaintly arrogant telegram, are not more remarkable than the obvious eagerness of the rank and file to declare themselves supporters of Lord Salisbury. Fear had consolidated these opponents of Home Rule, that is clear; but fear of Home Rule? Surely not.

For if they had no enemy save Home Rule the game for these patriots to play would be support of the tenant-farmers against the landlords; to be able to say, 'What do you want with a Dublin parliament when we will give you all you ask for, and as an instalment, to show that we mean it, will stave off the landlords from you at this pinch, so that you may make *some* livelihood out of the land?' Surely this would have been the card to play for a party calling themselves Unionists. And to an outsider it seems as if it would have been so easy, too. The National League with its 'Plan of Campaign' would appear almost to have been asking the *Liberal* Unionists to dish it. At least Mr. Bright might have been expected to be on the side of the tenant-farmers.

After all, our Irish friends seem to have understood the people they were fighting against, and that they could be trusted to plunge deeper and deeper into the mire. And as for Mr. Bright, he is one of those persons who roar out for sweeping reforms as long as there is no chance of their being realised, and draw back in terror as soon as they seem likely to come about.

In short, there are no two words to be said on the matter. The terror arises from the attack on property, as it seems to their eyes; though to ours the 'Plan of Campaign' seems rather a recognition of the rights of property, and therefore to be deprecated. But it is clear from the speeches that Socialism was the bugbear, and Lord Salisbury once again echoed the feeling in his speech to the Conservative Club; in which, by the way, he was naturally jubilant over the definite adhesion of the 'Liberal Unionists.' He has a strong party to lead now.

Neither are there wanting signs that the greater part of the Gladstonian Liberals will soon be in the same camp. The avidity with which they will seize on an excuse to go over to the safe side was well illustrated by the article in the *Daily News* following Lord Kilcoursie's letter on Mr. Dillon's speech. It meant once more: 'Yes, we will do what Mr. Gladstone wishes as long as the natural results don't seem likely to come of our doing so; but then – .' The Gladstonian

Liberals also are beginning to understand what Irish affairs mean; and when they have come to understand fully that it is not a question of Parliamentary politics, but of property, then, except for the Irish themselves and a few Radicals, there will be but one party in Parliament as far as Ireland is concerned. But, meantime, how the Irish party must despise their Liberal allies!

Yes, the Tory party seems safe, and it would be unreasonable if it were not so, since except in this matter of Home Rule, in which they are not in earnest, the Liberal party has nothing to propose which the others are unwilling to accept. Take as an example Mr. Arnold's ridiculously misnamed 'Free Land' scheme, and here is Lord Salisbury's remark on that point: 'Anybody must be absolutely ignorant of the history of this country who believes that the desire to make the acquisition of land easy' (to those who have the privilege of money understood) 'is inconsistent with the principles of the Conservative party.' Perhaps Lord Salisbury had better let history alone. But 'the principles of the Conservative party' at present need no stretching to enable them to accept a scheme which would strengthen the power of capital, as the 'Free Land' business certainly would.

To those who wish to retain any respect for human nature, the stupidity exhibited by the speakers at meetings like the Poor-law Conference is somewhat of a blow. Meantime, it is not worth while to hunt these people through the labyrinth of lies which they construct so elaborately. Yet, fools as they are, it is strange that even they cannot see that their arguments against the exceptional nature of the distress, which no one denies, form the heaviest indictment possible against the cruel fraud which they call Society, and which they sustain so persistently. If this is to be our ordinary condition in the future, and if you have no plan for getting rid of this 'chronic' and necessary misery and degradation, what scheme of revolution can be too wild for us to try? In sober truth it seems to most thinking people that we are being pushed down a long incline, and that before long we shall look back to this dismal year as one of comparative prosperity. What is the remedy for the present condition of the poor? To get rid of the condition of the poor; and we know how to do it if we will, by getting rid of the condition of the rich, to whose existence as a rich class the poor are necessary.

Commonweal, Volume 2, Number 49,
18 December 1886, p. 297.

CONTRIBUTIONS TO
COMMONWEAL

1887

POLITICAL NOTES

There is naturally great commotion in political circles about the resignation of Lord Randolph Churchill, and speculations about the result; as far as we Socialists are concerned we need not trouble ourselves much about it. It emphasises the idiocy of our Parliamentary struggle, that the resignation of a man who is looked upon by every one as a mere trickster, who openly repudiates the folly of having principles to trouble himself with, should be a matter of such mighty importance. Further, it is an indication of the disintegration of parties which is caused by the shadow of advancing Socialism, and which has been going on at such a great rate recently.

But although it is really a sign of this decay of party government, it is probable enough that its first results will be the uniting of the Liberal party on the basis of the surrender of the Gladstonian Liberals. Mr. Chamberlain's speech at Birmingham had a tone of confident triumph about it which is somewhat justified by the situation. The Liberals are quite prepared for this act of ratting; indeed, Mr. Gladstone himself has given the signal for it by letting it be known that he too condemns the 'Plan of Campaign.' The Jonah of Home Rule once thrown over, nothing prevents the Union of the two sections of the Liberal Party, who can then set to work about the business which the more enlightened of them see to be their true function, of widening the basis of exploitation in these islands in various ways. The attempt at the creation of a new lower middle-class to stem the torrent of Socialism will be the serious business of this new party (for in spite of names it will really be new), of which the two brothers-in-arms, Churchill and Chamberlain, are such distinguished leaders.

Mr. Chamberlain's very clear statement on the necessity of turning the Irish tenants into owners of their holdings was very significant of this aim. As far as Ireland is concerned it must be said that dismal as is the prospect which the realisation of his views would put before that luckless country, the turning of the Irish tenants into peasant proprietors is only too likely to take place, whatever political party may get the upper hand. It is the new misery which Ireland is bound to go through, unless the new social order is realised in civilisation generally in time to prevent it. Nor is it by any means unlikely that the promise of such a change may break up the Irish Parliamentary Party, and leave the New Liberal Party free to do its work in Parliament. That party will be the then Intelligent Reactionary Party, the great enemy of progress expressed by Socialism. But so fast are things moving that its great men will not be the Hartingtons and Goschens, who were once called Liberals and are now mere Tories, but the Radicals old and new, among whom, I suppose, we must now rank Lord Randolph Churchill.

But meantime what is this ominous sound in the air? War is threatened again, and this time more determinedly and clearly than ever. On all sides one hears that this time it is certain, and that spring will see murder afield on the monstrous scale of modern times. How will our English parties deal with this horror if it comes? Will it afford a last chance to the old Tory party to do one more injury to the world before it departs for ever? Or will the Tories unite with the Intelligent Reactionary Party in one great flood of Jingoism?

At first sight, indeed, it would seem a mere act of madness for Bismark and Co. to provoke a hurly-burly which may well make an end of his firm and its aspirations. But one must remember that they are hardly their own masters in the matter. The monster of Commercial Militarism which they have created must be found work for or it will destroy its creators; and there comes a time when all must be risked – even revolution *behind* the invading armies.

Meantime, if war really becomes imminent our duties as Socialists are clear enough, and do not differ from those we have to act on ordinarily. To further the spread of international feeling between the workers by all means possible; to point out to our own workmen that foreign competition and rivalry, or commercial war, culminating at last in open war, are necessities of the plundering classes, and that the race and commercial quarrels of these classes only concern us so far as we can use them as opportunities for fostering discontent and revolution; that the interests of the workmen are the same in all countries and they can never be really enemies of each other; that the men of our labouring classes, therefore, should turn a deaf ear to the recruiting sergeant, and refuse to allow themselves to be dressed up in red and taught to form a part of the modern killing machine for the honour and glory of a country in which they have only the dog's share of many kicks and few halfpence, – all this we have to preach always, though in the event of imminent war we may have to preach it more emphatically. Also, since if any English government allows itself to be dragged into war it will as a matter of course be on that side the triumph of which would mean reaction – *i.e.*, Bismark and Co. we may have to protest specially and definitely against such a proceeding, and probably we should have to put ourselves forward somewhat prominently in such a protest, from which respectability of all kinds would be very apt to hang back.

Commonweal, Volume 3, Number 51,
1 January 1887, p. 1.

[UNTITLED PARAGRAPH ON TRAFALGAR SQUARE]

'Three copper-plate engravers' were regarded by Mr. George Sampson in Dickens's immortal work as 'a large number.' Two hundred and fifty 'bankers and West-end tradesmen of influence' may also be looked upon as 'a large number' of such cattle; but an ordinary citizen of no special influence may doubt whether the number is large enough to dictate to the whole of London terms on which it may express its political and social opinions, and whether or no it is preposterous impudence in them to meet for the purpose of egging on Government to attempt to close Trafalgar Square to public meetings; and an attempt in which they will undoubtedly fail.

Commonweal, Volume 3, Number 51, 1 January 1887, p. 5.

[UNTITLED PARAGRAPH
ON THE CZAR]

The *Pall Mall Gazette* has been sending to Madame de Novikoff to ask whether it is true, as is generally supposed, that the Czar of all the Russias has been driven out of his senses by that very human but not very dignified passion, terror. Everybody outside the *Pall Mall* supposes Madame de Novikoff to be a Russian political agent. The *Pall Mall's* proceeding, therefore, is, to say the least of it, grotesque. It is much as if he had sent to the devil's varlet to ask the truth about those awkward rumours of hoofs and horns, and those rumoured strange views of his majesty's about the welfare of the human race. The varlet, as in duty bound, replies that it is all a foul lie; that his Satanic Majesty has ten toes like other people, and is a prince of well-known benevolence. Of course the public is satisfied with this answer!

Commonweal, Volume 3, Number 52,
8 January 1887, p. 11.

NOTES ON NEWS

We can believe that our old acquaintance Mr. Phillips really
was sorry that he could not help the unemployed men who
applied to him to help them, and were waiting to see if they
could get a job in clearing off the snow, because he seems to
have some appreciation of the condition of the unemployed
at present. He appeared to relish the job of blowing to pieces
a lie that appeared in the respectable *Times* to the effect that
'although a large number of persons were wanted to clear the
snow from the streets on Boxing-day, only three applied, and
they were under the influence of drink.' Mr. Phillips said that
the Town-hall was not open on that day, neither was any
notice given that men were wanted on that day. Mr. Phillips,
much to his credit, stigmatised this as a deliberate lie, and a
libel on the working classes – 'in fact a malicious libel.' It is,
however, the kind of lie which is very commonly accepted as
gospel truth in these winter days, as anybody can bear
witness who has an opportunity of listening to the conversation in a second-class carriage on the District Railway.

'Infamy' has different meanings to different minds, it would
seem. To Mr. Mansfield, for instance, it appears to have
meant the other day the extremity of poverty which forces a
man to beg in the streets in order to get a little victuals for
himself and three little children. 'Your conduct is simply
infamous,' said the 'worthy' magistrate. On the other hand,
others (myself amongst them) might think the title of 'infamy'
fairly well earned by the magistrate who from his
unanswerable position goes out of his way to insult a poor
man, even supposing that he was compelled by a stupid and
brutal law to send him to prison for what was no offence.

Commonweal, Volume 3, Number 53,
15 January 1887, p. 17.

THE POLITICAL CRISIS

It is difficult to write about the 'Political Crisis' seriously, except so far as contempt may be serious. The bespattering with flattery for their patriotism of those members of the Government who are wanted to take themselves off; the flutter among the lesser men lest they too should be pulled off their perch and be boiled down for gravy for the new coalition pie; the terror of some Conservatives, like the *Standard*, lest Mr. Chamberlain should climb half-way down the tree; Mr. Goschen's anxiety that his position should not be misunderstood, whereas all the while it is as plain as the nose on Mr. Goschen's face that he is a high Tory reactionist. All this is sufficiently grotesque, and once more illustrates happily enough the dignity and honesty of Parliamentary Government, but otherwise does not concern us in the least.

All this on the Tory side; the Liberal position is perhaps a little more noteworthy, but also considerably more discreditable. The confusion in the Tory camp has given them hopes of success once more, and it is quite clear that most of those who may be called the responsible men of the party do in consequence look upon 'compromise' in quite a different light from that in which it showed a few weeks ago. There are rumours afloat that Mr. Gladstone is prepared to cut down his Home Rule Bill, feeble as it is already, so that it would amount to nothing but a perpetual English-Irish squabble in the Westminster Parliament. This rumour the *Daily News* denies with all official solemnity; but as it admits the almost plenary power of the 'Conference' to be held presently, which will have only one sincere Home Ruler (Mr. Morley) in it, this denial is not of much significance. Mr. Labouchere put the matter on a reasonable footing in his

Reading speech when he practically pointed out that no conference between those who were for Home Rule and those who were against it could mean anything but surrender on one side or the other.

Clearly whatever comes of it the Gladstonians are anxious to surrender, if only they can put a good face on it and hoodwink the rank and file of their party to the extreme baseness of the proceeding; otherwise they would have insisted on genuine Home Rule being made the basis of the Conference. It can scarcely be doubted that the Responsible Liberals will, if they dare, heave the Irish Jonah overboard; the only thing which will prevent them from doing so will be their fear of the consequences of their being accused of his murder when they reach the shore. Even if they do not they will have weakened themselves by their shilly-shally ways; if they do, no man with even the remains of wits in his head will take the trouble to distinguish them from their Tory competitors for loaves and fishes.

The moral to be drawn from these corrupt and degrading dodgings and shirkings is simple. Let the genuine Radicals turn from the collection of incompetent tricksters, and the battered and disgraced idols whom they hold up to our worship, and concern themselves with the serious questions of the day. Shall England make alliance with reactionary powers to crush out Revolution? Must we always have some piratical war on hand in order to conquer a fresh cheating-market for the harm of barbarous countries and our own unhappy population? Must we always have a mass of unemployed workmen hanging about, till to many of them, by the force of habit, work becomes impossible, and they are turned into mere loafers, a constant disgrace and a periodical terror to Society? Are we to be for ever satisfied with bestowing 'mere subsistence livelihood' (*i.e.*, semi-starvation) on the lower part of our labouring classes? Are the members of the artizan class for ever to be condemned to live poorly, without leisure or pleasure, in constant anxiety of falling into the gulf below them? Is the lower middle-class for ever to be stupid, vacant, and vulgar, and the upper middle-class to oscillate between blank Philistinism and simpering preciosity? In fine, why are these 'classes,' and what end do they serve? Let them face these questions unconventionally, and in the spirit of men who have abandoned the idea of finality in politics and social matters, and the old parties will soon be united in desperate opposition to the one Party of Progress, the Socialist Party.

Commonweal, Volume 3, Number 53,
15 January 1887, p. 20.

NOTES ON PASSING EVENTS

Prince Bismark has made his speech, set all Europe guessing as to what it might mean, had his Army Bill thrown out, and dissolved the Reichstadt, and now he is to have another by March; energetic work enough, but what does it all mean? First, one may suppose that he knows he is not going to live much longer, as he said, and that he wants to leave the German army still the tremendous engine for the purpose of reaction which it has been for so long; which it cannot be unless it is systematically increased and perfected. As to his speeches, so plain-spoken and yet so capable of reading between the lines, doubtless a great deal of the threatening and ominously warning tone of them was due to the fact that he wanted to scare, not the present Reichstadt (for doubtless he expected the hostile majority), but the electors of the new House to assemble in March. Therefore, no doubt he was bound to make the most of the possibilities of a French war, of the prowess of the French army, and the terrible results of a French victory; and that all the more as he was also bound to parade the good understanding between Germany and Russia, so as at one blow to destroy the hopes of Austria for German help against the advance of Russia in her direction; and also to point out to the French that when the day for the advance of the German army came no attack on their rear from the Russians need be expected. Since it had to be made clear that no danger was to be apprehended from that quarter, the danger in the other quarter had to be made the most of.

Nevertheless, all deductions made, the speeches of Prince Bismark were ominous enough; let everything be ready they seemed to mean for the demand on the French of disarming under pain of invasion; and who shall say how long it will be before that demand will be made? Nor need any one think that Prince Bismark's defeat the other day means relief from imminent war; the army is to be duly augmented, vote or no vote; and the necessities of electioneering will force the Chancellor to appeal to the Jingo spirit in the forthcoming contest, so that we may expect an increase and not a decrease in the fever of German 'patriotism'; as it is pretty certain that Prince Bismark will sweep the table clear in the coming elections and have a big majority at his back.

And what then? Will not this be the position? The German bourgeoisie will practically say, Germany as she is is too poor to bear this big army ever crying out for fresh steps towards perfection; in order to avoid its eating its head off, it must undertake some expedition, the result of which will be expansion for German commerce on the grand scale.

'Thou hast a fine sword, my son,' says the father in an eastern tale, 'but where is the head for the shearing?' 'Doubt not, father,' says the son, 'but that I shall soon find a head for the shearing.' No doubt the primary use of the German army is the upholding of 'law and order' in its own land, but to find 'a head for the shearing' is necessary for it as for all other such weapons in the hands of reactionary Governments.

The 'great Liberal meeting' of January 12 was of course a regular caucus meeting. No doubt from that point of view it was a success, the present staggering of the Tory party being an encouraging sight for Liberals, as they are beginning to feel sanguine (rightly or wrongly) of having one more innings as a party – perhaps as a 'united' party. All, however, was not unity at the meeting; a section of the Radicals perceiving that the fate of their party would be to be smothered under the incumbent weight of conventional Liberalism, moved an amendment, put forward by a prominent Chelsea Radical and Mr. Foote on behalf of the Metropolitan Radical Federation, which had the fate of Cassandra's warnings, as might have been foreseen. Mr. Bradlaugh, in a speech which gave the *Daily News* ecstasies of delight, took the side of respectability, and practically begged the Radicals to allow themselves to be smothered, lest the party organisation should be weakened before the Tories. So the London Liberals and Radicals are declared 'united' – until next time.

There were some demonstrations in the hall, however, with which the more respectable part of the meeting could only have been half pleased. But it is a pity that those genuine Radicals who were there couldn't see that it will not advance things much to merely hiss 'God save the Queen' and cry out for the 'Marseillaise.' Strange that they don't understand that the changes which such demonstrations hint at will not be allowed to be furthered in the party of such respectable persons as Mr. Bradlaugh and Mr. Shaw-Lefevre! The Liberal Party is willing to use the Radicals to attack the Tories on the one hand and snub the Socialists on the other; but mighty little of their own way will they have, till at last they will look round and find the Liberal Party gone and themselves a weak army indeed before the united forces of Reaction, and weak not only from want of numbers or cohesion, but from what is worse, lack of definite principles.

The best advice one can give to Radicals at present is to stick tight to genuine Home Rule and the attack on landlordism in Ireland, and to see where that will lead them – it will not be into the arms of the 'Respectable Party.' Unless they make up their minds to give up all their aspirations towards freedom, and all attempt to look seriously into social questions, the Respectable Party will not want them long.

Meantime the Conference of Conciliation has met and – parted – till after Parliament meets, or the Greek Kalends, as the case may be. The idea still seems to hold that Jonah is to walk the plank with all decency, in the interest at once of the Unity of the British Empire and the Unity of the Liberal Party. Truly our recognised political parties are running an eager race towards the goal of Unlimited Shabbiness, and 'tis hard to say which will get there first.

Our comrade Mahon tried to get a hearing at the Mansion House meeting about the Colonial Institute, but of course was not allowed to speak to foregone conclusions. In fact the promoters of this scheme are quite right to do their best to prevent all discussion on the subject, as even the sheep-like general public are beginning to see that it is nothing but a barefaced job, bolstered up by servility and flunkeyism of the basest kind. However, since the money to float it will only be a part of the general robbery of labour, it would be scarcely worth while noticing it if it were not for the astounding impudence of it, and its connection with the humbug of Imperial Federation which is being so busily pushed forward by one of our Philistines. A scheme which, with much parade and volumes of clap-trap speeches from those who are paid to lie to the people in various ways, proposes to collect money and do with it something (not specified) for the honour and glory of the empire, is worth noting as a triumph of jobbery, even in these days.

Commonweal, Volume 3, Number 54,
22 January 1887, p. 25.

NOTES ON PASSING EVENTS

Mr. Justice Grantham, in charging the Grand Jury at Norwich, apropos of the events which so unhappily delivered two of our comrades to the tender mercies of that strange specimen of humanity, the Special Fool in a high place, sung a song of triumph over that glorious institution, the workhouse. Oddly enough, in the issue of the day before of the same paper that gave us the solemn wisdom of this genius, there is printed a paragraph which is a good commentary on that blessing of modern times – that refuge for the unlucky which, according to his lordship, affords such a firm and satisfactory stand-point from which to aim at the conquest of health and wealth – the workhouse. We give the passage in full:

'WANDSWORTH. – CASUALS AND THEIR FOOD. – James Harding and George Wright were placed in the dock charged with refusing to work while casual paupers in Wandsworth workhouse. – George Cheshire, the superintendent, said the prisoners were admitted on Saturday night, and that morning he set them to work. Both refused to work. – The prisoner Wright said he could not work on the food given to him. He had dry bread, and was put in a place where he was perishing with cold all night. He would not do it for the Queen of England. – The superintendent said the wards were heated. The food consisted of eight ounces of bread for breakfast, half-a-pound with $1\frac{1}{2}$ ounces of cheese as dinner, and eight ounces of bread with hot water to drink for supper. – Mr. Bennett: Not any cocoa, nor anything of the kind? – No, sir, – The prisoner said he had a pail of hot water and dry bread. A pail of hot water was brought in as if to a horse. – The witness stated that the diet was given by direction of the Local

Government Board. – Mr. Bennett said if the prisoner had any ground of complaint he must go to the Local Government Board. – The prisoner said he might as well go to Buckingham Palace, and knock at the door and ask for the Queen. – Mr. Bennett committed the prisoners for seven days.'

The only comment on this paragraph that is possible is to ask if there is not some mistake in the report that the prisoners were sent to prison for seven days?

Mr. Justice *Nupkins* (we ask pardon, Grantham), being in a jovial and joking humour apparently, was so pleasant as to say that certain persons who misled the people and told them they were badly treated – to be sure: badly treated when going to the workhouse they can get their water *hot*: hot water, the drink at present of the more refined among the 'cultivated classes' – that these persons told the working-classes that they ought to have money whether they worked for it or not. Setting aside Mr. Justice Nupkins' confusion of ideas about the working-classes who don't work, which is of itself pretty to behold, his lordship has only to attend a few Socialist meetings (he might draw up his carriage at the edge of the crowd) to hear those who want to have money without working for it pretty sharply denounced by these very misleaders of the working-classes. He would there learn that the living on other people without working is the very thing we demand to be abolished, though it must be admitted that at present it is the very foundation of that society of which his lordship is so startling an ornament.

It was announced last week that the Government were going to make a new departure in coercion, and would bring forward a regular gagging Bill, which would serve for arranging Irish affairs at present, and would also be available for dealing with English, Scotch, or Welsh discontent, as it was to be made applicable to the whole of the United

Kingdom. Socialist organisations, we were told, might expect to be particularly honoured by the notice of this new Act.

This news seemed from the first almost too good to be true; but it seems it was true for the time, and that the Tory Government, on the look out for something to damage their really strong position, had hit on this device as a satisfactory one. But unluckily it is almost impossible for them to go on with the gagging enterprise, as it would stir up the vigorous opposition of the Radicals, and even the Liberals would be shamed into voting against such a measure. Accordingly they are now backing down: are going to begin with the bill on procedure, and will *only* make their gag for Ireland, though even on these terms they have very little chance of getting it through Parliament.

Mr. Goschen is carrying on his candidature for Liverpool merrily, and in spite of the result of the last election, in which the Liberal candidate was successful, he will probably get in, owing to the servility of all parties towards 'a distinguished official,' 'a man of so much importance,' and so forth. Meantime this light of intellectual finance has introduced himself by making a long speech down there which was really remarkable for emptiness, dullness, and twaddle, even among election speeches.

Apropos of Members of Parliament, the following story told by Mr. Labouchere at Spalding on Thursday week is too good to be lost. He said:–

> The atmosphere of the House of Commons does not seem to agree with Radicals. They soon want to become fine gentlemen. He remembered a case in one of the divisions with regard to the admission of Mr. Bradlaugh. About ten minutes before the division a highly respectable gentleman on the Liberal side of the House came to me and

said, 'You know I have been thinking this over, and my conscience won't allow me to vote for Bradlaugh.' I replied, 'I have not got time enough to talk about your conscience – what do you want?' The Member said, 'What do you mean? I am not that sort of person'; whereupon I said, 'Do you want to be made a knight?' and the gentleman replied, 'No, you are entirely mistaken.' I next asked him, 'Have you got a wife?' and he answered, 'Yes.' 'Well, do you get asked to those crowds, those receptions, at the Foreign Office?' The hon. Member admitted that he and his wife rather complained that they had not, and then I said, 'You go in and vote, and I'll see that you are asked to them in the future,' and in about ten minutes afterwards I polled that patriot in.'

Walpole, in the good old bribing days, would have been happy if he could have bought his votes as cheap as that.

The Commission on the Depression of Trade has issued its report. It will be criticised hereafter in these columns in some detail, so that it may go for the present with a few words. It is a matter of course that the Commissioners try to put the best face possible on the state of things commercial, though they do not succeed very well in the attempt. They say, 'There can be no question that the workman is in this country, *when fully employed*, in almost every respect in a better position than his competitors in foreign countries.' The italics are our own. Will the Commissioners pretend that they do not know that even in good years the great mass of working-men in and about London are unemployed for four months out of the twelve? that the workmen of the great industries have to 'average' their wages, have to insure, so to say, against the months that they are 'at play,' from strikes and lock-outs and the like? Will they say where in Europe or Asia they can find a workman more miserably pinched and resourceless than the south-west country labourer with his income of 10s. a-week when things are going well?

Or need one keep one's patience any longer with those
miserable fools and liars, paid to lie and paid to be dull by a
blind society amidst its last corruption? It is true that they are
not paid to be imaginative; but a little imagination is
necessary to most men, if only to keep their bodies from
stinking in default of salt. Let them, then, bring their imagination to bear upon facts, and try to picture their noble and
cultivated selves reduced to the condition of those workmen
whose lot they are so contented with. Let them think of
themselves as living and keeping a home together on 10s. a-
week in a Gloucestershire cottage, or worse still, on 16s. in a
London slum; and if they have really tried to do so and have
any honesty left in them, if they can do nothing else, at least
let them hold their tongues and live silently on the proceeds
of the perpetual *robbery* which habit has made them look
upon as a holy right and the cement of society.

Commonweal, Volume 3, Number 55,
29 January 1887, p. 33.

NOTES ON NEWS

Mr. Chamberlain waxed almost pathetic in his appeal for the gratitude of constituencies to their representatives for *past* services: a very convenient feeling to establish on behalf of 'rats' and dishonest politicians, and I fear a feeling rather strong amongst voting working-men. I fear, because as a matter of fact such a feeling at best means a weak doubt of one's own principles, and at worst (and oftenest so, probably) means mere servility and stupidity. Gratitude to traitors and turn-coats! Sham sentiment of the nineteenth century, you do indeed get into curious corners when politicians deal with you!

Mediæval sentiment was at least more logical than this. An old chronicler puts into the mouth of an orator pleading a cause some words like these: 'Why do the heralds at the tournaments cry "Honour to the *sons* of the valiant" (preux), and not "Honour to the *valiant*"? Because a man that has been valiant may do amiss, and spoil his valiancy, and then he is valiant no more; but when he is dead, and has not spoiled his valiancy in aught, then you may call him valiant indeed; and to think of this is great encouragement to younger men, so that they may endure to the end.'

Certainly in politics 'we have changed all that'; and the rule now is that when a man has once got a reputation as a leader he may indulge himself in almost any shabbiness and sneaking ways, and injure his reputation scarcely at all; always so long as he brazens it out, and keeps himself well before the public – advertises himself, in fact.

Mr. Chamberlain, for the rest, said very little worth noting. His scheme of peasant-proprietorship, which he has always before him, is really reducible to this: the creation of a class of small owners who would (somehow) have bought their holdings, and the driving those who could not (somehow) buy them into the class of day labourers. This would certainly be an advantage to both landlord and capitalist, but it would hardly turn Ireland into a heaven for the working man, whether he were a labourer or a small proprietor with a millstone of mortgage round his neck.

Commonweal, Volume 3, Number 56,
5 February 1887, p. 41.

[UNTITLED PARAGRAPH
ON WILLIAM BLAKE]

William Blake was almost the first, if not the first, of those poets who drew English poetry from the slough of conventional twaddle in which the 18th century had sunk it; and visionary as he was, he was able to look at realities, and to make his words mean something; whereas it was an understood condition of the so-called 'poetry' of the 18th century that they should mean nothing.

Commonweal, Volume 3, Number 56,
5 February 1887, p. 43.

NOTES ON NEWS

Parliament has offered us a sort of stage-battle over the Egyptian rascality. No one, of course, thought that anything would come of it, though 97 members voted in favour of immediate withdrawal; some of whom perhaps would not have done so if they had thought that their vote would have had any influence in bringing about a withdrawal.

Some of the Radicals were, though they knew nothing would come of it, rather afraid of pledging themselves against our piracy wholly; and moved another amendment, substituting the Yankeeism 'in the near future' for 'immediate.' This raised laughter from the Ministerial benches, as it well might; though probably it would be found that 'immediate' would have the same meaning as 'in the near future' in the mouth of any capitalistic government.

One of the mediæval Joe Millers tells of an inn which bore the following inscription: 'Good wine given away for nothing *to-morrow.*' Of course when the sanguine toper who had seen the promised blessing on Monday called for its fulfilment on Tuesday, he was told that *to-morrow* was still ahead. So it will be in Egypt till the bayonet of some other robber is applied to the rear of the British Christian.

A modern American traveller in Persia, after giving an account of the arbitrary and violent acts of the rulers of that strangely long-lived kingdom, which are of the sort with which students of ancient and mediæval history are familiar, and after saying of the peasant, 'that if he produced upon land so rich that it easily produces enough to meet his humble wants, any more, it would be simply to render him the victim of extortion,' goes on to say, 'the people of Persia are as happy as the average of other people!'

This fact, which is borne out by the observation of travellers among peoples under similar conditions, is not so difficult of explanation as the bourgeois observer sometimes thinks it. The Persian labourer works lazily to supply his humble wants, and then stops, *knowing* that anything more he produces will be taken away from him. But we have got our labourers into better order than that. We make the English labourer work industriously *after* he has supplied his humble (very humble) wants, and thereby make him supply our own not so humble wants. The Persian labourer *knows* that everything that can be taken away from him will be taken away, and therefore doesn't vex the kind earth and his own body too much. The English labourer is in exactly the same position of being robbed of what he earns; but then he does *not* know it, and so he sweats away and tries to keep out of the workhouse. Fraud is out and out a better weapon than force, it does the cleaning-out job so much cleaner, let alone its being so much safer – till it is found out.

Among the advantages offered by emigration agents, a free passage to Davy Jones' Locker should figure prominently. Yet it will not be long before the horrible murder of the Kapunda will be forgotten by all classes just as dozens of other like cases have been. Nevertheless, while it is remembered (if it is still remembered by those not directly interested in it) let us ask what it was that drowned all those poor souls without remedy, and the answer must be Commercial Profit!

No one who thinks about the event can doubt that it was possible by spending more money to have contrived that the ship should not sink in a few minutes without any chance of getting her boats out; and if people will think a little more they will have to come to the conclusion that in these matters as in others the one thing sought after is 'profit.' Ships must be made safe enough not to frighten freight and passengers off them, and also not to make them uninsurable, or to risk too much loss if they are not injured. Outside these necessities 'applied science' will not be *applied* to the making of people's lives as safe as it knows how, but to making of the owner's profits as safe as it knows how; and if you please, as those profits are made on the *average* of ships and voyages, the loss of a cargo of human beings now and then can be borne by the enterprising owners without their purses or capitalistic lives suffering much. But what fools *we* are to bear it!

In the first of the debates on the subject 'Is Socialism Sound?' between Mrs. Besant and Mr. Foote, Mrs. Besant sustained her part well. Mr. Foote threw no new light on the objections to Socialism, and, as often happens with a clever anti-Socialist debater, he made too much use of the *argumentum ad hominem*, a very feeble weapon if applied to anything more important than a Parliamentary debate.

It was curious to see Mr. Foote in his quality of Land-nationaliser so very bitter against Socialism; in him the lower middle-class prejudices and shibboleths seemed to unite readily with the acceptance of Mr. George's nostrum. Mrs. Besant's exposition of the fallacy of detaching the land from the other means of the fructification of labour was very clear and satisfactory. She also made her position as to the relation between Socialism and Communism clearer than it is in her pamphlet, and I should say had advanced from that position. Mr. Foote, of course, twitted her with this, but not very fairly. Socialists will follow with much interest the progress of this debate.

NOTES ON NEWS

Sir Charles Warren (no doubt in self-defence and defence of the police) has given a blow to contemporary history as written by the daily press, by a sudden demolition of the very rapidly growing myth of the *Wicked Socialist and the Heroic Butcher*, which is, after all, perhaps the very latest example of the solar myth. The bright and ruddy hero dispelling the murky crowds of the cloudy night with the shooting forth of his bright rays must be, according to the solar theory, what is really typified by this apparently historical incident. Mr. Andrew Lang perhaps could tell us what it might signify according to the explanation of the 'customary' theory of myths.

To one person it must have signified victuals and drink, temporarily at least; to wit, to the ingenious gentleman who produced the detailed and dramatic 'Siege of a Butcher's Shop' in the *Daily News*. I hope I have all due professional sympathy with our injured contemporary, but I really cannot help saying with Mr. Bounderby in 'Hard Times,' 'We are waiting to hear what apology you are going to offer us for going about the country express with no other luggage than a story of a cock and a bull!'

The *Pall Mall Gazette* gave us lately the account of interviews with various business men as to the present condition of trade. The views of these gentlemen were mostly what under the present circumstances may be called optimistic, that is they all seemed to think that things were mending a little. But, after all, what they said amounted to little more than that the public were getting rather eager for investments, which fact may mean nothing more than the beginning of a brief swindle-period.

Judging by the condition of production, which is indicated by the plain statement of facts given in the columns of our own paper under the heading 'The Labour Struggle,' this seems to be all that it does mean. The hunger-riots of the Scotch coal miners also do not point to our nearing a period of plain-sailing prosperity.

Mr. Bright 'is at it again.' He really does seem as if he were determined to show that his claim to have been a popular leader was mere moonshine; it would be difficult for any enemy of his to be as successful in this demonstration as Mr. Bright himself.

The *Daily News* the other day was righteously indignant with the sentence of a country magistrate on a labourer, convicted of the terrible offence of setting traps to catch wood-pigeons, for which in the upshot the poor man got two months' imprisonment. Probably, however, such sentences are as common as frosts in winter, and not nearly so much noticed. Our own experience has taught us that, since neither the *Daily News* nor any other bourgeois paper made any comment on Judge Nupkins-Grantham's sentence on Mowbray and Henderson; the *Pall Mall Gazette* joining in the conspiracy of silence, although when convenient it can say a good deal about the doings of one section of the Socialists.

The Chiswick poisoning mystery has been explained, say the daily papers: 'the Government analyst has failed to detect any traces of irritant poison of (*sic*) the contents of the stomachs of the two children...having regard to the fact that the mother and six children slept in a single bed in a room only measuring 8ft. by 9ft., and that the cold and the scanty covering on the bed and the clothing generally in the house compelled them to huddle together to keep themselves warm, shutting out at the same time all ingress of fresh air into the room where for hours there had been a lamp burning, he has, it is reported, come to the conclusion that the cause of the death of the two children was vitiated atmosphere.' Misery is a shorter word than vitiated atmosphere, and yet a more explanatory one. I suppose these victims of vitiated atmosphere will not be set among the record of those who were starved to death? (I have not patience to remember the euphemism for that), but starved to death they were.

In his first debate with Mrs. Besant, Mr. Foote affected (surely it was affectation) scorn at those who distinguish between competition and emulation, and asked what was the difference between them. Mr. Foote knows well enough that competition, as we use the word in English, means seeking one's own advantage at the expense of one's neighbours (compare the French *concurrence*). As to emulation, judging by the tone of his attack on Socialism, it is probable that he does not understand what that means, as it is certainly a generous quality. To give the difference between the two shortly, emulation means making the *best* of one's own capacity; competition, making the *worst* of one's neighbour's.

Mr. Bradlaugh was enthusiastically cheered at a meeting held on behalf of the crofters for saying amongst other things 'that we had no right to pauperise the crofters by law and then send them into others lands to die.' Most true; but how strange that Mr. Bradlaugh should object to the substitution of the word 'working-men' for crofters! He has been lately taking some trouble to attack those who are trying to show that we have no right to pauperise, not the crofters only, but all workers, by forcing them to yield to 'capital' a tribute for leave to work – that is, to live. How utterly illogical it is in him to attack also a small section of the monopolists of the means of production!

They have exactly the same 'rights of property' as every one else has, neither less nor more; and those rights leave them free to use or *abuse* their property according to their own will. If the abuse of their property should be interfered with, why not other abuses of property? And is it not an abuse of property to employ it as a mere means of compulsion to force other men to work for the compeller – or privileged thief? How can it matter whether the instrument of violent robbery is called 'land' or 'capital'?

Commonweal, Volume 3, Number 58,
19 February 1887, p. 57.

NOTES ON NEWS

The hocus-pocus by which the debate on the gross jury-packing in the Irish State trials was set aside, seems to have pleased the Tory mind; and it ought to please us Socialists also, because so far as it goes it is a sign of the growing decrepitude of our great enemy, or rather the great instrument of our enemies, the middle-class Parliament. In short, the disgrace of such a scene as that of the 17th is so clear, that one is really driven to wonder that it could be cheered even by the greatest idiots of the idiotic party of the most idiotic assembly in the world.

The release of the 23,000 odd prisoners in India as a compliment to the Jubilee flunkeyism has a queer mediæval smack about it, and of itself disposes of our pretensions so often put forward to governing India on modern principles of 'Justice.' Indeed, to some people it will reveal depths of tyranny undreamed of before. Here is a dilemma for our Jubileeists: 'If it was dangerous to the public that these men should be at large, why do you release them for the danger of the public? If you can safely release this host of poor miserable tortured people, why did you torture them with your infernal prison?' There is no answer but one: 'Because we are unjust, tyrannical, muddling fools!'

The Lake railway scheme has scored a success at last, but one may hope that the bill will yet be thrown out, as such misfortunes must be averted by any means possible, as they are lasting and irremediable.

It would be hardly worth while noticing Mr. Labouchere's bad arguments in favour of the railway if they did not illustrate the anti-social temper of the ordinary bourgeois so-called Radical. Because, of course, Mr. Labouchere is always playing a part, and he is no more the brutal and stupid bagman which he posed as being the other night, than he is the virtuously indignant democrat which he plays on other occasions. He is a very smart and handy person, who has chosen the democratic side of the political game, and is determined to play his part thoroughly and without flinching. So that we can see that his conception of the democratic bourgeois involves a grovelling and sordid utilitarianism, and it is to be feared that he scarcely overdid his contemptible part in speaking as he did on the 17th.

Meanwhile, I would appeal to all Socialists to do their best to preserve the beauty and interest of the country. It is true that it is a part of that wealth in which the workers under our present system are not allowed to share. But when we have abolished the artificial famine caused by capital, we shall not be so pinched and poor that we cannot afford ourselves the pleasure of a beautiful landscape because it doesn't produce ironstone, or of a beautiful building because it won't do for a cotton-mill, and that pleasure will not then be confined to a few well-to-do people, but will be there to be enjoyed by all. Of course, as things go now, the Lake railway is not a question of the convenience of the Amblesiders, or the pleasure of the world in general, but the profit of a knot of persons leagued together against the public in general under the name of a railway company.

Commonweal, Volume 3, Number 59, 26 February 1887, p. 65.

NOTES ON NEWS

I have seen more than once Mr. Jones, the manager of the London Co-operative Society, quoted as saying that capitalists will be glad to allow labour to use their money for nothing on the condition that the principal shall be secure. Here is another case (with a vengeance) of 'Good wine given away for nothing – to-morrow'? Meantime will Mr. Jones explain how these two sanguine 'capitalists' propose to live while they are neither buying victuals with their money or being paid for the use of it? Let us take, for instance, the poor-widow-small-shareholder of whom we have heard so much: will she send here money to a co-operative society and accompanied by a letter couched in such terms as these: 'Kind gentlemen, I send you my little all, and trust that you may find it useful; to me it is no longer so, since I am told (and believe it) that people can now live without either working, begging, or stealing; therefore pray send me no dividend, but whatever profit *you* make of it by employing people to work and taking from them a part of what they produce, keep for yourselves with the blessing of the widow and the orphan.' I wonder what her next letter would be like.

Commonweal, Volume 3, Number 60,
5 March 1887, p. 73.

POLITICAL NOTES

The 'row' in the House of Commons of March 3 gives us an indication of what is coming, if we take it along with the hints as to what the Coercion Bill is likely to be. The Chief Secretary's insults and tall talk mean pretty much the lion lashing his tail just before his wrath (or hunger) takes the practical form of a spring and a blow. Or perhaps it may with greater accuracy be compared with the demeanour of the Highlanders, walking about and snorting to stimulate their warlike spirits before they pull out point-and-edge, as described by Walter Scott in 'Rob Roy.'

The Tory supporters of the Government have bidden them to get angry and act. They are trying to get angry so that they may act, since there is no way out of it; but no doubt their feelings are not very enviable at present. They must be full of dismal forebodings that their action will draw on a state of things which only strong men could deal with and avoid the mingled curses and laughter which accompany absurd failure in 'strong' – *i.e.*, tyrannical – measures.

The Irish nation have shown such admirable qualities through this struggle, such steadiness of purpose, and persistence in union, that they may be trusted to deal satisfactorily with this long expected crisis; all the more as they must be seeing clearly final victory drawing nearer and nearer to them. But what allies will they have among English parties outside the sympathy of the outcast Socialists?

As parties or sections what allies can they have? It would be absurd to appeal to the Liberal party to further those aspirations towards freedom which it is its very business to restrain. And as to the Radical party, where is it and what is it except the feeble tail of this same feebly reactionary Liberal party?

The only appeal that can be made is to those few Radicals who have any title to the name to break off from their Liberal party if it shows, as it certainly will show, the slightest sign of wavering in steady opposition to coercion without any great nicety as to the means. For in good truth, if the Government are going to put forward an effective Coercion Bill, as according to all reports they are, they will give the signal for civil war.

Here is the position in all its simplicity. On the one hand a people determined according to its lights to win freedom for itself. On the other hand a government which is determined that this people shall not be free, and after having exhausted all half measures of mingled chicanery and force, with a thin gloss of professed respect for 'constitutionalism' (whatever that may mean), is now driven to throw off the mask, and to say there shall no longer be any semblance of freedom in Ireland, and the expression of opinion shall be considered, or even the implication of opinion shall be considered, as treasonable action in the egg and shall be suppressed and shut up in jail accordingly. What is to come out of this position? Who is to give way, Ireland or the reactionary party of Great Britain? If the former is to be crushed, the struggle will not be long before it reappears, not as civil war in Ireland, but as civil war in England.

Commonweal, Volume 3, Number 61,
12 March 1887, p. 81.

NOTES ON NEWS

Our heavy contemporary *Punch* has lately had a cartoon a long way 'after' Albert Durer's marvellous cut of the Knight and Death, illustrated by a 'free adaptation' from Fouqué's Sintram, to commemorate Bismarck's victory (?) over the Socialists. Our wooden friend with a naïve stupidity quite characteristic of the professional bourgeois jester, had had the impudence to omit the not unimportant figure of Death from his cartoon, although if he had not been quite so dull or so impudently lazy he might have extracted something from Fouque's romance which would have helped his lame allegory to totter on a step or two.

However we may leave Fouqué's gratuitous interpretation of Durer's immortal work to ask what Durer really did mean by it. For the imagination of the honest and serious craftsmaster of old Nuremburg, fertile as it was, and though it led him into wild and strange places, was free from any touch of the hysteria which disfigures Fouque's elegant and even beautiful romances. Durer always meant something definite; and in this case modern historical research has found out what he did mean: his cut is a commemoration of a notable victory over a robber-knight who had long plagued the good town of Nuremburg, and implies a warning to those in high places who live by violence and robbery. The armed man on the war-horse is riding towards no victory, but a shameful death; he has come to 'the net end of all his villainies'; and the aweful *thing* that follows him is a tangible image of the crimes of his past life; his greed, rapine, cruelty, fraud, and reckless violence.

So that we may be well content after all to take Albert Durer's 'Knight and Death' with his own meaning still cleaving to it, as a figurement of the doom of Blood and Iron of our own day; especially if we look not so much upon the man Bismarck, whom the course of circumstances has so curiously placed in his high position of infamy, but rather upon the type of the armed bourgeoisie, 'the strong man keeping his house,' which to-day owns all that is made and all that makes, and which after a long period of that confidence of living for ever, which is the natural gift of youth and manhood, is now entering the valley of the shadow of death, and has become conscious of its coming defeat, and of the companions it has made for itself, and so rides on warily and fearfully, Crime behind it, Death before it.

Commonweal, Volume 3, Number 61, 12 March 1887, p. 84.

[EDITORIAL ON THE
AMBLESIDE RAILWAY BILL]

It seems to me that our friend in his enthusiasm for railways is unconsciously playing into the hands of the capitalist robbers, who are the only persons who will be really benefitted by it as things go. In the first place this railway is meant to be the first step in the invasion of the Lake country, and will certainly not stop at Ambleside if the projectors can help it. The question is nothing less than this, Is the beauty of the Lake country, and the natural wish that people have to see it and enjoy it, to be handed over to be exploited without limitation by a company who looks upon the public as so much material for exploitation? If it is to be so, its beauty will soon be a thing of the past, and when you have taken the trouble to bring people into the once lovely and romantic country they will find that they have come indeed, but come to nothing, and might almost as well have stayed at home, and had far better strolled into some country side less renowned for beauty, and therefore not so tempting to the runners of those horrible pests, the tourist railway and the tourist hotel. The intention of the capitalists in this matter is to make the Cumberland and Westmoreland 'show-country' a mere appendage to their filth-heaps of Manchester and Liverpool, and they allege the necessities of their filth-heaps as a reason for this. But the rest of the country have a good right to say, The concoction of your filth-heaps is no valid reason for your destroying the wealth of the whole country, nay, the wealth of the world; something of the natural beauty of the face of the country has been left in spite of your foul greed and disregard of other people's rights, and that, wofully (*sic*) little as it now is, we are at last impelled to guard against your greed. For my part, while admitting that it is seen in queer places, I cannot help thinking that the spirit which takes this view is a part of the great wave of social feeling which will one day sweep away monopoly and enable every one to have his due share of the pleasures of the world; whereas the feeling of jealousy of local interests and prejudices, even when expressed by a Socialist, is but the remnant of the unsocial feeling forced upon him by the present conditions of life. One may say in passing that the presence of the railway in a new district is *not* a benefit to it; it brings more trade to it, more employment, and therewithal more competition for employment; it cheapens one thing and raises the price of another; or, if it cheapens things generally, it is clear that it will lower the wages of the labourers, though doubtless it will increase the incomes of those who live on them, which once more is its object. I entreat our friend not to help in killing the goose that lays the golden eggs; it is true that to the company which wishes to exploit us it is of no importance that the golden eggs should cease to come, since they will be other people's eggs; but to us the rest of the public, both that are and that are to come, it is of much importance. Short-sighted brutality wherever it is met with, and whoever and whatever its source may be, is *unsocial*, and should be attacked by all Socialists.

Commonweal, Volume 3, Number 61,
12 March 1887, p. 85.

POLITICAL NOTES

The past few days have brought about a change in the political atmosphere, which may perhaps have startled some persons; but it is not difficult to explain. The Government placed between the devil and the deep sea, have been screwing up their hearts for a Coercion Bill. This seems at first sight a simple and natural proceeding for a Tory Government, a thing which everybody would expect from them. But to pass an effective measure of coercion against such a solid opposition as the Irish nation offer to it, and to carry it out when passed, is an adventure which needs the courage of the past ages or of the future – the aristocratic period or the revolutionary one. The age of political farce in which we are now living in England cannot deal consciously with tragedy, though the actors in it can sit and watch many a farce-born tragedy go on before their eyes calmly enough. In fact, the Government swaggers coercion boldly enough but doesn't mean it; all the more as it has no shadow of a Strafford to carry out the policy of 'thorough.'

Meantime, the 'Liberal Unionists' are preparing for a 'new departure.' Mr. Trevelyan has practically declared himself reconverted to Gladstonian policy, and the greater portion of his party will follow him, since the course of events of late has convinced them the cat is going to jump in the Home Rule direction. Some of the most sanguine of the Liberal prophets are even speculating on the return of Lord Hartington, and have already discounted that of Mr. Chamberlain, whose position, if he does return, would be a rather curious one for a sensitive man, until the lapse of time – say three weeks – shall have reinstated him in his old position of an infallible leader of the democratic party.

The Tory Government then are beaten, and the only question is how they will take their beating, whether they will on the one hand judiciously determine to do nothing, in which case they may yet have a longish lease of life before them, as it is a matter of course that the Liberal party 'united' or disunited can have no wish to come in again yet awhile, to accept the responsibility of making peace with the Irish by passing a compromise Home Rule Bill – a somewhat delicate operation.

Or possibly they will ride for a fall by bringing in a fierce Coercion Bill without any hope of passing it, and back this by the promise of a Land Bill to follow it, which the report of the Commission gives them an opportunity of doing. This would give them the chance of appealing to the country with law-and-order in one hand and 'remedy' (of the well used delusive kind) in the other; and it is not all so sure, in spite of the Liberal rejoicings now on hand, that they would be beaten in a general election. Yet if they (the Tories) win, what next? And how would they deal with a still unpacified Ireland? And what would their Land Bill amount to? These are questions which they will have to answer if they succeed, although they will certainly forget them deliberately till the moment for answering them comes.

Nor if the United Liberal Party comes in again will its position be either an easy or a triumphant one. The Home Rule Bill must be a compromise, and as such will be accepted by the Irish only as a lever to bring about the full accomplishment of their aspirations. But even before the half measure of Home Rule is gained the underlying question of land and livelihood in Ireland will have to be faced; a question which involves that of the land and livelihood elsewhere. This fact does enlighten a little even the dastardly short-sightedness of Parliamentary politics, as may be noticed in Lord Salisbury's last speech, in which he had the impudence to impugn the patriotism of the Irish, because they have found out that they cannot separate the cause of self-government from that of the livelihood of the people.

Though perhaps he really was saying what he thought on this occasion; for naturally to a Tory the mere *superstition* of nationality is a more important matter than the *reality* of the necessity of dealing with the sufferings of an industrious and honest population.

This necessity will be the Nemesis that will presently overtake not only the Tories and the Whigs but the Liberals and Radicals also; unless those last named will face the real difficulty. When Home Rule has been gained and the party question has been laid, we shall then see if the sympathy now so widely expressed for the cottars of Glenbeigh and elsewhere in Ireland was genuine or not. If it is not extended to the dwellers in the Wiltshire village and the London slum, and if the same kind of remedies are not proposed for these latter as for the Irish cottars, it will be proved to have been a mere piece of party clap-trap got up for the occasion. We need not fear but that the occasion will be afforded for such practical sympathy: the Irish question will help to sow the seed of revolution throughout the British islands.

To be sure if the Whigs, Tories and Liberals had any foresight or any courage they would have united to stamp it out this time as they have done before. The Unionist Liberals *were* wise in their generation when they turned on Gladstone; they are now in coming under his wing again going to exhibit themselves as fools and cowards as well as reactionists.

Happily it always happens so in revolutions; the nearer the time comes for the defeat of reaction, the more pressing its necessities grow, the more the courage of the reactionists fails them, because they begin to be conscious that their cause has become a mere mass of found-out lies and helpless hypocrisies.

Commonweal, Volume 3, Number 62,
19 March 1887, p. 89.

NOTES ON NEWS

The press has of course busied itself over Mr. Gladstone's speech, and various meanings favourable to this or that hope in the present crisis have been drawn from it, with more or less ingenuity; which ingenuity, to say the truth, has not been less wasted that (*sic*) that which enables people to write the Lord's prayer on a threepenny piece. Any one of the guests at the dinner might have said, like Tennyson's Northern Farmer, 'I thought he'd said wha a' ought to have said, and I comed awa.' Mr. Gladstone had to say something, and make some show of seeing through a grindstone, and giving those not gifted as himself the advantage of his vision. It was a matter of course that he should accomplish this feat with his usual skill in such exercises.

What his speech really amounted to was party defiance to the Tories; civility to the wavering Unionist Liberals; and a statement that he was in favour of Home Rule, and was prepared to make some concessions. Since all this had to be said, let those of us who have read his speech be glad that we have not got to do so again, and forget it.

Speaking, after all, will not change the position of affairs, which quite simply is this. The feeling for Home Rule is spreading among the English democracy; everybody is noting that; therefore the Unionist Liberals are in terror for their seats, and in terror at the prospect of eating their bold words. The Tories, who vaguely hoped that they wouldn't have to bring in a Coercion Bill, find they have got to do so, and know that it will undo them; and all English political parties are shuffling about from one foot to the other in an anguish of doubt, because they know that the land question must be dealt with by one party after the other, each of whom will make a helpless mess of it.

Needless to dwell long on the fact that all this is accompanied by rather more than the usual amount of conventional twaddle and lies to conceal the fact that the mighty British Empire and its glorious Constitution is being pushed against its will into what, considering its circumstances, are revolutionary measures.

The new Irish Secretary is beginning about as well as possible for the Nationalist cause. The arrest of Father Keller will answer its purpose as far as the Irish are concerned. The setting the seal of Peterloo on the police murder at Youghal by open approval of it, the threats of violence and 'thorough,' – all this will help to bind the English democracy to the Irish cause. Certainly Mr. Balfour is turning out the very man that the Parnellites would have picked out if they had had to choose.

Commonweal, Volume 3, Number 63,
26 March 1887, p. 97.

NOTES ON NEWS

The Government have got through the first stage of this new coercion adventure with no very triumphant success, though only one Liberal Unionist voted for Mr. Morley's amendment; Mr. Bright in his new character of definite Tory voting for the government as a matter of course. There was nothing very remarkable in the debate that preceded the division. Mr. Gladstone spoke bold words enough as to the opposition which his party were prepared to make to the bill, and it is to be hoped that they will be made good; but one must see it done before one can be sure that it will be: meanwhile, of course, the Tories raise the cry of 'obstruction'; as if it were not the business of any minority in the House of Commons to obstruct the passing of any measure that they thoroughly condemn.

A great part of Mr. Gladstone's elaborate speech was taken up with trying to prove that *his* coercion bill was quite a different thing, and put forward under quite different circumstances than this new measure; and the orthodox Liberal papers were in ecstasies over his success in this attempt. But a reasonable man would think this ingenuity wasted: the Coercion Act on one hand and the action of the National League on the other, are simply acts of war; and it was just the same thing when the Liberal Government passed their Coercion Act. To speak plainly, all this side of the debate *pro* and *con* was simple twaddle; the mere lawyer-like stupidity of never making an admission, which is a habit in Parliament, too. Really, Mr. Gladstone need not be ashamed of changing his mind with the example of Mr. Bright before him, who has become a Tory simply because he could not change his, when things were changing around him.

It would be refreshing to find somebody who would say, when challenged as to the relation of his present to his past opinion, 'Yes; I did think that, but I have changed my opinion now,' but that seems to be as rare a bird as the man that will say 'Yes; I said so-and-so, and I meant it then and mean it now.' And it would take a strong lantern to find a man in Parliament who could say either of those things.

As to Mr. Chamberlain, he seems determined to go deeper and deeper into the mire; and surely a man who had been away from the country for two years, and had not seen any newspapers during that time, if he happened on any of Mr. Chamberlain's present speeches, would be likely to say, 'Pray what Chamberlain is that? Is it any relation to the Joseph Chamberlain who, when I left England, was going about the country making demi-semi-socialistic speeches?'

The thoughtful soul, may, if it pleases, debate with itself whether the German or English people have scored in the game of flunkeydom by the last two exhibitions of that art, the celebration of the Kaiser's birthday, or the Queen's visit to Birmingham. Certainly, the German transaction was on the larger scale, and so more offensive, and there appears to have been an outpouring of sentiment on the occasion, not easy for a sane man to understand, if he chance not to belong to that parish; neither is the superannuated drill-sergeant who was worshipped by the German population – (What were all the Socialist voters about, by the way?) – a very worthy idol. Still, the man is a kind of a real king, and represents, at any rate, the memory of a set of desperate battles, and, 'tis said, does his joss-business of being seen with much assiduity, and his position altogether is not so preposterous as that of our own special joss, which does *not* do its business even of being seen (if that mattered at all), and cannot do anything else of a public kind without being called over the coals for it as an unconstitutional act.

Doubtless, also, a good deal of the enthusiasm at Berlin was of police creation, and it is to be thought that the Birmingham loyalty was more genuine of its kind, and at the bottom of it, probably, lay the hope of the quickening of business a little.   Finally, when we take into consideration that Birmingham is a Radical town, I think the palm must be given to the English professors of flunkeydom; their faith is purer, and shines brighter through the wrappages of individual character, political creed, and other accidents than that of any other nation.

Commonweal, Volume 3, Number 64, 2 April 1887, p. 105.

THE REVIVAL OF TRADE (?)

The promised revival of trade is long a-coming, apparently. Here are some cuttings from the *Daily News* of Monday 28th March, chiefly concerning the textile trades.

Cotton Goods, Manchester. – In the cloth market the week has been on the whole rather dull but firm; business for the larger eastern markets much restricted by the uncertainties of exchange.... The home trade is doing rather more.... 'printers' quiet.... Business in yarns has fallen below an average in most departments.

Woollen Goods, Leeds. – The week's turnover, all kinds of cloth, has been far below average, buyers being very cautious in their operations, and showing not the least disposition to speculate.

Wool and Worsted, Bradford. – The wool market has a rather more cheerful tone; but the business is still of a restricted character and to cover orders recently taken in yarns.

Leicester. – In the hosiery [trade] business as a whole is quiet.... Orders are scarce, *and profits narrowed by the keenness of competition.*

The Boot and Shoe Trades. – But the chief drawback is – not any despondency as to the outlook for the second quarter, which is cheerful – *but the narrowness of profit owing to the activity of competition.*

In elastic webs the recent revival has not been maintained, there being now a lull and dullness all round.

Nottingham. – Nothing very cheering can be said of the lace trade this week. Although the season is advancing, the business does not appreciably increase. Indeed, so far from business expanding, it is doubtful whether orders are coming to hand so freely as they did earlier in the year. The local manufacturers, as a rule, have little reason to congratulate themselves on the aspect of commercial affairs.... Accounts of the hosiery trade are somewhat discouraging.

Birmingham, Hardware Trade. – ...New orders are not coming forward very freely, *and prices are kept on an unremunerative level by the keenness of competition....* The shipping trade continues abnormally quiet.... Travelling-trunks of the cheaper kinds are in brisk request, *though the profits are limited.* The fender and fire-iron branch is rather dull.

Sheffield. – There is a decided check in the progress of the iron and steel trades.... Steel makers are experiencing a rather slacker demand for the best qualities. The production of heaving steel castings is fully equal to the demand, which is less boyant (*sic*) than of late.... For bar and hoop iron there is a rather better demand than for some other kinds of manufactured iron; but business is not so brisk as it was hoped it would be.

The italics in the above cuttings are, of course, my own.

Commonweal, Volume 3, Number 65,
9 April 1887, p. 115.

[UNTITLED PARAGRAPH ON FLOGGING]

Some villagers in Egypt have been flogged and their sheik imprisoned for six months *because* a party of British officers first wounded a villager and then on a disturbance arising shot another dead. Justice can scarcely go further than this; even flogging the whole population for having the rebellious impudence to exist, though it would be harder on them, would be a trifle more logical. It will now be a sacred social duty for the Arabs to avoid being shot by British officers, lest their recklessness should involve the whole of their village in a flogging. Bah! the man of modern civilisation is a sickening animal to contemplate.

Commonweal, Volume 3, Number 65,
9 April 1887, p. 117.

NOTES ON NEWS

The agitation against the Coercion Bill is going on quite as briskly as might have been expected; but of course it is not the kind of opposition which will prevent a parliamentary majority from passing the Bill. Whether the Government will venture to put it in force when passed is another matter. The popular opposition, respectable as it is, does not seem to be of that volume and energy which implies a threat of consequences beyond the ballot-box; and as to the vote, the agitation is discounted by the Tories because they know that a very large proportion of the agitators have not got it, in spite of the assertion of our 'light and leading' friend the *Spectator* that 'every man has the vote or could have it if he would,' – an assertion, by the way, which those who do not know that estimable journal might suppose to be either a joke or a deliberate lie, but which I may assure our readers is made in good faith, and in the exercise of that curious fatuity which is the chief characteristic of that 'official organ' of the Prigs.

This much may at least be said about the anti-coercion agitation (no doubt it has been said often already, but may well be said still oftener), that the wall which parted the Irish from the English democracy has been thrown down. Here at least, if no otherwise is, *union* – that kind of union which comes of men respecting each others' rights.

Nor should the Tories hug themselves too much on their majority. There are not lacking signs that the pendulum will swing Gladstone-wards at the next election. The defeat of the Unionists on the Birmingham Caucus, Mr. Trevelyan's anti-coercion letter, the 'raising of Cain(e)' at Barrow, and so forth, are the kind of things that go before the fall of a big parliamentary majority. Of course it goes without saying that a great many Liberal M.P.'s – those chiefly who are not marked for office – will be bitterly disappointed at their success. If only the Irish would turn tail, and accept some 'compromise,' and then never be heard of again, how glad would these gentry be! Liberalism might then be purified of its last taint of reality.

The way in which the coercionist press tries to belittle the quite successful Easter Monday demonstration is a good example of the by-ways of party guidance. The *Standard* may be taken as the type of these optimists, or rather would-be optimists, whose fury betrays the fact that they are miserably disappointed with our success. One point is worth noting which is expressed in the following sentence in the *Standard*: 'The preponderance in the huge crowd of the class which needs no oratory, honest or dishonest, to whet its animosity to law and order was a sinister symptom.' Now not even amidst its foaming-at-the-mouth-disappointment can the *Standard* pretend to take exception to the behaviour of the very orderly crowd of Easter Monday: it is agreed on all hands that there was an entire absence of the horse-play which generally winds up these Hyde Park demonstrations. So what the *Standard* means is that the revolutionists and their sympathisers were in the majority there; and the whole coercionist press makes a handle of this fact against the Gladstonites.

Well, well! times are changed, it seems, since the last Hyde Park demonstration which I attended – the Franchise one – where the banner of the Labour Emancipation League was destroyed, and our comrade John Burns hustled by a Radical mob, because he had said a few words of blasphemy against Mr. John Bright. Would the Easter Monday crowd have hustled any one who had taken the trouble to call in question the infallibility of the Quaker pope?

It is much to be hoped that all friends of freedom will rally to our meeting in Hyde Park on the 24th, to sympathise with the Northumbrian Miners. A stronger case for sympathy and help could scarcely be put before the public, as the readers of *Commonweal* must already have noted. It would be shame to us in London indeed if working men here were to allow the political prize-fight to absorb all their attention, when such worthy men as these are suffering so unworthily, and struggling so hard against the tyranny of our idiotic system of sham society.

The *Pall Mall Gazette*, while it is had done good service in some directions is certainly curiously inconsistent. It has most rigorously sustained the battle against coercion in Ireland, and apparently is prepared to go on doing so; nevertheless in the very same issue which contains an attack (most justly deserved) on Mr. Chamberlain for his newly-developed love of the fairly complete form of 'freedom of contract' known as the Crimes Bill, contains also a letter, printed with all the honours and obviously with editorial approval, from Madame de Novikoff, the acknowledged agent for quite the completest form of coercion yet known in this world – the modern Government of Russia. This is really rather too grotesque.

On the other hand I read in the *Daily News* that the whole Russian press condemns the Coercion Act!!! It really is too quaint.

Mr. Baggallay asked Mr. Labouchere if he was prepared to repeat in the House his saying in Hyde Park that the policy of the Government was one of the ruffianism of Bill Sykes.

'Beyond all question,' quoth Mr. Labouchere. This is a pleasant hearing, after the usual explanations and eating of words which are the custom of the House. But then Mr. Labouchere has been always careful to show that he is not a fool; as careful as most M.P.'s are to show the contrary – though certainly they need not labour hard at that business.

———————————————

Apropos of this subject, Mr. Conybeare should learn to understand that a man should not be too greedy of humble-pie if he wishes to retain any respect from those who in any way profess to be fighting the popular cause. Explanation on the top of apology is – Well, we really want Sam Weller to characterise this excess in the banquet of humility!

Commonweal, Volume 3, Number 67, 23 April 1887, p. 129.

NOTES ON NEWS

The great event of the last few days has been the attempt on the part of the *Times* newspaper to climb a step higher towards the place of irresponsible dictator of the United Kingdom by dint of what can only be called a piece of cowardly slander; and the name will apply whether the 'accusation' is true or false, since a print that could plot an anonymous accusation of this kind has no longer anything to lose as to character or honour.

As to its truth or falsity, it certainly seems out of character with Mr. Parnell's astucity that he should have written such a document at the time; and that all the more as the killing of Cavendish and Burke was obviously aimed at the very party of which Mr. Parnell is the leader, in order to break up the alliance which was being formed between the Irish Parliamentary Party and the Gladstonites: it was a sore blow to Mr. Parnell. But if it would have been stupid to write such a note then, what can one say of Mr. Parnell if his denial of it now is false? Simply that he is the stupidest man that ever pretended to lead a party; which if far from being a likely story.

As to the challenge thrown out to Mr. Parnell by the Tory party to attack the *Times* in the law-courts under penalty of being considered guilty, this is illustrating our friend Bax's view, expressed in these columns, on the necessity of abolishing the libel law, with a vengeance! So it comes to this, that the enemy of any man, public or private, can trump up an accusation against him, and if the injured man does not submit himself to all the chicanery and uncertainty of a law-court, he is to be held guilty, although nothing whatever is proved against him; and that though his slanderer may have at his back almost unlimited capital to carry on the battle with!

But perhaps the malignity and dirtiness of the *Times'* attack is scarcely equalled by its stupidity. What honest man not blinded by party feeling would think the worse of Mr. Parnell if he had written the letter? Was it not at least a common opinion even in England at the time that Burke had got but what he had long been asking for? And was not this opinion expressed by numbers of people who were shocked at the murder of Cavendish, and thoroughly disapproved of the whole affair; who thought it in fact a disastrous business? I say that this was an opinion often to be met with among persons of by no means extreme opinions at the time.

It must be repeated that the whole business is one of the basest party moves ever made. A baseness in which Lord Hartington must henceforth share after his shuffling with Mr. Dillon the other night: his Whig worshippers must now leave off putting him forward as the soul of honour, as it has been their fashion to do.

It is to be hoped at least that even this dastardly episode may do some good in helping to disgust people with the tyranny of the anonymous press; future ages will scarcely believe the story of our having submitted so long to it. And how puzzled they will be in trying to square the ethics preached throughout society with the conduct of our most respectable, most majestically successful journals.

It is pleasant to turn from these sickening intrigues to the humanity of the Irish police-constables, who have resigned rather than dragoon their fellow-countrymen; as far as it goes it carries out the hope so often expressed by Socialists, that when the uniformed instruments of capitalism come to understand what it really is that they are paid to do, they will refuse to do it. All honour to our Irish friends for showing the way in this matter!

As to the position of the two parties in Parliament since the second reading of the bill, there is not much to be said about it. In spite of his letter to the *Pall Mall Gazette*, Mr. Gladstone seems to be hanging back somewhat; as indeed he is wont to do in a crisis. He seems to think that the chapter of accidents may have something hidden in it which may turn out the Tories without his committing himself any more. The Tories have at least this advantage over their opponents, that they *are* in, and that the others are not very anxious to take their place. It will be curious to watch the lengths of cowardice that want of confidence in the principles which they profess will drive the Liberals to. Undoubtedly they need have no difficulty in bringing on a dissolution if they wish it; and if they shrink from doing what they can to deliver us from the disgrace of the Coercion Bill, they and their leader will earn a title to feebleness and cowardice which one may hope they would seek to avoid – though one cannot help fearing that they will not care much about it.

There may be some meaning in the arrest of the French Commissary on the frontier or there may be none. It scarcely seems possible that such a trifle can really be taken seriously in itself; but it may be a link in a chain of irritations which will lead directly to war. In any case the perturbation it has caused in Paris shows on what ticklish ground the peace of Europe stands.

NOTES ON NEWS

Mr. De Rutzen's sentence on the so-called rioters by the
Marble Arch is a fitting *pendant* to the Norwich affair in
which the members of the League suffered; and though no
doubt Mr. De Rutzen can lay claim to be represented by Mr.
Nupkins as well as Justice Grantham, one cannot help
thinking that there is something behind that, and that the
'worthy magistrate' has had a hint to do a little terrorism,
and that the unfortunate persons who were not Socialists,
who have found themselves in the same prison-van as the
Socialists, must do their best to console themselves with the
fable of the cranes who suffered for being found in the same
net with the more game birds who were the hunters' real
quarry: the members of the S.D.F. were of course the real
persons aimed at.

One advantage the 'rioters' have at all events, that the affair
having happened in London, and chancing to coincide in
time with the growing feeling against the Tory government,
the press have been compelled to take it up in some way or
other. The *Pall Mall*, for instance, has a leader on the
subject, which does it much credit, while it had not one word
to say about the equally monstrous sentence passed on our
comrades at Norwich, prefaced as it was by Grantham's
charge to the jury in which he coolly prejudged the case.

As for the disavowal by Government of its agents Poland,
Matthews and De Rutzen, which the *Pall Mall* cries out for,
that can hardly be expected, unless a general public outcry
forces them to give way when the appeal is tried: they have

done what they were told to do, and are in their places to exercise arbitrary violence whenever it seems advisable to do so; and the 'respectable' mob that backs them is both too stupid and too truculent even to note the grim joke of De Rutzen kindly consenting not to send the accused to a jury, on which they might at least have had a chance of finding one or two honest and unservile persons who would have listened to the evidence and tried to find out what it was worth, instead of taking their opinion from that gross abuse, the summing-up of the judge: they would, I say, have had that chance, though it must be admitted that English juries are grown so servile, that it would be but a chance.

The reactionists are getting on, that must be allowed; to take advantage of a mere slight disturbance, provoked by what was admitted on all sides (except Poland & Co.) to have been the bad conduct of the police, to strike terror into the Socialists, is a considerable advance on their part. Their next step will probably be to drop all pretence of defending the rights of the public to the free use of the highway, or of supporting the police in quelling a disturbance, and to attack opinion directly. There is plenty of law for it, and they will have no difficulty in getting a conviction, if the unsupported evidence of policemen is to be accepted as good enough for the purpose.

The disturbance on Sunday at Kennington was the natural outcome of the police magistrate's decision of the week before not to defend a Socialist from violence. At the same time it may seem to some persons as the result of a deliberate plot on the part of the police to get rid of a Socialist preaching-stand without incurring the trouble and odium of a prosecution for obstruction. In that case it is a simple dodge and seems likely to be an effective one, since there can always be found handy a genuine collection of idiots under the name of a branch of the Primrose League, who, having nothing to say, don't want to hold meetings except amongst themselves, and so need not fear reprisals.

Commonweal, Volume 3, Number 69,
7 May 1887, p. 145.

NOTES ON NEWS

The Tory Government, it is generally said, has made a great
mistake about the Privilege episode; even their own papers
have blamed them for their conduct, and the whole country
will endorse that blame. That may be, and certainly such are
the tight places into which *stupid* lying leads most commonly.
Yet after all the Tory Government is very strong against any
mere constitutional attacks. It has a well-grounded confidence in the strength of party feeling, and the very common
wish of the flunkey of all classes to vote for 'the Gentlemanly
Interest,' like the innkeeper in 'Martin Chuzzlewit.' And the
Liberal Unionists who hold the balance for it, are prepared to
wade through any amount of dirt in defence of their
'principles.' The division on Mr. Gladstone's amendment
moving the appointment of a select committee, and that in
the teeth of the *Standard's* disapproval, shows that the
Government has some reason for its recklessness, and that we
shall have a Tory Government in for some time to come – a
matter of small importance, since the alternative is a Liberal
Government.

To return to the matter of questions in the House.
Honourable members are more easily satisfied with the
answers given than a believer in the benefits of Parliament
would be likely to expect. Take for example Sir H. Holland's
answer on May 7 about the flogging in the Hong Kong
prison. Considering that we all know how little a Chinaman
can live on, and also that of all scoundrelly oppressors the
English colonial or crown-colony one is the vilest, does it
not seem as if 'the reduction of the diet, the existing scale of
which was considered excessive' – prison diet excessive – O
Lord! – meant an attempt to starve the prisoners to death?

Yet the answer was accepted apparently as satisfactory –
probably because the same thing is done here at home both in
prison and out of it, and no one is called to account for it –
not yet.

———————————

It doesn't, perhaps, much matter what a bishop says
nowadays: yet if a bishop could have any moral sense at all,
he might consider the extreme unfairness of telling lies in the
pulpit, where he cannot be contradicted, as he might be at a
public meeting. A bishop preaching at the Chapel Royal,
Whitehall (not a bad place for lies, by the way), the other
day, 'urged that the logical conclusion of Socialist views
would be the practical carrying out of the motto, "I squeeze
all things flat"' – in short, Mr. Bradlaugh's dull level of
mediocrity. Now, there is plenty of Socialist literature for the
bishop to read, and if he has read it he lied in his statement;
if he has not he is an imposter for preaching on a subject of
which he is ignorant. Let him take his choice of either horn
of the dilemma.

———————————

Some of our Socialist friends may have noticed the attempt,
which has already partially succeeded, to force the older
universities to set up a new 'Honour school' – *i.e.*, a new
school of competitive examination – in English literature,
and may perhaps have wondered why it has been taken up so
excitedly by part of the press. The reason is obvious to those
who know something of the universities and the higher class
of literary hacks: it means the pushing of a great new *job* for
all the clan of log-rollers in literature. The dishonest and
conventional twaddle which has been poured on to the public
on this subject is thus easily accounted for; as the professional
and other hangers-on of capital have an innate sympathy for
any one who is job-hunting. All the big-wigs who have
written with such portentous solemnity on the neglect of
English literature at the universities know perfectly well that
English literature is a thing which can be *learned* but cannot
be *taught*, as language and the sciences can be; but they will

not interfere with a poor job-hunter who wishes to feather his nest out of those institutions which our forefathers founded for the education of the *people*, but which, like all other expensive things, are now monopolised by the rich classes.

Commonweal, Volume 3, Number 70,
14 May 1887, p. 153.

NOTES ON NEWS

The Coercion Bill is being slowly dragged through committee, and attacks are being made on its details with more or less success, so there are not wanting genuine anti-coercionists who are beginning to feel elated at the prospect of the bill coming out of the mill something quite different from what was intended. I would remind these persons that it will in any case still be a coercion bill for Ireland; that is to say a bill for the manufacture of special crimes in that country, which do not exist in England, Scotland or Wales, and that the Tory Government and their Liberal allies will be quite satisfied with it in that form: a few words more or less, what do they matter?

In fact this struggle over the bill in committee illustrates very well the impotency of minorities in Parliament, even when they are important, respectable, and numerous, and the futility of attempting to use that body as a means of safeguarding the people from oppression. The bill becomes law after all this sifting out of parts of it that are any way siftable; nor, as the division on Sir W. Harcourt's amendment shows, can the Opposition get rid of any of its principle; nevertheless anti-coercionists, and those as aforesaid, not of the mildest, are already beginning to look with a kind of complacency on the altered bill, are considering it to a certain extent as the work of their own hands, as indeed it is or will be; the effect of their guardianship of the liberties of the people will be visible in it, and will take the edge off the resistance of moderate opponents of the measure, or timid people, who will say, we have done all we can in the matter – through our representatives in Parliament – and it isn't so bad after all: now let us go eat our dinners and forget the Irish question.

That is of course just what all Governments reckon on in such cases; they don't expect to carry a measure condemned by the democracy by the mere force of the accidental majority of that odd jumble of a body, the voters of the United Kingdom; they have always the fraud of Parliamentary representation to help that force, and can depend on the juggle of 'determined opposition in committee' to do all they want for them and enable them to pose as persons who are carrying out the will of the people and are trying, so far as is possible, even to satisfy the perhaps not unreasonable prejudices of the minority.

How different a figure the bill would have cut if instead of going night after night to fight the air in committee, the real opponents of coercion had said after the second reading: Well, the force of the majority is yours and the bill is carried; we have opposed it as well as we could, and henceforth will have nothing to do with it, there is none of our handiwork in it; the whole measure is yours, face the public with it in your hands as the only persons responsible for it. If they had said that and then gone home till the business was over, would not anti-coercion have been by now in a better position than it is? Possibly in that case the Government might have put forward the bill in all its hideous nakedness and so have courted open revolt, thereby shocking the moderates into serious opposition: more probably they would have felt extremely nervous under their ill-omened freedom from opposition, and would not have ventured as far as they are venturing now under opposition; but in that case the public would have understood clearly enough that their forbearance was caused by cowardice, whereas they now suppose that they have yielded to reason as expressed by the Opposition. In either case the Coercion Bill would have been much more obvious for what it is, an impudent attack on the most

elementary liberties of the country. The Parliamentary sham-
fight of compromise and expediency has once more served
the purpose it is sustained for, that is keeping the people
down; and that in spite of the thoroughly organised and
sincere opposition of the Irish members, who have done
everything that they could have done – as a Parliamentary
party. For the kind of abstention I have alluded to could *not*
be done by a Parliamentary party.

Something has already been said in the *Commonweal* about
the case of the pit-brow woman; but owing to Mr. Burt's
amendment to the Mines Regulation Bill the matter is again
before the public, and is now put before them with senti-
mental and even theatrical embellishments which tend to
obscure the real question at issue, which is briefly this: Are
these women to be used for doing work which is unfit for
women *for the purpose* of reducing the wages of working
people? The capitalists very naturally answer 'Yes,' the
working men as naturally answer 'No.' The public, confused
as it well may be by the fact, amongst others, that the women
engaged in this beastly work (also quite naturally under the
present muddled slavery of labour) do not wish to lose their
employment, doesn't know what to say. It may therefore be
explained to them once more that the women would not be
employed unless at lower wages than men would have to be
paid, and that this is the case whenever women are employed
on work which they are not especially fitted for. Whatever
boon, therefore, may be conferred on the women by allowing
them to work amidst filth for a small wage, it will be no boon
to the working people in general.

A word may here be said to the 'women's rights' group.
They are far too apt to put women forward as *competitors*
with men, and thereby injure the cause of the emancipation
of women which every Socialist is bound to further. They are
therefore blind to the fact that the capitalist employment of
women for the general cheapening of labour is founded on

that very dependence of women which they (and we) want to get rid of. Under reasonable conditions of society every woman will be free to earn her own livelihood as every man will be, but for that very reason there will be no competition between the sexes; and women will neither get nor seek employment in work which men can do better than they can. Capitalism *forces* them to accept such work now – at starvation wages; just as it forces males to accept work which is not fit for human beings. As long as men are slaves, woman can be no better. Let the women's rights societies adopt that last sentence as a motto – and act on it.

The East-end people may be congratulated on the new 'palace' they are getting, though the word is an unsavoury one in the mouth of the people. But what a number of East-enders there will be whose poverty will prevent them from using it! People too ragged, dirty, ignorant – in a word, too *degraded* to use it. And even those of the workers who can use it, can they do so with due pleasure and content? Surely not, when they contrast its magnificence with their own narrow, inconvenient, sordid dwellings and their wretched surroundings. Until their private houses are roomy, comfortable, and pleasant, they cannot really enjoy splendid public buildings; they have got to go back again to their narrow, shabby lodgings, and beastly workshops – and live there. Surely when true society takes the place of false, we shall raise beautiful and magnificent halls with their surroundings for the use of all. But the contrast will not then be between splendour and sordidness, but between splendour and special beauty and the due simplicity of the dwelling of a private person which is quite consistent with beauty and convenience.

Commonweal, Volume 3, Number 72,
28 May 1887, p. 172.

NOTES ON NEWS

Speeches of Mr. Chamberlain; letter of Mr. Bright; Birmingham meeting, and solemn sermon by the Birmingham organ of Coercion Joe; Glasgow anti-coercion meeting; progress of Mr. Gladstone, once the Liberal King, now a kind of rebel leader, striving rather for a glorious end than for his lost crown. These are the preparations for the Liberal reunion, the hope of which some persons cling to so fondly. It does not directly concern us Socialists much, as after all it only forecasts the formal inauguration of the reactionary party which has been in working order some time already. But indirectly it will, one may hope, add to the confusion and ineffectiveness of Parliament, and so tend to disgust the people, and at the last disgust them so much that they will relegate it to its due place as a mere rowdy debating society, that sensible persons will give a wide berth to, till the happy day comes when one can squelch out its noisome existence.

Over the whole plain of labour and trade you saw society in conflict. No arms were used, and yet men were struck down; no blood was spilled, and yet men died. Neither giant nor feudal lord was any longer there; a new tyrant reigned in their stead, more omnipresent and pitiless than they, whose name was Capital.

So says Mr. G. J. Holyoake in his prose poem on co-operation; nor is the picture overdrawn. But will not his words serve to describe the present as well as the past? Surely our own Labour Struggle column is enough to answer that question. It is true that the rule of the 'tyrant' is now questioned, but no longer by the co-operationists but by the Socialist. The former seem to have a veil cast over their eyes which makes them see their old tyrant in very different colours to what they used to; for they can scarcely deny that he is there still.

_____

The fact is, the very success of co-operation shows how very far it is from being a solution of the labour question. Let us admit that they have exploded the superstition that workmen could not combine in production and distribution, that the autocratic one-man capitalist was a necessity for carrying on a business successfully: but with all their success, what else have they done? They have shown us that co-operation is desirable; but they are not allowed to co-operate: they must borrow money and pay interest, they must hire premises and pay rent to an individual or a company, they must buy the land that is theirs and the factories that they have made; they must pay a profit on every thing they buy outside their own association, either to consume or to transform into other wares. In short, not being allowed to co-operate, they have acted as all people *must* do under our present system – pay tribute to the owners of property for being allowed to live. And meantime they have established a form of joint stockery differing slightly (scarcely at all in most cases) from that already established; which to some of us cannot but seem a rather pitiful outcome of those perfectly genuine hopes for the regeneration of society which they began with earlier in the century, and all the energy developed from those hopes. Let them now, without casting aside the individual advantages they have gained, turn their eyes to Socialism, the real movement of labour, which will make the workers the arbiters of their own destinies.

_____

The *Engineer* says, apropos of the Belgian strikes:

Capital does not receive the common interest of the country when laid out in the coal mines, the workmen and their families cannot possibly subsist on a pittance of 1s. 6d. to 2s. 6d. at most a-day for ten hours' work in a deep mine, and the price of coal cannot be raised if it is to be disposed of. If economy in plant and working is no further possible, the look-out is a dreary one indeed.

Just so; and if 'economy in plant and working' can be carried further than at present by squeezing the ingenuity of the capitalist and the terrible dull patience of the workman to the utmost, how long will the new improvement in the prospects of the coal capitalist last? Just as long as the increased competition which will immediately spring up will allow it. The look-out is dreary indeed – to the capitalist. But to the Socialist, even when viewed through all the suffering of low wages and strikes, and riots consequent on the tyranny of the last squeeze of despairing capitalism, it is not so dreary – because he can see the end drawing near: the capitalist, finding his profits cut down by competition, while the workman, growing more and more enlightened, claims more and more.

Mr. Haigh, of Barnsley, in speaking to a large number of miners and the officials of the Yorkshire Miners' Association, complains bitterly of the bad effect on trade of the high mining rents and royalties in Great Britain. He explains the depressed state of the coal trade by the depressed state of the iron trade, and he uses the following remarkable words:

Whilst as a nation we were almost the sole makers of iron and steel, and had no foreign competitors, we could supply our home trade and other countries without feeling the effect of these royalties and charges quite so much; but the moment we are face to face with a foreigner in the markets of the world, who has very small rents and royalty charges to pay – and even these charges go into the national exchequer to assist in meeting the expenses of the State – we are run out of the foreign markets, and even driven from our own.

The readers of the *Commonweal* are pretty familiar with this view of the state of trade and the prospects of capitalism in

Great Britain; but as an utterance from the capitalist side it is worth noting. And what is to be done, pray, Mr. Capitalist?

For why should we take the profit from the poor land-owner, who is already moaning dejectedly in another corner of the field about the pining away of his rents? Some of our non-Socialist working-men friends will say and think that the British working-man will get something out of it. Will he? To do justice to the paper who reports Mr. Haigh's speech, *The Engineer*, it can see through the flimsiness of *that* hope: 'The speaker did not explain how it was that in spite of all this, the Belgian workman works for starvation wages.'

Yes, indeed, that is what it must come to in one way or other as long as we work for the profit of a master. At the best, one group of workmen thriving somewhat at the expense of another, that is what *has been* in this country, and what the 'patriots' of all countries put before them as an ideal to be striven for, blind fools as they are! What most certainly *will be*, and before very long too, if the Social Revolution does not intervene, is that all workmen throughout the world will be reduced to a 'dead level,' not of 'mediocrity,' but of starvation for the satisfaction of the tyrant, Capitalistic Competition.

International Capitalism and the workman a hungry machine; International Socialism and the workman a free man and the master of his own destiny – it must be one or other of these two. All the feeble compromises that aim at checking the power of the capitalists, and yet allowed them to keep their position, will be speedily found out, one after another, by the monster which the Age of Commerce has made by dint of such mighty effort and cleverness, and which it must now feed by anything that may be handy. Honour, justice, beauty, pleasure, hope, all must be cast into that insatiable maw to stave off the end awhile; and yet at last the end must come, and the sooner it comes the less of a desert the world will be after the storm which is inevitable.

Commonweal, Volume 3, Number 74,
11 June 1887, p. 188.

[UNTITLED PARAGRAPH]

A section of the Indian native press is against the extension of railways, on the grounds that they only benefit British capitalists. The *Bangabasi* says:– 'The English merchants wish the Government to extend railways on its own responsibility, and borrow money from British capitalists. Their desire would be satisfied if the Government would borrow forty crores of rupees. They have raised the question of the welfare of both England and India. They wish to prove that the natives of India will be benefitted by the extension of railways, and that the English people will also be benefitted by it. We have already shown that the English people only will be benefitted. We wonder at the argument set forth with a view to betray the natives of India and the Indian Government. The extension of railways will increase the sale of English goods. There is no necessity for raising the question of the welfare of the natives of India. Our Government will not do any good to the natives, even if it has the desire to do so. It must undertake work which will do good to the English people. So the railways will be extended. It is idle to talk of the welfare of the natives of India.' – *Engineer*. – True, doubtless, but for one correction; it is not for the benefit of the people of England, but for the governing classes of England that all this is done.

Commonweal, Volume 3, Number 74,
11 June 1887, p. 191.

NOTES ON NEWS

The O'Brien incident in New York is worth noting. It must be admitted at once that Mr. O'Brien would have injured the present prospects of the cause of Home Rule – that is, more explicitly, the establishment of a semi-independent Irish parliament at Dublin – if he had identified himself with the Land Nationalisers and semi-Socialists of New York. But on the other hand, his refusal has also injured the cause of Irish independence, looking at it from a broader point of view. The Land Nationalisers and other more advanced politicians may well say, Is it a foregone conclusion, then, that all the Irish Parliamentary Party look forward to is an imperfect form of peasant-proprietorship – *i.e.*, the creating of a number of small landlords in place of the few big landlords already existing?

Well, as a matter of fact that *is* the idea of the parliamentary Irishman; and if he went further than that he would be ahead of the ordinary Irishman – in Ireland, at all events. Nor need we wonder at that. The land question is the side of the question of exploitation which naturally thrusts itself forward in Ireland; and the share that the cottar tenant has in it is a war between his industry on one side and a poor soil and a coarse form of robbery on the other; and any alleviation of his lot will for the time put him in heaven, so to say, and make him a very conservative and property-loving character. All this, of course, is what the parliamentary Irish politician is reckoning on, and consequently he won't trouble himself to even consider the landless labourer who will still remain after the advent of peasant-proprietorship, or indeed the future of the peasant proprietor himself, which will, in two words, be ultimate ruin.

Perhaps sometimes we Socialists have been tempted to envy the simplicity of the one-plank platform of the Irish agitator, but such an incident as this of Father M'Glynn *versus* Mr. O'Brien shows the dull side of it. In fact revolutionists cannot evade the duty of keeping their true aim clearly before them, and asking themselves if it is worth the trouble, and they must accept as a necessary consequence of the carrying out of that duty all the unpopularity and lack of support and jeers at their want of practicality which they are sure to encounter if they go straight to their object.

Meantime a Socialist can hardly help chuckling when he thinks that Father M'Glynn, who has really made a straight revolutionary hit at that terrible revolutionist Mr. O'Brien, may in his turn find himself denounced as a capitalist-saver one of these days: may, or certainly will, unless he moves forward with the times. To-day there can be found respectable people who are moved to indignation by the spectacle of a certain class of landlords exercising their undoubted legal rights to the full; though the greater part of landlords, since they are not driven to act so dramatically, are allowed to do as they please without comment. At some future time not far distant there will be found probably respectable persons who will wish to take away this legal power from all landlords. There, however, the respectable people will stay their advance, for the next step will be the attack on all capital – that is, really, property; and all respectable people have capital in some form or other. Well, so it goes – he that endureth to the *end* shall be saved.

The triumphant Tories are determined to show us how feeble a barrier Parliament is between any faction that may have crept into power and the liberties of the people. By the time of the date on this number of *Commonweal* the parliamentary resistance to the Coercion Bill will be at an end, and for all practical purposes it might as well have never been begun. As to Mr. Smith's urgency resolution it was taken sheepishly enough by the House, and was clearly looked upon as a matter of little consequence. And indeed it is not of much consequence, considering what Parliament is.

———————————

It may well be hoped that one day the people will take possession for their own use of the noble buildings which their forefathers built in the days when they were striving to break the bonds of feudal tyranny, and had not yet foreseen the straiter bonds of capitalism. All Socialists therefore should join in the protest which Mr. Frederick Harrison made at the meeting of the Society for the Protection of Ancient Buildings against the destructive tomfoolery now going on at Westminster Abbey. It is an easily read token of the sincerity of the *conservatism* of the bourgeois, when a building, which is still perhaps, in spite of all the degradations it has suffered the most beautiful in Great Britain, is to be subjected to the risk of total destruction, and the certainty of great damage for an idiotic piece of Court humbug that nobody, not even the very flunkeys themselves, care a rush for.

———————————

Apropos of this grievous nonsense our readers may have noticed some of them perhaps with disapproval, that there has not much been said about the Jubilee (one is really ashamed to write the word) in the pages of *Commonweal*. This is to be explained, I suppose, by the mere contempt with which Socialists look upon the whole subject. But the 'great event' of it is so near that one may perhaps say as much as this, that the powers that be are determined to use the opportunity to show what a nuisance the monarchy and court can be as a centre of hypocrisy and corruption, and the densest form of stupidity.

Commonweal, Volume 3, Number 75, 18 June 1887, p. 193.

NOTES

A writer (anonymous) in our contemporary *Justice*, has found out a new definition of Anarchism. According to our friend Anarchism means abstention (for whatever reason) from parliamentary action. I fear this new definition is scarcely exact enough to satisfy either Anarchist or Collectivist.

———————————

Our friend also writes as if the Socialist League had made some new departure at the late Conference. He had better read again the resolution of the Conference as printed in the *Commonweal*, which will set him right in this matter, since it asserts the indisputable fact that the policy hitherto pursued by the League has been one of abstention from parliamentary action.

———————————

I must venture to call the end of his note as to the constitution of the Council of the League impertinent, since the domestic concerns of a body with which he has nothing to do, do not concern the writer. However, it may be as well to remind our friends that while our Council sits in London we have Branches in various parts of Britain, who cannot possibly send up one of their members to sit on the Council once a-week. A real delegate Council would be impossible under such conditions, and a bogus one would not be desired by a body like the Socialist League, which has always shown what I must consider a very laudable objection to 'bossing.'

Commonweal, Volume 3, Number 75, 18 June 1887, p. 196.

THE NORTH OF ENGLAND
SOCIALIST FEDERATION

We have received the following Principles and Programme of the North of England Socialist Federation:

PRINCIPLES.

The North of England Socialist Federation has been formed to educate and organise the people to achieve the economic emancipation of labour.

While fully sympathising with and helping every effort of the wage-earners to win better conditions of life under the present system, the Socialist Federation aims at abolishing the Capitalist and Landlord class and forming the workers of society into a Co-operative Commonwealth.

An employing class monopolising all the means of getting and making wealth, and a wage-earning class compelled to work primarily for the profit of these employers, is a system of tyranny and slavery.

The antagonism of these two classes brings about fierce competition – for employment amongst the workers and for markets amongst the capitalists. This gives rise to class hatred and class strife, and destroys real independence, liberty, and happiness.

The present system gives ease and luxury to the idlers, toil and poverty to the workers, and degradation to all; it is essentially unjust and should be abolished.

Our aim is to bring about a Socialist System which will give healthy and useful labour to all, ample wealth and leisure to all, and the truest and fullest freedom to all.

All are invited to help the Socialist Federation in this great cause. Adherents shall acknowledge truth, justice, and morality as the basis of their conduct towards each other and towards all men. They shall acknowledge NO RIGHTS WITHOUT DUTIES: NO DUTIES WITHOUT RIGHTS.

PROGRAMME.

The Socialist Federation seeks to gain its ends by working on the following lines:–

(1) Forming and helping other Socialist bodies to form a National and International Socialist Labour Party.

(2) Striving to conquer political power by promoting the election of Socialists to Parliament, Local governments, School Boards, and other administrative bodies.

(3) Helping Trade Unionism, Co-operation, and every genuine movement for the good of the workers.

(4) Promoting a scheme for the National and International Federation of Labour.

All Socialists will wish the new society success; to which wishes I must add for my part the hope that our friends will find out the futility of sending (or trying to send) Socialists or any one else to Parliament before they have learned it by long and bitter experience. They will find their work cut out for them in carrying out Nos. 3 and 4 of their programme, and useful and necessary work it will be. At the same time I heartily congratulate them on not holding out the bait of a long string of 'stepping-stones'; measures which no bourgeois Parliament would pass, and which yet would be out of date in the very first days of a Revolution; promises not capable of fulfilment, nor worth fulfilment.

Commonweal, Volume 3, Number 76,
25 June 1887, p. 205.

NOTES

The *Pall Mall* is sanguine enough to see a hope of Liberal reunion in Lord Hartington's speech; a less sanguine supporter of Liberalism would see in it the ordinary utterance of a Tory in Whig's clothing (which is the wolf and which the sheep?). But really to take any serious notice of such people as this lazy Whig-Tory lord would be beneath the part of the mere journalist even, if it were not for the worship of Parliament which is such a curious part of the modern Englishman's creed. Meanwhile there is one comfort, not all the Queen's horses (even with artificial tails and stuffed ears) and all the Queen's men can put the Liberal party together again. There is an-end of that piece of humbug at any rate.

It is said in the daily papers: 'An illuminated address of congratulation on the event of the Jubilee will be presented to her Majesty to-day by Sir James D. Linton and Mr. Alfred Everill on behalf of the Royal Institute of Painters in Water Colours. It is bound in the form of an album in crimson plush,' etc. Only by a printers' error, I suppose, the statement is omitted that the plush was cut from the seat of a pair of breeches of that material hitherto reserved for the wear of the President of the illustrious society – the loss will be supplied.

The amendment to the Mines Regulation Bill designed to put an end to the work of the pit-brow women was thrown out. This was a foregone conclusion, considering the amount of ignorance of economy shown on both sides of the question, mingled with the determination to do nothing likely to put a spoke in the wheel of capitalism, which is the natural atmosphere of the House of Commons. Mr. M'Laren, apparently quite innocently, gave the key-note to the whole debate when he said, 'No objection has been urged against the employment of women on the pit-bank that could not be urged, with as much force against the whole factory system of this country.'

To Mr. M'Laren that seemed a conclusive argument; – and to us it seems so also. It would not be worth while attacking here and there a special abuse, a special horror of the present labour system, unless through it we were attacking the whole capitalistic system; we don't want to improve the system which Mr. M'Laren obviously thinks as necessary to the production of commodities as the sun is to the production of plants, but to sweep it away.

The case of the pit-brow women has been put more than once in the *Commonweal*, but as not everybody who may get hold of this number will be a subscriber to the paper, it may shortly be stated again thus: that these women are employed on work unfit for women in order to reduce the wages of men in the coal industry. That is the whole matter in a nutshell.

Commonweal, Volume 3, Number 77,
2 July 1887, p. 212.

NOTES ON NEWS

The Irish members the other night abstained from voting on the Coercion Bill, and thus took the step at last which they ought to have taken at first; but the ugly words 'too late' will pursue them; the mischief is done, the time for a great demonstration is lost, and at the cost of great trouble and expenditure of energy, they have been playing into the hands of the Tories all this time. Once more the moral: when you are in Parliament you must play the parliamentary game, even if you know you are throwing away your hand by doing so.

The Federation of Radical Clubs having met and discussed the advisability of holding another great demonstration against the Coercion Bill, has decided to forego it. This sounds disappointing enough; but they were probably right; at the best such a demonstration would not have come up to the Easter Monday show; and even if it had surpassed it, it would have been [of] little use unless the agitation could have been kept up and gone on increasing, and developed into threatenings of something more serious than Hyde Park and Trafalgar Square meetings. For all this the Radicals are not prepared; so they must take the Tory rule quietly, and will probably have plenty of opportunities for the exercise of the useful virtue of patience.

The Unionist chuckers-out at the Kensington Town Hall, who like the honest bravo of past times who insisted on killing his man when paid for it, even when his employer had changed his mind, thought that they were bound to give value for money received, and chucked out chiefly the wrong persons, have had a narrow escape from gratis lodging in a public building, but are quit for the fright. One of them in his account of his secondary use of a brass curtain rod, embellished the story unnecessarily; but it must be admitted that it is not easy to get clear evidence of what has happened at 'a rough and tumble.' At the same time one can't help thinking that if they had been Socialists accused of rioting, much clearer evidence would have been forthcoming in all due abundance, and the jury would not have been so scrupulous as to the identity of the rioters.

The frightful sea-tragedy that has just come before the public is miserable and depressing to hear tell of; an under-manned ship and overworked men were probably at the bottom of the slaying of the Malay. But from the first I couldn't help asking myself if the crew would have treated in the same way an English shipmate who from drink-madness or other madness had become dangerous to them? Isn't the jingo spirit which has given us much bigger horrors, from blowing mutineers from guns down to flogging a whole village because one of the villagers has foolishly allowed himself to be shot by a British officer, responsible for this last wretched piece of sordid misery on the high seas?

The tribe of Nupkins seems to be increasing, and the last specimen brought forward (by himself) for exhibition is certainly not a pretty one. One can judge by the behaviour of Nupkins-Newton in this 'mistake' which he has made, what his usual conduct is to poor girls who are not 'respectable,' and who are guilty of the crime which under various names is almost the only one punished by our robber-society – poverty to wit.

It is a curious characteristic of the present day that the stiffest defence of the rights of private property is blended with attempts towards crude State Socialism not merely in the same society, or in the same assembly, but even in the same man. Here is Mr. Bradlaugh, for instance, the doughty champion of the rights of monopoly in one form of the means of production, bringing in a Bill to force people to use their land in the way which he thinks that it ought to be used, or else give them up and be 'compensated' for it. It doesn't matter that such a Bill is not likely to pass and would not be effective if it were passed; the intention at any rate is to *compel* people to give up something which they call their property and don't want to give up. It seems not unlikely that Mr. Bradlaugh and Mr. Henry George will presently be running in the same coach. After that we shall see.

The improvement in trade that many persons were so cocksure of a few months ago, has gone to join the majority of prophecies now it seems. As guaged by the railway returns we are pretty much where we were last year. Most of those who have anything to do with business, either as employers or employed, will make rather a worse tale of it than that. We were promised a miracle and it hasn't happened. There will be plenty more of that before we have done.

Commonweal, Volume 3, Number 78,
9 July 1887, p. 217.

NOTES ON NEWS

When one has said that the Coercion Bill has passed its third reading, there seems little more to be said on the subject at this stage of the proceedings, except perhaps to express wonder at the meaning of all the fine phrases about the civilisation of the times, the freedom under which we live, the progress we have made in the toleration of the expression of opinion, the power of rational minorities, and the like. It is as well to descend to earth after all those fine flights, and to remember what the whole event means. Simply that political changes which are purely political and seem to lead nowhere, are accepted with little struggle as mere shifting in the rules of an amusing game, in which there must be a certain amount of give and take; while on the other hand changes that threaten ever so little the sacred 'rights of property' are to be defended by any means, fair and foul.

And these means are really only manifestations and forms of one when once the possibilities of fraud are exhausted, and that one is mere brute-force. That really lies behind all the junketing and gentilities of modern society, all its philanthropy and cant, and self-satisfied priggism. Brute-force is the foundation of all that, neither more nor less than it was of the devastations of Atilla or Timur: neither is it any more forgiven than in the days of the older brutalities, when once it is known for what it is. From that point of view we owe some thanks to the Tory Government and its steady majority of nobodies; in this instance of Ireland they have stripped the veil of pretence off their actions, and they say to the Irish, 'Dog, do this because it is profitable to us!' It will be a good day for the Social Revolution when the masters of society generally are forced into the same course, and dropping all pretence, to say openly to their slaves, 'Work for me (mostly gratis) or die.'

The Liberal successes at Spalding and Coventry, and the reduction of the Tory vote at North Paddington, are no doubt promising to the 'outs' in the game of 'ins and outs' as it is now being played. But hear the *Daily News* as to the spirit abroad among the working men at North Paddington: 'A number of working men who possessed the vote could not be got to use it, being swayed by an overmastering impression that in regard to the two parties in the State it was "six of one and half-a-dozen of the other," and that neither cared a straw for the interests of the working man. "Why should I trouble about voting? What is it to you or me who gets in? They're both a set of humbugs, promising you anything and everything to get in, and doing nothing when they get there."'

Yes that is why the Tories are able to keep their places, and why their party is being continually helped by persons once called Liberals and Radicals: because the working-men voters have got hold of one truth at least, that Parliament, with its parties, auxilliary newspapers, and the like, is not kept going for them but for their masters. This is encouraging to Socialists and other honest men – who will all be Socialists presently.

The Government has sustained a sharp defeat, owing to their own inconsiderate folly and want of foresight in not seeing how probable it was that the Cass incident would be taken up by the shop-keeping group, and what dangerous enemies they are. On the other hand, so good-natured and easily-pleased (and one must add so stupid) the general English public is, that the House of Commons has considerably reinstated itself in public opinion by voting, by a very narrow majority, that it may be wrong for a policeman and a magistrate to commit an act which is at once (for a wonder) illegal and unjust, and for a great official to decline to consider such a proceeding.

Again wonders will never cease! The martinet Sir Charles Warren has issued instructions to the police not to go beyond the law in persecuting poor girls in the streets, who are doing what our present society insists that some women shall do; that is, to serving as a safeguard to the chastity, or a veil to the respectability, of their richer sisters.

As to Mr. Newton, what can one say but that he has acted after his kind? What he did in the case of Miss Cass he does, no doubt, every day: only this time to injustice, brutality, and cruelty he added a mistake. He thought he was dealing with a defenceless person, and lo! the shopkeeping class spring up behind her like a jack-in-the-box. No doubt he will take care not to do it again; – that is the mistake, not the injustice, brutality, and cruelty.

Commonweal, Volume 3, Number 79, 16 July 1887, p. 228.

NOTES ON NEWS

The Government Land Bill does not need much comment from a Socialist; it is all that might be expected of it, and is in fact so bad that it will at least injure the Tory party, and may turn out a biggish nail in the coffin of the Government, though perhaps hardly so big a one as the Cass case, because the average English politician will not take the trouble to go into its details; nor indeed has he any occasion to do so: it simply means trying to do nothing under the guise of doing something.

The mountains are now in labour with a new(?) National Party, which, if it ever comes to the birth will, as a novelty, be a ridiculous mouse indeed. But setting aside the novelty, and the absurdity of making that which is already made, the party is a formidable one, and Joe Chamberlain and Co. are wise in their generation to take care to belong to it. It has long governed England under various names, and for convenience sake one must call it by the one under which it has hitherto been most respectable, the Whig Party. It may after all be worth the while of the reactionists to sacrifice such an empty thing as a name to it, and to admit, what is obvious, that the whole of the Tory party that has any power or capacity belongs to it. Ye shall know them by their fruits.

The charge against our comrade Williams has been quashed at the appeal, a fact of which every honest person, Socialist or not, will be glad; but it is doubtful, if it had not been for Mr. Newton's good deed in the guise of a bad one, and his rashness in meddling with a person who had the shop-keeping class behind her, whether the bench would have considered the evidence so carefully. I must also call attention to the fact (and all papers that do not aim at being considered supporters of injustice should do the same) that there are still two men in prison working out their sentence who were convicted on similar evidence to that on which the 'learned' magistrate convicted our friend Williams. And lastly, I must once more call attention to the EQUAL LAWS under which we *free* people live, which condemn these innocent men to a cruel punishment simply because they have no friends rich enough to be responsible for paying the expenses of the appeal if it chances to fail. Nor must we forget even if these poor men are released now, they will have been in prison for many weeks; the injustice remains in any case. Well, it is but what must be looked looked (*sic*) for; for a society founded on robbery must be sustained by violence and wrong.

Commonweal, Volume 3, Number 80,
23 July 1887, p. 236.

NOTES

Mr. Walter Besant, as hon. treasurer of the Working Women's Conference, is appealing to people in general to give him information as to the wages and conditions of life of working women. The result of this may be useful, or it may not be. In the first place it will be useless if the information is not thoroughly genuine, if it is allowed to be influenced by the spirit that often creeps into such collections of 'information': the spirit that tries to create the impression that things are not very bad, and that even if they are bad they can easily be altered for the better a little, and that – there, that will do.

But supposing a great deal of genuine information gathered and published; what will be the use of it, and to whom will it be useful? It will be absolutely no use unless it is used, so far as it goes, for the purpose of putting both sexes of workpeople into a totally different position from their present one. And under those circumstances it is hard to see how it can be useful to any but those who are striving to change the basis of society, to make all women working-women, and not force either marriage or prostitution on any of them as a profession – in other words, to free labour from the tyranny of monopoly. Those people who are trying to do this are usually called Socialists, and I fear that Mr. Besant can hardly be classed as one of these, in spite of his apparently genuine sympathy with the joys and troubles of working people.

Apart from those middle-class persons who have had the good luck to be convinced of the truths of Socialism and are actually working for it, I have met with two kinds amongst persons of good will to the popular cause: first, persons of very strong and marked advanced opinions who are so far from thinking that the holding of such opinions involves any sort of action on their part, that they rather (or indeed very much) plume themselves on their superiority over those who act on their opinions, whatever they may be; – of course, such persons are desperate pessimists. The other kind are persons whose opinions are not very advanced, but have a sort of idea that they should act upon them, such as they are, and will undertake cheerfully any little job that may turn up, from total abstinence to electioneering, with a cheerful confidence in the usefulness of their work: but all the while they have not even faced the question as to the necessity of changing the basis of society; they suppose that the present system contains in itself everything that is necessary to cure the evils which they are to some extent conscious of; and indeed some of them are very anxious to stave off the radical change which Socialism proposes by exhibiting the said evils in course of being cured by – well, I must say it – rose-water.

I know this latter group of well-disposed middle-class people exists, and I rather think Mr. Walter Besant belongs to it. If I wrong him by so thinking I shall be glad to be convinced to the contrary. And meantime this group of people may yield converts to Socialism when they have found out by practical experience that the evils they are good-temperedly attacking are not accidents of the present system but essential to it. Then they may make up their minds to attack the system itself.

Till within the last few years St. Alban's Abbey used to be one of the most interesting of the historical monuments of England; not because it was the longest church in the world, nor even altogether because it comprised some of the most beautiful work of the most perfect period of architecture, but also because all kinds of varied historical interest centred in its site and building. Partly built of materials from Verulam, it became in the early part of the Middle Ages the refuge and home of the chroniclers of the time. Some of the most interesting and heart-stirring passages in the Peasants' War, that outburst of Mediæval Communism, took place around it. It witnessed two of the battles of the Wars of the Roses, the second of which was the bloodiest of all; and till within the last few years, though it had suffered some indignities, was still the stout and beautiful old building that had seen so many dramas played round about it. It is not too much to say that it stood in the homely Hertfordshire fields one of the wonders of the world.

Well, to-day it has been deprived of most of its beauty and two-thirds of its historical interest. How and why? Insurrections, battles, changes of religion, had left it pretty much unhurt; but the damage they couldn't do has been done quite lately by such a thing as a common parliamentary lawyer, a cleverish vulgar man, once called Sir Edmund Becket, now Lord Grimsthorpe, who coveted the glory of 'restoring' this ancient monument; and although the ruin he proposed to make of it was disapproved of by most of those who had the guardianship of this piece of public property, all opposition went down before the shaking of his money-bag, and 'tis all done, or on the point of being all done; and the whim of a parliamentary lawyer has proved to be more destructive than miller Grindecobbe's bills and bows, than Henry the Eighth's greedy barons, or Cromwell's lobster-tails! Truly the money-bag has more to answer for than the destruction of works of art and monuments of history; yet the wantonness and irremediable character of this kind of destruction, joined with the preposterous vulgarity of the instrument of it, makes it hard to bear.

Commonweal, Volume 3, Number 82,
6 August 1887, p. 249.

NOTES

The hot words and straightforward quarrelling which took place at the miners' gala on July 31st at Blyth Links, were not more than might have been expected from our downright brethren of the north. Some people will be lamenting the appearance of disunion amongst a most important body of workers after a defeat in an ordinary labour struggle. But it is rather a matter of certainty than of hope that there is more at the bottom of it than that. That the indignation of the more thoughtful of the men at the 'soft-fighting' of their leaders shows a gathering determination for real union founded on a complete sense of the fact that the interests of all workers are the same, and that workers' organisations cannot stop short at merely fighting a matter of wages in the passing day; but must aim at the one thing worth aiming at, a condition of things in which the workers should control their own affairs, and not as now pay the heavy price of slavery to the employers for managing matters for them.

Mr. Fenwick who (very naturally certainly) seems to have got very angry at the attacks made on him, and who attacked our comrade Mahon in turn, got much mixed up in talking on Socialism. He seemed to feel that a defence of the capitalists as masters was not likely to be well-received by such an audience, so he attempted the defence of capital by enrolling the workers also in the capitalist army on the grounds of their invested savings. This sort of thing catches those who do not understand (as probably Mr. Fenwick himself doesn't) that it is the individualistic capital itself and not the holders of it, that is the enemy we are fighting against. The working classes by the practice of 'thrift,' which to a man who knows what the life of an honest man, duly contributing his share of labour to the world should be, is horrible even to think of, manage to save a little money, which under the present system they are compelled to 'invest,' that is, to hand over to be used by the very monopoly which prevents them from managing their own affairs.

The capital earned by the labour of the working-classes will not be taken away from them; on the contrary, it will be resumed by them. Each man will not have a special portion of it to call his own, *i.e.*, to have the power of preventing other people from using it; but each person will have the full share that he needs for developing his powers of producing wealth in concert with his fellows – that is, *he will have as much of the means of production as he can use.* Which means in other words that not only he need no longer have a scanty livelihood won by over-toil, but also that his livelihood *will be no longer precarious.* 'Thrift'[1] in the sense in which that much abused word is used, meaning saving, will be transferred from the individual to the community.

In short, instead of the chance which Mr. Fenwick offers to the workers as bait to them to hook themselves on to capitalism – the chance, viz., of becoming owners of a very very small share of the privilege to make people pay for the right of working, Socialism offers to every one of them his full share of all that he needs in order to work like a man and live like a man.

There is an interesting article in the current number of the *Contemporary* on the Great Depression in Trade, by Mr. Wells, which is well worth the attention of a Socialist. Beginning by pointing out what a serious blow the opening of the Suez Canal was to the warehousing business of England,

---

[1] 'Thrift' means the art of thriving, not the practice of starving yourself into a mummy while you are young to prevent the robber class from sending you to the workhouse-prison when you are old.

he goes on to show the great 'displacement' of human labour which has taken place during the last ten or twelve years, owing to the rapid strides towards the perfecting of machinery which has been forced on civilisation by the competition of the world-market. The facts he gives tend to show that the last decade has introduced a new revolution in industry (a new phase in its evolution, to speak more correctly) approaching in importance to that of the introduction of modern machinery itself, the phase of the perfectioning of machinery and the acquirement of the knowledge of its full commercial use.

Mr. Wells is a cheerful specimen of the commercial optimist, and does not trouble himself with the consequences of this new phase, except to sing in an undertone, as it were, a quiet hymn on the enormous cheapening of wares that is resulting from it. But a Socialist will be inclined to ask him, 'How long do you think you can prevent those that do work and those that could work if you would allow them, from sharing in these advantages? For if you the monopolist owners of the civilised world are so incapable of organising the labour whose fruits you are so jubilant over, that there are vast numbers of unemployed and starving people in civilised countries, and a far vaster number much below anything approaching to a reasonable standard of well-being, amidst all this so easily created wealth, then the facts condemn you as incapable to carry affairs on much longer, and you and your monopoly are hastening to an end.

One other Socialist deduction from such facts. The pace of the march towards the change in the basis of society is increasing decade by decade; if we are not prepared to deal with the crisis when it comes, we shall make but a sorry job of 'the morrow of the revolution.' Surely we ought to make no delay in doing our very utmost in getting the workers to see their real position, and as a consequence uniting together in a great and inclusive federation of labour which should form a new society under the old dying one with its parliaments and artificial 'laws' – a new society which would form habits of thought and action that would be 'laws' indeed without being called so, and which would take the place of the old society of monopoly and usurpation naturally and surely, whether that takes place with or without a dramatically obvious crisis.

Commonweal, Volume 3, Number 83, 13 August 1887, p. 257.

NOTES ON NEWS

The Government are taking credit to themselves for their Allotment Bill; and Mr. Jesse Collings, ex-Radical and now coercionist, has been buttered them all over for this 'popular' piece of legislation. Sir William Harcourt has nothing better to say about it than to twit his political opponents with inconsistency, reminding them that when a similar measure was talked of before, its furtherers were called Socialists. 'But now,' says he, 'it seems we are all Socialists.' Really this is very poor stuff; it will not be the last time by a great many that the Government, Liberal or Tory, will bait their hook with similar pieces of 'Socialistic' legislation. All one can hope is that those whom they are fishing for will learn to suck the bait off the hook without touching the latter, like wily old carp, if it is any use to them.

But as to this allotment scheme, J. S. Mill said all that was necessary when he said it was simply allowing the labourers to work to pay their own poor-rates. The bill is really in the interests of the employing farmers and the rack-renting landlords.

Mr. Bradlaugh, lecturing at the Fulham Liberal Association on 'National Economy,' is reported to have said 'that working-men were quarrelling about a small percentage on wages while they allowed this monstrous war-expenditure to eat up the bread-and-cheese that should be in their cupboards.' Yes, doubtless, the war expenditure is monstrous. Don't let workmen believe that supposing it were put an end to they would be any better off while labour and its earnings is forbidden to any one who cannot find a capitalist who can employ him. If the war-expenditure were stopped it would be necessary to find some other means of wasting the working-man's labour that would put money into the capitalists' pocket; and meantime until that others means was found, trade would be the duller for it. Under the idiotic system which oppresses us, all destruction of wares, all consumption of them, however consumed, is temporarily 'good for trade,' advantageous to the actual producer in the lump.

But, after all, it is impossible to get rid of war expenditure or of war as long as all Society is based on war, commercial war; it is the struggle for the market that arrays the battalions in the field; the *necessities* of the capitalist is what brings on war now-a-days.

As to 'the working-man quarrelling over a small percentage of wages,' if he did not do so, if he had not been doing so ever since the birth of commercialism, bread, or rather skilly without the cheese would have been his roast meat by this time. Commercial war compels the capitalist to cheapen production to the utmost, the method of cheapening it is to reduce the amount of human labour to the utmost; the ensuing competition among the workmen for employment (for since they are slaves they cannot employ themselves) keeps down wages. Any combination among the workmen checks this tendency, and is good as far as it goes; but the partial combination of trades' unions and the like *must* develope (*sic*) into general combination, which will at last assuredly destroy the war of classes which is the foundation of our Society of waste, strife, and robbery – at last – might the workers but see it at once and set on foot that great combination before the pinch of utter misery which will come of the breakdown of our short-sighted system of commercial war, a war which Mr. Bradlaugh looks on with complacency, although, as aforesaid, it is the parent of the open war which he has (very rightly) been denouncing.

The *Daily News*, commenting on the meeting of the S.D.F., which demanded the release of Pole, is really a trifle too absurd even for a bourgeois print on a Monday morning. It admits the strong case of the Socialist, but says, alluding to the hanging of Endacott in effigy: 'If they had asked for it in another way, the appeal must have commanded wide-spread attention.' In other words, according to the *Daily News*, the justice or injustice of the sentence on a citizen depends on the good or ill manners of certain other citizens who demand his release, and not on his own conduct. Really, is the *Daily News* then to be made responsible for Lord Salisbury's Coercion Act? or are we to be made responsible for the Monday morning fatuities of the *Daily News*? Here is solidarity with a vengeance.

Commonweal, Volume 3, Number 84,
20 August 1887, pp. 265–6.

NOTES ON NEWS

Mr. Thompson has been able to lay before the public in the columns of the *Echo* the evidence in the case of our comrade Pole of the S.D.F., and it must be said that if the magistrates who sentenced him to two months' hard labour have nothing to say in contradiction of the facts as there stated, they cannot clear themselves of the crime of sending an innocent man to prison, whom they must have known to be innocent.

The public can scarcely fail to see this, and another blow will be struck at this monstrous abuse of the magistrates' court with its bodyguard of professional witnesses, who, like all policemen, consider, and are bound to consider, that it is their business, if there is any breach of the peace, to get hold of a prisoner and convict him when they have got hold of him, at whatever expense to truth and justice may be necessary.

The stupidity of the police in the case of Mdlle. Drouin is only what might be expected of these gentry, and no doubt many dynamite scares have had about as good a foundation as this one; but how are honest citizens to guard themselves against it? Are we to have an artist and a chemist attached to every police centre to inform the guardians of law and order what modelling clay is, and to assure them that the only danger it is fraught with is that it may be worked up into futile and ugly images?

Among other cases of legal oppression comes the hideous tale of Mr. Justice Field and the luckless Welsh girl;

concerning which what can words do to express due indignation against such a sentence? But one thing we must
remember: these and similar cases of the injustice of the law
are being brought to light plentifully now; but we must not
suppose that they are uncommon, and that there is only by
some accident a passing shower of them at present. It cannot
be doubted that they are of constant occurrence. Nay more,
bad as they are, they are only extreme examples of the
ordinary deeds of the law; it works in this way habitually and
can work no otherwise; it is a machine constructed for the
production of injustice; that is the sober truth.

Whatever may be thought about the guilt or innocence of
Lipski, the whole circumstances of the trial call for a remark
on one point in criminal trials which jurymen should
remember, and which they are too apt to forget, that it is *they*
who are the *judges*; they, not persons educated by professional experience and – cant, into callousness and disregard
of everything but the rules of the game; but citizens and
neighbours discharging part of their daily responsibility for
the good of the community, and judging the matter by the
rules of common sense and the experience of ordinary daily
life. This is still the theory of the jury, and before centralised
bureaucracy had quite overlaid the customs of the freemen of
the tribes it was the practice also; but as things go now, the
judge oftenest usurps the function of the jury, and his
summing up is the real verdict. Let any one who sits on a
jury, especially in a criminal case, take this to heart, and, as
far as he is personally concerned, redress it.

Meantime it is a good thing that the public are having their
attention turned to its worst abuses; they will soon see that
they are helpless to cure them, if only they begin to try; for
their conception of the law is that it is an impartial power
that enforces respect to the due rights of the citizens, that it
arranges personal differences between man and man. This is

just their mistake, its real business is to defend property at the expense of personal rights.

Mr. Bradlaugh has received what may be called a new title at the hands of Lord Wemyss; he has been dubbed the 'defender of the faith,' so to say; protector of the sanctities of 'free contract' (*i.e.*, the leave to whack one's own nigger) against the original sin, which is now discovered to be a part of nineteenth century human nature, of paying some attention to the general welfare of the community. It may be doubtful as to how much Mr. Bradlaugh relishes this distinction, in spite of his anti-Socialist proclivities; it is not doubtful that the whirligig of time brings about curious revenges. Who are to be the next allies, I wonder? – Chamberlain and Salisbury, Wemyss and Bradlaugh! It is no use hazarding a guess; yet strange things may happen to Socialists if ever they get into the House of Commons, and they may have queer distinctions thrust upon them; they had better keep out of it altogether.

Commonweal, Volume 3, Number 85,
27 August 1887, p. 273.

NOTES ON NEWS

A newspaper correspondent, on a visit to the City dust-bin, seems to have been a good deal filled up by the boss there, who vaunted the superior attractions of the occupation of – well, *dirt*-shifting and stink-smelling. So that it seems we are all wrong together in our attempts at sanitation; or perhaps the dust boss was a liar, which seems on the whole the simpler explanation. Anyhow this job of dust-shifting is one of those concerning which one gets asked after lectures as to who is to do such and such things under Socialism. Well, however hard the question might be to answer as to the future, it seems to me that at present M.P.'s might work at it between the squalls. It would teach them the difference between metaphor and fact for one thing, and probably they would prefer their old habitual way of eating dirt after all. To be serious, the real job is not fit for anybody else – except the lawyers.

Mr. Bradlaugh is in luck; after being canonized by Lord Wemyss, he has received a still more important testimonial from the *Daily News* which classes him amongst 'thoroughly sound and moderate politicians'! After this it will be strange indeed if he is not a member of the coming Gladstonian Government. Some persons will think indeed that it must be rather a strain to keep up a reputation for 'soundness and moderation;' and whatever has been in the past, that will probably be true in the future, and even before very long, when when (*sic*) there will only be two parties – the party of the people and the party of reaction. You can only be moderate when it is possible to say 'perhaps' instead of 'yes' or 'no.' Which of these two latter will Mr. Bradlaugh say?

Meantime, on this Irish matter there are Gladstonians with greater claims to moderation than Mr. Bradlaugh. The meeting Liberals held recently to discuss the help to be given to the Irish in the present stress was in its moderation worthy of the study of a Moliére. Even allowing for the disclaimer of the accuracy of the report in the *Daily News*, the general tone of it must have been pretty accurately given in the report, and it is curious how anxious certain members were – especially Mr. Howell – not to commit themselves to anything definite. One need hardly warn the Irish party not to trust too much to the Gladstonian M.P.'s, they will have reckoned them up long ago; but the English democracy, which is sincere in its conversion to the cause of Irish independence, should look a little sharper after its 'representatives.'

The delusion as to the recovery of trade which was spreading, or rather, perhaps, being industriously spread, a little time ago, probably as a part of the Jubilee decorations, is vanishing with the brilliant memory of those decorations; and it has now to be confessed for one thing that the falling off in the railway receipts is serious. The coming winter will bring home the fact of the failure of expansion in English trade very sharply to the millions of the slaves of commerce. And the trading class also will be feeling more and more the result of the revolution which is going on, though neither class will know what is the real cause of the pinch, but will put it down to 'free trade,' the immigration of foreigners, and other sticks and straws that are floating on the vast current of fully-developed commercialism.

It is Socialism only that can explain the conundrum offered to us by the capitalists, 'Livelihood is so cheap that it is hard indeed to live.' Truly even when thieves are disreputable persons they are inconvenient members of society; but when successful stealing is the aim of all *respectable* persons, and thieves have got to be looked upon as benefactors of society; when legalised theft is so gloriously organised, and the art has reached such a pitch of refinement that the thieves steal their slaves ready-made, instead of buying them honestly in the market, or boldly risking their lives in battle to conquer them; then indeed the less successful of us may well find it hard to live.

Indeed even the stealing is accomplished vicariously by these full-blown geniuses in the art, for, as Mr. G. B. Shaw was explaining to us the other night, the slaves themselves are forced to offer themselves as unbought property to their masters. Ancient society, with its brutal chattel slavery, did its business with discreditable want of economy compared with capitalist civilization.

The captive Salvationists are being championed by mightier prints and persons than we can bring forward. So, little need be said about their case, though it cannot fail to be interesting to us who have been in the same trouble and shall be again. The crime for which they are punished – of speaking in public on ground that belongs to the public – is familiar enough to us, and the cause for the attack on them is one of the causes for which we were attacked – lack of respectability, to wit. We can only hope that those who are defending freedom of speech in this case will do so again when our turn comes round.

Commonweal, Volume 3, Number 86, 3 September 1887, p. 281.

NOTES ON NEWS

Mr. John Bright is very anxious to extinguish all chances of open war between England and America. To many people it seems strange that he is not equally anxious to put an end to the war which has been so long going on between England and Ireland; or rather that the only way in which he would allow it to be done would be by crushing Ireland into sullen subjection to her slavery. This is strange to many, but not to Socialists, who understand that Mr. Bright's Internationalism is, and always has been, a very one-sided matter, as one-sided as his love of peace. The Internationalism of bourgeois interests is what he is enthusiastic for, and in that cause he would try to join all the nations in the world, ignoring the fact that each nation is composed of two other nations, the nation of the poor and the nation of the rich; and the peace that he would have between these two nations is just that which he would have England give to Ireland – the peace which the master is always willing to give to his submissive slave. Mr. John Bright is a thoroughly consistent person.

The miserable optimistic twaddle of Mr. Gladstone's Jubilee speech (what, another of them?), which would have disgraced a Sunday-school teacher, is sickening enough to read for those even who have thought of the condition of the workers without the knowledge that it is caused just as much and as little by 'the infliction of the Providence of God' as the corn-laws; even when they don't know that the 'follies of men' which produced the window-tax or the corn-laws, are just as much responsible for the 'unemployed' of our present winters (of our summers, too, if well-to-do people only knew it); even to such people there seems little occasion for an optimistic hymn.

Not much of a triumph for fifty years of reform are the results of all the progress told of to his henchmen by this Conservative gentleman who has been too busy with politics to follow the struggle between capital and labour which has been going on all the time. The time remembered and contrasted with our times by the model contented old workman that he spoke of, was of the darkest days which the workmen of this country have ever known; the country had just passed through a frightful war; the robber class had begun to use the new and terrible instruments of robbery, which had recently been invented, with the utmost recklessness, and without the checks which the governing classes were terrified into applying to them afterwards; and as a consequence of the unchecked competition which Mr. Gladstone regards as 'providential' and opposes to 'the follies of man,' the whole working-class was miserable, starving, and rebellious.

Such a state of things could not last; it must either have come to a break-up or some improvement, and the improvement came through the conquering of the world-market by Great Britain, which produced such a prodigious amount of wealth for the country in general, that even the workers profited by it and became 'contented'; since the contrast between their present and the immediate past was really considerable, and their past misery so great, that they felt the same kind of happiness which the tortured man does when he is allowed some little rest. Breathing-time was thus gained for the two combatants, Capital and Labour, and the proprietary classes on their side began to see the necessity of palliation if the game were to last, and hence all those reforms of which Mr. Gladstone boasts.

But these reforms were not the cause of the 'prosperity' of the last forty years, but the prosperity was the cause of the legislation. The governing classes were frightened at first, careless afterwards since they were so rich. Like the pirates in Defoe, who had fought like devils when they were poor, they did not care to show fight when they had such a glorious cargo aboard.

Thus we came to the period of the advance of wealth 'by leaps and bounds,' which made Mr. Gladstone so joyous a little time ago; and the question one would think even for a politician to study is not so much whence we have come, as where we are now, and whither we are going. Would not the story of the last seven years furnish Mr. Gladstone with some thoughts on that point? It needs no man risen from the dead, and no half-dead old man to teach him something if he will contrast his 'leaps and bounds' year with this present Jubilee year and its blessing.

At any rate, very little consideration will teach him that the nation (of the rich) came out unscathed from the disorder of the first years of the great machine-industry revolution, because of the expansion of its profitable trade, which was then so huge that most people could see no end to it. They can now both see and feel the end to it. That ally to the exploitation of labour by the capitalists is dead. Prosperity can indeed be regained, and go on once more by leaps and bounds; but only on terms which Mr. Gladstone has not even thought of, viz., that the workers should employ themselves, or in other words, form a new society in which monopoly would be not a crime but an impossibility.

What does Mr. Gladstone, and the middle classes which he leads, think of the 'propriety' which forces people to accept the position of tramcar drivers and conductors, or servants in their yards under such conditions of slavery, and such insulting and degrading regulations that one would think that nobody but those in the very last stage of destitution would accept such an occupation? And yet we are told that free citizens of our free and improved country crowd into it, partly because it is a respectable occupation! Still more respectable, and as complete in slavery and insult, is the position of assistant in the establishment of the Universal Provider; and for this position it is necessary to share the blessings of education, and, in fact, to belong in some sense to that triumphant middle class which has improved the world into its present condition. Isn't it worth while for that class itself to look about it, and notice that it too is making a new proletariat out of itself, which at its worst degradation is worse than the fringe of labour deduced from the artisan and labouring class.

Commonweal, Volume 3, Number 87,
10 September 1887, p. 289.

NOTES ON NEWS

The affair at Mitchelstown is bad enough, but just what must be expected; quite apart from any design, from any intention on either side, such wretched murders are sure to spring out of the present state of affairs in Ireland. The people *will* meet together in spite of the Coercion Act, or even because of it; the police have orders to disperse them on some excuse or other. You can't disperse a gathering of excited men (and women) by mere politeness, and policemen, under the circumstances, knowing their position, don't waste any time in trying to do so, but throw themselves on the crowd, and hustle and hit and knock about in a way that would irritate a crowd of Jobs to resistance; and patient and over-patient as Irishmen have shown themselves, the Irish peasant is a traditional hard-hitter, and understands hand-play. So the police get their share of knocks, and get driven off perhaps, as on this occasion; and then comes the next act, which is more likely to turn the affair into a tragedy in Ireland than would be the case in a similar affair in England.

For in England, if the police were beaten off the red-coats would come on the stage, if sharp shot and cold steel were to be used or threatened; and as they would be fresh men unexcited by a preliminary contest of dry blows, they would feel their responsibility of firing on an unarmed crowd far more than men who had already come out of a rough and tumble, in which their official pride and *espirit du corps* had been humbled. In Ireland, on the other hand, the event is likely to happen which happened at Mitchelstown; the beaten police come back as soldiers, armed with deadly weapons, to take their revenge on the people, who for their part, unarmed and unorganised, feel the full force of the fierce words of the

Gothic king before Rome, when he was warned of the huge mass of people he had to deal with, 'The thicker the hay the easier to mow.'

And that all the more, by the by, if the police shoot from behind the shelter of their walls, as they did at Mitchelstown.

As to the government that allows this sort of thing to go on, by-standers can see, if they cannot, that they are not strong enough to go in for a series of new Peterloos. Probably the Irish will stand it without breaking out into open insurrection, because, as has often been said before, they have no opportunity of setting a serious rising on foot. But general public opinion in England is not in favour of government by massacre, whatever the passions of a few landowners and their backers may urge them on to. It is not difficult for an English Radical to conceive of himself in a similar position to that of the Irishmen at the Mitchelstown meeting; and he would at least be ashamed of himself it in such a case he had not gone about as far as the Irishmen did in resisting the first attacks of the police; and under the orders which the constabulary now have in Ireland from the government, it seems that murder may be expected to follow the exercise by peaceably assembled citizens of a little manliness in resisting outrage.

But the Government may say: 'Did we not pass a Coercion Bill? And does not Coercion mean killing in the long run? What are we to do?' One is driven to answer the last question by saying: 'Well, gentleman, I must say it is difficult to point out to you any course of action which would at once satisfy your desires and ours. Perhaps the least harmful thing you could do would be to hang yourselves. But even then there would still be so many fools left in this country that there would still be a government; and that government, after having performed the deeds of the new broom with applause for some time, would presently be in much the same mess as you are in, or indeed, maybe worse; for it perhaps would not have the Irish Question conveniently at hand to take people's attention off the affairs of the whole working population of these islands.'

Meantime, once more the Tory Government will soon find out that a Peterloo policy can only be carried out by the thoroughest of the thorough.

The terrible calamity at Exeter, which has taken up so much of public attention lately, is simple the outcome of the commercial system as applied to the construction of theatres: it is just of a piece with the wreck of a ship sent to sea for profits' sake unseaworthy and under-handed, or with an explosion in a mine ill-ventilated for the same reason. Profit-grinding has murdered all those unfortunates, just as certainly as it murders thousands every day by the slower death that at every step besets the life of wage-slaves, of those who allow masters to muddle away their lives for them, who allow the hurry and heedlessness of irresponsible gamblers to settle for them how they shall live and how they shall die.

The orthodox Liberal *Daily News* has been rather amusing in its utterances on the Trades Union Congress. It began by an article in which it made what was no doubt intended to be a serious hit at the Socialists: told us that the theory that we hold of the rank and file of the trades'-unionists looking doubtfully at their leaders, and beginning to consider their real position, was a delusion; that they were all of the orthodox faith, – and in short, the usual good-boy patronising exhortation. But then came the resolution of the Congress to set on foot a Labour Electoral Committee, and the *Daily News'* good boys had to have a little lecture read to them on their foolishness in taking this very mild step towards choosing their own 'representatives,' of separating themselves from 'the two great parties.'

Not very wonderful if the workmen are at last beginning to find out that the 'two great parties' are like 'the two great parties' that form up in a field before a football match – to play the game! The only pity is that they do not let them play their game all by themselves, and form their Labour Party without reference to the football-field called Parliament.

Meantime it may be said for the benefit of those readers of the *Daily News* who may also read the *Commonweal* and who do not know much of Socialism, that Socialists are not hostile to trades' unions, but to those who wish to prevent the trades' unions developing with the times. Their real enemies are those who would crystallise them into mere societies for the guaranteeing of the privilege of capitalism, and recruiting grounds for 'the great Liberal party' – that is, Whig vote-preserves. This would be an ignominious end to such an important association of workers; but it need not be dreaded. The trades' unions *will* develope (*sic*), even if in doing so they have to change their old form and be no longer recognisable by their once enemies, now their anxious allies, the Whig politicians.

Commonweal, Volume 3, Number 88,
17 September 1887, p. 297.

NOTES ON NEWS

The present example of the sickening conventionality, called a Queen's Speech, is a fine specimen of its loathsome kind, but there is nothing in it to surprise anyone. Its framers are, of course, bound to praise themselves, whatever crimes or blunders they may have committed, but that people should tamely bear such a ridiculous and preposterous piece of nonsense is a sign, if but a small one, of the rottenness of the society we live in, and a token of the baleful officialism of our dead-dog constitutional monarchy, that finds it useful to have a cloak behind which to shelter its misdeeds; even when it is a cloak that would be openly laughed at but for the cant that guards English bourgeoisdom from every breath of common sense.

Mr. Balfour's speech on the Mitchelstown massacre is accepted as meaning an endorsement of the murderous conduct of the police; that was all we wanted to know of him. His *tu quoque* to Sir William Harcourt was as effective as you please in the atmosphere of the House of Commons, but has nothing whatever to do with the question which all honest men are asking: Are you going to govern Ireland by Peterloos? Mr. Balfour answers 'Yes, if my colleagues' courage does not collapse.' A very big 'if' is that. If the age of miracles does not come back on us, the responsibility of Ireland will presently be shifted from the Tories to the Gladstonites, though perhaps the very confidence that most people have in the rapid approach of Home Rule, acting on the habitual laziness of the English papers, will yet delay it somewhat.

The feeble forcible government has made another step in Coercion by specially proclaiming illegal the Clare branches of the National League. This will make no difference to the work that body has been doing (except to keep its name before the public), since it will be taken up in another form.

Mr. Cunninghame Graham is to be congratulated on his suspension at the hands of the pantomimic actor who serves the House for Speaker at present; it is the only honour which an honest man who has strayed into that assembly can receive from it.

That political prisoners should be treated in our jails on the same footing as ordinary criminals, is certainly a piece of English brutality; but I think it is so principally because it is intended for an insult against freedom on the part of the coarse blackguards who govern us. On the other hand, if the political prisoners protest against prison-torture applied to themselves only on the ground that they are high-minded and superior persons, they show their unfitness for citizens, and their fitness for governors. To treat *any* set of men in the brutality-plus-science manner that prisoners in English jails are treated, degrades the whole nation; not merely the poor devils of warders, jailers, and the semi-military fools of governors, but the whole of society, that in its indomitable cant takes it for granted that here as in other matters England is ahead of the rest of the world, is thoroughly respectable.

Indeed what words can express the baseness of the *vicarious* cruelty that sets a body of poor wretches of the 'lower classes' to do the prison-torture for the behoof of the respectable; and these all the while know perfectly well, if they know nothing else, that their prisons are breeding-places of crime and slaughter-houses of the hope of a return to decent life; and if they choose can know that our English prisons are about the worst in Europe, and a disgrace to humanity. 'Am I my brother's keeper?' quoth Cain, and the same sneer is practically the answer which our vile respectability makes to any doubts that may be suggested to it on this matter.

The appeal of the Chicago Anarchists has been rejected; but they have a further appeal to the Supreme Court of the United States. Our friends, it may be hoped, will remember that the evidence on which they were convicted of the bomb-throwing or complicity with it, was quite worthless; and that the conduct of the police on the occasion was simply an exaggeration of that of the police in the first act of the Mitchelstown tragedy; only the American police used deadly weapons from the first. In spite of all this, it is only too probable that these men who have dared to speak of freedom to the republican people of America, will be sacrificed to that spirit of cold cruelty, heartless and careless at once, which is one of the most notable characteristics of American commercialism.

Commonweal, Volume 3, Number 89,
24 September 1887, p. 305.

NOTES

Mr. Chamberlain's meeting at Birmingham went off as well as might be expected; the malcontents were few, although the meeting was a free open one (according to Mr. Chamberlain, although admission was by ticket) and it was scarcely to be expected there would be no malcontents. As to Mr. Chamberlain himself he chiefly dwelt on the blocking the way by the Irish question, though he gave no sign of recurring to his demi-semi Socialism of two years ago.

The truth is, all that is a mere pretence for carrying on a private and personal war, and it must be once more said of the Chamberlain section as of their allies, the Tories and Whigs, and of a great part of their enemies, the Gladstonians, for the matter of that, that the Irish Question is a godsend to them simply *because* it blocks the way to the consideration of English matters.

If English matters are at some future time to be dealt with, to judge by one part of Mr. Chamberlain's speech, he is anxious that they should be dealt with 'sweetly as to manner' at least, however strongly as to matter. Since, perhaps somewhat stimulated by the frankness of the wording of the interruptions, he expressed himself anxious for fresh and thorough gagging arrangements in the House itself.

He did not suggest any improvement in the office of Speaker in that august assembly, no doubt because he felt that from *his* point of view an improvement was scarcely possible. After all in this matter Mr. Chamberlain is logical; if coercion is good for those who differ from Mr. Chamberlain in Ireland, it must also be good for those who differ from Mr. Chamberlain in the House of Commons. His weak point is that to insist on good manners in the House will hardly suit his Tory friends.

Michael Lane and his brother-in-law O'Grady, not forgetting his wife, are champions after the heart of the old Norse story-tellers, whose matchless talent in that line is much needed in the tale of these Irish matters; and the kind of fighting courage of the opened door and the charge on the police explains the story of many a desperately won victory of the *English* army in which *Irishmen* were the main actors; but doubtless strong faith in the goodness of the cause must have been at the back of such courage, which could drive a man on to have at least one blow at his oppressors, even when he knew that if he escaped alive from the mauling he was sure to get, the prison was to follow.

How *very* queer our English has come to be in the penny-a-liner's hand by the way; the newspaper report of the affair told us that Lane beat the police *mercilessly* about the head. Spirit of Defoe, teach us some other word for the charge of two men on two hundred!

The Lord Mayor of Dublin and Mr. O'Brien are to be prose-cuted for publishing reports of suppressed branches of the Land League in their respective papers, 'United Ireland' and the 'Nation.' This is as it should be; this is to understand coercion as far as it goes. When shall we see a Lord Mayor of London in the dock for resistance to arbitrary authority?

In our debate on Socialism, Mr. Bradlaugh took exception to Bax's statement of the tendency of manufacturing capital to aggregation; and our friend Bax, when challenged to produce examples of this process, did not go much out of his way to do so; probably because he did not think it worth while to defend a statement which he might well think that nobody but the Pope (or Mr. Bradlaugh) would be bold enough to attempt to controvert. But since some persons are staggered by the use of a distinguished name, however reckless or foolish the bearer of the said name may be, I venture (once more) to supplement my friend Bax in this matter, and quote again from Mr. David A. Wells' article in the *Contemporary Review*.

Says he: 'The now well ascertained and accepted fact (not accepted by Mr. Bradlaugh it seems) that power is most economically applied when applied on the largest possible scale, is rapidly and inevitably leading to the concentration of manufacturing in the largest establishments and the gradual extinction of those which are small. A cotton mill which with a profit (formerly not unusual) of a half-penny a yard could easily pay 10 per cent. per annum on a given capital, with a reduction of profit to a quarter of a cent. per yard would have to make and sell four times the number of yards to earn the same gross profits; which even then would fall very far short of paying the former rate of per-centage on the increased capital, machinery, buildings, etc., necessary to effect the increased production.'

He goes on to show that this concentration is *forced* on the manufacturers, and takes sugar as an example, pointing out that the turn-over which some time ago would have made a decent business would not now enable it to live. 'The successful refiner of sugar to-day in place of being, as formerly, a manufacturer exclusively, must now as a condition of full success, be his own importer, do his own lighterage, own his own wharfs and warehouses, make his own barrels and boxes, prepare his own bone-block, etc. etc.... It is not therefore to be wondered at that under the advent of these new conditions, one half of the sugar refineries that were in operation in the sea-board cities of the United States in 1875 have since failed or discontinued operations.'

He quotes the *Statist*: 'It is a characteristic and noteworthy feature of banking in Germany, that the bulk of the business is gradually shifting from the small bankers, who used to do a thriving business, to the great banking companies, leaving quite a number of small customer[s] almost without any chance to prosper in legitimate operations – concentration of capital and business in the hands of a limited number of powerful customers being the rule of the day.'

Small ships, he tells, are no longer built, owing, amongst other things, to the economy in manning, brought about by the use of large ones. 'The Directory of American Millers for 1886 shows a decrease in the number of flour mills in the United States for that year as compared with 1884 of 6,812 out of a total in the latter year of 25,079, but an increase at the same time in capacity for flour production. The legitimate inference from these statistics therefore is that the small flour-mills of the United States are being crushed, or forced into consolidation with larger companies.'

He says that it was hoped and thought that one result of the war that ended in 1865 would be the substitution of small yeoman farmers for big plantations in cotton cultivation; but that it has been found by experience that the small cultivator cannot live at all. I could go on multiplying these examples, but I have perhaps said enough to prove that water does not naturally run up hill, even though it may be necessary for the theories of Mr. Bradlaugh that it should. Both these two articles by Mr. David A. Wells are well worth studying by a Socialist.

Commonweal, Volume 3, Number 91,
8 October 1887, p. 321.

NOTES

Mr. Champion's address at the Church Congress was as well received as could be expected, although very naturally a meeting largely composed of officials, was much disturbed at his attack on the head official, the Queen. A more or less friendly critic remarked that Socialism proposed to give plenty and wealth to everybody, but neglected their spiritual condition. To a non-ecclesiastical mind a good foundation for a sound spiritual condition would appear to be the common-place virtue called honesty, and, unless the Church Congress is much belied by the reporters, that virtue seems to be too common-place to be noticed by these providers for the spiritual life of the nation. The spirit of the meeting, especially during the discussion of that most spiritual question of tithes, was decidedly in accordance which (*sic*) the ancient motto, Get all you can, and keep what you get.

A Mr. Grier said, however, with much truth, that the English people, from the days of Hengist and Horsa to those of Lord Randolph Churchill and Burmah, was always ready to take everything they could lay their hands on. Well, the proverb, 'Like people, like priest,' is a good one, but Mr. Grier must remember it has two edges; and I must come back to my text and say that the most spiritual persons *ought* to be the most honest – though they seldom are.

One genius said that he feared that behind the apparently-innocent appearance of Socialism the livid spectre of Communism lay hid. This reminds me of an agreeable scene enacted at a rather stormy open-air meeting at which I was present, when a furious opponent said, 'Why, at this rate you will be approving of the deeds of the Paris Commune.' Whereat a reverend and much respected comrade sprang forward and addressed this retailer of stale news much as follows: 'Sir, you have made a most remarkable discovery, a most remarkable discovery! Sir, I beg to congratulate you on your remarkable discovery! Sir, you are a fool!'

Mr. Arch, in addressing a great meeting of field-labourers, has been lamenting the sacking of Messrs. Fenwick and Burt, and, taking his cue from the respectable Liberal papers, has been telling them that it is probably a piece of treachery – the work of Tory intrigue and so forth. Why does Mr. Arch talk such nonsense, when he either knows the real facts or can easily find them out if he does not? He need not profess fear of the Northumbrian miners turning Tories: but if he thinks it a misfortune that they should turn Socialists he has considerable cause for fear.

Perhaps no Government ever took so little by an attack on freedom as the present Tory Government have taken in prosecuting Lord Mayor Sullivan; the defeat was so overwhelming that the only excuse the Government prints could find was in the stupidity of their own officials. It has given the Nationalists an opportunity for a most successful demonstration at the cheapest possible price. For the rest, though one finds it hard to help smiling at the spectacle of the Lord Mayor, attended by mace and sword, a prisoner in the police court, yet it is a good augury of the time when local bodies shall find themselves in formal opposition to the stupid centralisation, which a little time ago seemed to be all triumphant.

The news of the 'Socialist Disturbance' in New York demands explanation. That the American police should break up a Socialist meeting with the most brutal violence is nothing remarkable, unfortunately, even setting aside their exploits at Chicago, for they are on the whole the most brutal of all the defenders of law and order. But what explanation can there be of Mr. Henry George's followers attacking the Socialists except that that gentleman has ratted and joined the Capitalist camp? Definitely as we Socialists differ from Mr. George, this would be a great disappointment to some of us, since he has always been put forward as a specially honest man and a lover of progress in all forms.

Commonweal, Volume 3, Number 92,
15 October 1887, p. 329.

NOTES ON NEWS

The bourgeois press is very busy in making the least of the demonstrations of the unemployed in London and in telling us that the crowds who assemble to show themselves in the streets are composed largely of persons who would not work if they could. Now it may at once be admitted that there are such men among them, although the crowd is mostly composed of men only too anxious to work. But who makes these loafers loaf? That is the question. Everybody knows that when a manual worker has been long out of work he gets 'soft.' The terrible discouragement of having to look for work day after day with very slight prospect of finding it takes the heart out of him; and in time he loses all capacity of seeking for work, and is then the loafer whom false society has made, and whom she punishes for existing.

Also, trite as the observation is growing, one must really say that it ill befits a 'society' that rewards some people so munificently for doing nothing, to insult and oppress the *poor* people who won't work to earn the semi-starvation wages which it offers them. Let us admit that it *is* a crime to live without producing, and accept the consequences that flow from that admission, to wit, that a society that will not allow men to work though they want to is the very essence of this criminality, and is of no good except to rebel against.

The police-onslaughts of Friday the 14th inst., and the following days, is of evil augury for the coming winter. They are to be, it seems, as ever, not the servants of the public, engaged in guarding peaceful citizens against accident, but the servants of a peevish and easily frightened minority, and the masters of all the rest of us whose arbitrary bidding we are to do under penalty of suffering immediate corporal violence, which as G. B. Shaw said at South Place, we may seek a remedy for *after* we have suffered it. Really if this is to go on we might as well live in Moscow – or Chicago. We might as well be Russian peasants – or American citizens.

The accompanying extract from the Chicago *Morning News*, shows how right the speakers were at the South Place meeting in their view that the prisoners were condemned not for their deeds but for their opinions:

> The address of A. R. Parsons, the condemned Anarchist, to 'the American people' is by no means unworthy of perusal. For the most part, it is quite as argumentative and dispassionate in tone as could be reasonably expected from a man who stands in the shadow of the gallows. We doubt not it will evoke sympathy from very many who are incapable of coping with the adroit reasoning of the author. Beyond the line covered by this special pleading, however, there remains the great, stubborn fact that Parsons cast his fortunes with the enemies of law and order; that the whole drift of his life during the two years which preceded the Haymarket horror was in the direction of anarchy; that his teachings, if they meant anything at all, were provocative of riot and murder. Such at least was the judgment of a jury of his peers. Such also was the judgment of the highest court of appeals. The law which Parsons sought to overthrow is rightly regarded as the great bulwark protecting the rights of the citizen. With scrupulous regard for his every equality the verdict has been made up. Nothing is likely now to alter his fate.

A friend told me this morning that speaking to some American acquaintances on this subject they answered his expostulations by saying something like this: 'Ah, but you forget that Most has published a most atrocious book against society.' This is exactly the spirit of the Chicago trial. One man has written a book, so seven others are to be hanged for it. The American bourgeoisie are well know to be an inventive set of people; but surely this 'short method of dealing with political opponents' is the cutest of all their inventions. Mr. Balfour had best learn from such passed masters in the art of suppression of free speech.

Commonweal, Volume 3, Number 93, 22 October 1887, p. 337.

NOTES ON NEWS

The continued violent and brutal attacks made on the public by the police have added another element to the demonstrations of the Unemployed: a deliberate attack on the freedom of speech is now being made. The respectability of London is, it would seem, so terrified at the sight of the misery it has created that at all hazards it must be swept out of sight. So the police have, it cannot be doubted, received orders to fall upon any assembly of ill-dressed persons who may have the temerity to assemble together to try to find out why they are ill-dressed and half-starved. These wickedly rash people they are to beat, kick, and otherwise ill-use as much as possible on the spot, and they are also to bring home a bag of game in the form of anyone they can catch who is ill-dressed enough to be considered a criminal at sight: it being quite a minor consideration as to whether he has taken any part in the 'riot,' since the police themselves are always ready with any amount of evidence that may be necessary for the conviction of the criminal (who has certainly committed the crime of being poor) before the Nupkins of the hour.

All this is done, it must be repeated, just to drive the symptoms of the disease which is eating out capitalistic society below the surface – for a month or two; and if in the process the right of public meeting and free speech receives such a blow as nothing but the most vigorous protest will remedy, what does it matter? For these people are not a long way off, like the Irish cottars; their woes are very unpicturesque; and though in fact they bear the old historic name of proletarians, well known to Rome when she was sickening for her death, the English Liberal thinks not of the history but the nuisance of them, as, if he were living in Ireland, he would think of those valiant Celts, over whom Mr. Gladstone has thrown his cloak, and thereby made them respectable.

This is a very poor game for the Great Liberal Party to play, but it seems it is good enough for persons blinded by the base political struggle, the great game of ins and outs. Meantime, are there no Radicals who remember something of their old traditions, of dislike of officialism, of resistance to arbitrary authority? If that is so, then it is a clear case that the Socialists are the only body of men in these islands who have any regard for liberty.

Or what do they think about the dictum quoted by the Bow Street Nupkins in sentencing the 'rioters' for allowing themselves to be knocked about by the police? which, stripped of its verbiage, amounts to this, that when the police (the servants of the public) are running a-muck it is the business of peaceable citizens to prove on the spot, when they are under the batons of these philosophers, that they are peaceable citizens, and, if they don't, that they may be sent to prison for their carelessness: so that they had better not go out of their houses at all, for fear lest they should fall in with one of the guardians of Law and Order.

On this maxim the police are now acting; but fortunately in the hurry of the moment they have sometimes attacked persons of undoubted respectability. More power to their elbows in so doing! since if that goes on we shall still be allowed, perhaps, to hold out-door meetings without the accompaniment of a probable cudgelling on Saturday and a sentence on Monday.

Our friends of the Social Democratic Federation have issued a manifesto concerning the unemployed, which all Socialists must read with interest. It must be said of it that if it were possible for a bourgeois government to carry out the proposals contained in it, they are very reasonable ones considering the present condition of society; and one would think that the bourgeois themselves, those of them at least who have any real good-will towards working-men, and don't class them all as mere necessary nuisances, would be of that opinion. But then no capitalist government will attempt to carry out any one of them, and in truth it *could* not do so. These proposals all attack the sacredness of 'free contract' between the master who gives men leave to work on payment of a sufficient tribute, and refuses it on any other terms, and the workman who must work or die; and the maintenance of this holy law is the one function of a capitalistic government.

Therefore, it seems to me that our friends ask either too much or too little. Even a transitional administration (if such a thing be possible) would give much more, because it must be said (as our friends would doubtless admit) that if all these demands were granted the workers would still be in a condition of miserable slaves; while on the other hand, as aforesaid, the maximum which a capitalistic government would or could grant would be a wretched concession of mere 'charity' or out a-door relief. That concession will have to be made, whether or no, and therefore to my mind it is a mistake for Socialists to take steps which may mix them up in the granting of this misery of a concession.

One can easily imagine the song of triumph and self-congrat-ulation which the capitalist government will set up when it has been forced to set on foot a few relief works with pauper wages for payment of the workers. 'We are all Socialists now,' will be the cry, 'what do you cantankerous revolu-tionists want now?' 'What do we want?' we shall have to answer, 'Why all that we have always wanted, the Freedom of Labour, the abolition of private property in the means of production?' I think that answer will come clearer from us if we have allowed the capitalists to grant the palliatives they could not help granting. Don't let us mind their gaining what transient credit they can gain from such measures; it will soon pass away. 'The poor ye have always with you,' is the doom of capitalism.

'The police have adopted a milder bearing towards the crowds,' say the *Daily News* of October 24th, after Sunday's events. In other words, the police have been beaten once more, and have had to give way before the gathering indignation of the public, and probably also before the task of bludgeoning a *Sunday* crowd, more numerous than a mere week-day one. The *Daily News*, the advocate of free speech in Ireland and of the suppression of free speech in England, has a good deal to say on the subject, which, however, doesn't come to much in the teeth of the fact that all that the objectors to police violence put forward has been proven true by events. During the week small bodies of men met, and were attacked by the police, so there was 'rioting'; on the Sunday large bodies of men met, and there was apparently well-founded fear in some people's minds that there would be a great disturbance, but there was none. Why? Because, in the words of the *Daily News*, 'the police have adopted a milder bearing toward the crowd' – that is, they have not made a riot as they did on the other days.

Now that the police have proved themselves a set of ruffianly rioters, and that Sir Charles Warren has written himself down an ass in characters which he who runs may read, surely even the Law-and-Order (in England) *Daily News* will admit that it is preposterous to keep the citizens in prison whom the Bow Street and other Nupkinses have sentenced to one, three, and six months' hard labour for performing their duty as citizens. The only question is what compensation is to be made to them for the ill-treatment of the police and the police-court, and with what amount of ignominy Nupkins and Co. are to be dismissed.

The scene has shifted to Ireland again. Mr. Wilfred Blunt has received the diploma of honour which the policeman's hand gives now-a-days, and with him Mr. John Roche, the President of the local Association. The *Daily News* will (of course) condemn their resistance to undoubted *legal* authority, but we shall congratulate them for serving the same cause as the poor workmen in London are serving.

Once more an Irish policeman, Connor, has shown that he is a man by refusing at his own peril to fall on harmless and unarmed citizens. Such men give one hopes for the Social Revolution, and the heroism which will be necessary to carry it through.

I see that one or two geniuses have been writing to the *Pall Mall Gazette* proposing a scheme for inveigling the unemployed into the ranks of the British army: that noble body of warriors which is at present to act as burglars abroad and bum-bailiffs at home – since Ireland is still 'united' to England – and whose future function will be perhaps the attempted suppression of rising liberty in England. Well, I doubt if the cock will fight; but if any workmen are driven by starvation into the army, let them at least remember what they were, and like the gallant man mentioned in the note last above, refuse to attack their brethren if they should be called on to do so.

Commonweal, Volume 3, Number 94,
29 October 1887, p. 345.

NOTES ON NEWS

Mr. Wilfred Blunt is to go to prison for asserting the rights of free speech in Ireland. Well and good so far; but surely he is not to be the only one of the English Home Rulers who is going through this business: one could name half-a-dozen who would be fitter for the task than Mr. Blunt, who is a 'faddist', which is the political jargon for a man who has some idea of justice outside mere party necessities, as witness Arabi and the Egyptian matter. Let some of the orthodox show the genuineness of their convictions on coercion, and for once be of some service to the cause of progress that they profess. It will be a shabby business indeed if they don't share the glory and discomfort with the candidate for Deptford.

Or the Balfour will score a victory, and the process may be a long one. But once for all there is a method of shortening the struggle, or rather of finishing it at one blow, which, strange to say, has not suggested itself to any Gladstonian partisan yet. Though I believe my following suggestion will not be accepted as the Columbus egg-trick by the whole Home Rule Liberal Party if, as is doubtful, they happen to read the *Commonweal*, yet it certainly should be so accepted.

Let Mr. Gladstone go over to Ireland and follow Mr. Wilfred Blunt's example, and coercion is at an end, and the Tory Government along with it.

Yes, I know the orthodox will receive this as an unworthy joke; but the very fact that they will do so, and that I have been obliged to put it as a joke, shows how lightly politicians treat the matters which they talk about so solemnly. Here we have them gravely discussing the legality or illegality of Mr. Blunt's action when they know very well that he went to do what was at once illegal and reasonable. If Mr. Gladstone were to do the like, how the unreasonable legality would vanish amidst roars of laughter, and the discussion about Home Rule and the squeezing of rent from people who *can't* pay would enter on a new phase. But it is a joke to propose if for that very reason. It would crush the Tory party, and to do that is exactly what the orthodox Liberals will by no means do. A famous chess-player doesn't want to exterminate his adversary; or who is he to play with? He wants to beat him at the *game*, that is all. If there were no Tories to play with and make about the same moves as the Liberals, the latter might have to deal with *realities* – and what would they do then?

I repeat, let the great man go to Ireland and get arrested for speaking on the side of freedom at Woodford or elsewhere, and thereby put his political opponents in the deepest hole any government were ever in, and himself become the most popular man of the century.

Says a correspondent of the *Daily News*, 'When any disturbance does occur it is the police that begin it.' It is not London that he is speaking of but Woodford in Ireland; that is, doubtless, because he has not been in London for the last three weeks.

Mr. Chabmerlain's (*sic*) expression of passionate devotion to law-and-order is touching, coming as it does from the man who gave that warning to the rich about ransom. And it must be said that, if there is anything genuine about him at all, probably this latter view of his is a genuine one; he is

what the cabman once called the almost forgotten Robert
Lowe (now Lord something or other) 'a harbitrary gent.'

———————

Poor Samuel Huby has had very bad luck with Mr. Nupkins-
Mansfield. The policeman in the attack on the citizens of
October 20th, hit him and he very naturally hit the
policeman, who being knocked down either received or
imagined a kick. Huby explained that the policeman hit him
three times and knocked him down; but though his old
master came forward and gave him a good character, and
though the policeman himself said: 'he seems to be a
respectable and very good lad,' yet the *thing* on the bench
paid no more attention to his statement than if it had been
the wind blowing, and had the impudence to remark in the
true Nupkins style, 'It would be a most improbable thing for
the constable to strike you without provocation.' So Mr.
Huby got three months' hard labour in order to increase his
affection for the beauties of law and order. I don't know if
he was a Socialist before his introduction to the Nupkins of
Marlborough Street; but I should think he would lose no
time in becoming one now.

———————

The *Daily News* is very severe on the deputation sent on the
28th October to the Board of Works, for what is called their
'Jack Cade' behaviour there; but may there not be another
side to that story? Suppose that the deputation were treated
by the majority of the board with that circumlocution-office
off-handedness which is a standing insult to the citizen, and
which everybody having business with an official body is
sure to receive, as I by personal experience can declare, unless
he is known as a 'person of importance'. If that were the
case, is it wonderful that men on such serious business as the
trying to get work in order to prevent them from starving,
should show some resentment at this supercilious bad
manners, not knowing perhaps that such bad manners are
habitual and a part of what we pay for. The representatives
of a vast body of starving men don't to my mind need

forgiveness if they lose their temper when brought face to face with the brazen wall of official impudence and unreason, which even Dickens' immortal humour failed to shake by a hairs'-breadth.

———————————————

The police have been spinning if not one of the longest, yet at least one of the stupidest of galley yarns on record about Clan-na-Gael conspirators and jubilees, and lodgings and swell hotels, and the Lord knows what, clearly under instructions and for the purpose of discrediting the Home Rule agitation. Stupid as it is, it will no doubt be an effective weapon as far as it goes, that is, it will frighten some timid voters who take everything for gospel which they see in an official report. But, really, was it worth the wear and tear?

Commonweal, Volume 3, Number 96,
5 November 1887, p. 353.

NOTES ON NEWS

The Supreme Court of the United States has refused to grant
a writ of error in the case of the condemned of Chicago, and
as I write there is nothing between them and the gallows
except the will of the Governor of Illinois, who can, if he
pleases, commute their sentence. The Press is already
gloating on the preparations for their slaying with that base
pruriency which is one of the most horrible symptoms of the
degradation which the criminal law-courts brings on civilised
humanity. Before the date of this issue of the *Commonweal*
the people of America will have decided upon one of the
most momentous events in their history. It is a hope against
hope that they will yet give themselves a chance of repairing
the injustice they have already done to our friends, and that
yet some ray of intelligence may pierce to the dull brains of
the money-lords there; so I will yet express a hope, so likely
to be falsified before this appears in print.

If not, what can one say but that social crimes do of necessity
bear their fruits and prepare a natural and inevitable
punishment which no institution or law can bar. I say this to
the well-to-do people of America: If you are sure that henceforward the working-men of your country will live placid and
happy lives then you need think no more of the murder you
have committed; for happy people cannot take vengeance,
however grievously they have been wronged. But if it be so
with you as with other nations of civilisation, that your
workers toil without reward and without hope, oppressed
with sordid anxiety for mere livelihood, deprived of the due
pleasures of humanity, if there is yet suffering and wrong
amongst you, then take heed! increase your army of spies and
informers, hire more reckless swashbucklers to do your will,

guard every approach to your palace of pleasure without scruple and without mercy – and yet you will but put off for a while the certain vengeance of ruin that will overtake you, and your misery and suffering, which to you in your forget-fulness of your crimes will then seem an injustice, will have to be the necessary step on which the advance of humanity will have to mount to the happier days beyond. You yourselves will have made it necessary by making people unhappy and then punishing them for their unhappiness. You have sown the wind, you must reap the whirlwind.

The shopkeepers in the neighbourhood of Trafalgar Square are once again very angry; and under the very natural impression that the Square belongs to them and no one else, or at anyrate should do so, they are petitioning to prohibit meetings there. Before the meeting at Exeter Hall took place they are reported to have determined that if the request was not acceded to they would take other and more drastic measures for helping themselves. I don't see how they can take more 'drastic' measures for helping themselves (to other people's earnings) than they already have taken; but I suppose they mean that they will hire roughs to keep the peace in Trafalgar Square by breaking heads; which may turn out a rather dangerous game for them. Perhaps they will go further, and imitate their brethren on the other side of the Atlantic, and get up another Pinkerton army here; they will find that very convenient no doubt; but it will have the disadvantages of war – in the long run the knocks wouldn't be all on one side.

In the meantime if their businesses have suffered from the meetings of the unemployed, whose fault is it? Whose, but those who raised the ridiculous outcry in the press about the dangerous attitude of the demonstrators, who were perfectly peaceable until they had to defend themselves against the police? Whose but those who hounded on the police against the peaceable people?

And yet it lies deeper than that; if there were no unemployed, no poor in short, there would be no rich shopkeepers dealing in wares that nobody wants, but for which they can manage to teaze a price out of the vacant lives of the rich who live on the labour of others.

However it is not unlikely that this Exeter Hall attack on free speech is part of a regular conspiracy of coercion, which the Government and its allies are on the point of setting on foot, irritated by their disgraces in the Irish campaign. The double arrest of our comrade Allman and the arrest of others points to this; and the morning's paragraph makes its pretty certain that so it is. 'It is understood that the matter under discussion [at the interviews between Matthews and Lord Salisbury and Matthews and Warren and Howard] was the measures which the Government are resolved to take regarding the continued assemblies in Trafalgar Square, and the use of seditious language.'

We Socialists will have every reason to thank the Government if they put such a clear and simple issue before us as the freedom of speech, and we believe that we also shall find allies in this case as in the affair of Dod Street. The Tories should remember that what drew that enormous crowd into the streets was the certainty in the public mind that the police had interfered with the meetings not because they inconvenienced the public, but because the authorities did not like the opinions of the speakers at them. Since then, when we have been harassed by the police, we have been informed with all official solemnity that we were brought before the magistrates not for opinion, but for that remarkable elastic offence, obstruction. It will be a good thing if the mask is at last stripped off, and we find ourselves attacked for doing what we *must* do, telling our fellow-citizens the truths we have learned, and urging them to accept their consequences.

At first sight all this fussing and fuming at the peaceful meeting of a few hundred unarmed and unorganised men in the streets seems so cowardly and foolish as to be difficult to understand. But what we have to remember is this. It is not a riot, even a serious one, which the authorities are afraid of; they have ample force to quell it at once; and perhaps would not be sorry to show what organised force could do, and to have an opportunity of striking terror into the hearts of the discontented. It is not what goes on in the open street that is alarming our masters, but what is happening in the workshop, the factory, and the counting-house. The spectre of coming *ruin* is rising up behind the dusky procession of the unemployed, and its 'still small voice' is being heard amidst their cries and the answering bluster of the lords of society. Coercion is a good weapon in the hands of a class whose business is going well, and when all is prosperous with it; but then in such times it seldom has to be used, for then the poor are helpless. When the complaint of the poor forces itself on the ears of the rich it is a certain sign that, however unconsciously, they are aiming at better days to come. The Fear of the Rich is the Hope of the Poor.

Our masters are not so much afraid of what their slaves *mean* to do as of what they will be *forced* to do. It was not the hope of the glory of conquest that urged the tribes of the North to fall on the effete Roman Empire, but hunger rather; and so it will be again. And yet in our days when the force behind the workers grows strong enough, their aim will grow clear, because they *are* the workers and must reconstruct as well as destroy; the stir amongst them throughout civilisation is as much a sign of their growing knowledge as of their growing necessity. The Government will do well to put down *sedition, i.e.*, the *sowing of revolt* – if it can.

'Bombs have been "discovered" in Lingg's cell,' says an American telegraph, 'and a revulsion of feeling has been caused against the condemned man.' Indeed! Who put the bombs there? Is this not proof rather of the disgrace of the American capitalists? Does it not make it certain that there was no case against the men when authority is forced to resort to such base and clumsy shifts as this to justify its murder?

Henry George approves of this murder; do not let anybody waste many words to qualify this wretch's conduct. One word will include all the rest – TRAITOR!!

Commonweal, Volume 3, Number 96,
12 November 1887, p. 361.

[UNTITLED PARAGRAPH]

The Bermondsey Radical who wrote to Mr. Gladstone was doubtless disappointed with the answer, but it was very simple of him to be so. The question of the rights of the people is not a party matter, and therefore Mr. Gladstone can pay no attention to it. Nevertheless, the answer is useful; and there is even a glimmer of honesty about it, since Mr. Gladstone really says in it that if he were in the same position as the present Government is, he would do pretty much the same, *i.e.*, put down public meetings when they were inconvenient to 'Society.' Radicals might take note of this!

Commonweal, Volume 3, Number 97,
19 November 1887, p. 375.

CORRESPONDENCE

Will you kindly answer the subjoined questions in the next issue of your paper? I am preparing a paper on 'Socialism Practically Considered,' as you will see by [my] enclosed card. An answer to my inquiries will materially assist me in the formation of a correct judgment of the issues involved:–
1. What is Socialism?
2. Its aim and object?
3. How to be attained?
Also quote a work that would give the information I require?
– I am, etc.,
78A, Park Street, N.W., Nov. 9th   T. H. S.

[The above is a genuine example of a class of letter we are constantly receiving. We do not wish to discourage any enquirer, hostile or otherwise, but must point out that it is hopeless to attempt to master a subject like Socialism in a few days, and then to get up and explain it all! Those of us who have spent years in the study of the social problem, and who find every day new fields for study and research, are aghast sometimes at the unreasoning audacity of those who expect to deal with Socialism as lightly as a juggler with a handkerchief, and who expect the whole matter to be pressed into three small pills to be swallowed at a gulp! Knowledge, *even* on Socialism, must be *learnt* to be of use, and not taken ready-made. Grönlund's 'Co-operative Commonwealth' (Sonnenschein, 2s), and Mrs. Besant's 'Essays on Socialism' (Freethought Publishing Company, 2s.6d.) may be recommended to a beginner.]

Commonweal, Volume 3, Number 97,
19 November 1887, p. 375.

NOTES ON NEWS

The swearing-in of the Specials will recall to some of the older amongst us the similar panic caused by the last great demonstration of waning Chartism in 1848. But the rush into the ranks of the amateur police was much more energetic then. A certain amount of fun was poked at these heroes by the *Punch* of the period, which though bourgeois enough was both funnier and less completely flunkey than it is now. *E.g.*, one drawing of Leech's exhibited an unhappy little Special about to enter into conflict with a brawny and contemptuous drayman, and fortifying his courage by saying to him: 'Now, you know if I kill you it's nothing; but if you kill me, by George, it's murder!'

It is much to be hoped, by the way, that the real police, who, as we have abundance of reason to know, are in a very bad temper, will not vent any of it on their amateur brethren; that they won't look upon them as 'knob-sticks' and interlopers; that they won't in consequence hit them a knock on the sly when their badges are not very visible; that they won't detail them for warm corners amongst Socialists and Irishmen, and let them take care of themselves there, to find out by experience that 'the policeman's life is not a happy lot.' This would be spiteful and unpleasant of them, but *so* natural, that we are bound to hope that it won't take place.

On the other hand are the special constables all prepared to imitate the conduct of the police, now become so flagrant to all honest people? Is Sir Frederick Leighton going to knock down a woman; to scale a tottering old man, some relic of '48 perhaps; to beat a man on the ground wherever the baton can be got in when he is held by three or four other defenders of law and order; to thrash a defenceless prisoner in the midst of his foemen; to insult a high-spirited and brave man in the police-cell, and to beat him into senselessness if he retorts by word or look? Because all this is Sir Charles Warren's view of the duties of the English policemen at present, and as long as they have to deal with unarmed men.

I can suggest another course of action which really might come well within the four corners of the oath which these British Lions have to take before they can be trusted with the baton and the badge. How would it be if they were to translate 'keeping the Queen's peace' in this way?

> If I see the police attacking a procession of unarmed men going on their lawful errands, even if I don't agree with their political opinions, I shall feel it my duty to take their side and help to defend them from the police.
> If I see a policeman knock down a peaceful defenceless person I shall feel it my duty to arrest him and call on all citizens to help me.
> If any such horrors of cowardice come to my notice as beating and insulting prisoners, either when just taken or (still worse) in the police cell, I will pursue the wretches who practice such shameful atrocities to the utmost.
> If I am told off to prevent the people from making use of their own property, I will not prevent them, but will do all in my power to help them to keep the meeting orderly.
> In short I will do my best to keep the peace and to hinder peace-breakers even if they wear blue coats and numbers.

I offer these suggestions to Sir Frederick Leighton and the other military bourgeois now invested with the badge. But I confess I am afraid that they understand that the Government has called on them to *break* the peace and not to *keep* it. Yet even so I do still call upon them to act according to some of the hints above given. At least let them determine not to strike non-combatants, and not to maul men on the ground or insult helpless prisoners, and so be honourable enemies if they must be enemies. I admit that even if they go so far as this they will run some risk of finding themselves prisoners; for they will be expected to do the worst of all these things. Indeed it is for their own sakes and not for ours that I make this appeal to them; for I cannot think that they will be a very dangerous army. I wish them to spare themselves the dishonour of going down to posterity as the most shameful set of fools and poltroons that have ever disgraced English history – scoundrels as bad as the whores and pimps of Versailles in '71, or the cold and bloodthirsty cheats of Chicago to-day.

———————————

As to the professional police, what are we to liken them to? There is a story of the Wars of the Jews, I think in the book of Maccabees, of King Antiochus their great persecutor, and how he made his elephants drunk and then set them on a defenceless crowd. Just so has the Woman-queller Warren made *his* elephant, the police, drunk, opened the door of its cage, and bid it run amuck; and no doubt, being a religious man, as I hear, thanks God for the victory thus won. So I think it is not so much the unhappy drunken elephant we can hate, though we must certainly defend ourselves against him, as the king who has set him on – if indeed we can hate even him, a lump of wood and pipeclay, inspired with military duty, so-called, to take the place of intelligence and conscience. How long are we to be forced to bear the dominion of the class which in its turn has made him?

———————————

Concerning the sentence of Ingham and Vaughan at their drum-head court-martial – their stupid iniquity; the gross flunkeyism which drew from Mr. Poland an elaborate apology to Mr. Burleigh for the same offence for which Oldland had a year's imprisonment allotted to him; the collapse of the prosecution against Mr. Saunders, and its idiotic comicality – what are we to say of all this, except that it reveals even to the simple and unsuspecting the foundation on which 'Society' (so-called) is built – to wit, fraud and brute-force.

Cunninghame Graham has done his utmost to wipe off the reproach of the Radical M.P.'s. His conduct will be long remembered, one would hope, by lovers of freedom; but he must expect for some time to come to be a pariah among M.P.s. To do him justice he is not likely to care much about that.

Commonweal, Volume 3, Number 98,
26 November 1887, p. 377.

NOTES ON NEWS

One lesson, and a very valuable one, the authorities have been giving us by their recent conduct. They have, so to say, preached us a practical sermon on the value of the vague something called 'moral force.' This time surely the 'moral force' was on our side, and it was natural that many should have thought that the affair of Dod Street would be repeated, and that the Government, glad enough to harry and bludgeon a small band of poor unemployed voteless men here and there, would draw back when the Radical clubs entered the arena. Well, on this occasion they did not draw back, and many people are astonished at it. But they must remember that it was convenient for the then Government to draw back at Dod Street, while it was inconvenient for the present Government to draw back at Trafalgar Square. That is just as far as 'moral force' can push Governments who have in their hands physical force.

The Government with their big majority in Parliament felt perfectly safe against any mere talk, even though Mr. Gladstone himself and the United (?) Liberal Party were the talkers; therefore they thought that the opportunity was good for striking a blow which should encourage their friends and cow their enemies, and so far from drawing back they have been acting as an 'agent provocateur,' and would have been only too glad if they could have had an opportunity for shooting as well as bludgeoning the people. They believe themselves safe behind their bludgeons and bayonets against any 'moral force' that can be brought against them; and so they are until the 'moral force' arrayed against them means a corresponding amount of physical force, until apathy is turned into determination, timidity into despair, and organisation grows out of necessity.

Meanwhile, there is nothing to discourage Socialists in all this; we have known our present physical weakness all along; and the action of the Government has at least shown us that the classes are afraid of something, that they are beginning to forecast the inevitable trouble which the approaching break-up of wage-slavery is brewing; that forecast will almost certainly as it grows lead us into a period of persecution, and that again to a general knowledge among the workers of what Socialism aims at, and the threat of physical force (or let us say at once of *force*) which that knowledge will imply, will either make the oppressors waver, lose counsel and conduct, and so at last give way; or the oppression will become so unbearable that it will *force* the revolution to break all bounds and sweep it away.

A writer in the *Daily News* is sorely grieved at Sir C. Warren being called a martinet, a mere official soldier, in short, a lump of pipe-clay, and sets forth, at length his amiable and humanitarian qualities. Surely this is either a day too late or too early. The *innocent* Arabs who were slaughtered because their tribesmen slew the briber Palmer may be forgotten, and at any rate they can tell no tales; but how about our kind-hearted friend on the 13th and the 20th of November, 1887? Really Sir C. Warren's love for humanity took a strange form on those days; we have not yet forgotten all that so cleanly that we do not also remember that passage from an old book: 'By their fruits ye shall know them. Do men gather grapes from thorns or figs from thistles?'

The police, as we know too well, are, to put it mildly, very much irritated against the people in the streets, whether they are unemployed, or processionists, or what-not short of respectability. Naturally irritated, say some people, since they have been hustled about from pillar to post, overworked, kept without their meals (except when fed by the shopkeepers and the Prince of Wales). Well, you see, since they are 'naturally irritated,' they can be *depended upon.* I was talking about these matters to the son of an old chartist the other day, and he said that in the '48 time the soldiers were kept at extra drill for some time before the Kennington Green meeting, and in consequence were 'naturally irritated' against the people. There are more ways than one of killing a cat.

The Liberal leaders are in a terrible fright of being involved in a contest against law and order. Harcourt, Morley, and others have been speaking about the country, and not a word have they to say about the state of things in London. The Tories are not so reticent: they are naturally crowing over the victory of force over reason. The clever cartoon in *Punch,* which is really the illustrated *Times* in a political sense, puts the point to Mr. Gladstone in an unanswerable way. Only he *won't* answer it, or indeed think of the matter as long as he thinks it can be safely disregarded from the political or vote-catching point of view.

The 'unemployed' agitation has got as far as the setting on foot of a census of them; which to my mind does not seem very far; but if they themselves want it done, as it appears they do, all one can do is hope that something, however little, for their benefit will come of it. But how shall a census be made of men (and women and children) working for the wretchedest of wages? The wages now being offered to men on the ship canal works now beginning in Lancashire are 4½d. an hour, and I hear that thousands of men are eager to accept this 'reward of labour.' There is *employment* for you! I want to know also if a man who is an artisan, a carpenter, cabinet-maker, weaver, or what not, is set to do navvy's work, whether he can properly be said to be 'employed'?

Once again, it means but one thing – out-a-door relief. This is what the Captains of Industry and their governing committees, parliament and the rest of it, have to offer the people they lead. That is *their* way of organising labour.

It is curious to see the eagerness with which well-to-do people accept any scheme short of the one obvious remedy for dealing with the 'unemployed' business. You would think, to see the high spirits of some of them over this census business, that the men were by now not only numbered but also set to well-paid remunerative labour. Again the 'beggar colonies' scheme, here called politely 'home colonisation,' has been received with a kind of enthusiasm in some quarters. Mr, Herbert Mills set the ball a-rolling with his scheme, which was to be an imitation of the Dutch beggar colonies; and then there was an account of a similar scheme in work at Berlin, whereby people by dint of working eleven hours a-day and a strong dose of church to boot, all under strict discipline, were to earn a splendid livelihood of 6½d. per diem. That such schemes of slavery can be received as 'palliatives,' that they are not received with universal horror and disgust, shows how miserable our condition is, and what a tremendous upheaval it will take to amend it.

The Liberty and Property Defence League cannot be congratulated on the result of the 'big name' they got to lecture for them. Mr. Froude, almost of course, showed complete ignorance of Socialism and its aims, and quite of course violent prejudice in favour of reaction; and in short his address was a queer performance for a man with a reputation. And yet he gave his friends a hint or two worth their remembrance, when he told them, *e.g.*, that the rich had in these latter days surrendered political power in the hopes of preserving property, and that in all probability they would as a consequence *temporarily* lose their property. Some of their faces must have fallen at this *temporary* prospect. What Mr. Froude really meant was that liberty and private property are incompatible, – who shall say him nay?

Commonweal, Volume 3, Number 99,
3 December 1887, p. 385.

NOTES ON NEWS

A certain Mr. Pynes offered a petition to Lord Hartington as he made his triumphal entry into Dublin the other day, and his lordship declining in a royal way to accept it, Mr. Pynes adventurously threw it into the carriage, whereupon the police arrested him and he was brought before a magistrate next day; but luckily for him he was in Dublin and not in London (where there is no Coercion Act), *so* the magistrate dismissed the charge.

'The police, excited by the hooting, behaved like ruffians, and dealt blows with clenched fists to utterly harmless individuals who had remained within arm's length.' – *Daily News*.

What! is the *Daily News* coming round, then? Why, we shall have Mr. Gladstone next taking some notice of the bludgeoning of 'harmless individuals' by our 'admirable police' – Nay, stop a little! This report is from *Paris*, not *London*!

For the information of our comrades and other readers in the country I should mention that, however incredible the account of the behaviour of the police to the prisoners of Bloody Sunday, as published by the *Pall Mall*, may seem to them, there is no doubt that it is true, and they must believe in it. Indeed, after all, is there anything to wonder at in it? Such brutality is the blossom of the slum-life enforced on the 'lower classes' by our civilisation. Enlist that brutality in the service of a class whose one business is to uphold the oppression on which it lives; when occasion demands it, harass your enlisted brutality be sending it fools' errands up and down, and down and up; make it clear to the servants of law and order that in such service they can only commit one fault – to wit, behaving civilly and decently; promote men like Mr. Superintendent Shepherd, to show your 'admirable police' what model they should follow; and then sit down quietly and without fear, enwrapped in your respectability, and you may be quite sure of the results.

The preliminary trial of Cunninghame Graham and Burns in Bow Street was curious to witness and sufficiently damaging to the Government and its tool Wooden Warren – *i.e.* it would have been if the evidence for the defence had not been suppressed by the daily papers. Of course if Mr. Vaughan had not been practically under orders he must have dismissed the case, but equally of course it was more than his place was worth to do. The police gave their evidence in the usual way, and if there is any truth in an old saw, there must be few pots in the neighbourhood which have kept their legs, especially after Shepherd had done *his* duty. He was well 'sorted' by Mr. Asquith in cross-examination: the latter, by the way, was a brilliant contrast to that Knight of the Doleful Countenance, Mr. Poland, and I am really sorry that he is a lawyer.

The evidence for the defence was so clear and unanswerable that Poland had nothing for it but the regular traditional brow-beating, which served his turn very poorly, not only, as was to be expected, with such an old stager as Mr. Bradlaugh, or with Mr. Hyndman (who he had the impudence to ask to give the names of the others who formed the group about Mr. Graham and Burns), but even with the ordinary witnesses. In short, Poland tried hard to establish that the Government had with great difficulty quelled a dangerous riot headed by the defendants, and only succeeded in showing that the police attacked Graham and Burns as they attacked other citizens on that day.

Of course, unless the jury is very well packed, our friends will
be acquitted; but one can't help asking, supposing Burns had
been by himself, what would have happened? And again,
how about the victims of the drum-head court-martial, with
no clever Mr. Asquith (he is clearly very clever) to defend
them, and no respectable witnesses like Sir E. J. Reid and Mr.
Bradlaugh on their side? We shall have to ask, as we asked
before, if these men are acquitted or only have a formal
sentence, what is to be done to compensate the defenceless
men who have been sentenced, and what ignominious
punishment is to be meted out to their sentencers?

I came in for a quaint little piece of coercion last Friday. I
had been invited to lecture on Socialism and the 'disturbances' in London in the parish school-room at Buscott, a
little village high up the Thames, by the rector, our friend Mr.
Oswald Birchall. It had been agreed some little time back by
the squire and other village magnates, who at the time
wanted the said school-room for Primrose League purposes,
that it should be free to speakers of all parties, so I went
down expecting the usual quiet meeting; but at the last
minute the said magnates forbade the meeting, I believe on
the grounds that they expected a riot if I showed there. Then
they stole a march on Mr. Birchall by locking up the room
and taking the key away and 'picketing' the room to send
away anyone who might come to the meeting. We tried to
get the publican to let us have a room, which, however, he
declined to do, fearing, not without reason, the wrath of the
squire and farmers. However, things went pretty well, as, in
spite of all precautions, a few of the right sort had gathered
round the school-room and with these we adjourned to the
rectory, where we had a very useful meeting, the men
listening very attentively and sympathetically. The true story
of the 'riots' was clearly quite new to them, the *Pall Mall* (not
to speak of the *Commonweal*) being of course tabooed in the
neighbourhood; but they were clearly much impressed by it,
and will spread it about wherever they go. I may say that
men like this are not slow to learn the facts of their present

position, their slavery to the farmers being so direct that it presses on them every day. A good distribution of leaflets would be fruitful among such men: though many of them cannot read, they would get them read to them.

Mr. Thompson did his best to get a mandamus to compel Mr. Vaughan to hear evidence about the police attack on November 20th on a band of harmless processionists. It was a matter of course that the two 'Justices' stuck close to their brother Nupkins of Bow Street, but it is not a very cheering protest for those who believe that the law will do anything to protect 'discontented' people; whether they are 'discontented' at having the results of their labour stolen in the lump, or at having their musical instruments stolen every now and then directly to the tune of 'Wigs on the Green.'

A show of pet dogs opened at St. Stephen's Hall is a good example of the way in which labour is organised amongst us at present, to produce luxuries and to stint the people of necessaries, to say nothing of comforts. Perhaps Alderman Knight will suggest that some of the unemployed should have the job of combing the dogs.

Meantime, poor Linnell lies dead, slain by what I suppose the bourgeois press, when they are forced to say something about it, will call a 'lamentable accident.' It is, however, the kind of 'accident' which is likely to become common enough as, on the one hand, the workers become conscious of the fact that they are robbed of the greater part of their earnings, and become less and less inclined to put up with it, and as on the other hand those who live by the robbery get more and more frightened and therefore more and more repressive.

The Lord Mayor of Dublin is sent to prison, in spite of all his state in a sort of mediæval fashion: but the authorities have been afraid of sending him as a proper prisoner, and so have spoilt their joke in a very contemptible manner. I remember when I was a boy I used to hear a good deal about 'gentleman-farmers' (a profession which I suppose has now ceased to exist, what between agricultural depression and the elevation of all farmers to the rank of gentlemen). It seems as if a similar addition must be made in these cases also, and that some people must serve their time as gentlemen-prisoners. The Lord Mayor deserves and has our condolence in having to submit to this insult of gentleman-liness.

Commonweal, Volume 3, Number 100,
10 December 1887, p. 393.

NOTES ON NEWS

The Liberal Unionists had a great field-day at Westminster on the 9th. They seem to have been very cheerful about their prospects, and if they will but admit that they are a part of the Tory party, we on our part must admit in all honesty that they have some reason to be so – for the present – now that the Gladstonite Liberals have shown that there is no fight in them.

Lord Hartington made a long speech, as a leader must in spite of the torture he may inflict on his audience, of which torture his lordship is a master. The reporter makes the unfortunate Jesse Collings say that 'the *great minority* of the people of Ireland were loyalists.' And really since it was Mr. Collings, perhaps he did say so. Lord Selborne in attacking the worship of Mr. Gladstone as a pope (with which attack I cordially agree) held up Lord Hartington as a counter pope. Mr. Richard Chamberlain, in the absence of that illustrious humbug his brother, proposed 'extended organisation among the constituencies, not so much by holding meetings, as by private agency among the electors.' This latter phrase seems indiscreet. Might I as an interested person (possessed of six votes) ask Mr. R. Chamberlain, How much a vote?

Lord Derby's speech deserves more respect than these weary fatuities, although there was a hole or two in his logic even granting his premises; but at least it had meaning in it, and the moderates would find some of his taunts hard to answer. Yet one may remind him that if the Southern States put up (after a terrible war) with the coercion of the North, their struggle was for the continuance of chattel-slavery, which was doomed both by the ethical and economical circumstances, whereas the Irish are struggling for federalism, the feeling for which is obviously on the increase; it is not the form which a contest takes, but the reason for it which is important.

Lord Derby seemed conscious indeed that the tide was setting towards federation: 'Whatever was done for Ireland might be demanded for Scotland, certainly for Wales.' 'Were they prepared for four local parliaments with perhaps a federal council over all? it would be suicidal. Home Rule would lead to the absolute power of the Crown!' Well I don't see why, comparing it with what is, we should be terrified at the picture. The absolute power of the Crown would certainly lead to the abolition of the Crown, which would be a blessing, though a small one.

'Coercion in some form,' says Lord Derby, 'is only another name for civilisation.' I think he is right; civilisation means turning the whole world into a vast prison; the destruction of all manly ideals; the attempt to substitute 'comfort' so called, for happiness – the contented prisoner's ideal of life. I daresay Lord Derby would agree to that and say 'Well, what would you have?' But then, you see, he and those like him are withdrawn from the struggle like the popular gods of Epicurus. They are dull, but they don't suffer; they leave that to others.

After the Conference came the banquet at which Mr. Goschen made the conscious, and the Duke of Argyll the unconscious joke of the evening. A certain Mr. Sinclair had gone on his knees before the Unionist triumvirate – Hartington, Goschen and Chamberlain; so the midmost of those gods made the remarkable joke of picturing the feelings of those in the hall if they had the prospect of being governed by Hyndman, Conybeare and Cunninghame Graham, which to the audience of worshippers of the first trinity, seemed very funny; why, our readers can find out perhaps better than I can: I can only say that the *Standard* enjoyed it hugely, which is not much in its favour.

The Duke of Argyll's joke was better, much better. 'God save Ireland! to be for many years' (how many, your Grace?) 'an integral part of that Constitution which promises perfect freedom to all.' Apart from a country being an integral part of a Constitution a conception which people below the degree of a duke might find it difficult to master, this is a rich joke indeed. 'The promise of perfect freedom' is kept by enacting a stiffish Coercion Act in Ireland, and by doing without it in London and getting on pretty well by dint of open assault and robbery on the highway, backed up by drum-head court-martial afterwards.

By the way where is the Constitution and what is it? We hear a great deal of talk about it as a thing well known to all; but to most of us it keeps about as much out of the way as the sea-serpent. Perhaps the *Commonweal* might offer a price for the solution of the above question – if we could only find judges to decide it.

Another of the infamous sentences of the courts of 'justice' has fallen on Coleman – 12 months' hard labour for asserting the freedom of the highway – the jury giving Edlin the opportunity by not appreciating at its due value the official evidence of the police, which has to be bolstered up by signs passing between the witness in the box and the coming witness. Unluckily, quite apart from the prejudice of a 'respectable' jury, it has become the practice of juries simply to allow their ears to be tickled by the judges' summing-up, instead of carefully weighing the evidence themselves.

Trade is reviving – once more – perhaps. Or perhaps a ring or two are at work. Also, some person or persons interested, are working up the periodical war scare again; which is far advanced to have the honour of maps in the morning papers with the position of the Russian troops marked in them. Meantime the revival has not reached everybody; 'trade never so bad,' is the usual answer of retailers to any questions on the subject.

The attack on M. Ferry is a droll affair – hit by three bullets and never a hole in him – what *does* it mean? Is he like Claver'se and others in seventeenth century story, who had made a compact with the Devil and couldn't be pierced by any baser metal than silver? This would be rather suitable to his stockjobbing antecedents too.

Linnell's death is called, as one foresaw it would be, an 'accident' by the bourgeois press. Just so accidents happen when a hundred men pull the triggers of a hundred rifles loaded with ball cartridge, and other men happen to be standing opposite them. The general attitude of the press on this business is best characterised by the word *shabby*. The shabby dodge of reclaiming the body to prevent the funeral on the 11th! The shabby attempt to prove that Linnell drank, poor man! And again, in the case of Joseph Ellis, the harmless partyless man, the exultation of getting hold of a 'Socialist leader!' Shabby! Shabby!! Shabby!!! One is ashamed of having such enemies.

They are terribly powerful, though, in spite of – or rather, because of – their shabbiness. As witness the above case of Joseph Ellis: that such a piece of malignant injustice could have been perpetrated without an outcry even from the shabby classes shows how strong they feel themselves. To pass by other matters in the case – *e.g.*, the swearing through a brick wall, so familiar to us by now – let it be remembered that Ellis was charged with hurting Livingstone, and that he was obviously hurt with a *weapon*. Well, the jury, cowed and confused let us hope, by the style in which 'justice' is administered in that court, bring in a verdict of guilty; but the muddled Britons say at the same time that he did not strike Livingstone with an instrument, but with his fist: which, since Livingstone was not struck with a fist but a weapon, is tantamount to an acquittal. After which, Edlin (I regret to have to soil these pages with his name) sentences him to eight months' hard labour. This is what Palmerston's once famous '*Civis Romanus sum*' has come to! This is the protection of the law! Let us add as a crowning piece of shabbiness that the LIBERAL *Daily News* omitted in its report of the trial this quasi-acquittal of the jury.

Mr. Bradlaugh has been defending his conduct in Parliament before his constituents, who, it must be said, did not appreciate his reasons for voting against his colleague in the matter of cutting down the preposterous salaries of the successful lawyers called judges. He was in favour of women working at the pit brow, and thereby reducing the wages of the men of their own households; he is shocked at women being driven on the streets, but seemingly not so shocked at men knocking about the streets workless, which clearly must result in the women supplementing their scanty pay by street-walking. He objected to Land Nationalisation on the grounds that it must either be bought or stolen! Would he object to taking his fishing-boots back from a thief on the same grounds?

Commonweal, Volume 3, Number 101,
17 December 1887, p. 401.

NOTES ON NEWS

The tremendous mares' nest of the *Times*, big enough for the hatching of a division of cavalry, about the New York Dynamiters, is at first sight only a cause for laughter. One need not suppose that the wonderful and mysterious correspondent mentioned by that veracious journal manufactured the lie himself. He was (if he existed) probably some egregious fool on the hunt for something to please his employers, and glad enough to accept the wildest yarn of a Yankee joker. That is all very funny: but when one remembers that there are men on their trial for suspicion of plotting dynamite this idiotic lie wears another garb, let alone the convenience of pretending to believe anything that may be used as a weapon against the Irish party. However, it may be hoped that this time the story is too preposterous to have much effect.

The war scare is not subsiding – indeed, is rather on the increase; but perhaps, as we said last week, Bismarck's army bill will account for it. It is not easy to believe that the absolutist governments are really inclined to court the dangers of foreign war, with the ever increasing discontent which their armies must leave behind them when they march to the frontier; nor is it easy to see at present anything to force them into war.

But besides his army bill the German dictator has another bill on hand, a bill to make the anti-Socialist law still more stringent; amongst other matters in it is a provision for the International Congress of working men which is being organised for next year: it will be a penal offence involving loss of citizenship to take part in any Socialist congress. Perhaps some of our German friends can tell us what is likely to come of this. Meantime our own government is requested to take note and learn something new from this passed master in it.

The police are to have a medal for their services in last summer's Jubilee raree-show. Here is a chance for the Government: why don't they strike a medal and present it to the force for their services on November 13th? It would be quite according to precedent: the Treasury honouring the first Commissioner of Police; two such dignified powers as that. In like manner the Pope struck a medal in honour of the French King after the massacre of St. Bartholomew. If the medal is struck (and by the way, King Warren's face should be on the obverse), the poor specials also ought to be decorated with it.

Mr. Justice Stephen's sentence on Harrison, convicted on police evidence of attacking and wounding the police, is the most infamous deed yet done in the infamous chain of injustice and cruelty of the present Tory Terror. The cold and cruel pedant Stephen has at last earned a title to distinction. It is true that he is well known to a limited circle as a specimen of legal shoddy yarn, and I believe has enthusiastic admirers of his very commonplace feats in that line; but these fools, who are but few, will die presently and their hero will be forgotten as a pettifogging writer: as a cold and cruel pedant and enemy of truth and reason he may yet be remembered.

Yet if one could forget his existence it would be happier for us: so let us consider one or two things that soulless pedant said as spoken by the chair he sat on, and then say a word about them with less disgrace than if we spoke of him. The *Thing* laid down the doctrine that the 'law of England undoubtedly was that if the police or any other authority gave notice that any particular proceeding would not be permitted to take place it was the duty of the parties concerned to obey the notice and then to take any remedy which the law might give them if the notice was illegal.' Might I ask the *Thing* what remedy it advises Alfred Linnell to take?

It is well that we know the law, however, and that we understand how far we have drifted from the rough days of our forefathers, who with all their shortcomings never meant this, which simply implies that persons in authority by reason of their authority are free from the responsibilities of citizenship. The hide-bound pedant above-mentioned does us some service in stating this so clearly.

The coercionist rag the *Daily News*, with all the fervour of a new convert, very naturally highly approves of the law-grinder's sentence; which doesn't look well for the attempt which is to be made in Parliament to call attention to these shameful pieces of legal tyranny. Cannot we turn from such sneaks and try to find an enemy with some spark of generosity in him. Is there not some stout Tory hard-hitter to say, 'Stop that, you legal fools! The man held principles that I loathe, and if I had come across him in the row I would have given him one for his knob; but after all he did what I would have done, struck a good stroke or two in a shindy in which he was excited by seeing all sorts of violence going on. Don't be fools and call it a crime: say you have got him and mean to serve him out – though *I* should let him go since he got out of the scrimmage unhurt.' That's what a generous enemy lighted by the light of reason would say. Is there nobody to come forward and say it?

The bourgeois press is very naturally spiteful over the great success of Linnell's funeral, and of course the procession and the spectators are called roughs, rowdies, thieves, and the like. What a lie this is those know best who were eye-witnesses of this great demonstration, and saw the quiet but sympathetic behaviour of the crowd, incalculable as to number. However, let us not trouble as to the lie, for if all that crowd were rowdies and roughs, the *Times* supporters should be shaking in their shoes – as one hopes they may one day have to do with better reason. Meantime the words rowdy, rough, and thief are clearly changing their meaning, and are coming to signify an honest and hard-working man, as opposed to a useless person who lives on other people's labour; for such worthless rags who are our present rulers it is not worth while finding a name.

Commonweal, Volume 3, Number 102,
24 December 1887, p. 409.

EMIGRATION AND COLONISATION

The minds of the upper classes are still more and more turned towards emigration. It is true that they have not any wish to emigrate themselves, as one might suppose they would have, since they are always talking about their diminished incomes, and are never tired of dinning into people's ears the splendid career that lies before the emigrant. They are after all tolerably contented to live in the British Islands (Ireland excepted, where there are extra risks). But they have at last got to understand that there is a great mass of 'our poorer brethren' who have abundant reasons for not being contented with life in Great Britain and Ireland. The upper classes would dearly like to see the backs of these; for even in these early days they are sick of them and their troubles.

Enlightenment is, however, growing. Lord Salisbury at Derby had something to say on this emigration subject which, as coming from a Tory minister, was new. He would like to send a few more people out of Ireland, conveniently forgetting for the moment that the condition of the five millions now inhabiting Ireland was not so much better than that of the eight millions who once inhabited it. He said Mr. Tuke the Quaker Liberal told him that in large tracts of Ireland the people could not live upon the land. Exactly; because other large tracts have been stolen by the landlords and rack-rented to the tenants by them, just as the starveling larger tracts are.

However, this is not my lord's new idea. It is true that he seemed chiefly thinking about Ireland, because the Irish are better rebels than the English, but he was speaking of emigration in general; and thereon he said what certainly was remarkable for him. Quoth he: 'I am aware that emigration...happens not to be popular.... You will hear people say, Why should not emigration come from the upper classes? Well, I entirely agree with the people who make that contention, my idea of emigration is that it should involve all classes of the community.' And he went on to say that he thought it would be disastrous if only the unsuccessful and desperate took to emigration. It must be noted that these are the groups that the philanthropists of all kinds want to send away, and then we can give Lord Salisbury credit for a certain amount of enlightenment – for, in fact, recurring for the occasion to the older and more human Tory ideals of paternal government, which are assuredly far better than the new commercial absolutist ideas that have taken their place, whether their supporters be called Tory, Whig-Liberal, or philanthropist.

––––––––––––––––––––

However, it must be pointed out that Lord Salisbury didn't understand the popular cry he quoted, 'Why don't the upper classes emigrate?' or rather, didn't choose to understand it. His idea presupposes the sacredness of the present three-class society – nobles, tradesmen, and workmen – just as the Roman idea of colonisation did. The popular cry means 'Why don't the upper classes turn workmen?' And the answer clearly is, 'Because you, the workmen, don't make them do so.'

––––––––––––––––––––

After all, the difference between Lord Salisbury's grandiose, old Tory idea of the natural leaders of the people leading out a colony like the Romans of old, would mean in practice (if it could be put into practice, which it cannot) going out with ready-made somewhat old British bosses instead of stumbling on new-made colonial ones, or gradually evolving them from the rough and tumble of the early colonial gambling struggle for riches and position. There is little to chose between the two methods – the happy-go-lucky, and the paternal: all the more as the dignified paternal bosses would soon lose their dignity in the general scramble above-said. As things go, emigration must be a miserable, degraded scramble, a mess and a muddle that makes one sick to think of.

But our younger Socialist readers must not suppose that Socialists object to persons or groups changing their country, or fertilising the waste places of the earth. Granted that society really were the sacred thing it should be, instead of the mass of anomalies and wrongs that it is, the Roman idea of leading a colony is right and good, and it will surely be one of the solemn duties of the society of the future for a community to send out some band of its best and hardiest people to socialise some hitherto neglected spot of earth for the service of man. At present that cannot be done; all we can now do when pushed by our necessities is to waste and spoil some land which should be kept unwasted for the better days. As things go, we are as great a curse to the lands we overrun as were the Mogul hordes of the early Middle Ages – or worse, may be.

Meantime the 'remedy' of emigration is receiving rude blows. Lord Salisbury says the rich (perhaps the House of Lords) should lead our colonies. Others looking about them on the waste of the land in England itself, ask very naturally why *it* should not be cultivated. To set aside the direct answer which Socialists have to make, here is a scheme for Home Colonisation about which a few words should be said. It has been set on foot by Mr. Herbert V. Mills, who has noted with interest the Beggar Colonies of Holland, and being himself both by nature and profession an ascetic, has not been shocked at the slavishness and despair of the future of humanity which such schemes involve. The essentials of his scheme come to this: that charitable persons should subscribe a vast sum of money to buy land, which can be had cheap in England to-day and apparently will be cheap in times to come (unless Mr. Mill's scheme grows vastly and so raises the price), and that on this land certain families and persons are to be planted, having been chosen by the Charity Organisation Society (!). This community will feed, clothe, and house itself, consuming its own productions, and only sell to the outside world the surplus of what it produces. The colonists will be bound to work three hours a-day in return for subsistence (as I gather, at a low standard), and will also be allowed each to cultivate a plot of land for his own benefit. The first experiment is to be made on 500 persons, and £25,000 will have to be collected in order to set it on foot.

Now with all respect to Mr. Mills, who is undoubtedly a kind, disinterested, and devoted man, it must be pointed out, that while his idea of getting the people back on the land is a right one, and while it must be admitted that the members of such a community will be infinitely better off than their workhouse or slum-dwelling brethren, yet his scheme will not lead to any solution of the question between capital and labour. Not to make any carping objections, let it be admitted that the experiment gets over the natural difficulties and succeeds, *i.e.* that *granted the land given by charity*, the community supports itself; yet the colonists after all are slaves unless they succeed in producing more than a bare subsistence; and if they do so they then become capitalists also; and furthermore it must be asked what is the number of persons to be so benefited, and if that number is what it should be, where is the 'charity' to come from?

Clearly the answer must be that the 'charity' must be universal, in other words that *all* the land in the country must be given up to gain the end Mr. Mills aims at, due livelihood for the people, and along with the land all the other means of production. If 'charity' will do this, well and good; but it is not a matter of fear but of certainty that if Mr. Mills's scheme is taken up, it will be as an evasion of the demand of the Socialists that monopoly in the means of production should cease. And it is quite as certain, as has been said over and over again, in these columns, that this demand will only be yielded on compulsion. A proprietary class neither will nor can yield its privileges voluntarily.

A word with Lord Salisbury again; I must quote him. He says, apropos of emigration: 'Every year between three and four hundred thousand souls are added to your community. Do you believe that the means of supplying them grows, increasing as rapidly?' The answer is 'Certainly not, so long as labour is organised first to make profits for the idle rich, and next to supply them with luxuries, so long as it is organised wastefully: if labour were not so organised, or disorganised, then we should see.'

Meantime Lord Salisbury makes one admission of importance enough, and which if statesmen ever think, which is doubtful, must have made him feel how empty and hollow his suggestions of remedies were. Said he: 'We are in the most perplexing and anomalous condition – we are ruined because everything is cheaper than it was before – but of course you would at first sight imagine that when everything is cheaper everybody ought to be better off. Somehow everybody is not: everybody feels that his industry is checked and his income straightened, and we look round in vain to see some solution for our difficulties, some mitigation for our sufferings.'

In vain indeed, my lord! Possibly because when you speak about *our* sufferings, you are using rather an extravagant figure of speech. Oh, if only those whose sufferings are but too real would only 'look round' them, surely it would *not* be in vain!

Commonweal, Volume 3, Number 103,
31 December 1887, pp. 417–18.

[UNTITLED PARAGRAPH]

[The follow paragraph was written in reply to a letter from Reginald A. Beckett entitled 'Empirical Socialism'.]

I note here that the word 'religion' is often used very loosely; the *ancient* Jewish religion was not one of the 'religious' religions as Bax calls them. Also I cannot see how 'Internationalism' can fail to bring about the extinction of nations, and so give us the free communes of Lane's manifesto: the federal idea as opposed to the national is clearly growing even now. The centralisation of production and distribution is no doubt hastening the advent of Socialism; but it is in itself an evil, just as the class war is which is doing the same thing; true society once realised, we should get rid of such evils.

Commonweal, Volume 3, Number 103, 31 December 1887, p. 421.

CONTRIBUTIONS TO COMMONWEAL

1888

NOTES ON NEWS

Gladstone-worship is well on now among the faithful of the Liberal party, and is carried to such lengths that one cannot help thinking that some of the party must have doleful forebodings as to its future when their god takes his departure from the earth. What will be left of Liberalism when this one old man has gone; with his astonishing physical vigour, his belief in himself, his capacity of shutting his eyes to everything that his momentary political position forbids him to see, and his keen delight in playing the political game?

However, at present, there seems little need for us to speculate on what is to happen after him, and one is tempted to think that he may out-live the present political and social system now growing so crazy. May it be so!

His Dover speech will be thought a fine specimen, I suppose, and indeed it was brisk and combative enough from his own point of view, though he announced his intention of fighting after the fashion of the pre-Napoleonic generals and keeping all rules of the game: he boasted of his doing so in the Jingo period and chuckled over the result. Well, his soft fighting was discouraging enough in those days, but after all it was perhaps good enough for the occasion, for the Jingoes and Dizzy at their head, never intended to go to war; they only meant bragging – I admit that we didn't know it at the time.

After all this fine rhetorical oracle of the Liberal Idol, in spite of all its words, was as far removed from any practical and

social aspect of things as if it were delivered in another
planet: except perhaps when he touched on the Protection *v.*
Free Trade matter, he didn't talk about what people are
thinking about, but what they are *talking* about, and indeed
that is usual with him, and with all popularity hunters:
because by the time a thing has become generally talked of
the thinkers have got to the next subject.

The Tories have been trying a little 'dishing' in Ireland, to see
if it may count for a make-weight against their 'resolute'
Government there; they have reduced the judicial rents in
the teeth of Lord Salisbury's declaration that they were to be
considered fixed. The result of their experiment is not
encouraging at present; the Nationalists do not accept it as a
blessing, very naturally, looking at it as at once a blow at the
Plan of Campaign and a base plagiarism on it; and the
Loyalists also very naturally are in a fury at it, and are pulling
themselves together to claim compensation from the British
taxpayer, which indeed Lord Salisbury promised them. If he
redeems his promise the Tories had best arrange for the fresh
varnishing of the opposition benches for their behoof.

This matter is a fresh example of the slippery muddle which
our present system of property always makes; it allows a
privileged class to rob the people of the means of production,
asserting in high words and hard deeds 'the rights of
property,' and then from time to time takes arbitrarily from
one group or another of the privileged some small portion of
the plunder it has allowed them and encouraged them to
acquire; and all the while, whatever it does, insists at least
upon this, that there shall always be a class of hewers of
wood and drawers of water to be benefitted by this –
Socialism as some sanguine people are pleased to call it.

The death of John Frost in Pentonville prison is one of those
events which would let in a little light on the public as to the

prison system and its administration, if people were really trying to see; but probably as it is there will be little learned by it. An obviously sick man is condemned to 20 months' imprisonment, and when he gets to prison is treated as if he were not sick but shamming; but at last 'shams' so persistently that he is clearly at the point of death, when he is taken to the prison hospital and 'treated kindly,' but carried on his 'shamming' till he dies. No one who knows anything about our prisons can doubt that this kind of thing is common enough; only the victims don't always die in prison.

It speaks volumes for the way in which the prison officials treat the luckless men who have fallen into their powers, that the wife after 'trying to see the governor and being told that he was away,' in addressing herself to one of the nurses, '*softened her communication* as much as possible, so that matters might not be made worse for her husband.' And that the prisoner told her 'to make no complaint to the prison authorities lest he should fare worse in consequence.' Do smug well-to-do persons, who have little more chance of going to prison than they have of being made kings, understand what that means? It is time that they should learn this amongst other pieces of knowledge, in order that they may understand what class-hatred means and what it may lead to.

Commonweal, Volume 4, Number 104, 7 January 1888, p. 1.

NOTES ON NEWS

Mr. Blunt's appeal has been rejected, and he is in the jail where he is to expiate his 'crime.' No one, I suppose, expected any other result from the appeal, although a good deal was said about the illegality of his arrest both before the trial (if we must needs dignify it with that name) and afterwards. What is the use of passing a Coercion Act if it has meshes wide enough to let such fish slip through as one's avowed political opponents? Meantime, let us say that now Mr. Blunt is in prison, we will not forget that he spoke out well and boldly for the poor people in Egypt who were condemned to similar torture there by our English stock-jobbers.

Apropos of the trial, the *Pall Mall Gazette* asks in a straightforward leader, 'Is there any right of public meeting?' Our contemporary, one would think, does not ask the question because it does not know the answer to it, which is a short one enough, 'NO.' But one may expand the answer by explaining to those who have not thought about the matter, that in a 'constitutional' country there is liberty enough for every one belonging to the privileged class, but no liberty for any one else; and what sort of liberty of public meeting is that privileged class likely to allow to 'any one else' who is attacking its privilege openly?

The Radical clubs of Hammersmith have sent a delegation to the Metropolitan Board of Works asking them to adhere to their bye-law as to the newly-acquired Ravenscourt Park, setting aside a portion of it for public meetings, whereas the Hammersmith Vestry have passed a resolution asking the

Board to alter this. I may inform those who do not know Ravenscourt that it is a very large tract of ground, and that it would be easy to set aside a part of it for public meetings without in the least spoiling it for recreation. In fact, the Vestry are simply following their kind in trying to put a stop to public meetings in Hammersmith. Considering how much recreation ground will be in and about Hammersmith, it will be preposterous if the inhabitants have no regular meeting-place allotted them; but no doubt the local curmudgeons will take any excuse they can to put a stop to free speech in this neighbourhood. One would think that there was something hurtful to the public pleasure in a political meeting judging from the way that our Bumbles are dealing with the matter; whereas, to put it on the lowest grounds, a political meeting is a pleasurable excitement to most people who are not *very* 'superior persons.' The Hammersmith clubs must be congratulated on taking action in this affair, and it is to be hoped that they will not let it drop.

Commonweal, Volume 4, Number 105,
14 January 1888, pp. 9–10.

NOTES ON NEWS

There is plenty of talk at present on the revival of trade which will bring back 'prosperity' to the country; it is well to watch the trade accounts in the press, so as to get some idea as to what this revival and 'prosperity' means, and also the strange confusion of ideas that are usual, and which naturally come from the conflict between the view of the real needs and desires of consumers for goods, and the view taken by those whose real business is *investment* and not *production*, and to whom said consumers are just so many milch-cows.

'Concerning food products, it is satisfactory to find in Beerbohm's corn-trade list the remark that a return of firmness is expected in the trade, accompanied by some improvements in the prices.' (Note: 'improvement' means rise in price; good luck to the seller, ill-luck to the buyer.) 'In the sugar-market there has been since the autumn a rise in prices, based in part on a reduced estimate of the beet-crop, partly on the formation of syndicates for the rise in the market in Europe as well as in America' (otherwise, 'rigging'). In coffee it appears that short crops in Brazil, Java, and elsewhere have so raised the price as to check consumption, and a further rise is doubtful. In tea the competition of Indian growths has prevented the more distinct rise in prices which might have ensued upon the poor quality of the China leaf during the season.... In tobacco the crop in the United States promises to be but a fraction of the average, and prices have distinctly risen.'

'Short crops and high prices' therefore are still what we must pray for, as in the old days of the Corn Laws, to bring back prosperity to the world – the world of forestallers and regraters, at least. Yet such is the amazing power of cant that those very same thieves profess to be afraid of the political outlook and to dread a European war; though it is absolutely certain (as indeed our forestaller points out in the case of canned meats) that a war would raise prices and increase 'consumption,' and so help us forward to the longed-for 'prosperity.'

How often the blessings of the cheapness of wares are dinned into our ears as a reason for the workers accepting their slavery quietly! But now it seems that we are to rejoice in the rise in prices. May a plain man ask *which* of the two is the blessing, since both can scarcely be?

If Mr. Froude had not lately been taking up the cudgels against Socialism we might have looked upon him as a possible convert, judging from the account of his diatribes against the commercial sham democracy which at present rules the British Empire. But it is to be feared that he sees Socialism to be a step by the way to the overthrow of the authority, the complete despotic development of which is Mr. Froude's god.

Yet it is somewhat doubtful to my mind whether the paternal government, the decease of which Mr. Froude laments, is the hierarchical authority founded on *status* which was the full development of feudal society. I rather suspect his hobby to be a thorough good rattling bureaucracy of the 'superior persons,' not yet realised in history, and now for ever impossible of realisation. Much as we suffer under the present shabby tyranny of the Society of Contract, we must admit that it is something that it has destroyed the holiness of the superior person, and forces him, if he is to be something, simply to exhibit himself as a leader of shabbiness. Mr. Matthew Arnold must go arm in arm with Mr. Podsnap if he is to succeed now. The great preacher of refinement must back up the sordid wretches who steal two-thirds of the Irish peasant's porridge with a long spoon indeed – viz., the whole power of the British Empire. The scorner of philistinism and the vulgar middle-classes has to throw in his lot with the thing he loathes and be a defender of sweating, or his *refinement* will find no great market for it.

We can bear the tyranny of contract the better because, unlike Mr. Froude, we know that it is not going to lead to a mere exaggeration of all its stupidities and miseries, but to a contradiction of the system that produces them. It will lead us rather to a condition of life the very struggle for which will be fertile of the heroisms which Mr. Froude regrets, and which when realised will give every opportunity to the 'superior person' for exercising the talents he may really possess, while it denies him opportunity for the practice of the tendency to imbecile domineering which not uncommonly goes with his better qualities.

Lord Salisbury on the stump again! He has been playing the return match to Mr. Gladstone, but in part his speech at Liverpool has a look of definite anti-Socialism worth noting. He begins by pointing with joy to the present signs of 'prosperity,' and makes this remarkable admission: 'In this country and in Ireland what we really need to solve the difficulties – to undo and end the many insurmountable (?) troubles – is one touch of the magic wand of prosperity.' In other words, that statesmanship has nothing to do but wait upon some fortuitous turn of the world-market which can neither be foreseen nor understood. A curious confession of imbecility, certainly; what a fall from the old high Tory theory of government of the Gods and heroes! What a helpless condition for thirty odd millions of the deftest and most resourceful people in the world! However, we need not dispute with Lord Salisbury that statesmen are useless.

Another point on which we can agree with his lordship is that 'Our principles with respect to property are not the same as when this depression commenced.' That is, of course, true enough; nor can it be denied that if the new wave of 'prosperity' should reach far enough; if the dogs do get any of the crumbs that fall from the children's table, we may expect to find the attack on property slack off somewhat; but apropos of this let our readers note our New York letter of last week, and the fact therein mentioned that the effects of the good trade of the past year had by no means reached the working-classes.

––––––––––

But what are we to say to this? 'In these days, whatever may have been the result in the past, property can only be acquired as the result of the accumulations and exertions of industry.' True, not of these days only, but of all days; and yet a very dubious sentence capable of more than one interpretation. It reminds one of the old Joe Miller of the doctor advising his patient to take exercise on an empty stomach, and the prompt answer, 'Yes, doctor, but upon whose?' Whose industry gave Lord Salisbury the 'accumulations' which form his personal property? I am told that large as the salary of a Prime Minister may look to us others, there is little to be saved out of the job.

––––––––––

'In proportion,' says the most noble, 'as your laws assure to property its security, they assure to industry its reward?' Oh, most noble! you speak queer English and you have got on ticklish ground! What is the reward of the Irish peasant whose unassisted industry has made fertile land out of a patch of mountain bog? That his landlord shall force rent out of him when there is no rent, shall make him pay for being industrious. What is the reward of the English mechanic, who has made the capital and machinery which enables him to work, and has then to pay for leave to use it to a man who cannot use it, but who – has got it? His lordship's boldness can only be explained by his thinking he was speaking to fools – as he was.

Nothing can excuse, however, his dastardliness and snobbishness in leading cheers and laughter, from the despicable snobs who formed his audience, directed against the persons he has put in prison. There are degrees in baseness, but surely the superlative degree is jeering at prisoners, at men whom you have made helpless by your brute force.

Lord Salisbury finished by hints at the necessity of compromise in order to sustain the alliance with the Coercionist Whigs; and by promising not to go out of office for a small defeat – in fact, not till he was forced to. In brief, the meaning of his speech was a chuckle at the Tory good-luck of a revival in trade coming to help their big job; Lord Salisbury well knowing that the Government that finds itself in when a wave of prosperity comes on, is firmly seated on the content of the great mass of the middle-class, and can afford to scoff at all the misery that lies below it. Well, the game is good while it lasts, but in the nature of things it cannot last long; suppose the most sanguine expectations of the traders realised, what does that mean? Simply the preparation for a deeper depression on a wider scale than the last – and what then? Why, we may well hope to repeat that 'our principles with regard to property are not the same as they were when this *inflation* commenced.' The card-castle that Lord Salisbury is so busily engaged in building will go down then; and meantime our duty is to see, whether it be in times of depression or inflation, that our principles with respect to property are the not the same as they were before.

Commonweal, Volume 4, Number 106,
21 January 1888, p. 17.

NOTES ON NEWS

After a three days' trial, a jury have found our friends Graham and Burns guilty of 'unlawful assembly,' and a judge has sentenced them to six weeks' imprisonment. As both of our friends are emphatically *men*, they will not expect a long Jeremiad from us over their fate specially, since so many people are sharing it; and they will no doubt take it as part of the day's work, and a natural reward for courage and conduct exercised on behalf of the people. The real interest in the event to them as to us is as to what is to come of all this, what was intended by the closing of Trafalgar Square and the police onslaught of the 13th of November. No one can doubt who looks on the matter fairly, whatever his political views may be, that the intention is the suppressal of all meetings in the open-air that may seem inconvenient to the Government; and the Government, I may add, has now got an instrument in its hands which it can use whenever it pleases. The right of public meeting which our Radical friends fondly thought we possessed, turns out to have no existence; a practically irresponsible police officer can take upon himself to forbid any meeting, and can order the maiming or slaying of as many people as he pleases in the exercise of his *discretion*, if he chooses to disperse such a meeting.

This is Mr. Justice Charles's law, and certainly he is nobly earning his new promotion by laying it down so clearly, and by acting so frankly as the senior counsel for the prosecution, though this latter proceeding we are well used to by now. Let us have a sentence or two from his remarkable charge to the jury.

'He reminded them also, and he could not repeat it too strongly, that it matters not whether the purpose was lawful or unlawful…it did not matter a pin's head what the purpose was.' 'He had carefully considered Mr. Asquith's contention as to the right of public meeting in the Square, but he could find no evidence of the right on the part of the public to hold meetings in any thoroughfare…he could find no right to hold meetings in them [thoroughfares] for the discussion of any question at all, whether social, political or religious.'

To us Socialists this is no news: we all remember the trial of our comrades Williams and Mainwaring at Clerkenwell in 1886, where similar doctrine was held, though nominally our comrades were tried for obstruction and not for 'unlawful assembly'; we were then told that it was no use our bringing evidence to prove that there was no real obstruction, that the meeting itself was the offence although it gave no inconvenience to any single person. We knew well enough why our meetings were interfered with, but the press and our middle-class acquaintance rebuked or jeered us for saying that it was because we were Socialists, and they kept saying that we could not be allowed to hold meetings which 'inconvenienced the public,' and that that was the only reason why the police interfered with us. The recent events prove beyond a doubt that we were right: if the Radical meeting called on Bloody Sunday had been merely a political one, even though it was connected with the Irish revolt, it would not have been interfered with: our Radical friends became on that occasion Socialists; and it must be said that the authorities are doing their best to keep them so.

In truth all discontented members of the lower orders are now looked on by the middle classes as Socialists, and there is reason in that too; since where else can they look save Socialism for a remedy?

Mr. Justice Charles repeated the well-worn lie that the crowd in Trafalgar Square was largely composed of roughs; and said that there was no doubt that it was true: he must be a credulous person indeed if that is really his opinion. The fact was so notoriously the reverse of that, that we may be excused for pointing out to those who may still suppose that they will have any defence from law on such occasions, that if the police will stick to such an obvious lie as this and a judge will profess to credit it, it is clear that no meeting big or little can be safe from the charge of its being 'largely composed of roughs.'

Meetings in the open-air, therefore, are unlawful, and may be dispersed at the discretion of the police, whether they are social, political or religious. That is the law. The practice will certainly be that some unlawful assemblies will be winked at by the police. Tory or respectable Liberal meetings will not be meddled with, nor, as a rule will religious meetings; but Socialists will be put down whenever convenient as a matter of course, and Radical meetings also will often be harried when they are not consecrated to the cause of law and order by being called under the auspices of the Liberal leaders.

Thus at one stroke vanishes the dream of bringing about peaceably and constitutionally the freedom we long for; (and we may hope not we only but many of our Radical friends also, although they have but a vague idea of what it means;) for if they do these things in the green tree what will they do in the dry? 'Society' was a little alarmed, and much disgusted by the now regular unemployed agitation, and by that slight fear has been impelled to act in a way worthy of an ordinary absolutist government. Let the slight fear become a big one, the hand-writing on the wall grow clearer, and then we shall see suppression of indoor meetings also; suppression of associations, press prosecutions, and the like; and there is plenty of law for all that. What lies ahead of us is rougher work than languid 'constitutional agitation'; passive resistance first, with the usual incidents of jail and fine and ruin, until our educational agitation has had its effect; then increase of reaction, increase of resistance; the occasion given by some special stupidity of reaction, not for one crisis but for several; apparent defeat maybe at first, but always as the seed of victory; till at last the reactionary brute force of the executive finds itself helpless even in the hour of its triumph. This is the vision our enemies are forcing us to see by their present contemptible tyrannies, which seem so safe to them.

Meanwhile Graham and Burn's sentence has turned all but the strongest stomachs for Coercion; the *Daily News*, the special Mr. Facing-both-ways of the party, calls for their immediate release. So we all do, but also for the immediate release of the victims of the drum-head court martial and of Edlin and Co., condemned on the evidence of the police who manufactured the riot and the tales against the 'rioters,' at once.

One word about the 'gentlemen' who have been sent to prison. Their friends have been very busy trying to get them special indulgences in jail, naturally enough; but the result of this will be to make many middle-class people think that they are being treated worse than ordinary prisoners, since I now discover that it is only those who have a chance of being sent to prison who have any idea of what imprisonment means. Well, the fact is, as one of our comrades was saying to me the other day, that no 'gentleman' would be treated as badly as any working-man. I add to this that when a 'gentleman' comes out, unless his health has suffered, he is no worse than before; whereas a working-man is stamped by his imprisonment as a jail-bird whatever he has done. The subject of the prison system, however, is too wide a one to be treated in a mere note. Mr. Graham's spirited letter to the *Pall Mall* gives a hint of what lies at the bottom of it.

Meantime, we say with our new contemporary, the *Star*,
Remember the unremembered!

No doubt many Socialists were surprised that the jury did not
find our friends guilty on all counts of the indictment; all that
can be said about them was that they were commonplace.
But the Edinburgh jury that acquitted our crofter friends
were a very different set of men, and have recalled the best
traditions of the days before '48, when the reactionists and
democrats were at grips. All honour to them!

Commonweal, Volume 4, Number 107,
28 January 1888, p. 25.

[UNTITLED PARAGRAPHS]

NEWSPAPER 'PLOTS.' – Some day we shall have to hang an editor or two, and a few correspondents, to cure them of wanton sensationalism. – *Weekly Dispatch*.

The *Evening Star* has risen and shines (at ¹/₂d. per copy) on the darkness of London. It has not appeared before it was wanted, and all who are on the side of freedom must fervently wish that the closing words of its first article may be fulfilled, 'We come to stay.' We urge upon every one of our readers who takes an evening paper, the *necessity* of supporting the *Star* rather than any of its rivals. It and the *Pall Mall Gazette* are the only dailies which have a word for the workers, and if it keeps on as it has begun, the *Star* will go far to achieve one great thing towards the higher development of society – giving a voice to the dumb driven millions.

Lord Henry Bruce, M.P., speaking at Malmesbury the other day chiefly in favour of protection, finished his speech by saying that 'the Government should place some restraint on the immigration of Socialists and paupers into England.' It is recorded that Balaam's ass once spoke, and to some purpose, as it warned him of danger. Lord Henry Bruce has followed his example, and shown us the meaning of Mr. Arnold White's anxiety for defending the poor people in the East-end against the competition of cheap foreign labour. It is not the welfare of the poor slaves in the East-end but the welfare of their masters which is aimed at: it is the fear of Socialism which *they* are to be guarded against. That may become necessary if Bismark's new coercion bill is passed intact.

Commonweal, Volume 4, Number 107, 28 January 1888, p. 29.

NOTES ON NEWS

Within two or three days of each other, Lord Salisbury has received two deputations, one asking him to consider the state of the London poor, and one to consider that of the Irish landlords. At first sight this would seem like a practical joke played upon the Most Noble by people with a sense of grim humour. However, that does not seem to have been the case, and both deputations put forward their cases with great gravity – even that sent by the Irish landlords.

The contrast between the reception of the two was, however, remarkable. The parliamentary sovereign of Britain let the first deputation see that, to his mind, the condition of the poor had nothing to do with him, whereas there was an air of cordial and affectionate sympathy in his address to the delegates of the landlords which must have warmed their hearts and made them think it the next best thing to a Bill passed by both houses to make the whole public compensate them to the full for their falling off in rents. In fact, his enthusiasm for the useless class quite carried him away, and made him optimistic as to the future of these poor sufferers; whereas he was pessimistic to the last degree as to the possibility of the 'Society' which he represented finding work for those willing to work, whom competition has thrust out of the labour market.

It must be said that he was right in his pessimism, and wrong in his optimism. It would be preposterous for the head of a bourgeois government to pretend to be able even to consider any scheme for benefitting the classes on whom his class – the class whose servant he is – lives; and scarcely less preposterous for any set of persons to ask him to consider it; unless, indeed, they were Socialists wanting to show him up for what he is. Yet on the other hand he cannot do much for his dear landlords, seeking rent where there is no rent. Even they in the long-run must come on the Socialists for 'compensation'; only the 'compensation' will not mean giving them back again the ownership of all the natural resources of the country which has been so ruinous to us all, and which is beginning to slip through their fingers, but assuring to them a position in which they will be able to exercise their capacities and earn themselves a non-precarious livelihood.

Meantime it is instructive to note the irresistible instinct which forces Lord Salisbury to exhibit himself in his real position, the head of a committee governing the country for the welfare of the proprietary classes. To Lord Salisbury, as to all who are not either consciously or unconsciously Socialists, it is only the members of these latter classes who are men and women with feelings to be considered and real lives to live: all others are only parts of the great machine, to be thought of only as a general thinks about his army: food for profit instead of food for powder: beings without property, of whom no account need be taken but as occasion calls on you to manipulate their votes.

The debate in the German Reichstag on the new anti-Socialist Bill, produced a remarkable exposure, from our friends Singer and Bebel, of the secret police system of Bismark. It is good that not only the German public but the public of England also should know what the cost of suppression is and must be; and that a part of it must necessarily be the keeping up [of] a system of espionage and provocation to deeds of violence which is absolutely sickening to think of, is a disgrace to human nature – even absolutist human nature.

One thing is clear, that in spite of Herr Puttkammer's rage and indignant denials, the statements of the Socialist deputies are believed by everybody. It is a common middle-class trick in this country to pooh-pooh all statements of this kind, and to assume that everything is managed in 'respectable' modern Governments if in a stiff and business-like, yet in an open and above-board manner. The reception even by the English public of these revelations of the 'frankness' of Herr Bismark, show how conventional this way of taking the subject is. The road of repression is a foul one, Bismark has doubtless long been callous to its worst quagmires; but our own rulers seem to have a taste for dirt, and if they go on as they have begun they will doubtless before long rival the 'Great Chancellor' in his disgraces.

He has been speaking once more to listening Europe, and people can make pretty much what they please of his speech as to the hopes of peace and war; but whatever he wanted various sets of people to think he meant by it, one thing is certain and may console those who are afraid of a coming war, and that is that war is the last thing he wants, and that he will go any lengths to avoid it. The German army is too useful an instrument for the repression of the German people to be wasted in foreign wars if they can be avoided.

I can imagine some of our friends grinning rather bitterly at the title of an article in the current number of the *Nineteenth Century*, 'How to live on £700 a-year,' and thinking that they would like to try the experiment. It should be explained that the title ought to run, 'How to live in the upper ranks of the shabby-genteel on £700 a-year.' This is a different problem, and a sufficiently tough one to those who are compelled to live in this group of curs. The receipt for it is much as follows: give away nothing; let your hospitality be merely conventional; take no pleasure except for the sake of gentility; never buy a book; look very sharp after your servants; in short, repress every instinct towards kindliness and generosity, and you may cut quite a good figure in the ranks of gentility, and be in fact a fine specimen of the genus 'snob.'

Commonweal, Volume 4, Number 109,
11 February 1888, p. 41.

[UNTITLED PARAGRAPH]

[*The following paragraph was appended to an article by Tom Muse entitled 'Suggestions on Decentralisation' which suggested a system of local government to alleviate the worst excesses of the capitalistic system.*]

We print the foregoing communication as containing interesting information and suggestions; but Socialists will be apt to doubt whether it would be worth while elaborating a new machinery for dealing with the present conditions of Society. The demand for decentralisation must spring from the same source as, and be put forward simultaneously with, the demand for the freeing of labour from the monopolist rule. A system of 'local self-government' might, it is clear, become a very dangerous instrument of oppression in the hands of our present rulers and the proprietary class which they represent.

Commonweal, Volume 4, Number, 109, 11 February 1888, p. 43.

NOTES ON NEWS

Parliament has met once more, and to all appearance the coming session will be as hopelessly barren of any performance as the most sturdy Tory or the most constitutional Whig could desire. The over-whelming majority in favour of 'resolute government' is still there, of course, and is not likely to be altered by the results of the bye-elections. But that is not all: the minority, if it had any cohesion or sincerity, might doubtless 'keep the dull times off' their enemies in one way or other; but here is the rub, that they are *not* their enemies. By far the greater part of them are only awaiting a decent opportunity to declare themselves against the one measure before Parliament which tends towards the popular side, and which the chapter of accidents has forced them to put forward as a party test – Home Rule, to wit.

That is the reason why the leaders have passed the word to fight soft; but after all it is a futile expedient, now that the subject has had every word said about it that can be said. What will happen? Much what happened when Mr. Gladstone brought in his Home Rule Bill. He will come into office again sooner or later, and will be obliged to put forward his Home Rule measure, no doubt as strenuously as he knows how, since the rest of his life is pledged to carrying the matter through. Well, then up will jump a new section of the Great Liberal Party, men who are all Home Rulers now, and will cry out, 'Oh, but we didn't mean this by Home Rule; this is disintegration of the empire, Socialism, Communism, and the devil knows what!' And they will turn Liberal Unionists, or whatever the name may then be for newly-declared reactionists, and the G.O.M. will be on his

back in the road once more as a result of 'strictly constitutional' opposition – otherwise fighting soft.

What is the alternative? Why, fighting hard. Mr. Gladstone
is, without knowing it, engaged in rebellion – that is the plain
truth; and his chance of success lies in his rallying to him all
the elements of discontent and revolution throughout the
country. These are growing on the one hand, just as the
reactionary elements, the instincts towards absolutism, are
growing on the other, and between them they make Mr.
Gladstone's constitutional position an impossible one.

What could he do this session? it may be said. Well, two
courses were open to the minority if they had (as they have
not) any heart in them. In any case they could have said,
How can this be a parliament when its very members are
lying in gaol and are liable to be arrested on the threshold of
the House for asserting their elementary rights as citizens?
We do not acknowledge the authority of such a parliament.
Then they might have proceeded to systematic obstruction,
and prevented any business being done as long as the
executive upheld its present tyranny.

Or, which would have been better, they might after making
an emphatic protest, have all marched out of the House in a
body, leaving behind as traitors any of their party who had a
mind to stop, never to return till coercion (in England as in
Ireland) was at end, and invited the majority to make any
new little laws they chose; they in the meantime meeting as a
committee of freedom and giving advice and help to their
constituencies.

Both these courses are, it seems, impossible, the first no less
so than the last. Therefore the parliamentary opposition is
worthless. Nay worse, it is actively harmful, because it

prevents people from stirring who might otherwise be driven to do so; since they depend on the action of their precious 'representatives.'

One disappointment there has been already for those who were sanguine enough to hope for even a good wrangle in Parliament over Trafalgar Square. In spite of the brave words of Messrs. Russell, Pickersgill, Stuart and Bradlaugh, it has gone down the wind. For I suppose few can be found so – well, green – as to imagine that the appointment by the Government of a day when a substantive motion on the subject can be put, means anything else than the shelf.

After all something may come of all this; because though we are used to this miserable shuffling and thrusting aside of the people's needs and aspirations at the hands of all parties in Parliament, we are not so used to the assertion of the power (and therefore the right) of the Executive to treat us all like puppets, and our 'constitutional safeguards' as pretty pictures. In order to understand what real freedom is it was necessary for us to learn what middle-class democracy means by freedom, and to feel the full weight of the tyranny of a parliamentary majority, and to learn by bitter experience that it may be as tyrannous as the rule of any despotism of the earlier days. We are likely to grow wise in this knowledge before the end of this year.

Mr. Shaw-Lefevre has held *his* meeting without interference: can it be really true that this is because he is an ex-Cabinet Minister? One scarcely likes to accuse even Mr. Balfour of such mingled shabbiness and stupidity.

Bismark's new Socialist-Coercion Bill has missed fire, and our friends in Germany are not to be subjected to any more stringent repression than they are used to, – which is stringent enough in all conscience. There can be no question but that Singer's and Bebel's speeches in the Reichstag, mentioned in our columns last week, and their showing up of the inferior working of Bismark's police, have been in the main the cause of what under the circumstances is a Socialist victory.

The Bermondsey Board of Guardians have been making a good thing out of the 'relief' of the poor men employed in their stone-yards, – buying cheap and selling dear to them, as the way of the world is. The chairman thinks that the question was who should reap the benefit of a fall in prices - the ratepayers or the men? He was more of a man of the world than another member of the Board, a Mr. Bedding, who cried out, 'Then we are actually making a profit out of our own poor on our own goods. I call it a robbery on these poor people.'

It is creditable to Mr. Bedding that he could not take the matter coolly, and that this piece of shabby extortion startled him; but pray how do all capitalists live, except by 'making a profit out of their own poor on their own goods'? May we not call it, like Mr. Bedding, 'a robbery on those poor people'?

The jury find Arthur Gough guilty of 'assaulting' the police (according to the story of the police), but think he did it 'in a moment of excitement,' – *i.e.*, 'Guilty, but we don't think he did it.'

Commonweal, Volume 4, Number 110,
18 February 1888, p. 49.

NOTES ON NEWS

Mr. Commissioner Kerr deserves to be long remembered for the language of his sentence on our friend Gough. Mrs. Gamp at her best could hardly have achieved a greater success than this remarkable production: that is, as regards its manner: as to its matter, Mr. Commissioner Kerr finds it extraordinary that anyone, still more several persons, could be found to swear that the police were – well, mistaken – in asserting that the prisoner committed an assault on a constable's – helmet. Amazing indeed that any citizen should venture on such boldness as flying in the face of police evidence after all that has passed during the last three months! I remember being rather surprised when a policeman who shoved me in the Thames Street Police-court swore that I hit him; but I was not much alarmed, because I thought a serious citizen's word would weigh at least as heavily as that of an excited policeman. We have changed all that now, and witnesses who contradict police evidence had better nerve themselves against indictment for perjury.

At the same time our comrade Gough must be congratulated for not being tried by Edlin, who would probably, after praising him for his good character and admonishing him for his rashness, have given him six months. Considering the times we are in, he probably thinks himself lucky in getting off with a month for *not* hitting a policeman. Great are the blessings of law and order certainly, yet it is now as in the days of David, 'The tender mercies of the wicked are cruel.'

This morning (Feb. 18th) the Government of the British Islands won a great and notable victory: the friends of two citizens who had been imprisoned for trying to speak on a piece of public land proposed to meet them and greet them at a tolerable early hour as they came out of prison, the hour being the usual time for such release and at which it was announced that they would be released. By a stupendous exertion of strategy the prison officials thrust out the prisoners an hour and a half before the appointed time, so that many of the friends aforesaid missed seeing the prisoners, and, triumph of triumphs, John Burns had to wait about the neighbourhood of the prison for his wife for some time! Such preposterous shabbiness shows how low prison life will bring the officials connected with it: the poor devils have to spend their days in carrying out the multitudinous petty tortures of the place, whose aggregate makes up a severe torture enough, and one can scarcely wonder at any shabbiness that they may perpetrate. But just to think of all the elaboration of officialism, the wheels within wheels, the whole force of army, navy, and police, not to mention the judges, lawyers, etc., brought to bear upon such a shabby little trick! For indeed it takes all that to do it.

Ireland has carried the day in eloquence at least, and the speech of William O'Brien will be long remembered as a mark in the record of her rebellion. Mr. Balfour must receive the kind of praise for moral courage and self-restraint for not answering him the same evening, which a duellist does who manages to walk away from the field of honour without drawing his sword; it was almost *too* courageous. Doubtless he thought it well to wait till the effect of O'Brien's speech had worn off a little, but the alternative was not very happy after all, and the effect of O'Brien's speech remains.

The Liberals have at last won an undoubted victory in the big majority in Southwark; but the big majority still remains against them in the House of Commons, and they may chasten their exultation by remembering that Disraeli pulled the string of the shower-bath upon him owing to the encouragement which the Southwark bye-election of that year gave him.

In any case how will they spend the time between the time of the hope of office and its fulfilment? Probably in thinking of nothing political except electioneering; as for other matters they will go on hoping that 'things will come round and be all square.' If they were wise (as they are not), they would reflect that though the relief from the very worst to something not quite so bad will give them a chance of popularity, yet the present period of resolute government has bred discontent that is gathering hopes and ideas, and that a compromise with the Irish demands, followed by masterly inactivity, will not satisfy those hopes or smother the ideas; so that they also will have their own crop of discontent to deal with.

The reception of the prisoners of liberty on the evening of the 18th was most enthusiastic, and the meeting was in every way remarkable. It is needless to say that both Burns and Graham spoke heartily and to the purpose, though their voices had been thinned down by 'prison discipline.' Mr. Blane, M.P. (condemned to four months for the usual 'crime'), made a very favourable impression on the meeting by a speech full of friendliness and good feeling, which was far more advanced and less national than the conventional Irish member's speeches are wont to be. The tremendous cheers that greeted him on rising, however, were obviously given to him as a rebel. It is worth noting also that while the cheers for the rebels, both Irish and English, nearly took the roof off the hall, Mr. Gladstone's name was only cheered by a small minority of those present, and that when the said minority seemed inclined to persist an ominous booing arose, which did not cease till the cheering ceased.

The meeting held on Monday to welcome Graham and Burns was a very remarkable one, and in most respects very satisfactory. But whatever differences of opinion there might be between different sections of the audience, some of them need reminding that a meeting assembled to defend freedom of speech should allow a hearing to any one who may differ from them, and that though they had a right to express their disapprobation of Hyndman's speech, they had no right to prevent other people hearing him. For the rest the fact to which he drew attention was obvious enough; it would have been strange indeed if the meeting had separated without noting that the Liberal and Radical members were conspicuous for their paucity, – if nobody had called attention to the conspiracy of silence on the part of the orthodox party (which aspires to be popular) on the subject of the Tory dragooning. Hyndman's indignation was felt by many other persons who had no opportunity of expressing it.

Commonweal, Volume 4, Number 111,
25 February 1888, p. 57.

[UNTITLED PARAGRAPH]

[*The following paragraph was written in response to T. Binning's reply to Morris's article on 'Practical' Socialists. Binning described Morris's socialism as 'Micawber' Socialism, and stated that as far as he was concerned 'Practical' Socialism should be aimed at the immediate relief of the poverty of the lower classes and the untiring improvement of their social and political conditions.*]

Comrade Binning having some fault with my article, I asked him as Editor to put his animadversions in writing: I must say that there is very little in his letter which I should quarrel with; but it seems to me beside the subject of my article, which does not profess to deal with the methods by which either transitional Socialism or the completed communal society is to be attained. To clear up any misunderstanding there may be between us, I should say that my remarks were meant as words of warning to those, on the one hand, who are blind to the ideal which we have before us, and to those, on the other hand, who seeing and knowing that ideal, are afraid to put it before persons lest they should startle them too much. I never supposed that comrade Binning belonged to either of those groups, the latter of which are composed almost wholly of middle-class persons: as to the former, I think it of great importance to put the highest ideal before them, so as to encourage them to the utmost.

Commonweal, Volume 4, Number 111,
25 February 1888, p. 61.

NOTES ON NEWS

The debate on the Crofters was treated as one expects important subjects to be treated in the House, and as a matter of course those who were anxious to keep these poor people from starving because they are not allowed to use their own land, had no chance at all before the advocates of the snob-made solitude called a deer-forest. The utmost that their rulers think they can do for them is to transport them (some time or other) to some place where they do not want to go. It is sickening to read the speeches of these tyrants and prigs, talking (but not understanding) scraps of Malthusianism, when one considers that the poor people are actually at the point of sheer destitution, and that if they were treated with something like reason, there would at least be breathing space for them.

There is a certain pleasure in being able to say to one's enemy, 'Well, do you know I quite agree with you there.' Mr. Balfour has given us the opportunity for this pleasure, since he has (at last) found out that the Irish agitation is at bottom socialistic; or in other words that its ultimate aim is not a parliament at Dublin more or less after the pattern of the ignominious assembly in London, but the welfare of the Irish *people*. Strange to say, his discovery leads to no practical consequences, and he remains still opposed to Home Rule.

Indeed he finished his speech in a way that would make even a propagandist Socialist stare with wonder who is accustomed to the humours of the debates which follow his lectures. Not even the man who says, 'Mr. Chairman, I have not heard the lecture and do not know what the subject of it is, but I should like to say a few words in opposition' – not even this genius can quite equal Balfour's impudence. 'The laws of property are made much more for the advantage of the poor than for the rich.' I am glad to say that the Irish members laughed at this joke.

If one believed that Balfour had not had his tongue in his cheek when he said this, one might ask him to alter this a little and say, 'the laws of property are made more for the advantage of those who have no property than for those who have it.' But as a matter of fact, his phrase is only a measure of bourgeois hypocrisy in this country, which not only knocks a man down and robs him, but is not ashamed to say at the same time, 'My friend, it is for your benefit I do this, in order to stimulate your industry.'

This is not the only country where the immigration of 'foreign paupers' is a difficulty. America has the same trouble, only the 'foreigners' there are many of them English. We are to have an article in the forthcoming *Century*, says the *Daily News*, which suggests a passport system for immigrants, so as to prevent the landing at American ports of all criminals, paupers (say Highland crofters), Mormons, Anarchists, and the depraved classes generally.

Good! So much for keeping out those who are *not* there, but how about getting rid of those that *are* there? What's to be done with the 'native American' thieves who live on other people's labour? the 'native American' criminals who murder their political opponents by the safe process of false witness in a law court? With the 'rogue and whore' varnished over with gentleman and lady, of which 'native American' society (like our's) is so largely composed? If the Americans set themselves seriously to getting rid of their 'depraved classes,' 'tis thought that house rent will fall heavily in the 'genteel' quarters of New York, and Wall Street will be quiet enough.

Well, well! so it goes on! let us pass our paupers on if our neighbours will but have them; and if they won't. Well, the Roman's fell before the barbarians whom they despised, but who were at any rate *without* their society; while our barbarians are *within* ours! Would it not be cheaper and safer (let alone humanity (*sic*)) not to manufacture paupers and criminals, if we find them so hard to deal with when made?

Do people doubt that our destroyers are in the midst of us? I fear they do. It was thought even by 'advanced' persons that John Burns was either joking, or speaking with the extravagance natural to a man who had recently suffered from the hideous den when he spoke the other day so heartily, and wisely also, about pulling down Pentonville. Will people never understand then, not even Home Rulers and extreme Radicals, what our prison system means? Must we Socialists teach them even this? Pentonville must not compete with the slums, or its terror will be gone; and a very little more and it would compete with them. Therefore its diet and discipline must be on such a scale as is a torture to a gentleman like Graham, or even an artisan like Burns. If only Pentonville could be pulled down before revenge overtakes us for this folly and cruelty!

Commonweal, Volume 4, Number 112,
3 March 1888, p. 65.

NOTES ON NEWS

The farce of bringing the matter of Trafalgar Square before the House of Commons, that is of asking the Government who ordered the arbitrary closure of it to consider what right they had to do so, was brought to an end on March 2nd. The Government very naturally put its foot down, and in order to put the screw on some of its supporters who used to be considered Liberals and even Radicals, announced their intention of making the vote one of confidence, thereby, of course, formerly declaring their approval of all the acts of law and order. Nothing less was to be expected of them, and they would have been fools indeed if they had hesitated in avowing their complicity with Warren, especially after their victory at Deptford.

Sir C. Russell's speech was of little importance; he was bound by convention to make a sort of legal case for the right use of the Square by the people, to which of course no Government need pay the least attention, since they have plenty of weapons in the legal armoury with which to annihilate any such right. Sir Charles finished fairly well by appealing to the true foundation of the right to speak in the Square, which is, in fact, simply public convenience – for which, of course, no Government cares one jot.

Mr. Matthews repeated the whole string of stale lies about the dangers of the unemployed meetings. He had the fatuity to quote some piece of speaking about the firing of London from an orator, whom Mr. Bradlaugh, interrupting him, said was an associate of the police. In the course of this speech, Sir C. Russell undid the effect of the whole of his action by admitting that the Government had a right to stop the meeting (in that case why not every other meeting?). His speech meant that Trafalgar Square is royal property, and that, whether or not, the executive had the right to stop any meeting they think fit to stop – as they certainly, at present, have the *might* to do.

It is this all-important fact which nullified Mr. Bradlaugh's powerful speech, which would otherwise have been effective and convincing. He was quite right in stating that besides the question as to whether the people had the right of free speech in the metropolis, the question as to whether they had the right of free speech in the country generally was before them; and the provincial Radicals who have paid no heed to this Trafalgar Square business should take note of the fact. Unfortunately, of what use is the verbal assertion of the right in face of a Parliamentary majority elected by the combined property and ignorance of the nation, and their committee, the Executive Government, who are holding their places on the condition that they will do the bidding of property and ignorance?

Mr. Bradlaugh on the 3rd brought the disgraceful fact of the assaults on prisoners by the police plainly and squarely before the House; but the Attorney-General showed by his speech that the Government understood too well the resources of law-and-order in the great body of professional witnesses at their command – whose idea of duty is to give the evidence that they are expected to give – to be much disquieted at his plain statement of facts. We can only hope that the country generally will take note of it.

Our friend, Cunninghame Graham, spoke as usual boldly and well, and did good service by pointing out the undoubted fact that the Government did their best to create a riot on Bloody Sunday, and that the 'hazing' of the police by Warren was a good means of ensuring this. Of course, Matthews denied it; but also, of course, who would play such a game would deny it with the holiest horror. The fact remains true in spite of all denials.

———————————

Graham was received with what may be called House of Commons manners, that is to say, more brutally than if he were addressing a crew of drunken roughs at election time. What on earth *can* one say of men who jeer at a citizen for being ill from the effects of police brutality and prison torture? To call them blackguards has no meaning; to call them curs would be gross flattery, since I have known several curs (real ones with tails) of high moral worth and pleasing manners. How long are we to bear this disgrace, the House of Commons?

———————————

So, after all, there was a division on the question; and it may be said as the net gain of the debate that besides the calling the attention of the Committee to the police outrages, it consisted in forcing the respectable Liberals to commit themselves to something, though not much. Whether they will remember this when they come into office is another matter; they have plenty of loop-holes at which to climb out of. Apart from this small gain the matter remains exactly where it was before the debate; the Government are prepared to resist any attempts to speak in the Square by the usual machinery of law and order, police, soldiery, drum-head court-martials, professional witnesses, judge-directed juries, and the rest of it. Who could expect anything else?

———————————

The Welsh Anti-Tithe rioters got off very cheap – since they had to pay nothing. If they had done the same thing in London they would have had various terms of imprisonment, from four months to two years for their boldness. What is the explanation of this, if it means anything more than that Mr. Justice Willis is a very much better fellow than his brethren, as we will hope and believe? I cannot help thinking that it means a recognition of the power of the Nonconformists, who are the strength of the respectable Liberals. Anyhow, glad as we must be that these good fellows have got off, we are bound to point out once more what a ridiculous tyranny our law courts are. A crime in London is a peccadillo in Wales.

That absurd body, the Convocation of the Province of Canterbury, has been receiving a petition from some wise-acres as to the Sunday amusements of the upper-classes. These amusements only concern us from the fact that they are paid for by the misery of the *lower* classes. But the curious *non sequitur* of the petitioners that excursion trains on Sundays should *therefore* be stopped, shows the cloven hoof under the garment of religion, and lets us know what these anxious Christians would do to us if they could.

Commonweal, Volume 4, Number 113,
10 March 1888, p. 73.

DEAD AT LAST

[*These two paragraphs appeared at the end of the above article.*]

The Government are determined that we shall not lack sensation. Mr. Snelling's sentence to seven month's hard labour for speaking his mind in Ireland, is quite on all fours with the sentences in London on those who tried to speak their minds in Trafalgar Square. Really we must repeat our advice to the G.O.M. to show that he is in earnest by going over to Ireland, and daring the Government to arrest him.

The House of Commons has at the instigation of Mr. Labouchere been debating as to whether it would be advisable to abolish the hereditary element in the Upper House – whether it would be advisable to spend a pound or two in mending a bad sixpence. Here is comfort for the unemployed, the men on strike, the hewers of wood and drawers of water!

Commonweal, Volume 4, Number 114,
17 March 1888, p. 81.

NOTES ON NEWS

There is a sort of feeling of expectation in the air of
something to happen in Germany, now that the ignominious
old man who has so long filled the joss-seat has gone. Some
hope that the new Emperor will go further than merely doing
his best to keep the peace of Europe unbroken; that he will
inaugurate 'reforms' in Germany itself, relax the oppressive
laws just re-enacted against the Socialists. An article in the
Pall Mall Gazette dwelt on the solemn position of the
Emperor Frederick, placed as he is between the new throne
and probable speedy death, and seemed to think that his acts
would be the more conscientious and beneficent for that
reason.

I don't know: I cannot help thinking that he will rather feel
himself an *ad interim* Emperor whose business it is to do
nothing. Besides, I doubt the effect of illness as a stimulus to
action: it seems to me that people who are ill and drawing
near their death are rather apt to think more about their
illness than anything else. It is from those who are vigorously
alive that one expects vigorous action.

And after all, is it to be believed that it will be so easy for this
one man and the clique in the Court that follows him to
break through the strength given by the long years of the
Bismarkian policy?

Finally, in no case, even if Kaiser Frederick lives and inaugu-
rates the reign of reform, will it be good for the cause of the
people or bad for it. May it not bring about a state of things

not better but only more plausible? a state of things like that which we have so long 'enjoyed' here; in which people are free – to starve; free also to speak – so long as their speaking does not annoy their masters too much. These are questions which we cannot help asking ourselves.

Commonweal, Volume 4, Number 115,
24 March 1888, p. 89.

NOTES ON NEWS

Mr. Ritchie's Local Government Bill is accepted everywhere as a progressive measure, and surprise is often expressed that such a measure should come from a Tory Government. It is hardly worth while for us to go into its details, especially since it is more than possible that, whatever Mr. Ritchie's intentions may be, the Government generally does not intend that it shall pass intact. Meanwhile the putting forward by the Tories of a measure which would have been thought bold by the Liberals, points to that confusion of parties amongst our governing classes which is the sure forerunner of the emergence of the great popular party – Socialism, as the only real opposition to the sham Toryism and sham Liberalism that are now really one party, the Obstructionists.

It must also be said that since undoubtedly this Bill is intended as a dishing measure and a bid for the popular vote at the next election, this betokens that the feeling for decentralisation, which has made the present form of agitation for Home Rule possible, is on the increase. It was understood by the Tories to be a certain bait, which it would not have been if the feeling in favour of decentralisation were not strong. Doubtless they also think it a *safe* measure; let us hope that it will turn out not to be quite so safe, and that it will be used for other purposes than electioneering.

Great news! An amnesty proclaimed in Berlin as the first-fruits of the new Kaiser's accession. 'It chiefly applies to political offences,' says the press; 'but is not extended to persons sentenced under the Socialist Laws, nor to those imprisoned for high treason.' To whom is it extended then in the name of patience? and how many first-class carriages would the non-Socialist political offenders fill? The Socialists, who are no doubt not at all surprised at this act of mercy, must feel themselves much honoured by the exception. Well, well! so ends any hope that may have been founded on the Liberal Kaiser – poor devil!

The consistent supporter of coercion in England, the *Daily News*, in reviewing the prospects for the hatchment of that bad egg, the Liberal Party, says that 'when Parliament met on the 9th February the Liberal cause had been seriously compromised by the follies of Trafalgar Square.' This is an Easter Monday paragraph, and no doubt in such holiday times the production of a paper has to depend on at least its *second*-rate writers, and I think we may fairly suppose that the writer in question has as good a right to give us his views about folly as a blind man has about blindness, or a lame man about lameness.

Yet one must agree with the words of our coercionist booby, if not with his meaning. Balaam's ass has spoken, and spoken truth too; the Liberal cause has been seriously compromised by the follies of Trafalgar Square. Such a folly as that committed by Mr. Gladstone and his followers has rarely been met with, when they fell into the Tory trap by not resisting coercion in England while they were going about bawling over the horrors of coercion in Ireland. Trafalgar Square has been the touch-stone of their genuineness, and has found them out, and they now stand proclaimed as mere politicians and humbugs, who have taken up the Irish question because Mr. Parnell forced their hand by making his party vote against them in 1885. They will find out their mistake at the next election and bitterly regret 'The Follies of Trafalgar Square,' as given for the first time by the G.O.M. and his world-renowned company.

Commonweal, Volume 4, Number 117,
7 April 1888, p. 105.

NOTES ON NEWS

The police have been at it again, and this time, as they have been bearing false witness not against 'revolutionaries' or persons who happened to be mixed up with them, but against ordinary citizens not guilty *à priori* of the crime of 'demonstrating,' they have got into trouble, and the public prosecutor is to look into the matter. Couldn't he go a few weeks backward and look into the cases of the 'rioters' of the past winter?

In all soberness, the attention which has been paid to Mr. Montagu Williams' scolding of the police brings out the cowardly injustice of society towards the victims of the raid on free speech into yet stronger relief than before. To judge by the tone of the press about this affair, one would suppose that no accusations had ever been made against the police, that the whole public are perfectly satisfied that their evidence against Harrison and Ellis and dozens of others was admitted to be spotlessly true, and that everybody 'run in' for anything (or for nothing) connected with Trafalgar Square was even himself persuaded that he had received a perfectly fair trial. Surely no hypocrisy has ever come anywhere near the Pharisaism of modern bourgeois England!

I get papers from candidates for the vestry shoved into my door at times, beside the voting paper. Some of the former are droll. One candidate appears to me to be at least frank; he says he shall consider it one of his principal duties to see that the contracts are given to persons in the neighbourhood, or words to that effect. The same gentleman says that he will do his best to see that those unfortunate persons who are in need of relief shall, as far as possible, be treated with a *fair* amount of comfort and consideration. Here is qualification with a vengeance!

The economics of some of our leading papers are wonderful indeed. The *Daily News*, for instance, says, quoting Major Roe about a work at Birmingham: 'The use of power-driven machinery is daily increasing, with the result of increased output and the substitution of women and youths for the skilled artisan; on the other hand, the men are more than compensated by the increased demand for them in the manufacturing of tools and machinery.' Which most clearly means, if it means anything, that the manufacturer, having got rid of human labour at one of the process, uses up all the displaced labour at the other end, and has besides saddled himself with machinery which he has had to pay for and cannot use, and that he does this without compulsion. On the whole, it is easier to believe that the *Daily News* gets its minor leader-writers from Colney Hatch than to believe this.

Indeed, this explanation gathers credibility as one reads further where the writer, having informed us of the first-quoted passage that women and boys are being substituted for skilled artisans, goes on to tell us that it is said that the days of *un*skilled labour are numbered. With a leer in his eye and a straw or two and a peacock's feather in his hair, he finishes by drawing a moral for us, the often-told tale that all is for the best in this best possible of worlds, wherein the capitalist can still make a profit out of other people's labour. 'Thanks to the Education Act, the condition of the working classes is better than it used to be; they spend both their wages and leisure better than of old. Technical instruction and sober diligence will be the salvation of many a British industry.' Yes; but he means the salvation of much British capital. Make technical education so common that it is no longer of any market value, thinks the capitalist, and then we shall be able to get the skilled workman at the cost of the unskilled; let every workman (that is employed) work two hours a day more than he does now, and it will put so much the more into *our* pockets, as we shall pay the same for the twelve hours as we do now for the ten. This is the way to safeguard British industry against foreign competition.

Yet education, technical instruction, and sober industry are good things – so good that it is grievous indeed to see them made use of to 'cheapen labour,' that is, to make legal stealing safer and more profitable. However, let us have courage; education is a dangerous gift to give to slaves. What does our author from Colney Hatch think will be the result (if we should come to it, and we *are* coming to it) of a class of skilled artisans unemployed, or reduced to the ranks, and at the same time 'educated' by book-learning as well as suffering? No men, surely, have ever set themselves more busily to sow the wind for the harvest of the whirlwind than our anti-Socialist 'Liberal' capitalists.

Commonweal, Volume 4, Number 118, 14 April 1888, p. 113.

NOTES ON NEWS

Mr. Arnold White has been giving evidence before the House of Lords on the sweating system in the East-end, which no doubt will shock the respectabilities of the middle-class – for a little time; until in fact they forget all about it, and then to them these miseries will no longer exist. Probably the fact that the 'sweater' is often as poor as or even poorer than the man he employs will come as a surprise to many who do not know the way in which the poor live. Now they know that fact might they not ask themselves the question, Who sweats the sweater? The question asked by a well-to-do person will have to be answered in the manner of the ancient Hebrew chronicler, *Thou art the man.*

Mr. Arnold White proposed remedies. We will not say that there are *remedies*, but there is a *remedy*, which Mr. White, it is to be thought would not relish, and that is the freeing of labour from privileged monopoly; all Mr. White can see as desirable to be done is to make a feeble attempt to stop foreign immigration, to crush out the small employer by a tax on workshops, and so forth, and then to stand by and see how much people would starve then – for they certainly would starve. What workmen should remember is that all this 'sweating' is necessary in order to [ensure] that 'cheap production of wares, which is still quoted as being a blessing to the working-classes (though scarcely I think with the same confidence as formerly). These cheap workmen must be cheapened down to their present misery in order that the more expensive ones may still be cheap relatively to the capital employed in buying them; so that this country may be able to compete with others, and other countries with this country; and in spite of all Mr. Arnold White's 'remedies,' this process will go on, and *must* go on until the whole cursed system breaks down – or blows up. The horror-stricken supporters of capitalism must not be so unreasonable as to expect to have an omelette without egg-breaking; or a capitalist without propertyless workers, the final expression of whom is this sweated East-end immigrant.

I should like, by the way, to ask of any of our friends that know the 'industry' in question, whether Mr. White's confident assertion that all the sweaters are foreigners is strictly true?

Mr. Saunders is going to try the right of free speech by a civil action against Warren & Co., and some think that if the judges are anything but the creatures of reactionary bureaucracy, something ought to come of that: but as a matter of fact, that is just what they are. If they cannot find law for any piece of tyranny which *our masters* have a mind to, they are not worth their salt, and out masters should dismiss them. But surely they have already abundantly proved that they *are* worth their salt. They are expensive but necessary to our masters.

A report of a traveller in Siam says of the Nan slaves: 'Every man of the lower orders must be enrolled as the slave of some master; but he is allowed to choose whom he will serve, and if he does not like one, he may enroll himself as the slave of another.... A slave is fed by his master while he is working for him, but at other times he must feed himself. No purchase money is paid for the slave by his master.' Dear me! Siam is a long way off, and supposing one were travelling to see diversities of the condition of workmen, I for one should scarcely think it worth while to go through so much to learn so little as I should have to do if I were to undertake the journey. For the condition of the Nan slaves is just that of the London slaves; except, indeed that the latter do not find it so easy to shift themselves from one master to another as their Siamese brethren do; for there seems a certain flavour of compulsion on the masters to employ in the hotter and happier country.   In fact the *Daily News* from which I extracted this good news of a better land, seems impressed by the fact, and says, 'We can even imagine many of our less fortunate countrymen envying their prerogative.' Would Mr. Arnold White like to take the place of agent for emigration to Nan-land! Or would he not think the workman *too free* there? The latter, I am afraid.

Commonweal, Volume 4, Number 119,
21 April 1888, p. 121.

NOTES ON NEWS

Our comrades of the *Social Demokrat* have received notice of expulsion from their asylum at Zurich, and will have to leave Switzerland. This attack on freedom by a bourgeois Republic is the sort of thing one expects in these days, but it may be ominous of something special in the welter of European politics, an indication that the huge tyranny of the German Empire is looking on a war as sensibly drawing near, and is putting its house in order, by a further attempt, which will certainly be as futile as the rest to stamp out the growing flame of Socialism.

Just as we are going to press we have received an interesting letter from a comrade on this subject, recounting the shabby pretexts of the Swiss Federal Government for this tyrannical act. Of course, as our comrade states, the Swiss Government is acting under pressure from the German Executive, and the *immediate* cause of the 'energy' of the latter is revenge on the *Social Demokrat* for the defeat sustained by Bismark and Co. in the Reichstag, when the attempt was made to strengthen the laws against the Socialists; which to any other Government or potentate, ancient or modern, would seem strong enough as they are. In fact, this expulsion of our comrades is just a part of that forward move in repression.

We may well wonder what Balfour and his mates believe in their hearts will be the end of their Coercion adventure in Ireland, or to what lengths they are prepared to carry it. They must, at least, have a deep faith in the want of generosity of the English bourgeois, and the impossibility of shaming him into anything like manliness, or they would at any rate have made haste to alter the sentence of additional imprisonment passed on Mr. Blane for having the hardihood to appeal against his conviction. Such conduct is worthy of an ill-tempered pedagogue, and no one but a man who considers himself entirely irresponsible to anything but his own indigestion, would dare to act in such a manner outside the ranks of the English or American fool, the quintescence of all stupidity past or present.

Yet it is probable that the Balfourian snobs think that something will come about from the imprisonment of Blane and McFadden and the onslaught at Ennis, and other deeds of a like nature. What is the something which they hope for? Surely that they may at last irritate the Irish into some overt act of rebellion, so that Coercion and its dirty tricks may be justified in the eyes of British respectability. Really if this is so, and all the recent events point towards it, the game hardly seems worth the candle to a calm looker on. For what will Balfour do next – and next – and next? Of course he has not troubled his head about that.

As to Mr. Blane, however, perhaps the Irish authorities may know what they are about, and have laid hands on the right person. Some of us will remember our introduction to him at the tea whereat Graham and Burns were welcomed, and the speech he made on that occasion, in which he spoke like a Socialist and a thoroughly good fellow. No doubt he is a dangerous man, and the opportunity of keeping him under lock and key a few months longer is not lightly to be forgone. Meantime, after what we saw of him on that occasion, our sympathy with him must be of the strongest character.

The meeting summoned by the Metropolitan Radical Federation to consider the Trafalgar Square business will, at any rate, have one good effect, that no Radicals worthy of the name can look with anything but contempt on their 'Liberal'

representatives in London. Mr. Foote's defence of them in
the letter which he wrote to the *Star* is as lame as anything
could be; and the round-robin written to the meeting fully
deserved the shouts of laughter with which it was greeted.
Men who will snatch at such an excuse as Mr. Saunder's
civil case will do anything in the way of excusing themselves.
If Mr. Saunders gains his case he does not establish the right
of meeting in the Square, but only settles under what quibble
it is most convenient to forbid meeting. If he loses it, affairs
are just in the same position as they are now.

We need not doubt that there is plenty of law to prevent us
meeting in the Square; or, indeed, anywhere else in the open-
air. For the matter of that a very little ingenuity on the part
of lawyers and judges would enable a government to forbid
us meeting *indoors* either unless we say there what pleases
our masters. There is still, for instance, an unrepealed law
which forbids Sunday meetings in places unlicensed for
public worship under penalties heavy enough 'to make your
flesh creep'; and it would be awkward, not to say impossible,
for Socialist branches or Radical clubs to get their lecture-
rooms licensed as chapels. We may be sure that neither this
government nor any other will ever be seriously embarrassed
by the laws. Whatever is convenient for them to do in the
way of keeping the people down they will do if the people lets
them – if they dare.

The rights of property take shapes as curious and shifting as
the wizard in the old tale. Here is a 'common-sense' public
horrified at Socialist propositions to meddle with the sacred
thing, and invoking the eighth commandment of a tribe
which, I think, in those days hardly held the same views
about property as the modern bourgeois does. Here is the
House of Commons, the judges, the lawyers, the magistrates,
the police, the army and the navy all engaged in the holy task
of safeguarding property, and yet the whole of this magnificent moral sense, the whole of this irresistible machinery,

quite capable of spending a hundred pounds in mending
sixpence beautifully, cannot get back for poor Mary Ryan
her property, which has been 'conveyed' from her by the
police; though a magistrate (a not very tender conscienced
species) gave her an order for it, the judges of a superior
court found they were not strong enough to let her have it;
and so hopeless is her case that questions have been asked
about it in the House of Commons! Her sole remedy now is
to bring an action against the police. What a night-mare of
stupidity and injustice!

It is puzzling to some brains why Mr. Peters should have
£300 as a result of Mr. Bradlaugh's assertion about Lord
Salisbury's cheque. It is doubtful if the conundrum is worth
much trouble to solve; since it is clear enough that the jury
awarded that sum to him to avenge Lord Salisbury on Mr.
Bradlaugh. I suppose precedent forbade their recommending
from the box that Mr. Peters should offer halves to the Most
Noble; but it may be hoped that Mr. Peters will see his way
to making the marquis a handsome present out of his
windfall: all the more as his lordship belongs to the neces-
sitous class whom Mr. Peters supports politically – the
landlords of Great Britain and Ireland. If that could be done,
it would be a case of 'all's well that ends well': Mr.
Bradlaugh's fine paid by M.P.'s who can afford it; Mr. Peters
happy; and Lord Salisbury content.

Commonweal, Volume 4, Number 120,
28 April 1888, p. 129.

NOTES ON NEWS

The Mid-Lanark election has resulted in a great Whig triumph, which will surely be not altogether unpleasing to the Tories, since it is at once a triumph of respectability over poverty, and a great blow to the prestige of the Irish Parliamentary Party, whose direct interference no doubt largely contributed to the Whig majority; henceforth it will be clear to the British Labour Party that the Irish leaders are simply using the democracy of this island for their own political purposes, and there cannot fail in consequence to be much soreness against the said leaders among the British workers.

We Socialists however appeal earnestly to the workers of Mid-Lanark and others who have suffered by these servile tactics, to take a noble revenge on the leaders, by looking to the Irish people themselves, and being all the more intent on freeing *them* not only from the tyranny of foreign centralisation, but also from the new tyranny that awaits them when they are victorious in the matter of Home Rule; if indeed they ever will get Home Rule until they acknowledge the full force of the class struggle and the identity of the interests of the workers all over the world. Undoubtedly when there is a parliament in Dublin the struggle of the Irish people for freedom will have to be begun again, and it is just because we Socialists want to see the real struggle for freedom begin, that we will do all we can to push on this preliminary stage of Home Rule.

Home Rule by all means; but not as an instrument for the exploitation of the Irish labourer by the Irish capitalist tenant: not as an instrument for the establishment of more factories, for the creation of a fresh Irish proletariat to be robbed for the benefit of national capitalists. Our Home Rule means Home Rule for the Irish people, that is to say *equality* for the Irish people.

A word or two to our own Socialist friends on this unpleasant Mid-Lanark business. They have entered on this electioneering struggle with a people at their back not yet educated into a knowledge of the reasons for the wrongs which they suffer, or the remedies for them, and as a matter of course they have been defeated. Is it too late for them to change their tactics and make up their minds to educate the people in the principles of Socialism before asking them to return Socialists to Parliament? I think Socialists sometimes forget what a great distance there is between them and the mere discontented Radicals who must form the mass of the voters they have any chance of winning over. The Socialist can no more forget his Socialism than he can the elementary facts of science when once learned. So that while *he* continually sees before him at least the first real Socialist measures, his Radical friend sees nothing but the preliminary steps to those measures, and is, in consequence, an easy prey to the false promises of the loose-tongued Whig and the dishing Tory-Democrat.

Of one thing I am sure, that if propaganda by electioneering is practised by any body of Socialists they will have no time for any other means of propaganda: they must begin at once and think of nothing else but getting Socialists into Parliament. The direct education of the people in the principles of Socialism must be the task of other Socialists who do not trouble themselves about Parliament; and unless there is such a body of Socialists our parliamentary friends will find their task an impossible one.

The Pope has now formally banned the Plan of Campaign and boycotting. This is good news indeed, and it is to be hoped that the Irish bishops will find themselves compelled to follow suit: it will be better news still when the parish priests declare against the people. The two curses of a reactionary religion and the national sentiment which has been forced upon Ireland have been a heavy drawback on the necessities and aspirations of the Irish people.

———————————————

It seems that charity is somewhat at a discount at present; there has been a great falling off lately; the Jubilee last year was bad for it, and so on, and so on. This means of course that the rich and well-to-do are determined not to lack their luxuries and comforts whatever happens. In short the more charity is wanted the less of it is to be had. In the long run this will be found out to be the case with all palliatives of our system of robbery. They cannot be applied just at the time when they are needed.

Commonweal, Volume 4, Number 121,
5 May 1888, p. 137.

NOTES ON NEWS

The alliance of the Tories with the Pope would seem to be a serious political event instead of a piece of meaningless tomfoolery as a reasonable man would expect. It has even been said that Mr. Parnell was going to advise backing down on the Plan of Campaign and boycotting; but in his speech at the Eighty Club he simple threw the responsibility on the Catholic members, with a prudent reserve as to the Plan of Campaign not being necessary to Irish agitation; he also somewhat deprecates the Plan as having led to coercion. This all looks somewhat like hedging; as if he thinks surrender may be necessary. But surrender won't do. Whatever may be said of the Plan, the boycott is a necessary weapon to a people who cannot fight and will not yield.

And all this fuss about an old man representing a superstition all but extinct; in fact extinct everywhere except in Ireland. The once redoubtable Pope of Rome has now become a *don*, and the expression of his opinions about as important as those of the Vice-Chancellor of the University of Oxford; or indeed of the head beadle of that reverent presence, the old gentleman in the gown and the round flat cap that used to be called the head gold-stick in my young days. Yet at least this sham of what was once a real power, dried up and effete as it is, is good enough to be used as a policeman by the reactionary party. What a desperately shabby resource to use. An innocent intelligent onlooker would say: My friend, as to the pure all things are pure, so to the shabby all things are shabby.

Anyhow this bugbear of a gold-stick has to be faced by the Irish people, and surely the sooner the better: a revolution led by an ecclesiastical hierarchy, even though the first grade is composed of the parish priests, many of whom are thoroughly good fellows individually, 'is to us suspect.'

Meanwhile the reaction is harping vigorously on the other string, and Mr. O'Brien is in for another three months. Of course whatever force there may be in Mr. Balfour comes of his obstinacy; he hopes to pit this quality in himself against the same quality in the Irish; and apart from his advantage that he has nothing to *suffer* in playing the game, he has an advantage in the stupid carelessness of the British nation which whether or no it be an original national quality, has been so much fostered by the commercial life which we have brought to such a perfection of degradation and cowardice.

For these imprisonments for political offences are now becoming so common that though they once shocked public opinion somewhat, they are beginning to wear it out, and people who are not put in prison, thinks Balfour, will soon cease to notice them, and then will begin their 'deterrent effect' on the offenders. Certainly he is justified in having such hopes. It *is* the custom of the British to be much impressed, and perhaps genuinely so with some disgraceful outcome of the system which enslaves us, and to make a great outcry about it for a little time, and then, the disgrace all the time going on, and even getting worse, to drop it all, as if there had been no disgrace, and no outcry. Balfour is probably right to count on this cowardice which has become so characteristic of us.

Besides why should we not get used to a few people being punished by prison-torture for their political opinions when we are quite used to a great many people having the same punishment administered to them for the crime of *poverty*?

Nay, can we say the *same* punishment? Our political offenders whether they have worn the prison dress or protested against wearing it, whether they have performed or protested against the 'menial labour' which by the way they condemn nice-looking girls to perform for them every day, when they come out of prison return to 'refined' homes and the applause of at least a wide circle of 'respectable' people.

The punishment of poverty is far different from that: tendencies harmless or even good in themselves perverted, inevitable degradation forced [on] many a weak good-natured, or self-indulgent, or hot-tempered person not worse than the average taken altogether; criminal habits forced on him, and then prison, and confirmation of the criminal habits and further degradation, and the man who might have been harmless or even useful has but one use now, and that a terrible one. He is 'an enemy of society.' This is the punishment of poverty, and yet we are so used to it, that we think we are living in a state of profound peace in England! Fools that we are!

Or indeed to many thousands, what is the earth on which we live, so full of beauty and such infinite resources for pleasure and well-doing as it is, but one huge prison? Listen once more to the often-told tale, that tale we have got so used to, and which we heed so little; this time told, I must say, by a person who has developed strange opinions out of the dreadful facts that he has seen and the conventional habits of thought which have been *forced*, we will say, upon him.

'The Rev. W. Adamson, Vicar of Old Ford, stated [before the Commission of the House of Lords] that his parish had a population of 11,066, and contained no middle-class. He said that the sweating-system had always existed, but had become aggravated from the results of civilisation, competition and early marriages, and necessarily from that [which?]

overpopulation. Large builders, though forbidden in their contracts, practised sweating by subletting at a mere fraction of the contract price. In the making of match-boxes 2½d. per gross was paid until the Salvation Army came into competition [the Army denies this] and reduced the price to 2½d. And now the making of the boxes was sublet for 1½d. per gross, the workers finding their own paste. A woman assisted by her children, when at home from school, could earn from 4s.6d. to 5s. a week. Early marriages arose from the two sexes herding together in the same rooms [What does *that* arise from?], from men marrying in order to be partially supported by their wives' earnings, and from men and women thinking [poor souls!] their united wages would be better, though poor, than single wages.'

Mr. Adamson then discussed as to whether clergymen are bound to marry people before the age of twenty-one, as though 'marriage' were necessary to breeding, and then gets on to the 'foreigner' question. 'He agreed with other witnesses that the immigration of paupers had an appreciable effect, and that the foreigners were at least as moral, and more sober than the English [what a curious concatenation!]; but they neglected sanitation, and might in that way be the means of spreading infectious disease.' (But then, according to the Arnold White theory, in this respect they ought to be useful in helping forward 'the elimination of the unfit,' because people die of infectious diseases pretty often.)

More sweating details: silk mantles for 7½d., sold (with the silk, such as it is, I suppose) at from 16s. to £1; asked if these were of the best class, thought they were the same mantles as were sold at £5. 'He disapproved of the present system of education, because it fitted boys to be clerks; 200 of them would apply for a boy clerkship, and some would offer to take it for nothing in the hope of getting eventually a few shillings a-week. [Yes, even education, the good thing we are all crying out for, is turned into a curse, when robbery is the foundation of society.] Girls learned only the theory and not the practice of domestic work, and therefore went into factories or were compelled [note the world] to lead an immoral life.' (Yes, people forgetting the merest elementary arts of life, as to my certain knowledge they are doing, in the country as well as in the towns: this is 'civilisation' – *i.e.*, a reversion to an inferior kind of savagery.)

'As an instance of extreme poverty, he gave the case of a person who sold 6 fibre bags for 6d., and out of that spent 3d. for new material, 1d. for coals, 1¼d. for bread, ¼d. for milk, ½d. for tea, to make a meal for four persons,' – and so on, and so on. (Remember, this is why Mr. O'Brien's rations will be so scanty; the prison must try not to compete in attractions with the workshop.)

'He admitted [?] that the middleman saved the principal a great deal of trouble, because the latter might not wish to have a number of poor persons about his premises. Teaching boys and girls to work for their own living might check the competition of unskilled labour [how? in the name of wonder!], but would have no great effect so long as over-population [*i.e.*, *unregulated* slave-breeding] existed. In this utilitarian [say thievish and murderous] age, the sweater wished to get his work done as cheaply as possible, and did not care whether it was done by horse, ass, or man.'

Now for the remedies: 'He would impose a poll-tax on foreigners, and would inflict a penalty on men marrying before twenty-one and girls before eighteen years of age'!!!

This is certainly a wonderful result to come out of all the reverend gentleman's experience, if he has not been misrepresented by the newspaper reporter, which after all is very possible; in which case the general journalistic conscience must bear the burden. In any case the 'remedy' means once more that we are engaged in slave-breeding, and have overdone it, and can now see nothing to be done but trying to regulate the slave-breeding, and if we possibly can, reducing the number of slaves to the limit of profit to us. We have got used to these horrors, and since they do not happen to ourselves, we find we can bear them pretty well – But patience! something will take place as a result of them which *will* be hard to bear, if we do not find better 'remedies' than Arnold White and Co. suggest to us: nor can we find any remedy, as long as such lives as these are necessary to the lives of those who are ordained to live on the labour of others.

Commonweal, Volume 4, Number 122,
12 May 1888, pp. 145–6.

NOTES ON NEWS

Mr. Parnell's speech at the Eighty Club has some interest for us, although that by no means lies in the long statement of his dealings with Lord Carnarvon. On that head, what does it matter what either Lord Carnarvon or all the Government said to Mr. Parnell when they thought the support of the Irish parliamentary party worth buying, since they now think they can do without it? Does anybody really suppose that the Tory party would be likely to turn Home Rulers without compulsion of some sort. The real interest in Mr. Parnell's speech hangs on the fact that having tried the Tories and found that nothing could be done in that direction, he was able to have recourse to the Liberals, whom he had *compelled* to become Home Rulers: and certainly his game was cleverly played, since the same stone killed both birds; tried the Tories and found them wanting, and drove the Liberals to support the Irish party on pain of having to endure an apparently perpetual Tory majority.

And now Mr. Parnell has to pay the price for this great parliamentary success, for this alliance with the party who a year or two ago were the coercionists, because they were the party in power, the rulers in England. What is the price which he has to pay? In the fewest words, he has to engage himself to the spreading of Whiggery in Ireland: a Whiggery indeed suited to the soil, including if necessary protection of Irish industries, but still Whiggery. He is anxious to show that all the Irish want can be gained by purely constitutional means, and to repudiate all revolutionary and illegal action. And yet he knows perfectly well that but for the revolutionary spirit in the Irish people, but for their many illegal acts, he and his party in parliament would have been nowhere; and as soon as that spirit of revolution dies out in Ireland, Home Rule will become a mere piece of political pedantry.

———————————

To tell men that it is 'their duty to suffer any thing and to dare any thing *within the law*' is sheer nonsense. Only those can suffer from the criminal law who disobey it. That sounds perhaps like a law-and-order maxim; but what it means is that there is always law enough in a society founded on wrong to make everybody a criminal who does not sit down quietly under his wrongs: or to put it in another way, no one either in Ireland or England can be a good citizen and a law-abiding person.

———————————

The Coercion Act is just as constitutional as the parliament which passed it; and parliament will be always ready if necessary at twenty-four hours' notice to pass any other addition to the 'Constitution' which will have the effect of keeping people down when they become conscious that they are wronged, as we are only too glad to think that the Irish people is conscious. Let it keep that consciousness till no man in Ireland is wronged, and then it may use Mr. Parnell and not let him use it. But if [it] does less than this it will have changed its tyrant but not its tyranny.

———————————

A defence-scare on again – and the defenders all by the ears. Lord Salisbury losing his temper and flying out at Lord Wolseley; the *Telegraph* with posters out calculated to make timid people take a ticket for some station in the north of Scotland, and inquisitive ones rush to Dover with the largest telescopes procurable. What will come of it all? Well, a job or two, or a job or twenty – that most certainly: probably absolutely nothing else. Luckily it is not possible to make the English army a perfect machine like the German one is. Let us be glad of that at least, that its power as a reactionary instrument is limited by our natural tendency to muddle and job.

Commonweal, Volume 4, Number 123,
19 May 1888, p. 153.

NOTES ON NEWS

The Liberals had a grand meeting at the Memorial Hall the other evening, to condemn the coercion and imprisonment proceedings of the Government in Ireland. This is well enough, and everyone who thinks freedom a matter worth considering must agree with their resolution against the stupid bourgeois tyrants who have set themselves the task of conquering a determined people by a kind of persecution, which proves conclusively that they themselves at home are the masters of a country nowise free. But there are one or two points to be considered before we can let our Liberals blow their trumpet too loudly. These very same men, when *they* were opposed by the Irish people, acted much in the same way as those whom they now condemn, and would do so again if occasion served. Far greater applause greeted the news of the imprisonment of Mr. Parnell and his colleagues at the hands of Mr. Gladstone than is now uttered at an anti-coercion Liberal meeting.

The truth is, once more, that the Liberal leaders only use this 'imprisonment for political offenses' as a stalking-horse for getting a shot at the official benches, and the ordinary Liberal follows his leader blindly and hilloas when he is told. This has been often enough said, but it is necessary to remember it in order to calm one's amazement at the shamelessness of Liberal politicians in holding a meeting about the prisoners of liberty and not saying one word about those who had suffered close to their own doors. So it is! Gladstone has given his fiat that nothing is to be said about Trafalgar Square, and all his following do his bidding with a tameness that has no parallel in the animal world; and poor Harrison must rot in prison and have his life worn out month after month, and no notice taken of him because his case doesn't come within the scope of 'practical politics.'

Commonweal, Volume 4, Number 124,
26 May 1888, p. 161.

NOTES ON NEWS

There is no doubt that the Southampton election is a heavy blow for the Government as things go; and little doubt that the election turned on the compensation clauses in that piece of humbug, the Local Government Bill. This is quite natural, since this question which is, we must suppose, beginning to excite people dreadfully, is after all and considering the bill it has to do with, a small matter compared with the independence of Ireland; and being a small matter, people are sure to take more interest in it, because the whole of their political education tends to turn their thoughts towards mere pettiness. It is a matter of course that if some piece of mere local politics, especially if it were a personal affair, of little importance to themselves and none at all to anyone else, could have been pushed into the front for the consideration of the good people of Southampton, they would have been more excited still about the election.

———————————

However the Government must not console themselves for their defeat on these grounds. On the contrary, the fact that the Southampton electors were thinking less of the Irish question than the Government bill is an unlucky sign for the Ins, and shows that their time for being the Outs is drawing near. The fact is that the Government has been compelled to make a show of doing something besides repressing Ireland and London, and is beginning to reap the harvest of its activity. This is an old story, and will have to be told of every Government in future: they come in on the back of a faction excited about something or another, and are happy and glorious; and could they remain with no other work than talking bunkum about the defeated faction, they might remain *in* happy and glorious for quite a long time. But there is a conventional idea that they must attempt to do something, and so they turn to; but as there is nothing to *be* done but an attempt to tinker that which only a few Whig pedants really believe can be tinkered, and which it is in the interest of most powerful people should have as many holes as a sieve in it, the first step in their attempt at doing something means their first step towards the door.

The Tories have now taken more than one step in that direction, so that we Socialists will probably soon have to be thinking as to what our prospects will be with Mr. Gladstone in office again; and the only question of any interest to be asked about this matter is, will the compromise which will in all probability be come to in the Irish matter let that question rest for a while, and so deprive politicians of a satisfactory refuge from the necessity of at least pretending to deal with the general condition of labour? Of course desperate attempts will be made on both sides to spin out the Irish question. How far will they succeed? Will Socialism become a matter of practical politics? If it does it will be very certainly dragged through the mud a great deal; and it will be especially necessary for all who know what they are striving for, to keep its true ideal steadily before people's eyes.

The Co-operationists have just had a very important congress. It would be impossible to criticise the speeches and addresses delivered there from the curt and garbled reports of the daily press; but pending the careful consideration of more trustworthy accounts of its proceedings, we cannot fail to note that there was a conflict of opinion there between those who have an ideal of Co-operation and those who have not. Our sympathies are of course on the side of those who have the ideal, especially as their opponents appear to an onlooker to be about as grovelling a set of profit-hunters as ever encumbered the earth. Nevertheless it is necessary to point out to them that they are in a false position, and that Co-operation is certain to drift completely into mere joint-stockery with minutely subdivided shares.

Since the days of Robert Owen the position of Co-operation has been quite changed by the uprising of *revolutionary* Socialism as a result of the application of the doctrine of evolution to human society, and the consequent perception of the class-struggle. The Co-operationists of Robert Owen's time did not perceive the existence of the class-struggle, and their Co-operation was but a part of their ideal of Socialism in the future, and a means to that end in the present. They knew that monopoly of the means of production existed, but they did not know (in spite of Adam Smith) that it was an essential part of the society, political and economic, under which they lived.

But now that a living and militant Socialism has made manifest the antagonism of the classes, it should be clear to our Co-operationist friends that true co-operation and privilege cannot exist together. The monopolists of the means of production will only allow the Co-operationists to rise out of their class misery *on condition that they themselves shall join the ranks of the privileged, and live on interest, rent, and profit*, thus forming a new class of *owners*, whose business is in the main keeping down the producers.

It is true, of course, that a great part of this new class would be living by producing, as well as owning wealth, that they would be exploited as well as exploiters; but there is nothing new in slaves owning slaves. That condition existed as long ago at least as the time when the 'Odyssey' was written. In that book, Eumæus, an obvious thrall, often complaining of his thralldom, has a thrall of his own, 'bought with his own money.' Surely the 'idealist Co-operators' cannot think this a high ideal to aim at.

If they will only look at the matter with eyes cleared from prejudice they will see that Socialism embraces in its programme whatever is really feasible in their ideal, and that the Socialists and not themselves are the true opponents of the sordid profit-grubbing which they are attacking in their own associations. Meantime, it seems to me that these profit-grubbing Co-operationists are doing a service to the Cause of Labour by pointing out the 'Thus far shalt thou go and no further' to those Co-operationists who really have nobler views, and are not engaged in the favourite scheme of the dominant class of to-day, to wit, the fashioning of a new middle-class out of the working-class, *and at their expense*, as a barrier to revolutionary Socialism.

Perhaps I may as well meet an objection likely to be made, and which was in fact made at a Radical club in my presence, that the Socialists themselves are establishing a Co-operative Society. That society (to which I wish all success) makes it an essential part of its plan that no interest shall be paid on money borrowed, and no dividends of profit made to individual shareholders, which is a demonstration on its part of its views of the impossibility of true co-operation under the present system; as it implies that it does not think it worth while to start a Co-operationist Society unless those that help it are content to sacrifice the *privilege of capital* which the laws of our modern monopolist Society confers on them.

Lord Salisbury's impudence and insolence really pass all bounds. When we heard that the Government had refused to recognise officially the Paris Exhibition of next year, everybody thought it only meant the usual official apathy and red-tape; and the matter might surely have been allowed to rest there unless some special fool could have been dug up for the occasion. However, that special fool *has* been dug up in the person of the most noble himself. He has thought it necessary to give a reason for the refusal, which is an insult to the French nation, and is clearly meant to be. His given reason for not appointing an English Commission to help to organise the Exhibition, is that it is intended to be a commemoration of the French Revolution! Such an answer almost makes one think that the Government is 'riding for a fall.' This is the day of panics. Some timid people will be thinking that when the *coup d'état* of Baker the First (Boulanger) comes off, we shall be sending a *corps d'armée* (if we have got it) to help that hero in putting down opposition. Really it quite puts one in spirits to see that our 'rulers' can be such blundering blockheads as this.

The Bishop of Limerick has fulminated against the Mayor of that city, who called a meeting to uphold the Plan against the Rescripts, which meeting, with several others, has been successful held. This as far as it goes is satisfactory, especially when taken together with the condemnation of the Plan by the Protestant Mr. Parnell, since it tends to stiffen whatever is revolutionary or at least progressive in the Irish movement. The cleavage between Whiggery and Revolution is growing wider daily.

Commonweal, Volume 4, Number 125,
2 June 1888, p. 169.

REVOLUTIONARY CALENDAR:
WAT TYLER

Wat Tyler. – Wat Tyler, *i.e.*, Walter, the tiler or thatcher, was an artisan of Dartford, in Kent, and became a leader in the great peasant rebellion which took place in England in the early years of Richard II (1381), and which was much more dangerous to the tyranny of the day than is usually supposed; it spread from the north of East Anglia, all through Essex and Kent, and along the south coast to Exeter. The immediate occasion of Wat Tyler's own rebellion as related by the chroniclers, was his resistance to a bailiff, who, calling for the poll-tax then being levied by the very unpopular Government, treated his young daughter brutally, and was slain by Wat with his lath-rending axe. The rebellion, however, in which the valiant tiler was a leader, had much deeper roots than resistance to a mere tax. It was a protest against the reaction of the landlords against the inevitable movement which was abolishing serfdom; the serfs were gradually turning into tenants, and much unfree *land* was being held by free *men*; and these the landlords were attempting to force into serfdom on the ground that their lands were the lands of serfs, and that therefore they must be serfs. Wat Tyler and the Kentish bands gathered at Blackheath on June 11, 1381, and on the next day marched thence into London, where the feeling of the people was with them and where they met with no resistance. The Court was terrified by a visit they paid to the Tower, and the King prepared to leave London; on his way occurred the celebrated scene in Smithfield, where Wat Tyler was basely assassinated while pleading the People's Cause under safe conduct. The King promised the enraged people whatever they demanded, and thus broke up their gathering, and as a matter of course kept his promise afterwards by wholesale murders amongst his helpless and scattered people.   Nevertheless, though the rebellion was put down it had slain the reaction it was aimed at before it died itself, and the extinction of serfdom in England went on faster and faster.

Commonweal, Volume 4, Number 126,
9 June 1888, p. 182.

NOTES ON NEWS

The Government have withdrawn their Compensation clauses – if anybody except the teetotalers cares about that, unless it is from the point of view of 'legitimate party warfare,' as it is called, and which is so contemptible that one wonders how people can be found who can pretend to look upon it seriously. Not unlikely that they put the clauses in so that the public might have something to ask for and have granted to them if by any chance the clauses could not be carried without any bother. But they have managed the whole affair ill enough to rejoice the electioneering gentlemen on the other side. A plague on both their houses!

A great Liberal-Radical meeting at St. James's Hall, and the utmost enthusiasm displayed against coercion – in Ireland. Mr. Morley as eloquent as such a man can be, but having the effrontery to say if such and such things had been done in London, it would have been in a blaze: and just the same things *were* done in London – but where's the blaze? Is it possible that Mr. Morley hasn't heard of all this? of course not. The man passes as a 'sincere' man; but no doubt he has long ago learned the lesson that a politician must only air his sincerity when it is convenient for practical purposes.

Lord Wolseley in fanning the somewhat cold ashes of the invasion-scare which is to put a job or two in the way of naval and military gentlemen and their friends, said one or two curious things. It was a matter of course that he would like a conscription if he could get it, so as to raise a really formidable army; and in order to make such a proceeding seem somewhat more useful to the ordinary civil mind, he dwelt on the physical advantages drilling would confer on the under-sized and stunted town population. All very well, my lord, but perhaps a little feeding from the cradle upwards would be of *some* use in the same direction, and a little better housing, and some more leisure: in short, to have a citizen-soldier you must have a citizen. But the army which Lord Wolseley would like to raise would be used chiefly for preventing the greater part of the population becoming citizens, for enforcing them to remain slaves – *i.e.*, persons to be used by 'the country' and not allowed to use it.

Luckily he won't get much of an army after all. The innate dishonesty of 'the shopkeeping nation' will compel them to have everything connected with the army and navy done at the greatest possible expense with the result of the least possible efficiency. That is too old a condition to be broken with before the pinch comes, and when it does come – well, let us hope that it will turn us into something better than a shopkeeping nation! After all, the terrified public (who do not care a twopenny damn for the whole business out of the newspapers) may be reassured. The reactionary military powers wouldn't ruin bourgeois England if they could; since they well understand that she is the greatest champion of reaction; all the more useful because of her cant over 'liberty' as over other matters.

Commonweal, Volume 4, Number 127,
16 June 1888, p. 185.

NOTES ON NEWS

The Kaiser Frederick is dead at last then, and we can all of us feel some pity for a man kept alive in a miserable condition by modern science and politics combined; and though no doubt many and many a man died on the same day that he did with greater suffering, who had been more useful to the world than he has been. For the rest, if the position of the man was an enemy of the people, the man himself was not so far as his intention went, he being of the good-natured bourgeois type: and at least he died with the good deed done of trying to get rid of Putkammer. It is hardly possible but that his successor will force all honest men to regret him; for if he had lived he would have stood between the outburst of the fresh reaction which is pretty certain to take place now.

Mr. Parnell at the dinner he gave to the jail-birds of his party dwelt much on the courage and steadiness of the other jail birds who are pretty much nameless as far as the newspapers go and have to forego the glory which those trumpeters confer on the illustrious; yet we need not suppose that they altogether miss their reward even apart from the satisfaction of doing their duty and feeling that they are not shabby wretches. It cannot be doubted that these obscure men are not obscure to their neighbours and friends, and we may well suppose that in the simpler society of the Irish country side a sort of tradition will arise which will not fail to do justice to their generous courage; which tradition will be none the worse history because it has not been written down.

The Gladstonites have won a considerable victory in the Ayr Burghs; one can only hope that it may mean that the electors are really convinced that that extreme form of tyrannical centralisation and landlord robbery is wrong, and that they repudiate it; otherwise it is a matter not worth considering. The successful candidate seems about good enough for a seat in Parliament, which is a serious accusation to bring against anybody who professes to be anything else than a digesting apparatus in the form of a man.

———————————

The Government don't seem to think it worth while to back up the Metropolitan Board of Works in the matter of the collections on open spaces. The present doleful position of those queer civic senators is perhaps almost too much for them. Perhaps, also, the recent Ayr Burghs election has opened their eyes on this matter. Will they be inviting us to Trafalgar Square next? Why not? Surely its closing against meetings 'has caused more vexation and annoyance than it has prevented' – and still will do so.

Commonweal, Volume 4, Number 128,
23 June 1888, p. 193.

NOTES ON NEWS

The defeat of the Government over the police-managing clauses was not a great matter in itself, as it might have been if the whole bill was anything else but a sham; neither is it by itself of much moment in the game of Ins and Outs: but taken with other matters it becomes a sign that the pendulum is swinging again towards the Gladstonian section of the Whigs.

Those gentlemen have a special opportunity now afforded them by the confirmation of the ferocious sentence on Mr. Dillon. They have been raising a great outcry on the illegality of this sentence. That would be a matter of importance if law were what it professes to be, a protection to peaceable citizens against violence and wrong-doing; but since it is in fact nothing but a machine for the support of the privilege of successful persons, the legality or illegality of an act of the executive is by itself not worth considering, since an executive which cannot find law enough to put down any act of rebellion is not worth its salt. If the force at its command is overwhelming, its acts will in any case be legal; if there is a general feeling that its acts are illegal, that means that its power is wavering. Mr. Dillon is in prison because he is an enemy of the Government, and, whether he is conscious of it or not, of the 'rights of property.' Harrison is in prison for exactly the same reason. It has always been the custom for persons in authority to suppress their enemies when they dared: but when their enemies are the friends of society, it is in the long run bad for the suppressors.

However, if the Gladstonian Whigs feel this affair so sorely, what are they going to do? They have done what the *Daily News* calls 'a very wise and very bold thing'; to wit, moved a vote of censure on the Government, which they knew beforehand they could not carry. This may be wise; though its wisdom is obscure to a simple person. As to its boldness, the said simple person wonders where that is hidden; its consequences do not seem of a nature to make even a new-born hare tremble.

A bolder course than that is conceivable and can be stated, though even this does not threaten the life, the limb, or even the next day's dinner of the champions engaging in it. If ever there was a case for abstention, here is one. Let the whole Gladstonian and Irish party walk out of the House after the due overwhelming majority has been recorded for the Government, and not come back again till at least the Coercion Act was repealed; leaving the Government and its friends to do the best they could without an opposition to help them in playing the game. If the Gladstonians are not bold enough for this, at least the Irish members might strike such a stroke; if they dared or could do so it probably would be enough, and Irish coercion would be laid aside, till a Liberal government found it useful, if indeed it were ever possible after such an act.

But it goes without saying that nothing of the sort will be tried. The Irish party are bound hand and foot to the great Liberal ditto, like the living to the dead in the old story. And as for the Liberals, they are only too conscious of their reason for existence as a party. Their business is to keep the game going steadily, and not to do anything to interrupt, far less put an end to it. Abstention would look like favouring revolution; it would have to be explained to the constituencies, and it could not be explained away; and explaining away is the great 'art and craft' of success in the game of Ins and Outs, of official success. Such a success as attaining to the end you profess (to your constituents) by the shortest road, being a thing by no means desired by the Liberal side of the game at any rate.

Meantime Mr. Dillon is in prison, and his strictly political friends don't seem in a hurry to get him out of it. It is a comfort to think that he himself must have known this all along and understanding his allies, has gone into the trap with his eyes open, knowing well that his imprisonment would further the cause he is striving for. All honour to him for that.

The proclamations of the Kaiser William II. to the Army and Navy and to the Prussian People may be considered by some as mere pieces of conventional official fustian; but they mean more than this both in what they say and what they refrain from saying; thoughtful persons scarcely need to read between their lines. Reaction of the coarsest kind is what they announce. It is possible that this will be less injurious to the cause of the people than the steady respectable bourgeois dead weight of inaction which would have been what the late Kaiser would have tried for, probably unsuccessfully as against the more open reactionists.

The proposal of the Rifle-shooting Association – or whatever it calls itself – to destroy Richmond Park for the benefit of its annual pic-nic, fair, and prize shooting match, would be a piece of impudence almost incredible if one did not remember the lazy and thoughtless stupidity of the public. There is any amount of space on the sandy wastes south of London – e.g., about Woking – of no use for any other purpose, since nothing will grow on these places and they are too hideous to be 'spoilt' by anything short of iron-puddling. They would seem to be providentially ordained for the requirements of modern sham-soldiering; and yet there are persons seriously taking into consideration the proposed ruin of one of the few solacements of our beastly muck-heap of a London! Really, the horrors of war are on us already.

Note that our friend the *Star* has the fatuity to favour this cruel injury to the democracy. I fear the reason why is clear – to wit, that it is a chance of attack against the Duke of Cambridge, and royalty through him, too good to be thrown away. '*Is* it worth the wear and tear?' There are so many occasions for the display of this kind of revolutionary fervour, that surely we need not cut the nose off our face to spite the face and *make* an occasion. See how foolish party spirit makes us! Surely we can despise the preposterous old martinet without destroying what in a fashion is our own, without handing it over to a private company to make money of.

Mr. Balfour gave an explanation the other day (probably untrue) of the circumstances of the imprisonment of Shane O'Donnell, imprisoned for refusing to give evidence against his fellow resisters to tyranny, and who was said to have fainted on the way between jail and court. In the course of this explanation, Mr. Balfour said that he could scarcely be called an old man as he was only 64. Pray, is Shane O'Donnell a working man? I ask this, since I have seen field-labourers in England who were old men at 50 and very old men at 64 – if they managed to live so long as that.

The Sweating Commission has been receiving evidence of a different character to some that it had received before. Mr. Lionel B. Alexander has tendered it what the press calls 'rebutting evidence.' But his evidence was in the main a defence of the Jewish workmen against the attacks of Mr. Arnold White, and a calling attention to the fact that the last link in the chain of sweating, the poor sweater, is not the criminal in the case, but the *employer* of the said sweater, who is himself sweated to the bone. As to his defence of

sweating, it amounted to little more than his perception of
the necessity for it in some form or other as long as competition under privilege exists. Cheapness at any cost he sees is
necessary to our system of manufacture, and he does not see
his way to limit it – nor will the Commission.

The position has often been stated, but one may be allowed
to state it again. Wage-slaves like other slaves can only
consume slave wares; but our wage-slaves are so numerous
that the production and sale of slave-wares is an important
branch of commerce, and any check to it would lead to a
great number of the poorest labourers being unemployed;
for none but those who are driven down by competition to
the lowest point can be used for producing wares cheap
enough for this shameful market, and these *must* take any
wages that will keep them alive.

Moreover since this mass of cheap labour necessary for the
production of slave-wares is offered in the market, and there
is still an excess of it, it is used for the production of articles
of comfort and luxury consumed by the richer classes, who
thus add to the income derived from their profit on slave-
wares by getting the wares they need at a price below the
average.

It is an old, old story; the poor always punished for poverty.
Those who have shall receive more abundantly, and those
that have not it shall be taken from them even that which
they have. Can a royal commission alter this? If so, how?
Yet it will be altered, and probably Mr. Arnold White will
not like either the alteration or the method of it.

Mr. Blundell Maple's 'evidence' was a curious business. If
the report of it may be trusted, he bullied the commissioners
and threatened all his enemies in a way that only a very rich

man dares to do. He also (like a good business man) did not miss the opportunity of puffing his firm gloriously; and painted his own portrait, so to say, as the true friend of the working-classes – even to the extent of working his sewing-machines by a gas engine for *their* exclusive benefit; and increasing his turn-over by thousands of pounds for the same disinterested purpose.

But even if Mr. Maple were an angel of light, and had absolutely *no* other aim in doing business than the welfare of his employés, he could by no possibility succeed in that aim. His gas-engine would benefit him and not the luckless sempstresses thrown out of work by it. He must use his enormous army of employés for producing wares at a cheaper rate than his competitors, or else his huge business, of which he gave such glowing account before my lords, would land him in bankruptcy and put an end to his career of usefulness. As long as he is engaged in making profits out of other men's labour, he is simply a helpless unit of a class, whose enemy is the class which it employs, and which employed class is engaged on its part in working *for* and fighting *against* the employing class.

The announcement of Court mourning consequent on the death of Kaiser No. 2 drew from the morning papers a regret for the state of business among the shopkeepers of London, and a further regret that it was absolutely necessary to make this worse by a period of Court mourning, which it was thought would certainly be the case. And indeed it seems that business is bad enough and that it is *not* the most advisable time for a person to die who must be mourned for publicly. I was told, for instance, by a person who knew the fact, that at a large optician's shop in London, conducted with all the usual pomp of manager, partners, and the rest of it, the whole take for one day a week ago was eighteen pence!

But here is a curious piece of folly, or rather two pieces, or indeed masses of folly: in the first place that the 'employment,' *i.e.*, the livelihood of a hugh number of deft, ingenious and industrious men, depends on the whim of certain idlers, and the empty inclination (scarcely to be called a desire) for such and such frivolities and luxuries; and in the second that when it is loudly declared by the rich that their luxuries and frivolities are a blessing to the poor, they nevertheless are quite prepared to interrupt the flow of such blessing by any little piece of official superstition connected with the Court; the very existence for which humbug and centre of corruption is often defended on the grounds that it is good for trade. Those that think so should try to get royal personages who are immortal – or as some would prefer, carve them out of lime-tree wood and paint and gild them duly. Such articles have been known to last for centuries.

Commonweal, Volume 4, Number 129,
30 June 1888, pp. 201–202.

NOTES ON NEWS

The opposition having struck the 'very wise and very bold' stroke we heard so much of last week, seems to have exhausted the arrows in its quiver, and no doubt hopes that the country will be satisfied with its last invention in the do-nothing business, and will wait henceforward for the bolt out of the blue which is to pulverise the Tories and raise the hopes of all those who may happen to be watching for the first time the going out of one party and the coming in of another. The hopes of those who have seen this process before will remain pretty much where they were.

Then there was what may almost be called a non-party debate and division on the Channel tunnel. The 'person from another planet' would have supposed that the scheme would have been discussed on its own merits; that the subject matter of debate would have been as to whether the tunnel was wanted; whether it could be safely made; how much it would cost, whether the expense of making it would be worth the advantage to be gained by it; and so on. The other-planeteer would have been disappointed; pretty much all that was talked of was whether or no the French would be able and willing to invade us by means of it. Here we are again under the horrors of war!

Anyhow it seems clear enough that a French or other hostile army who should be rash enough to trust itself to such a means of transit, would soon know as much of the horrors of war 'as the man who invented them.' The truth is that the whole pretence of fear of invasion through the tunnel is nothing but a pretence; it means opening up an opportunity to be used at some future time for pressing forward an increase of the army.

Lord Randolph Churchill was so candid as practically to admit this, and said that he voted against the scheme because if gone on with, it would give an occasion to a claim for more money for the army, which wouldn't suit him as he has taken a brief for economy just now. Which means in short that we must not consider whether the tunnel is possible or desirable, because if we do the jobbers will directly get their fork into us! O, British nation, wonder of the whole earth for your practicality and business-like habits, what a bragging, twaddling fool you be!

Government, determined to help its friends the publicans a little, has insisted on withdrawing its Sunday-closing clauses form the Local Government Bill. In spite of our friends the teetotallers, we must say that all this is a dismal and empty business. Really *is* it of so much importance whether a man determined to get drunk, performs that function on a Saturday or a Monday instead of a Sunday? After all, this is a clear case of a palliative that is useless and takes as long to get itself accepted as a condition of things which would not *drive* people to drunkenness as their only excitement, or as a mere drowning of their wretchedness for a little.

Mr. E. D. Lewis has had his answer at last from those two pillars of Law-'n'-Order, Mr. Justice Wills and Mr. Justice Nupkins – I ask pardon, Grantham – in the matter of Trafalgar Square, and the answer is just what might have been expected. Trafalgar Square was *created* by statute, and any right of meeting there must be similarly created. That is the gist of their answer. Of course if it had not been *created* by statute, common law would have forbidden meetings on it. Their lordships say that the right of public meeting is beyond discussion. On these terms it certainly is *at a public meeting*. You may meet in public whenever you please; *only* you mustn't meet here, nor there, nor at the other place. Where is the grievance? if you are starving and want to tell your rulers so, you had better buy a few acres of land: rents are going down in London now we believe.

The lamb going to law with the wolf is a curious spectacle to behold. The lamb must put up with it as long as he *is* a lamb. Perhaps evolution will change his wool into chain-mail and his feeble little shoulders of mutton into arms and fists with a chopping-stick in them one of these days. But evolution is a long job, thinks Mr. Justice Nupkins.

At the annual meeting of 'The National Association for the Promotion of State Colonisation,' or, as we should call it, the Society for the Punishment of Poverty by Transportation (at which it appears that the working classes were represented by Mr. Maudsley, of the Salford Trades' Council), there was much rejoicing at the progress of the 'work' (which, by the way, if it means anything, means that people are desperately hard up just now). A Parliamentary committee of 160 M.P.'s to help them (my word!); £10,000 granted by Government for getting rid from their own land of those inconvenient persons the Highland crofters, and all the rest of it. In short, these noble and gentle patriots, who love their native country so well that they want it all to themselves, were very happy, and their trades' union ally no less so.

A person not quite so happy, and whose share in her native country was but small, appeared before a magistrate next day with the following tale:– 'To-day, at Dalston, a poor woman asked the assistance of Mr. R. W. Bros to get her son back from Canada. He and another lad, both about seventeen, had been sent out by the East-end Emigration Society on a pretence that they would have plenty of work. The magistrate: You had better go to Captain Hamilton, the secretary;

but I should think there are many other lads who would be glad of the opportunity to get to Canada. Applicant: Yes, sir; if there was plenty of work, as they said; but my boy and his friend can neither get work nor food. The magistrate: I cannot give you anything. Go to Captain Hamilton.' The worthy magistrate did *not* add 'or hell,' perhaps because he thought that the poor woman was there already, as certainly her unlucky son was. It is almost a pity that this woman did not apply to the chairman of the meeting held the day before.

It probably would have done little to check the flow of their spirits, though, which were exuberant, as may be gathered from the speech of Mr. Maudsley, the trades' unionist, who said: 'The opposition proceeded chiefly from the Socialists, who knew that, if successful, the movement would cut the ground from under their feet.' Now, as the Association disclaims the intention of sending out paupers or ne'er-do-wells, the movement must mean the transportation of thrifty and industrious workers. Anyone but a very stupid person, one would think, ought to be able to see that if *this* is an advantage to the country, the country must be in a bad way indeed, and sorely in need either of Socialists or of persons who have some better scheme than getting rid of its producers of wealth. In fact, what these people really want to do (and they would say so if they durst) is to get rid of all elements of discontent, that is to say, those whom they and their idleness have made poor and helpless. A Helot-hunt, again, they durst not recommend, but it is what would suit them best. If they could kill one-third of the working population, it would for a time 'cut the ground from under the Socialists'' feet – but not for long.

The only way, Mr. Maudsley, to get rid of discontent is to remove the cause of it. Transportation of units of discontent is like the flea's funeral – a hundred more come to it. The abolition of the monopoly in the means of production, the freeing of labour, which the Trades' Council are doing their best to prevent, is the only thing that will cut the ground away from the feet of the Socialists, because it will make true society possible, and so make an end of our name of combat.

That friend of the working-man, Mr. Blundell Maple, has been disporting himself before the Sweating Commission again, and after some further glorification of his firm, was 'recalled' on his departure, and coming back said, 'that he had finished his evidence as to matters of fact, but there were other matters which he wished to go into.' So he went into 'these other matters,' that were not matters of fact, at great length. Some of these are old friends of ours, which we must admit are to be classed as Mr. Maple classed them, if the report of his evidence, once more, is correct; such as, for example, that the working-men earn as much as ever they did, although the prices of furniture have gone down; that their hours of labour are decreasing; that their skill as handi-craftsmen is on the increase, owing probably to the fact that it is not needed as much as it was; and so on and so on. It is, however, a matter of fact that the number of the unemployed is increasing, and Mr. Maple's admission of it, if it could by any possibility be denied, may be considered the one grain of usefulness in the clamjamfry of twaddle which this feeble committee allowed the workman's friend to shove down their throats.

Commonweal, Volume 4, Number 130,
7 July 1888, pp. 209–210.

NOTES ON NEWS

The great case between O'Donnell and the *Times* has come to
an end, with all its 'startling revelations,' 'sensational disclo-
sures,' and the like on the posters of the daily press. Of
course it was a political affair, and is to be judged accordingly; and it must be judged by all honest people who are not
rabid partisans as a disgrace even to the party politics of the
present day. The part of the daily press which happens to be
on the Irish side has stigmatised emphatically enough the
tactics of the counsel for the Government, and perhaps to us
the most interesting side of the event is the example it gives us
of the enormous power of a private corporation in governing
us so long as it is on the reactionary side. The *Times* is rich
enough and long-established enough to do what it likes, and
no dog may bark if Sir Oracle says 'Nay.'

What it has liked to do is to rake up the whole of its charges
against the Irish Parliamentary party in aid of the apparently
waning popularity of the coercionists. The English Home
Rule press professes to think that the attack has been unsuccessful; and of course it could not be wholly successful in the
nature of things. No person who thinks about the matter
could suppose that the astute, close, and formal Mr. Parnell
had written the letters in question; neither could any such
person doubt that the Irish Parliamentary party was more or
less in sympathy with the acts of war which preceded their
alliance with the Gladstonites. But that doesn't much matter;
the war-path which Parnellism and crime is on, is the vote-
catching road, and vote-catchers are not dealing with
thoughtful intelligence, but with impressionability to cries.

The coercionists have got their opportunity for a cry, and they will use it. All they have got to do is to treat every accusation they have made against the Irish party as a fact that cannot be disputed, to ignore the defence of the accused, and to keep on pointing out that Mr. Parnell refuses to clear himself in a court of justice – that is, to attack the *Times*, the representative of the great power of modern society, to which all that is reactionary will immediately rally, and which is inexpugnable as long as our class society hangs together. All this forms quite as good a cry as is needed, or can be got to carry on the coercionist battle, and doubtless will serve its purpose.

If you do doubt it, listen to the talk of business people, both principals and clerks coming home by the underground railway; and you must admit that the coercionists have pulled themselves together to meet the consequences of their recent defeats, and that this time they have struck a stroke.

But whatever damage has been done to the Irish party, it must not be forgotten that they have drawn it on their own heads by their eagerness to repudiate everything but consti-tutional means towards their revolution. That is the line they have gone on; they have claimed the support of the English people on the grounds of that repudiation, practically disclaiming sympathy with the enthusiasm of rebels, without which they would not have been able to obtain a hearing at all, and which could not be repressed because it was forbidden 'constitutional' means of expressing itself, and which will have to express itself again when the present constitutional gentlemen have made their Parliamentary revolution; unless, which is by no means likely, they cast aside all reaction and give opportunity for every Irishman to be truly free by destroying all monopoly of land and capital. And if they do that they will at once find themselves enemies of the constitution and *rebels* once more.

We have got another Zulu war on hand, which seems most likely to lead to another Boer war; this is only one of the indications of the way in which our commercial needs are pushing us on to grab what *we* can in Africa; other nations having their special ways. The sensational paragraphs lately published about the treatment of the Mahdi's prisoners, are doubtless an indication of that preparation of the public mind which we are so used to. Again, in the House of Lords, Lord Harrowby was very anxious about the growth of the slave-trade in Zanzibar, as interfering with 'British Commerce and British Missionary Enterprise' (sweet and holy couple). We know that two of a trade are apt not to agree; that is especially true of wage-slavery v. chattel-slavery; it is worth while putting down the latter in Africa if the result will be the strengthening the former in England.

Coleman, who has been in prison for assaulting a policeman on Bloody Sunday, and White, a dock labourer, 'and miserably poor,' says Mr. Bradlaugh, who brought the case forward, were to be further punished for the crime of poverty by being imprisoned for not paying £10 10s., the costs of the trial which they were so rash as to undertake against the police for assaulting them; and a similar punishment was to be meted out to Feargus O'Connor for a similar crime. Mr. Bradlaugh pointed out that these costs were exceptionally high, whereas in his own experience the Treasury costs were low. Probably this apparently wanton injustice is meant in kindness to the class of the poor if not to the individuals, in order to teach them once for all that they had better not indulge in the useless luxury of law, especially when a charge of offending against Law-'n'-Order has been trumped up against them.

And after all Mr. Matthews has turned tail; the three men in question appeared in the police-court in answer to the summons, there was no one to support it and therefore the case had to be dismissed; which it must be said would

certainly not have been the case if Mr. Bradlaugh had not
tackled Mr. Matthews.

Meanwhile, it does seem at first sight another instance of
the way in which the Great Shabbiness of the rich robbing the
poor dominates every incident of our society; it struck our
friend Cunninghame Graham that way. 'He repeated that it
gave him personally the greatest possible satisfaction that
this case had come up, because it was calculated to emphasise
that growing hatred between the rich and the poor, without
which no true reform was possible.' 'It would, he hoped,
serve to show that our British justice, like our Christianity
and our morality, was a gigantic fraud.'

His audience, since they were educated men and 'gentlemen,'
naturally laughed as his expression of both these truths;
feeling probably that the consequences of that terrible
growing hatred between rich and poor, which they could
scarcely deny would be long in coming, and their useless
lives would have come to an end before the crisis came; and
not caring for any consequences not personal to themselves
of the antagonism of classes which is the foundation of the
society amongst which they – stink.

Yet did they ever hear of the Welsh triad of the Three
Laughters of the Fool? It is worth quoting: 'The fool laughs
at that which is bad, at that which is good, and that which he
cannot understand.' All this the gentlemen of the House of
Commons have often done; there remains to them the other
laughter – on the wrong side of the mouth. May we all live
to see that!

Commonweal, Volume 4, Number 131,
14 July 1888, p. 217.

NOTES ON NEWS

The Government has offered Mr. Parnell a Commission of judges and others to go into the accusations made against him by the *Times*, and under the circumstances such a Commission would be as likely to be impartial as any Parliamentary Court of Inquiry would be. Of course if it were a case of trying a mere revolutionist the judges would almost to a man decide against him, whatever the evidence might be; but the chances are that since Mr. Parnell now belongs to a respectable Parliamentary party they will not look upon him as seriously as that, and that consequently their professional pride will act as a set-off to their political bias, unless, of course, the worst members of the bench are chosen. Mr. Parnell may be pretty well satisfied.

Meantime, the appointment of such a Commission, emphasises the fact alluded to in our last week's issue, that the *Times* as a great Corporation is practically above the law, as indeed all very rich people are. We are at the mercy of these money-bags, by whatever name they may be called. In the case of the *Times* the Government has now admitted this, as the whole country really does. Everybody knows that it would be sheer madness of an ordinary private person to attempt to bring such a huge power within reach of law. Rich people make the laws, but not for themselves – that's a very old story.

Commonweal, Volume 4, Number 132, 21 July 1888, p. 228.

[UNTITLED PARAGRAPH
ON THE MATCH GIRLS]

One of the firm of Bryant and May asked the *Star* interviewer whether Mrs. Besant would not be claiming presently a champagne supper for his match-making girls. A person who has not read 'Hard Times' would be apt to say, Why did not the interviewer retort, 'Do you drink champagne?' But one who has read that work and enjoyed the never-to-be-forgotten Bounderby cannot keep that worthy's gold spoon and turtle soup phrase out of his head. Really it was a fatal taunt for the match-making exploiter to cast at Mrs. Besant's head. What can one say, except that he has ticketted (*sic*) himself a Bounderby?

Commonweal, Volume 4, Number 132,
21 July 1888, p. 229.

NOTES ON NEWS

The match-girls have gained a victory over the blameless firm of Bryant and May. When one sees how small the gains to the girls are, how small their demands were, one is struck aghast at the miserable cheese-parings by which great fortunes are made. Truly, it well becomes Messrs. Bryant and May to characterise one of the grievances of the girls as 'trivial'! It is on these very trivialities, we repeat, that the splendour of the lives of these capitalists is built; and perhaps if such people ever trouble themselves to think, they may reflect on the curious fact that each 'trivial' atom of the huge mass of wealth which they monopolise and waste has been a matter by no means trivial to the atom of the industrial machine, the worker, who has had to keep his whole soul on the stretch in order, if possible, to compass a very 'trivial' addition to his income.

The daily press, of course, goes on buttering Messrs. Bryant and May for their generosity and the like, although their letter to the *Daily News* of July 19th is sulky and ill-conditioned in tone, and contains the kind of covert threats which employers are apt to use to those whom they employ; the 'Well, have it your own way then, and see what will happen,' which we so commonly hear; their innuendo against the 'agitators,' who first took up the case of the girls at their own risk, and worked with such untiring zeal at it till they at last got the London Trades' Council to step in, is just worthy of the whole shabby affair.

In short, it quite sickens one to have to call such a result of hard work for the girls and of courage on the part of the girls themselves, a victory; and yet it is one, for after all Messrs. Bryant and May's letter is the utterance of people taking a beating badly.

A desperate storm in a tea-cup has been going on. Mr. Balfour brought in certain Bann Drainage Bills, in plain terms a job for the advantage of Irish landlords; the Irish members seeing that this was going to be carried, whatever they might do, walked out of the House, as they ought to have done on more important occasions. Mr. Conybeare having been snuffed out by the closure, wrote a letter to the *Star* reflecting on the fairness of the Speaker, and by so doing committed a Parliamentary crime, although the substance of the letter was obviously true. The next day the House enjoyed itself by fixing on this Parliamentary crime, and so gaining the pleasure of a personal attack on Mr. Conybeare, who was suspended for a month, or till the end of the Session, if that comes to an end before the month. We do not hear that Mr. Conybeare has taken to his bed in consequence.

Neither, to say the truth, is the country likely to be much the poorer in any way for this 'waste' of a night in personalities. If the House of Commons had not wasted it in this way they would have wasted it in another.

Mr. Vaughan made short work of the summonses against the police for assaulting Mr. Borgia in Trafalgar Square. None, I suppose, expected any other issue of the attempt to bring Warren's lambs to book by means of law: for indeed such acts of arbitrary and irrational violence are the very foundation of law. Besides, let us look at it from the point of view of Law-'n'-Order. The police are told to do a thing; keep Trafalgar Square clear of meetings, let us say. They must do it at once or not at all: if, then, they are the stronger, can they stop to argue about it? They would be beaten if they did. Very well, then, they must break the head of any citizen

whose head is handy for breaking, and then take the responsibility afterwards. But if our magistrates and judges were to
make them bear the consequences of that responsibility, 'a
policeman's life would *not* be a happy one' indeed. And
where would Law-'n'-Order get its policemen then? The
necessary deduction from all which is, that whatever a
policeman does to a citizen with any pretext of legality must
be supported by the whole power of the law – or at any rate
is so supported. This is a very old story, and there is no help
for it but getting rid of the law which makes the policeman,
who in his turn makes the law.

The stories of dynamite plots from Chicago, with their
contradiction and vaguenesses, and criminals turned
informers, and the rest of it, have every appearance of news
got up to serve some temporary purpose: we have had plenty
of such 'discoveries' of late. It used to be thought by honest
middle class people that such infamies were used only by
absolutist governments. But it seems countries in possession
of middle-class political freedom have to tar themselves with
the same stick. Or after all must we not call the government
absolutist also? At least both it, and for that matter the
government of England also, will be practically absolutist
whenever their fears or necessities lead them into temptation.

We publish this week a paper by our comrade Bax on Africa,
which is worth very serious consideration. Even those of us
who are most sincere in their professions of internationalism
are too apt to limit our scope of vision to civilised countries,
forgetting that barbarous ones are at any rate of the kind of
importance that the lamb is to the wolf. Several questions
occur to us relative to this question of Africa as a possible
source of new life for dying capitalism which we should like
to see dealt with. *E.g.*, Whether the nourishment to be
afforded to capitalism by the Dark Continent is as great as
our comrade seems to think; whether the accelerated pace
which the impulse of huge new markets would certainly give

to competitive commerce would not go far to neutralise the advantages to capitalism of 'opening up' Africa – whether at least it would not make the break-up more complete when it came. Or again, if Africa is falling into the grasp of capitalism grown conscious of its necessities for new markets, is there anything which can prevent it from becoming the new nourishment for capitalism?

And that leads us to the practical moral of the question; that it is not our business merely to wait on circumstance; but to do our best to push forward the movement towards Socialism, which is at least as much part of the essence of the epoch as the necessities of capitalism are. Whatever is gained in convincing people that Socialism is right always, and inevitable at last, and that capitalism in spite of all its present power is merely a noxious obstruction between the world and happiness, will not be lost again, though it may be obscured for a time, even if a new period sets in of prosperity by leaps and bounds. We commend our comrade Bax's subject, and its consequences to the consideration of all our readers.

Commonweal, Volume 4, Number 133, 28 July 1888, p. 233.

NOTES ON NEWS

The Government have got what they wanted in the matter of the Irish Inquisition; but it is rather more than doubtful if they do not find they have got more than they know what to do with. We need not trouble ourselves as to any 'revelations' concerning Mr. Parnell and other Irish members; the best that the enquiry can do for the coercionists is to show that the Irish are determined at any cost to get rid of *English* landlord tyranny (would that we could say of all exploiting tyranny!), and also that they have every reason for their determination. If the knowledge of this turns the public opinion of this country, all that one can say is that it is the opinion of a public of fools and wanton oppressors.

Meanwhile what has come to light about Mr. Mandeville's treatment in Tullamore Jail will put a spoke in the wheel of Balfour's lot, and deservedly so. He was tortured so far as it was thought he could bear, and his tormentors went a little too far – and killed him. Do not let us forget, however, that the point of his ill-treatment was that he was to be made to feel that he was being treated like ordinary offenders, and that this means that 'ordinary offenders' are habitually tortured in our jails. With all its pretences to humanity (for our present prison system is the result of philanthropy), our modern sham society is forced to find some substitute for the rack and the thumb-screw.

Nay, it is not only 'convicted felons' that are treated as no man has a right to treat another, whatever his fault may be, but people arrested by Warren's modern miracles in blue, whether they have done anything or nothing, must be taught that they had best not be *suspected* of wrong-doing. The committee on the accommodation provided for prisoners has let some light on a very dark place. Dark very literally. 'The cells with very few exceptions imperfectly lighted, many quite dark.... The offices of nature must be performed under conditions of disgusting publicity.... Generally eight and sometimes twelve prisoners in a cell 12ft. by 15ft., the space not nearly so insufficient as in many cases'; and so on, and so on. In Manchester City Court, rooms 21ft. by 15ft., and others 15ft. by 14ft., as many as thirty men have been shoved into the larger rooms, and twenty women in the smaller. Hull as bad or worse; Liverpool and Sheffield as bad as the worst.

Truly 'Society' is in a bad way, if it wants so much taking care of! For my part when I consider the recklessness with which charges are made against *poor* people, I cannot help feeling some gratitude towards Balfour and Warren, and such like fools, for now and then shutting up one of the well-to-do. One almost feels as if one would like to do a good turn to those heroes, who are both rather strong in the educational line, by giving them a little education gratis, first in the elegant waiting rooms of the police court, and next in the salubrious and cool solitude of Pentonville or Tullamore. Yet, after all, even so I doubt if one could knock remorse or consideration into such blockheads.

Luckless Italians are being swindled into emigrating to America by emigration agents, and finding themselves workless and destitute when they get there. The Italian vice-consul says that 5000 Italians have applied to his consulate this year for assistance, and that there were 2000 destitute in New York now. So it goes on; in high places as in low; for indeed I don't see much difference but hypocrisy, between the agents above-mentioned and the delicate gentlemen and ladies who are so anxious to get rid of our poor people lest they should take money [out] of their pockets at home. Let us see your backs at any rate: if you thrive afterwards well and good; if not, your discontent will annoy and frighten *us* no longer.

But what's this? I read in the *Daily News* that people in the United States are extremely irritated with Colonel Ingersoll because he has stated that, 'The second generations of Germans and Irish in America are thoroughly patriotic.' This irritation is felt because people are so sensitive about immigration. Heavens! this is sensitiveness so great it is hard to understand. But at any rate, you transporters of the British and Irish, you had better look out, for clearly this door is going to be shut against your troublesome people soon. How would it be if you let them earn their livings at home, as they could so easily do if it were not for your idle lives which they have to keep?

Commonweal, Volume 4, Number 134,
4 August 1888, p. 241.

NOTES ON NEWS

Mr. Matthews, in giving a well-deserved tribute to Sir Charles Warren for acting up to the heart's desire of a Coercionist, denied that the police had lost their popularity with the great mass of the people. That may well be, as it is not easy to lose that which one has never had; but we may safely assert in Mr. Matthews' teeth that there are many thousands of people who used to think nothing about the police, or looked on them as a necessary useful machine, who now look upon them with active detestation. Many a worthy citizen has had his love for law-'n'-order shaken by the 'admirable courage' of Sir Charles Warren; indeed, that is the definite gain that we have got from Trafalgar Square.

The Government have driven the *Times* Protection Bill (as the *Daily News* happily calls it) through in the lump, and have thereby shown us once more, if we need another example, how tremendously powerful the rich men who govern society are, and in what a false position those men put themselves who attack some of the consequences of this tyranny, while they are not prepared to attack the tyranny itself. This wretched Bill provides a council of three to report on the hopes and necessities of the Irish, which everybody already knows all about, with the intention of swaying public opinion to the stark reactionist side again. Of course, the three will look at any evidence which is brought before them from the purely conventional point of view. It can only be hoped that the result of the humbug will be to push the Irish Question on a stage further by exasperating both sides a little more, and making the country feel more than it now does the idiotic dead-lock which greed and jingoism have got us into.

I must say that our comrade Bax's appeal to us to consider the Question of Africa is very timely. Here we have now the Pope taking the matter up, and urging the exploiters on to their task, and a Cardinal preaching on the subject to a most respectable audience anent it; an audience who were naturally, whatever their religious differences might be, most lovingly unanimous on this point. One paper says that this task of civilising Africa is well worthy of Modern Christianity. Surely that is undeniable. Tom Turnpenny never had a better job offered to him; 20 per cent. and the Gospel (or a thousand per cent. for what I know) are tempting indeed. To save your soul and your business at one stroke is certainly making the best of two worlds.

It is true that some simple people might say: Why are the English philanthropists and the Italian pietists so anxious about the interior of Africa, when the interior of London is so handy to them? Would it not be easier to deal with wage-slavery at home than chattel-slavery abroad? Would not a resolute attempt to get rid of that do away with far more misery than the abolition of the slave-trade in Africa? Is it not pretty certain that the extinction of wage-slavery would render all forms of slavery unprofitable, and therefore cut them up by the roots?

Well, these *are* simple questions! The philanthropists, Italian and English, Catholic and Protestant, are anxious about the African chattel-slavery just because they are anxious about the English and Italian wage-slavery – that is, they are anxious that it should continue without much friction, and allow them to go on living (as an Arab slave-dealer does) on other people's misery. It is true some of them who are able with a mighty effort to bring their minds to bear upon the condition of the Interior of London, and who are not more ill-natured than other people, are shocked at the consequences of wage-slavery. But then nature will not allow us to grieve too much over other people's misery (not even the best of us) if we cannot remedy it; and since these capitalist-philanthropists are *forced* to see that the only remedy involves the loss of their position of idle superiority, there is to them no remedy, and they soon cease to grieve or to think of the unhappiness of London.

Flatly it is much easier to deal with the African slavery than with that of London; always so long as you are prepared to make wage-slavery and its misery take the place of chattel-slavery and its misery in Africa, as it has done in Europe, and in the process to destroy whatever compensatory pleasure exists in the ruder form of servitude. The Cardinal drew a moving picture of the sufferings of the human merchandize in transit, and we have got that well into our minds now. But how can we who live comfortably ever get into our minds the multitudinous suffering, the forms of which are too numerous to reckon up, of the millions at home whom our philanthropists cannot deliver from their slavery? Or how many new forms of suffering, of which we at home should hear nothing, would not the importation of wage-slavery into barbarous countries create?

To put this matter in the fairest way possible – the present rulers of society are bound by their position to seek for new markets in order to work off the stock of wares which they go on producing by means of partly unpaid labour; they *must* do this whatever fresh suffering the process entails on the barbarous population they civilise, or the civilised population which they degrade far below barbarism. In the barbarism which they destroy they can only supplant one form of slavery by another; and in the civilisation which they uphold they are powerless to stem the flood of misery. In all this there is one element of good, that their necessities are leading gradually but swiftly to the extinction of the system which has produced all the misery and incapacity.

Mr. Balfour has further endeared himself to his countrymen and the world at large, by laughing in his seat in Parliament when he was questioned about a poor man who went mad in Limerick jail. No objurgatory words could add to the disgrace which the mere statement of this fact involves. This person afterwards said that Kennedy was treated with 'great kindness.' Pray, was that *before* he went mad or *afterwards*? We Socialists know pretty well what the 'kindness' of English prisons is, and the public have lately heard something of the 'kindness' of Irish ones. So the question is worth asking.

Mr. Wilberforce Bryant, in addressing the shareholders of his very prosperous and no doubt highly philanthropic concern, has really gone beyond the license which good-natured people are apt to allow to persons driven into a corner. As to his figures and explanations we know that every statement made can be figured and explained away, while the fact of dreary life-long torment, falsely called work, and something more than *semi*-starvation still remains, since indeed, as our comrade *Freedom* remarks, averages don't fill people's bellies. Let all that pass until Mr. Bryant chooses to explain why the 15 per cent. dividend lately declared does not go to the workers whose labour has earned it. And again, Mr. Bryant's coarse abuse of Mrs. Besant and Herbert Burrows is not difficult to bear, and no doubt our comrades look upon it as a certificate of honour, as showing that they at least have done something.

But the accusation which Mr. Bryant made against the Trades' Council, of admitting that the girls had nothing to complain of while at the same time they were supporting the strike, was a serious one; as, if it had been true, they must have been stigmatised as acting with treachery towards the workers who had trusted them, to say nothing about their humbugging the general public. Happily, in her letter to the *Pall Mall* of August 3rd, Mrs Besant disposes of this falsehood, and Mr. Bryant must finally be set down as a kind of champion of shabbiness, really a prize animal of his kind. Meantime, there are the match-girls, and many thousands like them, not to be disposed of so easily as Mr. Bryant! How long will it last? Can anything to come be quite as bad as our present 'Society'?

Commonweal, Volume 4, Number 135, 11 August 1888, p. 249.

NOTES ON NEWS

It is assumed by the speakers at a party meeting that the audience will stand anything, partly because as a rule if they are thorough partisans they only listen to certain party catch-words and cheer them; but in one of Mr. Balfour's late speeches he must have tried the 'thorough' party quality of his friends somewhat, and probably rather disappointed them, in spite of the loud and prolonged cheering which followed the remark, which we may assume was caused by the fact that the Under-Secretary spoke loud at this point of his speech.

Said Mr. Balfour: 'If it were true that the Union could only be maintained by taking away the civil rights of the Irish people, by putting in prison people who are innocent, by attacking those who are guilty of no other offence than that of differing from us in political opinion, I would not lift a hand to maintain the Union. I would rather that it was sacrificed, and that the greatness of the Empire were sunk in the dust, than that we should soil our hands by the political methods of which we are accused by our political opponents! *But it is not true.*'

How is that for high? One can imagine the fervour with which this flower of rhetoric was fired off at the heads of the Tory audience, and no wonder that they cheered. But on the whole it was probably *not* so much because Mr. Balfour spoke loud that he was cheered, but because his audience must have felt that they had come to the climax of the entertainment, and that no bigger lie could be told them that day.

What Mr. Balfour says he would *not* do under any circumstances is an accurate description of what he *has* done.

After all, why should Mr. Balfour be so earnest in disclaiming his acts, or trying to put another colour on them? It is his business as an officer of the Executive of our 'Society' to put his enemies in prison, and the legal accusation to be brought against them is a very insignificant detail of the matter. They are his enemies, that is enough.

In fact, all this business of careful discrimination between 'crime' and 'political offences' and the like is beside the question. What Mr. Balfour does with his Irish enemies 'Society' in general does with its enemies, only with far more cant and hypocrisy, since it feels itself safe in the absence of responsibility which its corporate quality gives it; and no doubt decent people are apt to feel as Mr. Balfour feels about Mr. Mandeville and others, that if they suffer in the process of slow torture, and sometimes die of it and sometimes go mad of it, so much the worse for them; that comes of their being our enemies.

For instance, when Judge Stephens the other day gave four lads fourteen years each for an act of brutality and robbery committed against an old woman, whatever enjoyment he might have had in the surprise of his victims, and the shrieks of their female relatives, which the reporter tells us rang through the Court, all that was by the way. As a judge (apart from the fact of his being Stephens) he had to make the accused feel that they were enemies, and were going to suffer the 'woe to the vanquished,' which is so old a story. It was not the brutality which he was set to punish, but the inconvenience to that abstraction, 'Society,' in which things are everything, persons are nothing, and to which Balfour sacrificed so recklessly in that prize lie of his.

Can we venture to hope that when the Irish have got Home
Rule, and before they have attained to social freedom, the
memory of Balfour's prison and its tortures and injustices
will make the then rulers of Ireland inconsistently merciful to
those other enemies, the enemies of 'Society,' who may come
under their hands, that they will rather remember the
suffering inflicted on persons, than the damage done to
things? We can almost hope that it will be so with such a
quick-witted and impressionable people, and that during the
space that intervenes between the attainment of Home Rule,
and the realisation of True Society, Ireland will be noted for
the lightness of its sentences on 'criminals.'

The Foresters have given a snub to American exclusiveness as
to colour by cancelling the Constitution of the subsidiary
High Court of the United States, which refused to withdraw
the exclusive word 'White' which had been put into the
clauses of its rules. This decision and the enthusiasm with
which it was done are creditable to the Foresters; but are they
going to stop at condemning the exclusion of 'men of colour'
from the advantages of Society? Won't they now protest in
some form against the exclusion of 'men of labour' from these
advantages? Surely this is their business if nothing else is.

Lord Salisbury has had at the Mansion House the usual
opportunity of uttering a manifesto on behalf of the
Ministers, if they have one to utter, and in any case of
blowing their trumpet before the fools who allow themselves
to be governed by them. His speech was not surprising, but
it is worth noting as giving a fair summing-up of the aspirations and covert fears of the stupider part of the middle
classes, of whom Lord Salisbury, in spite of his surface
cleverness, is a good representative.

He plumed himself on the passing of that piece of humbug,
the Local Government bill, and had the effrontery to hope

that it would be *final*. In dealing with the matter of Ireland he had the further effrontery to hint (he dursn't do more) that the opposition of the Irish was slackening. He said that the disease of Ireland was its poverty; and surely he might have added of England also, or else it is a delusion that the Government has been driven to hold a Commission on the sweating system (in London not in Ireland) and the resistance of the match-girls to the horrible shabbiness of the pious Bryant and May, and their poor little gain is a dream. He crowed over the diminution of boycotting in Ireland: but we Socialists can answer for it that it has not diminished in England; only here it is the boycotting of the oppressed by the oppressors and not of the oppressors by the oppressed. The hymn that he sung to the sacredness of 'free' contract no doubt was echoed in the breasts of his hearers, who rejoiced in believing that heaven would never sanction the abolition of *their* monopoly.

Then came his own subject, foreign affairs: 'Popular passion or popular feeling' may 'drive the vast force of nations' into war, 'but the object of the rulers of the world is to secure uninterrupted peace.' This seems intended as an insult to the people; but he is not thinking of them; his 'popular feeling' one can see means the feeling of the bourgeoisie only – the others – what others are there to this most noble man? For the rest he is right; 'popular passion,' *i.e.* the necessities of the competitive market may bring on war, and most bitterly will 'the rulers of the world' regret that they cannot help it, for who knows but that 'the popular passion' of the real people may then change the aspect of affairs.

Egypt, he said, is happy; that is, its accursed exploiters are: 'it is going on up to and beyond the utmost wishes we can have formed?' Yes, and what wishes can its luckless peasants have formed? I fear not much. I am sure that though Lord Salisbury has heard of them, he only thinks of them as a fact in the lump, and has practically entirely forgotten that this fact is composed of many thousand persons, each one of whom is a sufficiently complex fact in himself or herself. He said also that it was not the annexation of territory (in Egypt) that was desirable. Just so. To sneak a thing is much more convenient than boldly robbing it: besides, we have done that already: why steal it twice?

But enough about this grievous twaddle! The real thing to note in it is the complete ignoring of all but the middle-class and its rulers: the Marquis sneers at that middle-class, as his heritary position and politics compel him to do; but he is devoted to its interests, is its faithful servant; is, in spite of his sneers, an integral part of it, a result of its holy dogma of 'free contract.' Below that he knows of nothing but a machine which sometimes creaks inconveniently.

The *Daily News* says that the strike in Paris is a political one: that means in other words that the Paris workmen understand by this time what their true position is; that it is not a mere rise of wages that they need, but a change in the basis of Society. The *Daily News* further opines the strike and the 'riot' (*i.e.* the police attack on the citizens) at the funeral of Eudes are the results of Boulangerism – cause and effect with a vengeance! If the *Daily News* goes on like that it will presently credit the General with being the cause of the Revolution of 1798 – or in the long run of Noah's Flood. There is abundance of cause for a 'political strike' or an insurrection in Paris as in London. Slavery is cause enough for any amount of 'disturbance'; and we need not go from the grimly sublime to the loathsomely ridiculous by picking Boulanger out of the mud in order to account for it. After all, herein the *Daily News* is like Salisbury and ignores all classes but the Bourgeois, and thinks Society is composed of that – plus unreasonable, inscrutable disturbances.

Commonweal, Volume 4, Number 136,
18 August 1888, pp. 257–8.

NOTES ON NEWS

The verdict on Mr. Ridley's suicide, passing over the conventional phrase of 'temporary insanity,' will be endorsed by most men who are not rabid partisans. The poor man was too weak to play a part in the civil war which is now going on, and so was crushed out by an extra turn of 'the system' driving him up against his own conscience and that of the community amongst which he lived. It is a thousand pities that he could not have trusted himself to the good will of his fellow-countrymen, and snapped his fingers at the authority which bade him go a little further than usual in torturing a prisoner!

———————

The check to the share of Italy in the plunder of Africa will scarcely make a nine days' wonder, yet one cannot help feeling some exultation at the defeat of the armed clerks of the counting-house, under whatever nationality they may serve; though naturally one is most pleased when they belong to our own counting house, whose tyranny presses most nearly on ourselves.

———————

The new Kaiser's speech at Frankfort-on-Oder furnishes a curious commentary on Lord Salisbury's view of the pacific tendencies of the rulers of Europe at present; but it does not tell us anything new about the character or aspirations of the German demi-god. We have all known that he is a furious reactionist, who will do all the damage he can during his reign; but in this matter of war he will be rather driven than driving; the blind instincts of the commercial bourgeoisie, will force them to the worship of such men as this, will settle that matter for or against. It is at any rate pretty certain that if the Kaiser does fairly 'go on the rampage' in the temple of reaction, he will pull the roof down on his own head. So may it be!

The closing of the Landore Works is a good example of the position of the workman under nineteenth century capitalism. A thousand men employed in working at – in fact they know not what. Suddenly without warning the work comes to an end, and they are in the streets with a prospect of what would be indeed a cruel punishment for gross misconduct. And what can they do? They have never had the least control over their own work, know nothing about the market for *it*, or what may influence that market; nor have their 'employers' a grain of responsibility for them. They can do nothing but try to put themselves once more in a position, which involves helpless ignorance on one side and complete irresponsibility on the other. They are simple machines in helpless dependence on other men's wills, other men's necessities, of which they know nothing. When will the time come when they will make up their minds to employ themselves, and accept the responsibilities of their own lives? They will one day have to choose between that and sheer starvation.

Zola is being attacked in England through the publisher of his English translations, and there will doubtless be many pros and cons on the matter. The only one of his works that I have read is 'Germinal'. If that is a fair specimen of them, I must say that whatever grossness there is in it could do no harm except to those who are determined to have harm done to them. I feel sure also that the grossness is there not for 'nastiness' sake, but because it forms part of a true picture of the life which our civilisation forces on labouring men; and I hold that 'What is not too bad to be done, is not too bad to be told about,' though I find no difficulty in imagining that our rulers and masters take a very different view of the subject.

Commonweal, Volume 4, Number 137,
25 August 1888, p. 265.

NOTES ON NEWS

The discovery that our Secularist friends have treated Mr. Bradlaugh shabbily is surely of the nature of the (non-existent) enormous gooseberry, and Mr. Bradlaugh himself disposed of it speedily. Meantime a person with any sense of humour cannot help being somewhat tickled by the spectacle of the enthusiasm of 'the Respectables' for the man they once treated as an outcast such a very little while ago. It would be unfair to twit Mr. Bradlaugh with this sudden conversion, for he has never professed to be a Socialist; but it may have something to do with the discovery of respectability that an 'Iconoclast' is not necessarily a Socialist, who is the true dangerous person.

———————

Our comrades Cores and Reynolds are in prison for committing obstruction according to Nupkins. It ought to be quite obvious to those who, though not Socialists, are prepared to defend freedom of speech in England, that this is mere persecution for opinion. The 'running in' of a Salvationist at the same time is a blind, and nothing more; the fact that the police witness at our comrades' trial was allowed unchecked to spin a long yarn as to what they said on the Church Plain, shows clearly enough that 'obstruction' is a bare-faced excuse for attacking opinion. In my hearing at an obstruction case (at Marylebone I think) a London magistrate stopped a police witness who was running on in this way, and told him that the defendant was accused not of seditious speech, but of obstruction, and that what he said had nothing to do with the matter.

Commonweal, Volume 4, Number 139,
8 September 1888, p. 281.

NOTES ON NEWS

Baron Bramwell, the champion of the Liberty and Property Defence League, it seems, defends the present system of robbery on the grounds that the chief business of any community is to increase its 'pile' at the expense apparently of every other consideration; a theory which would lead to some curious consequences if acted up to without remorse or compromise, but which no doubt is a convenient one to those who may happen to be on the right side of the hedge – rich men that is.

The others, those who are not rich, *i.e.*, the vast majority of the population will hardly, if they think about it, agree with this theory of 'the whole duty of man.' They will be apt to say, 'However the "pile" of the whole country increases, though we are richer per head than other countries, though we are so much richer as a country than we were 500 years ago, yet this increase of the "pile" of the country has done *us* no good, we are just what we always were, labouring men, without property and without hope.'

To unprejudiced people who can use their senses, it is clear that life in a poor country is much more happy for a poor person than in a rich one; *e.g.*, the peasants of Norway and of Greece are far better off than those of England or France; better off in all ways, but especially in self-respect, simply because class society has not reached the same pitch of perfection as with us. I remember when I was in Iceland, whose poverty is deeper than most English people could conceive of, being much struck with this. In conversation with my guide, an intelligent and well-read man, I could not make him so much as understand the difference of classes in civilisation; and I say without hesitation that in that wretchedly poor country the people generally are happy, because they have not a trace of the degradation which our inequalities force upon the poor of a rich country.

———————————————

My Lord Bramwell, the truth is that no one in a poor country is rich enough to own slaves; and you are such a fool as to think that the ownership of slaves is necessary to the happiness, dignity, and elevation of character of a civilised man. Once more, what do the slaves think about it?

Commonweal, Volume 4, Number 140,
15 September 1888, p. 289.

NOTES ON NEWS

The controversy between the *Daily News* and Mr. Davitt
shows on what shallow foundations rests the hope that the
Liberal party will deal satisfactorily with the Irish question.
The whole matter for the *Daily News* is one of party politics;
to import any reality into the question and look facts in the
face appears, naturally enough from this point of view, an
impertinence. Mr. Davitt is an interloper, 'a dangerous
firebrand,' because he actually wishes to save his countrymen from the immediate miseries of eviction, and does not
hesitate to say what he thinks will stir up some honest men to
help in the matter. Anyone who has belonged to the Great
Liberal Party at a crisis and has had strong opinions of his
own at the time will at once recognise the true Whig flavour
in the wretched snobbery of the *Daily News* article the other
day; and Mr. Davitt's scorn which met it was most amply
justified, whether he was right or not in his estimate of the
present mind of English Liberals as to Ireland.

———————————

But surely he *was* right. No doubt the eyes of working men
who are true to their class have been opened on the subject of
Ireland, and Mr. Davitt can rely on these for support. But
what is their power in the Liberal party? Next to nothing.
Their enthusiasm has been wasted, they have been snubbed
and Trafalgar-Squared, and in short treated as inconvenient
persons – like Mr. Davitt.

———————————

The party, as a party, *is* apathetic, and the Irish constitutional
section is pinned on to its apathy. The truth is that these
Gladstonite Whigs can see nothing except the general

election, which they believe, and probably rightly, will bring them into power once more. The swing of the pendulum will then most likely give us a Liberal government again; but as far as anything they can do, that prospect is not encouraging even as regards Ireland, which is the only question the *Daily News* and its masters will allow us to look at. When one comes to think that the serious consideration of the relations between the Irish tenant and his landlord and the advocacy of some kind of land nationalisation makes a man a 'firebrand' in the eyes of the Great Liberal Party, one's raptures at the probable change of government are apt to be moderated.

What will happen? A compromise on Home Rule, a temporising measure in favour of the tenants, and the whole question as a real matter of everyday life handed over to the Socialists to deal with, and agitate upon.

Even the bourgeois papers call Mr. Saunders over the coals for his last appearance in the character of Nupkins. Of course people cannot help laughing at the monumental stupidity of the man; but it is just this stupidity which is the dangerous thing, for on such stupidity is based the immoveable cruelty of the governors to the governed. A man not irredeemably stupid could not help thinking, 'Here is a poor man in a foreign country, whose language he cannot even talk, who is extra helpless and has been wronged: if I am so hard-hearted as not to feel for him, at any rate let me *pretend* to do so.' Such wisdom is not to be had out of Nupkins; a hard fate drives him to proclaim his incurable stupidity, which has at least the effect of cruelty.

All this would not much matter if we read this week that Mr. Saunders has been dismissed in disgrace – which is not likely to happen; the freaks of an East End magistrate have nothing to do with the comfort of well-to-do people, for whom alone the laws are made, though they may inflict misery enough amongst the people whom he rules over, and who have no redress for his hard-dealing and insults.

The coming winter is not likely to lack its share of 'discontent,' which is becoming a thing to be looked for among the poor, just as 'the Season' is among the rich. We are beginning early too; the paupers refuges full, meetings of unemployed, police attacks on them; prosecutions for violent speaking; this does not look very like the peace and prosperity we have been promised.

As to the prosecutions for violent speaking, it is much to be wished that the authorities will attack us in this way rather than by means of their old sneaking obstruction tactics; it is much more satisfactory to go to prison for straightforward preaching of what is undoubtedly a dangerous doctrine, than for an offence which mixes up Socialists with Salvationists, etc. Only if we are to be run in for violent speaking, let it be for saying something that we shall not be ashamed to see quoted in the papers. Let it be for attacking the essence of our sham society, and not its accidents; let us in fact talk Socialism, for that may be both reasonable and violent at the same time. It is as well to have witnesses also, not for the sake of the police courts, where the magistrates will not heed them, but for the sake of putting ourselves right before the public and our comrades. As an author I know the unpleasantness of being misrepresented by newspaper critics; and I fear that police witnesses will not be much better than these.

According to the *Star*, the Salt Trust is to be succeeded by a Coal Trust, which will arrange matters (of course) for the benefit of the public, by taking care on the one hand that we don't get our coals too cheap, and on the other hand that the men shall be employed (as much as the employer finds it convenient to employ him). The promoters of the scheme are of course too modest to mention themselves, but clearly expect us to believe that they are actuated by the purest public spirit. The affair, along with others of a similar nature, is interesting to Socialists as showing in the first place that the unlimited competition on which our whole commercial system rests is beginning to break down, and in the second place the helplessness of the general public before the great capitalists: for of course, to drop irony, the real aim of these schemes is to rob both producer and consumer as safely and as much as possible. Meantime labour must pay for the whole game.

Commonweal, Volume 4, Number 141,
22 September 1888, p. 297.

NOTES ON NEWS

Mr. Dillon in his speech before the National League in Dublin, said all that he was likely to say, and no doubt said it well enough. He upheld the Plan of Campaign stoutly; as he well might, because at present, now the alliance between Parnellites and Gladstonians is so close, the Plan is the one distinctively Irish piece of strategy, and if it were gone, mere party politics would bury the whole Irish business under the usual mountain of procrastination and trickery.

On the other hand, Mr. Dillon deprecated 'impatience'; that is to say, in his position – very different to that of Mr. Davitt – he could not say anything that could be construed by stupid people into the beginning of a quarrel with the Liberal allies. This is the policy which Mr. Dillon is pledged to, and of course he cannot get out of it, unless the Gladstonites formally abandon the Irish cause, which probably they cannot do. When the fulness of time comes the electoral pendulum will swing the other way; Gladstone will be in, and Parnell with him.

But the 'impatience' of Davitt has another purpose than merely quickening the pace of the worn-out Liberal post-horse on the road to party victory. It is a warning to the Liberals not to be too liberal of compromise when their day of office comes. Of course what they will want to do is to grant the Irish the semblance of their claims without the reality, if they can thereby stop the mouth of the British democracy even though the Irish democracy is not satisfied. This is the reason why all Irishmen who are not precluded from it by official position should be steadily 'impatient.'

Those of our friends who are inclined to be 'impatient,' in another sense, of this long-dragging Irish Question, which bears with it so much that is indifferent or hostile to Socialism, should consider one remark made by Mr. Dillon in his speech which I believe to be made quite honestly and with a single heart. He said that all the old enmity which was once one of the master feelings of his heart had disappeared before the present action of the English democracy. So hollow, so easily got rid of, are these monstrous national antipathies which foolish people believe to be so deeply rooted. If the Home Rule agitation does nothing else than destroy one branch of this deadly upas-tree of sham patriotism it will have been worth all the trouble.

Moralists are trying to find out causes for the horrors which have lately shocked the sensibilities of 'cultured' society. Lord William Compton sees, as all people who have ever thought for a moment on the subject must see, that the condition of life in the East end slums is quite enough to account for such brutality, which is a necessary consequence of it. But what causes the condition of life in Whitechapel? The answer is plain: the *exclusive* culture of those whose sensibilities are so shocked by the brutality, the responsibility for which their greed and cowardice evades. These sensitive, moral, cultivated people are prepared to do anything (by the hands of others) which will sustain the inequality which is the foundation of modern society and which they glory in; and when the dark side of this glorious inequality is thrust on their notice, they are shocked and read moving articles in the newspapers – and go on eating, drinking, and making merry, and hoping it will last for ever, Whitechapel murders and all.

Have they considered a little event of which we have just had news, which comes of this determination of theirs to be thieves as long as possible? Another glorious victory for the British army, and indeed a real good cheap one, with the killing *all* on one side: 400 Tibetans killed and wounded and half a dozen slight hurts on the side of – culture. If the history of this slaughter had been given Homerically – *i.e.*, with abundance of realistic detail – it would have made a pretty good multiplication of a Whitechapel murder.

And was the reason for it any more excuse for this multiplied murder than the reason for the London horror? No. No worse cause could be found for a slaughter. It was perpetrated (and remember it is one among hundreds) in order to keep going that degradation of life with Lord William Compton so much deplores, which he would doubtless remedy if he knew how to without destroying our 'society' of inequality; but which under those circumstances he *cannot* know how to remedy.

Apropos of these 'little wars,' or great murders, our friend the *Star* has a well-meant article which misses the point disastrously. After having attacked the commercial Jingo policy, it says: 'Our profound conviction is that *as a rule*' (italics ours, in honour of journalistic qualification) 'warfare tends not to the advancement, but to the postponement of large commercial relations with another country.... Trade may be compared to a great natural force – silent, invisible, and invincible,' and so on after the Manchester manner. In short, our contemporary, for the moment at least forgetting the blessings of civilisation, such as Vandeleur evictions and London rent-grabbing from working-men, which it often laudably denounces, wants to purge the march of commerce of war and violence.

But unhappily it is *itself* war, and violence is of its essence, whether that violence takes the form of 'the soldier with his gun or the sailor with his iron-clad,' or the other form of the sword of cheapness and the spear of shoddy backed up by law – *i.e.*, the policeman *masking* the soldier and sailor – is a mere incident of its ceaseless, remorseless war. For as the aim is, so must the means be; and what is the aim of Commerce? Answer: to substitute its peculiar form of slavery for whatever it happens to find on the ground which it is bent on conquering; and that form of slavery is a 'Society' (or gang of robbers) governed by rich men, who shall make slaves of the producers of goods without the expense of buying the said slaves and without the responsibility of feeding them. Friend *Star*, the Sikkim massacre is bad, and you do well to object to it (though you do *that* very mildly), but the cause of it is worse – nay the worst.

Re the Salt Trust, the *Pall Mall* says: 'The syndicate will for a time have a depressing effect upon the labour-market in the salt districts of Cheshire, as the low range of prices prevailing for the past five years is directly due to over-production.... Owing to intense competition, prices have fallen 50 per cent. during the past ten years. Great confidence is felt in the future of the trust in Cheshire, where the money has been largely subscribed.'

I beg to propose a design for the seal or badge of this glorious modern gild, to wit: A Benefactor of Humanity with one hand in the pocket of a working-man, a salt operative, and the other in the pocket of the public typified by a respectable London mechanic. It is indeed pleasing to see the B.H.'s so naïve and outspoken as to the robbery which they are contemplating, and we Socialists should wish them all success. Monopoly has, unhappily, so far been made bearable by competition, but monopoly without competition will turn out to be altogether unbearable, and will help on the beginning of the end.

The vegetarians have tried to collect the London parsons to sing their praises, but the reverend gentlemen for the most part declined to be caught with chaff. Only thirty attended, presided over by Canon Farrar. I have not a word to say against vegetarianism voluntarily practised on the grounds of its suiting the health of the practiser, or of a natural sentiment against 'corpse-eating' as a friend of ours has called it; but in most more or less laudable associations that are not Socialist there lurks a snake in the grass; and the reptile is not lacking in the verdant meadow of vegetarianism. Canon Farrar, *e.g.*, not knowing, I suppose, what the devil to say, praised it because it would lead to simplicity of life, and because it would be a remedy for poverty.

Simplicity of life – good, most good, so long as it is voluntary; but surely there is enough involuntary simplicity of life, *i.e.*, hard fare, already; and to live poorly is no remedy against poverty, but a necessity of it. And really, hasn't Canon Farrar had time amidst his arduous ecclesiastical duties to learn that if our whole capitalistic society were to become vegetarian together, the 'poor,' *i.e.*, the producers, would be *forced* to live upon vegetarian cag-mag, while the rich, *i.e.*, the proprietary class, lived upon vegetarian dainties? When we are a society of equals we shall be able to consider all these niceties of life, and to do what we think best. Meantime, I bid Canon Farrar and the school of social reformers to which he belongs, not to *evade* the real question: Why are we not a society of equals?

Commonweal, Volume 4, Number 143,
6 October 1888, pp. 313–14.

NOTES ON NEWS

So we are on the verge of the sea of quibble and evasion and smothering of truth, which is called a political *cause célébre*. Fine times for the daily press indeed, certain copy, increased sale, and other soothing advantages for 'able editors'! Fine times also for the lawyers engaged on both sides! Though that is not much, for the sun does generally shine pretty bright on their side of the hedge, however cold the weather is for others. But as to supposing that anything else will come out of it, that is all nonsense. Arrangements will be made for the *Times* to fall soft; opportunities will be given to *respectable* Home Rule politicians to declare their unalterable fidelity to the rights of property and law-'n'-order, and we shall then pass to the order of the day.

Mr. Cunninghame Graham's letter to the *Pall Mall*, which had been in ecstasies at the prospect of something decisive coming out of this Great Evasion, was sensible and to the point. It is absolutely true, as he says, 'that the majority of the Liberal electors care not one farthing whether Mr. Parnell wrote or instigated the letters.' They are now Home Rulers, just as their opponents are Coercionists, whatever Parnell has done or has not done. And really when the *Pall Mall* is driven to say 'that the cause of Home Rule will be decided by the judge's decision' in this Great Evasion Case, it surely wants pulling up.

The fact is that Parliament and the Platform having been talked out on the very simple question of Home Rule for Ireland, the quarrel has to be carried on constitutionally by some other means, and the time 'put in' till the blessings of a

General Election fall upon us. What better means for procrastination could be found than that sire and dam of procrastination, the Law Courts?

———————————

General Gordon's statue has been unveiled with very decidedly 'maimed rites,' and there stands the Christian hero in all the dignity of modern realistic sculpture. Would not this be an opportunity for the revival of the plan for Hudson's Statue, which long ago succumbed to Carlyle's ponderous hammer-strokes of scorn? He might be taken, I mean, as the type of successful commerce; might be represented standing behind the soldier of Christian Commerce and pushing him on to – I was going to say victory; but that I admit is inappropriate – let us say pushing him on to thrusting his head into the hornet's nest for the advantage of 'progress' in Africa.

———————————

The claims of General Gordon, apart from his private character, to the worship of the centre of the empire of commerce are these: He served as a soldier of fortune in China, where he helped to put down what could scarcely be otherwise than a righteous rebellion against Chinese bureaucracy. He then 'got religion,' and became that most dangerous tool of capitalistic oppression, the 'God-fearing soldier'; in that capacity he allowed himself to be used to drive the wedge of profit-mongering into barbarous Africa, and was quite prepared to do all that a man must do in such a service if he is to earn the name of a good servant. As, for instance, his orders for the cutting down of the fruit-trees of the people whom he had come amongst as a benefactor. He might have remembered that the 'barbarous' Arab Calif Omar (who surely was as clear of his message from God as any modern 'Christian soldier' could be), in his instructions to his warriors, expressly forbade them the wanton damaging of the fertility of the earth and the cutting down of fruit-trees on any pretence.

———————————

The *Pall Mall* says that 'Gordon's whole soul would have risen in revolt' against Sir C. Warren's proceedings last year. Would it? That is a very rash assumption. I cannot help thinking that if he had any fault to find with his companion 'Christian soldier,' it would have been that he did not repress 'popular excesses' in a sharper way than he actually did. Studying Gordon's face by photograph and also by Mr. Thorneycroft's very good portrait of him, I see in it the modern soldier – nothing more; and his actions tell us whose soldier he was – the piratical capitalist's soldier. The centre of the accursed capitalism may well worship him, and say to others: 'Go thou and do likewise!'

Meantime a certain Mr. Manning has been holding up to our example the much abused Portuguese, who have been making a railway from Loanda to Ambaca (distance 225 miles, but called part of a very ambitious scheme). Mr. Manning is of opinion that this will do more to open up and civilise the country than formal missionary enterprises; though considering what missionary work is going on in other parts of Africa, and that the rifle is the principal tool used in it, that seems doubtful.

The *modus operandi* of the capitalists thus engaged in benefitting humanity is described with a *naif* simplicity which leaves nothing to be asked for. The Portuguese Government have guaranteed 6 per cent. to the shareholders during construction for five years. The contract was let to a Portuguese contractor, who in the first year of the work sublet it to an American – who sublet portions of it to other contractors – some of these again sublet smaller portions to small contractors. These men engaged their own labourers, *did the work* (italics mine), and received a lump sum on the completion of the work to the satisfaction of the engineer of the chief contractor.

Whether the labourers who did the work for the 'small contractors' who *did the work*, were satisfied is another matter. It seems that the chief difficulty is scarcity of labour. 'So long as the native can get enough to live on by cultivation or trade he will not do manual work' – for other people. Unreasonable black dog!

———————————————

Though the Japanese have been for long running after the foul skirts of our modern civilisation, and doing their best to lay hold of the filthy thing, they have not come up to us in the matter of prisons: not being afraid apparently of the competition of prison labour with 'free' labour, and not being under the spell of the fiendish stupidity of 'philanthropy,' which forces us to torture our prisoners by every respectable means (*i.e.*, any means which doesn't make blood flow and bones break), they set their prisoners to doing work which pleases and amuses them, and even teach them to do interesting work if they are capable of it. Only 29 out of 2,000 men in the prison visited by the *Pall Mall* Commissioner were set to the lowest work of breaking stones, and a great many were producing works of art. The Japanese after all have much to learn in the ways of civilisation. May they be long about it!

———————————————

It is asserted by those who are proposing the great coal trust – that is to say, a monopoly which will have the whole public in its power – that its effect will not be to raise the price of coal. This is rather a big pill to swallow; for how is the greed of the monopolists to be controlled? But the very fact that such an assertion can be made shows once more how the confidence in limitless competition is being shaken: for the contention is that the entire margin of profit would come out of the avoidance of waste, and that that waste is caused by the hurry of *reckless competition*.

———————————————

The following quotation, however, does not quite bear out the sanguine anticipations of the defender of the attempt to form a coal-trust: 'The oil trade in this country [America] is [owing to the 'trust'] in a more *satisfactory condition* that it has been in for some years. *Prices are higher,*' etc. In point of fact the 'more satisfactory condition' almost always does mean higher prices, and it is to this that all these combinations of capitalists are directed. They do not trouble their heads about anything else; for business men, like politicians, take care not to forecast matters for more than six months or so ahead – if even that.

Commonweal, Volume 4, Number 146,
27 October 1888, pp. 337–8.

[UNTITLED ARTICLE ON THE CHICAGO ANARCHISTS]

It is just one year since the tragedy of Chicago: enough time does not yet intervene to enable us to realise fully the meaning of the event we celebrate. Saddened by the yet fresh memories of our comrades' long struggle in the toils of bourgeois law, and the pain we felt when they at length fell victims to the deferred vengeance of outraged respectability; so many things combining to obstruct our view and distract our attention; we cannot for awhile see clearly the causes and the outcome of their death. Those things that have deepest significance when afterwards read in the light of history are rarely recognised by those who see them and pass by. It was not until negro slavery had been swept away in the fiercest civil war that was ever waged, not until the cause they died for was triumphant, that men understood why Lovejoy was assassinated and John Brown hung. Just as retribution overtook, and that not slowly, the great organised wrong of negro slavery; just as the martyrs whom it slew were avenged in its fall; so also will its doom come to the wider evil of wage slavery, and the upholders of monopoly be called on to account for the wrongs they have done in its defence.

The great god Commerce that rules wellnigh the whole world with an iron rod, is from one cause and another even more powerful in America than in the older countries of this continent. Reckless greed and sordid wealth are confronted by a larger and more desperate proletariat. There are less of the social gradations that here mask and seem to bridge the gulf between the millionaire on the one side and the pauper on the other. The masses are more educated and the classes less refined, the revolt against their rule more conscious and direct. The tramp of the men who struck down slavery still echoes in the ear of their sons. As America is to Europe, so is Chicago to America. There the social war is waged with greater fury, and its fruits are more apparent, than in any city in the world save London, and here it is not brought into so small a compass; in Chicago the opposing forces face one another within a narrower area.

There is no space here to re-tell the story of what happened, and there are but few words needed in which to explain it. The labour struggle was passing through an acute phase, and in all parts of the States there were strikes and lock-outs and threats on either side. Years before, the movement for an eight-hour day had become so strong that several States had fixed that limit for all governmental work, and Congress had followed their example throughout the whole country. But the law was not extended to the general body of trades, and an immense number of workers determined that it should be so; most of these recognised also that the law would be useless without an organisation to enforce it; that, given an organisation, the law did not much matter. In 1885 the general conference of the National Labour Union determined that next year the eight-hour day should be introduced all over the States by a universal strike on May 1st, and great preparations were made to that end. The agitation was hottest in Chicago, and the Socialists and Anarchists there were called on to take their places in the front of the battle. Seeing quite well that nothing short of the full resumption of the means of labour would benefit the workers for any length of time, but knowing also that any effort on their own behalf would elevate the masses and give them at least a passing relief, they encouraged the eight-hour movement by all means in their power; pointing out meanwhile the great ultimate goal that might by no means be lost sight of. So successful were they that it became plain to both sides that the real question at issue was little likely to be settled or even much affected by the immediate outcome of the eight hour strike.

As May-day approached the excitement grew, and strike after strike took place. At last the day came, and many thousands of workmen left their work; trade was paralysed; many employers grew frightened and made concessions; for awhile it almost seemed as if the cause was triumphant. But capitalism had not lost its cunning; it relied, and with reason, on its police, their weapons and their spies. The American Republic was to show that not Russia itself could surpass in treachery and brutal violence the behaviour of the ruling class of the 'land of the free.' A meeting of strikers on May 3rd was attacked by the police, who fired on men, women, and children alike, leaving six dead and many wounded. Next day a meeting of protest was held in the Haymarket, and this was again attacked; as the police advanced upon the meeting with loaded rifles and in fighting formation, a bomb was thrown by some one, traitor or fool, which killed one of them and threw many others to the ground. Firing began at once, and the flying unarmed crowd was followed in all directions by the police, who fired indiscriminately on all they saw. What followed is well known; how houses were ransacked and crowds arrested; how with small excuse or with none everybody was indicted who anyway could be; how a jury was packed, and how they earned the blood-money they afterwards received from the bourgeois of Chicago; how testimony was bought and witnesses made; how the whole 'legal' machinery was set in motion and well oiled with enormous bribery. It went for nothing that no connection whatever could be shown between the prisoners and the bomb; they were in the grip of the money-changers whom they would have 'scourged out of the temple,' and like their legendary prototype were condemned. Month after month dragged on, and appeal after appeal was rejected; the bourgeois would sate their anger on the men who had dared to teach the slaves to revolt. The one last appeal, to the workers of the world, was *not* fruitless; in their millions they responded, in vain as it seemed then, for unorganised right could not cope with organised wrong, and our martyrs died. But the appeal was not in vain, for the millions looked toward that gallows in Chicago on which four men had died for their fellows, and their 'silence was more powerful than speech.'

That silence has for us a message, the message of the Commune, the message of all the seeming failures that line the path of human progress: 'Agitate! Educate! Organise!' Agitate, that the workers may be stirred and awakened to a sense of their position. Educate, that they may know the reason of the evils that they suffer. Organise, that we and they may overthrow the system that bears us down and makes us what we are; that there may be no futile waste of individual effort, but that the army of the revolution may move forward united, steadfast, irresistible, 'for the Freedom of the Peoples and the Brotherhood of Man.'

Commonweal, Volume 4, Number 148,
10 November 1888, pp. 353–4.

NOTES ON NEWS

The *Echo* has been kind enough to advertise our approaching celebration of the Chicago martyrs and Bloody Sunday by a ferocious attack upon us, in which all the old calumnies against our comrades have been new burnished for the occasion, and we are held up to public reprobation as 'enemies of society.' All this is chiefly meant as an attack on Cunninghame Graham for his having the courage to be prepared to express in public what not only all Socialists, but all democrats who have enquired into the matter, must feel in their hearts. For the *Echo* believes Cunninghame Graham, though an opponent, to be on the same *plane of politics* as itself; in which idea it will I feel sure find itself mistaken.

Meantime let us say once more what was the real state of the case. Our comrades, the *Echo* says, were tried and found guilty of being privy to the throwing [of] the bomb. By whom? By the declared enemies of the people, who for long had no word in their mouths but 'shoot them down.' And on what evidence? On evidence rather less valuable than what would suffice for the condemnation of an English labourer before his squire of poaching a rabbit. There was *no* real evidence offered or required for the condemnation of our comrades: their guilt was clear already – they were the friends and fellow-agitators of the workmen on strike; that was enough.

Does the editor of the *Echo* know anything of that redoubtable weapon in defence of 'society,' the Law of Constructive Murder? It is a comprehensive one and by means of it any obnoxious person may be 'removed' by 'society' at a pinch. Any one taking part in a meeting at which loss of life occurs may be indicted for this wide-reaching crime. Supposing at some not very distant date the editor of the *Echo*, taking part in some Unionist meeting at which the audience gets too excited and shots are fired and someone is killed: how sad it would be if he was put on his trial for constructive murder!

'Enemies of society'? Of what society? Of the society which enables friends and kindred and fellow-workmen to live together in peace and good-fellowship, helping one another through all the difficulties of life; the society which gives every one an opportunity for living as well as the nature surrounding him will allow him to live? We are not enemies of this society, we are now devoted soldiers of it, and some of us may yet live to be happy members of it. For are we not Socialists – *i.e.*, people who want to realise true society?

But I suppose the *Echo* is thinking of another society; the society of classes: the society which insists that most men shall be poor in order that some may be rich. The society which as its culminating success in our own days takes care that poverty shall no longer mean, as it once did, mere rudeness of life and scantiness of possessions, but utter degradation of body and soul; the society which produces in one country, in one city, living under the same 'equal' laws, the coster's barrow and the duke's palace; the culture of the Whitechapel slum-dweller, and the 'culture' of the university superfine superior person. In a word, the 'society' that produces the rich and the poor, – that is to say, the suffering of the world.

Of such a 'society' as this – or rather of such a band of robbers and heap of corruption usurping the holy name of Society – every honest man must be the enemy, even if he is not conscious of it.

Mr. Balfour in his speech at Wolverhampton was very emphatic in showing that the difference between the Irish rebels of the present and the past, was that those of to-day were engaged in a socialistic agitation; the *Daily News* in commenting on the speech was naturally anxious to disprove this, pointing out that several of the Irish leaders are strong Anti-Socialists, that Mr. Davitt is not supported in his land nationalisation by his countrymen, and the Irish peasant is a fanatic for property in land.

All this is true enough on the surface; nor could it be otherwise, since the Irishman is conscious of having been thrust off the land by mere foreigners. The capitalist as he knows him is either an alien in blood or at least the representative of alien domination. Nevertheless Mr. Balfour is more nearly right than the *Daily News*, more nearly right then he knows himself probably. The agrarian agitation in Ireland *is* an attack on property, though its immediate results may be the establishment of a peasant proprietorship, a thing which in itself all Socialists condemn. The claim for Home Rule *is* an attack on the centralised bureaucracy, which is the palladium of the present robbery sham-society; although its realisation may lead at first to the establishment of another bureaucratic centre, which will be rotten long before it is ripe; and although the principle for exclusive nationality is abhorrent to all true Socialists.

But the Irish are being educated into Socialism by the force of circumstances whether they are conscious of it or not, and whether they like it or not. That is what Mr. Balfour means, and he is perfectly right.

We need not trouble ourselves about Mr. Vizetelly's 'punishment.' He offered his back to the lash, and is of course a mere capitalistic publisher engaged in bringing out what will sell, irrespective of other considerations. But a word or two may be said on the scene of ridiculous hypocrisy in which he played an unwilling part. M. Zola's books are horrible. Granted – but are they as horrible as the corrupt society which they picture? What is good enough to be done is good enough to be told of; and I think it is but fair to assume (since the books are undoubtedly powerful) that he is not merely wanton in writing them, but wishes to show modern Society what a foul beast it is. On these grounds he may claim at least the pardon accorded to the hearty good-humoured grossnesses of Shakespeare and Chaucer; and, as a matter-of-fact, the outspokenness of his books is not so provocative of lust as the veiled corruption of the ordinary erotic novels of the day.

As to whether all this is due material for art – that is another affair. But an affair to come before a judge and jury? Preposterous! Why the very reading of detached passages from the book as a method to found criticism on, shows how entirely outside the judgment of a law court such things must needs be. Really I think the position of the ordinary newspaper critic as compared with that of the author on whom he lives is already sufficiently imposing, without dressing him up in a gown and wig and giving him the power of sending his literary opponents to prison. In short, this trial of M. Zola (for he was the real person tried) is another indication, if but a small one, of the way in which our laws represent the worst side and not the best of modern life.

Commonweal, Volume 4, Number 148,
10 November 1888, p. 356.

NOTES ON NEWS

No doubt the great Liberal demonstration at Birmingham
was a very grand affair, and very comforting to the souls of
all those simple Liberals or Radicals at least who were not
behind the scenes, and do not know what a heap of money
these grand political demonstrations cost. Also it demonstrated at least the fact that Mr. Gladstone will disappoint his
Tory and Whig opponents and a good part of his Radical
followers in parliament by not being in any hurry to walk the
plank. On the whole, I think it would be safe to bet on the
G.O.M. reaching his hundredth year; and the greater part of
the time he yet has to live he will no doubt pass in sharp
political battle; and he may even, if things go quickly, find
himself driven to repeat like a parrot semi-Socialist phrases
expressing the aspirations of the rising democracy.

He wound up his holiday in the Midlands by a delightful
drive of fourteen miles through the Black Country, and was
received with all the holiday-triumph which the resources of
that shabby hell are equal to. I wonder if he enjoyed himself.
I almost fear that he did. I am willing to admit that Mr.
Gladstone is more human than most politicians; but all those
years of politics *must* harden a man's heart; and surely a
politician must go through such scenes as Mr. Gladstone
passed through the other day, with his eyes in his pockets, if
he has nothing better to do than return to his old party work
again with its leaden horizon of 'practical' politics shutting it
in on every side.

The reporter of the *Daily News* has a few sentences in which
the facts of the Black Country are alluded to in flowery

rhetoric. But there is all stops, though the writer has this (to the thoughtful) significant sentence: 'Wealth might be betokened by those furnaces, but it did not dwell amidst them.'

Mr. Gladstone does not, I fear, read the *Commonweal*, and if I were to write him a letter his secretary would return me a formal answer; but I wish I could convey to him somehow the fact that if he has a mind to gain popularity from a larger and 'lower' social strata than those who now adore him, he might occasionally give a lecture on social subjects; and I should like to suggest as a title for one of such lectures, 'Why those who profit by the labour of the Black Country do not live there.'

Warren is out; Mr. Matthews has hove over *his* Jonah. Probably the Government will heave over *their* Jonah – Mr. Matthews.

The International Trades Union Congress took the course which might be expected: that is to say, it was a contest between the reactionary trades unionism of the ordinary English workmen and the Socialism more or less pronounced of their Continental brethren. The officialdom of trades-unionism has of course a quite simple conception of its function at such a gathering – *i.e.*, the spreading of the idea that the English workman has no conception of the class struggle, but admits his dependence on his master. On this side the trades unions are a mere reflection of the conservatism of the non-producing classes; and the latter will be only doing as their position forces them to do in putting down sternly any attempt on the part of the workmen to better their condition by reducing the tribute with which they buy their position of irresponsibility. Slaves cannot dictate to their masters the terms of their slavery.

If the trades unionists have no other conception of their business than that which the majority of the British delegates have expressed, they had better give up all pretence at being anything but benefit societies: and *that* will be a useful function with a vengeance! Paying out of their wages part of their masters' poor-rates!

The amendment carried by Mrs. Besant seems to be pretty much the renewal of the International. At first sight the voting of the British delegates on it (11 for and 37 against) is discouraging enough. But we must consider what a 'slough of despond,' what officialism and bossing besets trades-unionism, and then we shall feel encouraged that it was even discussed at a trades union meeting, let alone carried by a united majority of the reasonable and independent delegates, British and Continental, who were present.

Commonweal, Volume 4, Number 149,
17 November 1888, p. 361.

NOTES ON NEWS

The Government have passed their bill for the relief of the Irish landlords to the extent of five millions, as they were quite sure to do in the teeth of all opposition, but their victory is not very likely to do them permanent service. Compensation to the Irish landlords at the expense of the British tax-payer is just the rock they are likely to split on, but they cannot help steering in that direction; so that before long they will probably have to make way for their opponents to try *their* scheme for peasant proprietorship in Ireland; or more plainly, for making a number of small landlords in Ireland instead of a few big ones. Needless to insist on the fact that this also will have to be done at the expense of the British tax-payer, whatever hanky-panky may be used to conceal the fact.

'The flowing tide is with us' (the Liberals) cries the *Pall Mall Gazette*. From the election agents' point of view that is probably true; that is, at present the chances of a Gladstonian success at the next election are brightening. But another metaphor more accurately describes the process by which the change of ministries is being brought about: 'The pendulum is swinging to our side again,' is the due figure of speech. That is not so encouraging perhaps to some of the members of the 'Liberal party,' that curious creature with a Whig head and a Radical tail; though I fear a very great many of them are much better pleased that so it is. When the 'flowing tide' of really advanced opinion sets in, these gentry will skip out of the way of it with all the nimbleness they are capable of.

Mr. Henry George has come to England once more with his old pretensions to Socialism abandoned, but clinging obstinately to his old economical heresies, with which in past days he used to weave a veil of vague socialistic aspiration and eloquence. Free trade and the single-tax, *i.e.*, what he used to call land nationalisation, but which he now more accurately describes as the taxing of land values, is his platform. He says it is but a step from free trade to the single tax, with a very curious oblivion of the not very recondite fact, that England has been a free-trade country for many years and is not very far on the road to the 'single-tax.'

Mr. George combats the cry of the land for the cultivator with the cry of the land for the people; but, unhappily, it is but a cry. What he really means is 'the land for the money capitalist'! And how he proposes to separate the land-capitalist from the money-capitalist passes human ingenuity to imagine. Is it possible for a man to be sincere, who with plenty of people teaching him, has not been able to learn this through all these years? To be a forward politician; to make a great agitation, clamouring for a great change which would change nothing in the life of the toiling people; but which happily cannot by itself be attempted even. This seems now Mr. George's career, after all his big words.

The frightful case of injustice perpetrated by 'justice' against the two poor men, Murphy and Branaghan, and the case mentioned by Mr. Bernard Coleridge, in which no pretence to remedy a similar injustice has been made (though, indeed, how can you 'remedy' the murder of so many years of a man's life?), shed a lurid light on all the ways and manners of our criminal law. For who can doubt but that many and many such cases have happened, and will happen as long as our sham society lasts, and calls for such a system of defence?

One remark in the papers about this shameful affair struck
me particularly. It was stated that there were serious doubts
at the time of conviction as to the guilt of the men, but that
they were overborne by the sympathy felt for the victims of
the burglary. Does not this show how the whole feeling of
the public is corrupted by our laws? An offence is committed,
and straightway in the interests of society a man-hunt is set
on foot; some one is arrested, and the public will be so
bitterly disappointed if nobody is caught that if the guilty
person cannot be convicted, at least convict somebody; and
then the whole machinery of the law is set at work to get a
conviction, of the guilty man if possible, but at least of some
one. A theory of prosecution is started, and the whole mass
of circumstantial evidence is manipulated by it; a sham jury
give a verdict which purports to be theirs, but is in fact
nothing but a deduction from the judge's summing-up – and,
as far as they are concerned, the play is over and the public
speedily forgets it, while the unhappy victims of its idiotic
thirst for theatrical revenge are rotting in jail if they have not
been hanged. The word *rotting* being no figurative word, let
us remember, but a literal expression of a fact.

Mr. Pyke, in his interesting volume on the 'History of Crime,'
notes that in the height of the Middle Ages in England juries
were very unwilling to convict. There is no more significant
token of the servile condition we have dropped into than the
ease with which convictions are got now-a-days; *per contra*,
when juries begin to think about their position, and the
Courts complain of the difficulty of getting convictions, we
may begin to lay some claim to be of the same blood as our
stout ancestors.

Commonweal, Volume 4, Number 151,
1 December 1888, p. 380.

NOTES ON NEWS

The School Board election for London has passed over, leaving behind it the usual electioneering dregs of defeated ambitions, empty boasts, compromises which no one believed in when they were made, and which will be sorely regretted hereafter by many who made them. As for the results, they are little except the dregs. For what does it all come to, this virulent storm in a saucer? In any case the children will be taught something; in no case can there be any satisfactory education under our present sham society; and the whole theory of School Board education is a bad one, even for our present system.

Setting all other considerations aside, is it worth the wear and tear for Socialists, who have so much work before them in merely putting before people the bare elements of their creed, to spend their energies, first in electioneering and next in the committee-room grind, in doing work which would be done quite as well, if external pressure were put upon them, by Radicals and Secularists, who otherwise hinder the work of propaganda?

The one thing of any real importance which could be done at once for the children is getting them the free meal, and it seems to me that with moderate pushing from the outside this could be got; not, of course, from pedants of the Lyulph Stanley kind, but from Radicals or even Tories not desperately committed to party shibboleths. The late cartoon in that very bourgeois print, *Punch*, in which the poor little advanced scholar claims something to still the cravings of hunger before going on with his 'intellectual' work (save the mark!), is sufficient indication that the suggestion of this piece of elementary humanity and common-sense is not so terrifying to the general public as it used to be.

Lord Salisbury has been bidding high for Whig abuse, and will probably have his belly-full of it in these current days. And indeed he may be always trusted at a crisis to say the most snobbish thing that can be said, and his 'Black-man' utterance quite comes up to the standard expected of him. The jeers at the Irish members, though rather stale now, and the heads on Temple Bar, are also reasonably good in the blackguarding line, and probably show that the most noble is not very hopeful of the coming election (when it does come).

But attack on this stupid reactionary 'splitting of the ears of the groundlings' does not come with a good grace from journals which are revolutionary in Ireland and Whig in England. Until the *Daily News* breaks the conspiracy of silence on the judicial murder of Socialists or Anarchists who were slain for their opinions in a crisis that coward society thought dangerous, it ought to hold its tongue on Lord Salisbury's ferocious but harmless hints. Until its brother Whig the *Star* has learned that the whole duty of man is not limited to the returning of Gladstonian Whigs to Parliament at any cost, it ought also to hold its tongue; unless it is prepared to admit the fact that as to morals and principles it heartily agrees with Lord Salisbury's 'short way with revolutionists' though the exigencies of party warfare compel it to pretend to be his opponent.

Commonweal, Volume 4, Number 152,
8 December 1888, p. 385.

NOTES ON NEWS

The Suakim business is growing, and England's hired slaughterers are lending a hand in getting rid of the Dervishes, of whose doings as much as possible has been made in order to give a fresh opportunity for pushing the fortunes of the market-mongers, and the persistent hammering at the story of this stupendous siege after the manner of the tremendous adventures of Major Geoghegan, appears likely to produce its fruits in some way or other. Only since the country is clearly not very anxious for any more 'glory' in the Soudan, the gist of the plan now is to keep up Suakim as a running sore, and to push traders up the country so as to involve us in a tangle which shall end at last in a new expedition for the smashing of the Mahdi. The plan is not very new or ingenious, but it is likely to succeed.

Mr. Henry James, the American novelist, has been writing an ingenious paper on the impression made by London on his feelings; but as a matter of course, his view of the monstrosity is taken from the stand-point of the superior middle-class person, who looks upon the working-classes as an useful machine, and, having no experience of their life, has not imagination enough to realise the fact that the said machine is composed of millions of men, women, and children who are living in misery; that is to say, they are always undergoing torments, the fear of undergoing which would make many a 'refined' person kill himself rather than submit to them. And to these torments they must get used, as the phrase goes; that is to say, hopeless suffering must be the element in which they live. It is this from which is born the 'dreadful delight' on which clever but dull Mr. James expatiates so ingeniously. Does he ever ask himself what is likely to be the final price which his class, who have created this Hell, will have to pay for it?

I should like a view of London from a quite different kind of man from the clever historian of the deadliest corruption of society, the laureate of the flirts, sneaks, and empty fools of which that society is mostly composed, and into whose hearts (?) he can see so clearly. I should like the impressions of London given by one who had been under its sharp-toothed harrow.

But he should not be a man born and bred in the slums, nor even 'used' to them, nor a man born poor anywhere, but someone who once lived in a pleasant place with hope beside him. From him I should like a true tale of the City of Dreadful Delight. If we could but have some new Defoe with the added bitterness bred of the tremendous growth of the burden of hideous tyranny to tell us such a tale! Or it may be rather that no words could tell it.

Besides, if it were attempted it would be brought into Court and judged by a jury of comfortable and respectable men, and a luxuriously-living judge, and be condemned as filthy literature, horribly indecent – in short, shocking, and its author would but add one fresh note to the song of suffering, which if it is good for nothing else, is good enough to tickle the ears of superior persons, more hypocritical and less naïve than the ogre in the Eastern story, who, when his captives awaiting the spit were lamenting and moaning, said: 'Hark how sweetly my nightingales are singing!'

Commonweal, Volume 4, Number 153,
15 December 1888, p. 397.

NOTES ON NEWS

The news from the Soudan is somewhat portentous, if, as seems pretty certain, Stanley as well as Emin Bey is in the hands of the Mahdi. It is in any case satisfactory that Stanley's expedition has fallen through; it gives us breathing-space, at any rate. Also as a matter of course the Soudanese are in a better position, for the present, for their possession of these important hostages. But on the other hand the danger of these 'pioneers of civilisation' (once called pirates) will be worked by the market-mongers and Christianity-shovers for all that it is worth, and the difficulties in the way of having a small half-responsibility expedition in the Soudan will tend to push us into a big affair in which we shall be fully responsible, and in which it would be almost too good to hope for serious defeat.

———————

Mr. Page Hopps' 'Radicals' Creed,' as printed in the *Pall Mall*, is as lamentable a piece of feebleness as a well-meaning person ever produced: the opening sentence of it convicts him at once of incapacity of understanding the whole social question. Says he: 'It is always foolish and wicked to set class against class, but the time has come for a resolute forward movement in favour of the toilers of our streets and fields.' Indeed the time *has* come, and long ago; nor for such a movement has the time ever failed. But pray, how can 'a resolute forward movement' on behalf of the toilers take place without its finding itself at once face to face with a class which says, 'Thus far and no further; we have won our position by a long struggle and have overthrown our masters; but now *we* are the masters. Your resolute forward movement must stop, unless it can go forward over us.'

———————

Will Radicals of Mr. Page Hopps' kind *never* learn that whatever is done to raise the condition of the 'poor' *must* be done at the expense of the rich; since the latter are only rich because the poor make them so by allowing themselves to be compelled into poverty? To waste their labour for the rich, and to be paid for their wasted labour with leave to live to waste their labour, that is what they are compelled to do. This is a fact, and there is no evading it. Let the 'Radical' read his Adam Smith, and see it stated there in plain terms before the days when modern social revolution was thought of and when there was no danger in stating it.

Who or what sets class against class? The whole evolution of society. That is, the existence of the classes. That is indeed a foolish and wicked thing, and since we now see that we can make an end of it, let us make an end of it at once. Here is a wall which hinders us from the use of a fair garden: there is the hindrance, and it is caused by the wall; which is there, whether we shut our eyes to it or not. Nor shall we be any more inside the garden because we turn round and dibble in a few potatoes outside it, and pretend there is no wall between us and the garden, and that we don't want to get in if we could. Moral – down with the wall! even if it is necessary to say plainly that it exists. More of the Radicals' Creed another time.

Mr. Arthur Arnold takes the trouble to attack Mr. George, over whom he, as a defender of capitalism, could win an easy victory, if he had taken the trouble to understand what the land monopoly really signifies, and how impossible it is to separate it from monopoly of the other means of production; but such a victory would not be a victory for the champion of 'free land,' but for the Socialist. Mr. Arnold tells us pretty plainly what his aim is when he says: 'Here, alas! the monopoly of the land is neither great nor wide nor deep; it is only narrow; I trust we shall make it great and wide and deep.' Just so; Mr. Arnold's aim, like that of many others whose instinct rather than their reason drives them to seek it, is the perpetuation of inequality – *i.e.*, the misery of the many, by means of the widening of the basis of robbery. He thinks (or feels), and rightly, that the more people you can get interested in the maintenance of oppression, the safer that oppression will be from the attacks of the disinherited. Plunder by all means, but don't let the few keep the plunder to themselves: if many share the plunder they will form a stout body of men who will be as firm in their opinion that 'the abolition of the monopoly is impossible' as the slave-owners of Aristotle's time were as to *their* monopoly.

Says Mr. Arnold, something or other 'would be cruelly unjust to the working-classes, and would impoverish them by enhancing the value of foreign investments.' How a labouring man on 15s. a-week can be impoverished by a rise in prices in foreign investments, is surely beyond the ken of anybody but a very wise financier – or a very great fool.

Mr. Arnold makes a curious quotation from J. S. Mill: 'The monopoly of land,' says Mr. Mill, in words which no accurate thinker can repudiate, 'is a natural monopoly…. which cannot be prevented from existing.' Well, I cannot, I fear, claim to be an accurate thinker, but I am in the habit of weighing the value of language, and I should say that a man who would use such a phrase as 'natural monopoly' might presently talk about 'dry water' without astonishing us much. To such a man I should deny the title of an 'accurate thinker,' were he Mr. Mill, or the Pope, or even Mr. Bradlaugh.

In plain words a monopoly can be maintained as long as the monopolists have fraud and force enough to hoodwink the most of men and bully the rest; failing that sufficiency of fraud and force, it is scattered to the winds.

But will Mr. Arnold, or any other Free Land Leaguer, tell us *why* the abolition of the monopoly of land (or say the means of production generally) is impossible! He might as well say that it is impossible for a man to touch his toe with his hand. It is impossible as long as his hand is tied behind his back.

Mr. Morley has been making what is conventionally called a 'great' speech in Clerkenwell. To judge by the reports and their many columns, it was at least a big speech; but there was in it little or nothing to note. Leasehold enfranchisement was the chief part of the song; and it is to be hoped that even advanced Radicals are not blind enough to see it as, what Mr. Morley half hinted he considered it, a step to the abolition of the land-monopoly. A measure to increase the number of landlords is about all that its supporters can claim it to be. But, as a matter of fact, it means merely aggrandising the capitalist, big or little, at the expense of the land-owner; and it is only meant to stop people's mouths, a make-believe of energy on the part of the 'Great Liberal Party.'

Mr. Morley put before [the] Liberals an ideal quoted from Shakespeare: 'I earn that I eat: I get that I wear: owe no man hate: envy no man's happiness; glad of other men's good.' Very pretty sentiments, but to whom are they addressed? To the workers? Well they certainly earn what they eat and get that they wear, but also what other people eat and wear. To the possessing classes? Well, when they can say that with truth it will be a changed world indeed. For they would be both naked and hungry if they only ate and wore what they earned; and if they were glad of other people's good, how about the Soudan, and Imperial Federation, and the whole disgusting war of the market, and oppression of that great tyranny the British Empire?

The *Star* has been doing a little bit of canonisation of Mr. Brunner as the worker's friend, which under all the circum-

stances it was bound to do, for where would the *Star* have
been without Mr. Brunner, or rather without Mr. Brunner's
money? But Mr. Brunner is a Gladstonian, so the *Evening
News*, which is no doubt quite prepared to canonise a Tory
or Unionist employer of labour, has taken the part of the
Devil's Advocate, and has taken pains to show that Mr.
Brunner is just about as good as might be expected from his
position, *i.e.*, a man belonging to a class which compel other
men to keep them gratis against their will, and competing
(*i.e.*, fighting) with other members of his class for the biggest
share he can get of this plunder. The motto of the *Star* is, 'a
Gladstonian can do no wrong even if he is one of our
owners,' and the *Evening News* has done some service to us
(unwittingly) by attacking this 'eternal truth' or infernal lie.
Let the *Star* do as much for the *Evening News* another time,
and so do honour to an ancient proverb.

Commonweal, Volume 4, Number 154,
22 December 1888, p. 401.

NOTES ON NEWS

Mr. Gladstone's answer to the unemployed was, I suppose, what the writers of the vague and quite desperately polite letter to him expected. If they did not expect such an answer they should have written a less vague letter to him, in which case they would have had no answer at all, or a very curt one. After all, the answer drawn from that venerable dodger is meant to amount to little more than staining white paper with a black pattern. There is, however, something more in it, which may fairly be translated from Gladstonian into English thus: 'Unemployed, what should I know about them? They are not my business. Parliament might – but no, they have something better to do than bothering themselves about the poor of London. So look here! I will call it [a] "local" matter just to make you know your proper places.'

The old gentleman has either quite made up his mind to ignore the fact that there are people who are discontented with the present state of society, and have learned by study of their own dreary conditions of life to know *why* they are discontented, and *how* they can alter the said dreary conditions; or else (and that really seems to me possible) he is genuinely quite ignorant of what Socialism is, and what its claims are.

One thing the unemployed may be quite sure of, to wit, that the governing classes are quite determined to do nothing for the workmen out of work except at the expense of the workmen in general. They would not if they could, and they cannot if they would, as long as the present system, that of capitalist and wage-earner, lasts. It is true that some

Government, Tory-Democrat or Radical-bitten-by-Socialism, may make a show of it in a desperate attempt to win popularity, but all they can do as long as 'society' is owned by the monopolists, is to shift the burden from one group of workers to another. Unless competition keeps down the wages of the mass of the employed to a bare subsistence wage, the capitalists of the country will be 'ruined,' that is, will cease to employ; and this glorious arrangement can only be kept going by dint of the capitalists holding in hand a large reserve army of labour. As that is absorbed into the active ranks of labour, the capitalists will be driven to fresh marvels of organisation, and fresh machinery to cheapen 'muscular labour' still more, and so remain masters of the situation.

The other day we had news that at Zanzibar, which for 25 years had been free from capital punishment (*alias* judicial murder), the Sultan had begun to imitate the foul deeds of English and American courts of 'justice' by striking off the heads of four of the 'natives.' Great indignation was expressed in our papers about this outrage, and surely this anger was but due against the wretched tyrant who was such a fool as to copy the customs of civilisation.

But what now? Who is the civilised English Government copying now? – Zenghiz Khan or Tamerlane? Scarcely even these; for these destroyers had their ideas stirred and their blood heated by the atmosphere of personal war and violence in which they lived, and at worst they were no hypocrites. But our black-coated, smug-visaged, dinner-party-giving, go-to-church 'scourges of God,' who have not even the spirit to plead for themselves that they *are* curses and must act after their kind, who can one liken them to? For the sake of what one cannot even call a whim – for the sake of one knows not what, they must slaughter a number of innocent persons whom they are pleased to call 'the enemy.'

Consider too that this Massacre of Suakim, whatever the Gladstonian party (equally guilty with the others) may say, will be heartily applauded by the average Englishman. Nay, it will be considered by the politicians who are now governing us as a stroke of good luck which will help to stay their failing fate, and will probably win them a seat or two of those that are agoing in the electoral scramble. This is the morality of the English nation, of which we have heard so much! Indeed, I admit that it is caused more by rank stupidity than by malicious scoundrelism; though there is an element of that in it also.

'The enemy' – Yes; if they are the enemies of such a nation as ours there must be some good in them I think, since commercial patriotism has brought us to this pass. Yet, indeed, once more it is no great wonder that the rich men who are callous to the murder of misery at home should be callous to the murder of battle abroad.

A meeting of the unemployed held some days ago, at which a resolution was passed calling on the Government to set on foot relief works, was stated by *Reynolds* to have been held under the auspices of the Socialist League. By the instruction of the Council, the Secretary wrote to disclaim this, as the Socialist League holds that the present system necessities the existence of an army of unemployed, and that no palliative will get rid of it; and that any attempt that a capitalist government might make to satisfy the claims of the unemployed would mean nothing more than helping labour at the expense of labour. This disclaimer was accompanied by the Manifesto on the subject published by the Council, Oct. 29, 1887; but we are sorry to say *Reynolds* has not inserted the letter, and thereby has refused to correct its inaccurate statement.

Commonweal, Volume 4, Number 155,
29 December 1888, p. 409.

CONTRIBUTIONS TO COMMONWEAL

1889

NOTES ON NEWS

A certain Mr. George W. McCree (who, since he says he has been a Christian worker in London since 1848, must now be an old man) has been writing an optimistic letter to the press, on the subject, 'Is London growing better?' which question he answers in the affirmative. He instances the growth of cheap literature; 'Every man can now have his newspaper' (mostly lies), 'his magazine, and his cheap edition of Shakespeare, Dickens, Burns, and Scott.' True, *if* he has got any surplus after feeding, clothing, and housing himself: but how is the cheapness got? Our friends the compositors, the hack literateurs, the girls in the 'doing up' binders, can answer that question partly I think. Dog-fighting is extinct, he says, and pugilism nearly so: yet Jack the Ripper is not extinct, nor the mass of brutality bred from a hideous life of suffering and squalor, of which he is but the blossom.

'For a halfpenny a tired work-girl can get a lift across one of the bridges on a rainy night.' Ah, Mr. McCree, *how* tired is she? *Why* is she tired? How many nights in the year is she thus tired? What kind of a life does she earn by her hopeless weariness? Does she ever think of this in the course of her lift across the bridges? – and do you and your like? 'An aged toiler with his bag of tools can reach home for twopence, often for a penny.' O noble boon, O glorious gain! Yet it would be more of a gain if that 'aged toiler' had a tolerable home to go to, instead of the dog-hole which serves him as a halting-place between the work*shop* and the work*house*.

'Clothing, food, fruit, and furniture are cheap.' Yes, how blessed cheap, and how damned nasty when they are

intended for the consumption of the workers, who have
made them, or grown them, and brought them to market! 'In
hundreds of tidy establishments hot coffee' (Ugh! what stuff
it is!) 'plumcake, peasoup, good milk, and a rare vegetarian
dinner on easy terms await the hungry man.' In these 'tidy'
establishments I note that dirt and stink are not expressly
charged for: and yet they *are* charged for, since cag-mag is
dear for what it is, and the poor man's penn'orths are but
scanty ones. It is sickening to think of this commercial dole
to the 'lower classes' of garbage not fit to be thrown to the
dogs: and to think that it has a price at all; that there is
anyone, I won't say to buy it, but to eat and drink it, uncom-
pelled.

'Many public-houses have been closed.' Yes, but many are
open, and are full too, beastly holes as they are, with not a
rag of comfort in them; which is worse (to my unphilan-
thropic mind) than their selling liquor – if it were good:
whereas that offered to the poor is just about good enough to
poison cats with – if it were strong enough.

'Ragged schools and refuges have almost entirely prevented
another generation of criminals.' Open Pentonville gates
then, and let out everybody but Socialists and rioters, since
there are no criminals! As indeed I think there are but few
who have not been *made* by that 'vastly improved' London of
yours, and polished up fine by Pentonville and its sister hells.

'The increasing sympathy between the rich and the poor, the
employer and employed.' Of that increasing sympathy, I
think I know more than you do, Mr. McCree; and I have
seen some curious examples of it, and heard some queer talk
on the subject both among the rich, and among the poor;
and, judging from all I have heard and seen, it has seemed to
me that that 'increasing sympathy' was about what was likely
to happen betwixt a mass of most miserable slaves, now

beginning to discover that they *are* slaves, on the one hand, and a body of slave-owners, blind and supercilious, but now at last beginning to see a possibility of their losing their slaves. Such sympathy as there can be between two such sets of men is likely to lead not to the continuous cheapening of cag-mag and shoddy for the benefit of the 'lower classes,' but to experiments in the streets of some new machine guns.

For a word here to those of our readers who belong to the rich classes, the well-off. Some of you prate about the virtues of the working classes, and doubtless they have virtues, in which lie hid the germs of our new society: but unless they are conscious and willing servants of your class, and on the verge of rising into it, they have not got those virtues which you think they have: commercial virtues, to wit, which *you* call, e.g., honesty, fidelity, and gratitude, but which others might call commercial foresight, servility, and prudent expectation of fresh benefits. No, the 'poor,' as you call them, are divided into two groups; those who are conscious of discontent against you, and would raise themselves at your expense by abolishing your class; and those who, without being conscious of their wrongs, work you and your wealth for what it is worth.

The first group are the intelligent and really honest among the 'poor;' the second (poor wretces [*sic*]!) have not intelligence enough to be honest and courageous, and are able to do nothing at present, but get out of you what they can by fawning on, and cheating you, taking your miserably shabby gifts with such 'gratitude' as can be imagined. Both these groups are your slaves and *therefore* your enemies; but whatever you may think, and in spite of all your efforts at stifling the free speech of the first group, it is the second that is the most dangerous to you, for it is by far the most numerous: and when the day comes, as it most surely will, unless you are wise in time, when these poor people can make no more out of you; when your 'captainship of industry' is discovered even by yourselves to be a fraud (*i.e.* when you can no longer live on it) when your charity doles to the poor have to cease, you will be face to face with the once-contented poor, those Englishmen whose patience and good sense you now contrast so proudly with the foolish visionaries of Continental Socialists, but who then will be 'contented' no longer; and who will, driven by their ignorance and despair to attack, not your position only, but your persons.

———————————

If you could but be wise in time! But can you be? My experience of the last five or six years makes me doubt it. Class prejudice is so obstinate, and so deceptive and insinuating, that in proportion as the movement towards equality grows and becomes more practical amongst the discontented 'poor,' the hearts of the rich are hardened against that movement. There are many in that class, some of whom I know, who six years ago were flushed with excitement over the rhetorical part (not the would-be economics, of that they knew little and cared less) of Henry George's 'Progress and Poverty,' who are now mere votaries of Law-and-Order. There was no appearance of the two camps being formed then; now there is, and they are being driven into their own camp. And these, mind you, are not mere hypocrites or tyrants at heart, they are simply people who cannot escape from their class. So strong that curse is!

———————————

London is better is it? We want more evidence than that of Mr. McCree to prove that. At least it is bigger, and who can really doubt but that with its size its suffering has increased? But if it is bigger, why is it bigger? Because the riches (far be it from me to say the wealth) of the country has increased enormously. Will anyone say that the improvement of London, 'vast' as it may be, is at all proportioned to that increase in riches? If he does say so he lies. What has been done then with that increase of riches, which should have been used for the bettering of London, *i.e.*, for the welfare of

those who made it? It has gone the way of all riches, it has
been wasted by the rich. We have been laborious, ingenious,
and commercially successful – what for? That we might
remain unhappy, and sing songs of triumph over the cheapening of cat's-meat for human beings. In a word, we are
slaves still, for all our 'vast improvement.'

Says the *Pall Mall* anent the police outrage of Christmas Eve:
'If they (the outrages) are not inquired into and punished
promptly and severely, Mr. Monro will pass as Sir C. Warren
has passed, for there is nothing more abhorrent to the
average citizen than organised outrage by a disciplined force
inflicted on law-abiding men exercising their rights of
citizenship.' I fear that the writer is judging other citizens by
himself; very few signs of indignation against these outrages
have appeared as yet. The events of the past two years in
England and America tend to show that whatever was the
case once, the average citizen is now always willing to hound
on the police against poor men who are not pleased with
their poverty. They expect the police to support law-'n'-
order to the utmost, by any means convenient to them at the
moment. Mr. Monro has been put in his place to see this
done, and for nothing else. I agree that the Christmas Eve
job is a test for him; but nothing would surprise me more
than his passing that test satisfactorily to honest men and
good citizens.

Commonweal, Volume 5, Number 156,
5 January 1889, pp. 4–5.

NOTES ON NEWS

The *Pall Mall Gazette* has been handselling its new and very disagreeable *format* by turning on its jingo stop most vigorously, though it is true that this is nothing new to it, as it is often smitten with a very acute form of the disease of loyalty to the British Empire. This time its old boss, Mr. Morley, comes in for it; and what seems a little ominous is that Admiral Maxse, a very hard-shell Coercionist, is turned loose on him and not rebuked for his snarl. Mr. Morley is compared, much to his disadvantage, to the Whig turfite, Lord Rosebery, and in short the ex-editor is well whipped for one of his merits, perhaps his only one, an instinctive dislike to Jingoism.

It is difficult to see how all this can go on along with the advocacy of Home Rule; for what it means really is 'our empire, right or wrong!' And no reasonable man who looks at the thing with other eyes than those of an election agent, doubts that the establishment of Home Rule would be a serious blow to that elaborate machinery of violence and fraud called the British Empire. Mr. Morley has the grace to see that it is a preposterous insult to logic to protest against coercion in Ireland when you are advocating coercion in Egypt and the Soudan, and therefore he certainly is guilty of the crime of anti-Jingoism.

It is a pity he cannot be a little more logical, and learn to see that our buccaneering wars and Christian heroes are just incidents in the huge commercial war that has made England so 'great' and so unhappy, and that those whose mission it is to 'civilise' barbarism by the introduction of wage-slavery cannot be nice about their means. One day it is rum-and-bible, another sword-and-bible, but cheap wares and sweating are what both these instruments are used for alike; and horrible as the slaughter of the bullet is, it is not more horrible than the slower process of the sweater if we could only see the latter as plainly. Mr. Morley can never answer Admiral Maxse and the *Pall Mall* effectively till he sees clearly that nothing can save the barbarians of Africa from the dreadful life which civilisation is preparing for them, but the speedy realisation of Socialism.

The papers which have been commenting on the last new Yankee joke, the electric sugar fraud, are astounded that people were taken in by an inventor who promised them to remove the dross from a pound of raw sugar without decreasing its weight. But this is a very mild form of a modern commercial miracle. Here is a much stronger one. You send a pound of thrown silk to the dyer, and he first takes from it something less than a quarter of a pound of gum which the worm has put on it, and then sends it back to you dyed black and weighing two pounds and a quarter; and you have no difficulty in convincing the public that the additional weight is all the work of the long dead silk-worm, instead of being, as it really is, made up of coarse materials and what-not of secret.

I call the Yankee inventor a very uninventive and timid person for not promising at least three pounds of sugar instead of one, without doing anything to it. It would only have been a parable of the present monopolist society.

Commonweal, Volume 5, Number 157,
12 January 1889, p. 12.

NOTES ON NEWS

There are curious signs of the time abroad, that show us pretty clearly in what an element of discontent we are living, *e.g.*, a leader in the *Daily News*, that pink of respectability, in lamenting the heavy record of murder of the past few months, does seem to be fairly shocked at the record of the gallows also. 'We are getting perilously near a revival of the good old hanging days,' is a sentence in strong contrast with the feeling of a large part of the well-to-do classes, whose word, like that of the king in the old romance, is 'Hang and head! hang and head!'

On the other hand, as a matter of course, after the burglary at Muswell Hill, the courage, humanity, and wisdom of the *successful* thieves of our sham society, the well-to-do, to wit, is illustrated by the loud cry for the flogging of burglars, and apparently of people (of the 'lower orders') suspected of being burglars. We must never forget that the boasted humanity and tenderness of human life of our century depends entirely on the feeling of continuous safety amongst the ruling classes; as soon as they are conscious of any hole in their rampart, of any enemy amongst them, humanity and tenderness is cast to the winds. 'To think that I – I should be subjected to violence, should be liable to be robbed or shot - I, amidst all my soft wrappages and the bosom of the family; I, who in my daily luxury and cowardice manage so success-fully to forget both death and the reasons for living! Hang and head and torture those wretches that have made me afraid!' That is the ordinary sentiment of the comfortable classes.

This is the constant tendency of the masters of society, of those who believe their position to be eternal; and who are so stupid as to fail to see that if they drive their enemies (on whom they live) to be conscious that there is no hope for them but the hope of revenge, they are building up for themselves a hell of daily terror; since, indeed, the one unendurable evil is *fear*.

The *Pall Mall* jeers at the *Daily News* for its exaggeration of the hangings, and laments not that so many people are hanged, but that so many are *un*hanged. It apparently favours the idea that it is possible to kill off so many of the bad specimens, that you will not only purify 'society' thereby, but also terrify those that are left of them into quiescence, thus killing two birds with one stone. This, after all, is only another way of accepting the eternity of sham society, mingled with the ferocity of the Christian religionist, who considers himself bound to be revenged on immorality.

For my part, I think the exaggeration of the writer in the *Daily News* is to his credit, as it is the result of the impression of loathing at the horrible judicial murders of the last quarter of the year, culminating with the slaughter of the two lads at Maidstone, which was obviously a judicial crime due to sheer cowardice.

Per contra the *Star* has some very timely and very sensible remarks on this matter of the 'punishment' of crimes against property. (Crimes against a crime? Can that be?) It is to be hoped that its working-men Radical readers will take them to heart, since I fear there are not a few of them who are inclined to share in the 'just indignation['], *i.e.*, the revenge for the terror of the 'plate-basket proprietor face to face with robbery.'

'There is no getting over the fact,' says the *Star*, 'that we have turned our burglars into murderers.' Just so; and also we have been driven into that idiocy by our initial idiocy of making them burglars. I quote the *Star* again: 'The trade of manufacturing and hardening felons at the greatest possible cost to the community (the main secret of the process is teaching them to associate the idea of labour with useless torture) goes on, whitewashed by the addition of a little hypocrisy to its brutality and stupidity.' Most true; and this no less so: 'Our penal system is an abominably cruel one; and it is made so for no other reason than that our honest poor fare so wretchedly, that if prisoners were treated with humanity, the victims of our sweaters would find in Pentonville a comparatively pleasant refuge from the miseries of their workshops and garrets. This is the naked truth.' It is indeed; the cruel judge with his solemn hypocrisy of morality is the necessary complement to the sweater of sweaters, the capitalist employer.

Sham society continuously revenges herself on the 'criminals' who she has created, and without whom she would cease to exist. How long will it be before all those who have a grain of honesty left in them, will understand this, and come out of her to become rebels against her?

Meanwhile, I think that for much of the change of feeling on this point of the treatment of so-called criminals, which to me (a middle-aged man or rather more) is obvious enough, we have to thank men like Sir Charles Warren and Mr. Balfour, and that never-enough-to-be-praised custom of our beloved country of treating political prisoners as mere felons. Some years ago none of us thought of a gentleman being sent to jail till he had been *ungentlemanned*. The fact that now we see personal friends who have worn the order of the Broad Arrow, and that we may wear it ourselves, has quickened the imaginations of us, the gentlemen, considerably.

Sham society is at work to try to purge itself of what every one must admit to be a crime, the condemnation and imprisonment of two innocent men, Brannaghan and Murphy, for burglary. The way it is setting about it is to indict four policemen for conspiracy to bear false witness. But no amount of revenge on the lower instruments of legal tyranny can undo what has been done, or give back the lost years of their life to its victims.

Nay, more: supposing these men are found guilty, let us not forget also that they are habitually encouraged to give false evidence by the very Law that tries them. They are not indeed encouraged to tell downright obvious lies, for they might be found out; but their statements as guardian of Law and Order are received in practice (whatever the theory may be) as facts that it is useless or dangerous to question. And surely to poor and ignorant men, degraded by their miserable profession of thief-catching, this is a mere invitation to the invention of falsity and the suppression of truth, and the general wresting of facts towards a conviction. Once again, if these men are found guilty and punished, sham society will punish them for the crime she has driven or allured them to.

The *Pall Mall* believes that the Puritan and the Socialist will meet on the common ground of Sabbatarianism! H'm, well; they may *meet* on that ground; but if they do, it will be to *fight* on it. We hope no enquirer into Socialism will be led astray by such nonsense into thinking that a Socialist can be either a Sabbatarian or a Puritan. I say flatly that the Puritan, as Puritan, is the enemy of the human race, his horrible galvanism of Christianity the worst religious trap which the world has fallen into.

Lord Rosebery and Sir J. Lubbock have been lamenting that the elections for the County Council cannot be wholly un-party-political. Here is the Devil objecting to sin with a vengeance! Are you tired of politics, Sir John? Do you want to keep politics all to yourself, my lord Rosebery? Probably. In short, what Lord Rosebery and the others mean on this head is, 'You County Councilmen, attend to your jobbery; you'll have plenty of it and you were made for it; but don't meddle with politics, that's for your betters. Look here, this is the way to do it! Ain't it funny?'

The Pope is laying a heavy charge on the bishops in America to do their best to put down the Socialism which is spreading amongst the Irish Roman Catholics there. This is good news on both sides; on one that Socialism is spreading enough to annoy his Holiness; on the other a sign that neither side of orthodox Christianity will attempt to draw us into entangling alliances. The Pope is right. Real Catholicism died with the Middle Ages: modern Catholicism is but a survival from it, kept alive on the one hand by its alliance with absolutist bureaucracy and on the other by its alliance with Puritanism, with which, though Catholicism is less revolting on the surface, it has much in common: the Salvation Army, *e.g.*, being a development quite in the manner of modern Catholicism. It is good to know our enemies; both these are of them.

The plot against humanity in Central Africa is going on briskly. The check given to the Germans has had its necessary result in stirring up those would-be masters of the world, the rulers of the German people, to set on foot a new expedition in regular military style, with twelve field guns to aid. At the same time we have news of a 'revolution' in Uganda. The missionaries have been driven away, and Islam has been proclaimed there; which means that the Arabs, the only people capable of organising opposition to the European pirates, have got the upper hand there. However, we must be cautious in accepting news from the tainted source of filibusters and filibusters' friends; for it will often be fabricated, or at least exaggerated, in order to stir public opinion into getting up fresh filibustering expeditions.

Commonweal, Volume 5, Number 158,
19 January 1889, pp. 17–18.

NOTES ON NEWS

The result of the elections for the London County Council and the Govan election, shift the scales once more toward the 'Liberal' side; for, as a matter of course, is spite of all disclaimers the County Council election was fought out in London on party lines. As to the Govan election, *if* the Liberal success tends at all to bring the Irish matter any nearer to a conclusion, it is so far favourable to us. As to the County Councils once more, it must be a very sanguine Socialist indeed who can really believe that they will have any inclination to go beyond the well understood lines of very moderate 'reform,' which will make no monopolist in the least in the world anxious about the safety of his heart – *i.e.*, his purse.

It is surely a matter to regret that our generous-minded and energetic comrade John Burns should be pitchforked into that thicket of red tape, which our new 'Parliament for London' is pretty certain to turn out; but, undoubtedly, the return of such a 'dangerous' man at the head of the poll is a sign of the times worth noting.

An account in the *Boston Investigator* of an interview with Colonel Ingersoll on the subject of Robert Elsmere, is interesting as showing the effect which the Socialist movement has had on that outspoken and eloquent Secularist. As far as I remember, in his early works Ingersoll shows no sign of being able to see beyond his own class; with him, as with so many intelligent middle-class men, the world was made up of the triumphant middle-class engaged in putting the finishing strokes to the work of demolishing feudal and absolutist oppression, and clearing away the cloud of superstition which yet hung over the latter end of the contest. The following sentence amongst several others has a very different ring about it.

'The poor man willing to work, eager to maintain his independence, knows that there is something higher than charity – that is to say justice. He finds that many years before he was born his country was divided out between certain successful robbers, flatterers, crawlers, and cringers, and that in consequence of such division not only himself, but a large majority of his fellow-men are tenants, renters, occupying the surface of the earth only at the pleasure of others. He finds too that these people who have done nothing and who do nothing have everything, and that those that do everything have but little.'

Again, as to 'charity': 'For instance in England, think for a moment of the manner in which charities are distributed, the way in which the crust is flung at Lazarus. If that parable could be now retold, the dogs would bite him. The same is the case in this country (America). The institution has nothing but contempt for the one it relieves.' It is much to be wished that all Secularist orators were as open to such generous ideas as 'Col. Bob' seems to be. More power to him!

Apropos of charities, I have been begged to contribute to the Providence (Row) Night Refuge and Home for deserving men, women, and children. I have no word to say against the charity in question, which seems to do what work it can with less expensive machinery than most, and at least is doing good service in stating the facts plainly; I notice also that it has no harsh words for the poor folk it succours; but I must emphasise the word 'deserving' by the way, for surely if there be any one who *deserves* less than the quite elementary help a night refuge can give him, what can that less be, short of a merciful bullet through his brains? Heavens! what strange words we use – about other people! The circular speaks about 'the *appalling* destitution which is in the midst of us; and the number of persons who are walking the streets for nights homeless.' Again, another word. Whom, I pray, does this appal, unless it be the sufferers themselves? Yet they, too, surely are long past being appalled. Will it appal the London County Council? I fear not.

And yet it well might if they could think of it. A hundred thousand people starving to death *is* appalling, I think, on any terms. One hundred thousand people is the population of a tolerably large town, even in the populous nineteenth century, if they were all brought together in one town. Reading, *e.g.*, has 42,000. Fancy living in Reading with *all* its population out of work, *i.e.*, starving! Think of yourself on a considerable island with no one in it able to do a stroke of work! Would that be less than appalling? And is it less appalling when this is happening amidst prosperous and respectable men going contentedly about their business and pleasure?

And why is not everybody who could by any chance amend it, always talking about it and about nothing else? Surely all business, public or private, should be but subsidiary to such a question as the solution of this 'difficulty,' this 'problem,' as we call it with lying cowardly evasion. For that is not all. Listen again: 'There are numbers of women under the sweating system working from 6 a.m. to 12 p.m., and sometimes till 3 p.m., can only earn from 4s. 3d. to 5s. 6d. a week.' We know the story, don't we? Or if we don't, *why* don't we, if it is true? As it is.

Do we know also that while business is improving, as is the word on all hands, 'the applicants for poor-law relief exceed by 3,000 the number last year, and the charitable institutions are besieged.' You capitalists, that is appalling enough if you will only consider what those two facts brought together mean. But you are not appalled, and I think will not be, until all doubt that your own skins are in immediate danger is at an end.

Again: 'The outcasts who were at a distance, at Stratford, Victoria Station, Hyde Park, New Road, Dalston, and Hackney, had the bus fare paid to them to Liverpool Street, were most of them so poor, ragged, and dirty, that the conductors would not admit them, etc.' Never mind, they were equal before the law to the Duke of Westminster and Mr. Blundell Maple. Oh pleasing and useful equality! Three cheers for civilisation! – with one cheer more for its – lice!

Yes, an old story indeed; and the why and wherefore of well-to-do people, not ill-natured or specially stupid above their fellows, looking on and sending from time to time a guinea to some such charity as this above mentioned, is not far to seek. No consideration of the subject, no talk, if it were continuous for a dozen years, would help. They would not know what to do, except by way of feeble palliatives, if they were to turn their whole attention to the subject. For they have not yet conceived the possibility of getting rid of the curse of private property and the struggle of the strongest for profits, which is its natural outcome. And the necessary outcome of that is that the extremely unsuccessful are not fit to ride in the same bus with even the moderately successful, or, if you please, even the moderately unsuccessful; so many minor grades there are in this hierarchy of the money-bag.

Most of all we have to remember that the only way out of this dreadful misery for the many, and the shame and crime for the few, of being forced to forget that it exists, is the attainment of a SOCIETY OF EQUALS. All inequality, whatever specious pretexts it may be veiled with, bears beneath the veil this grinning skeleton of stolid misery, side by side with soft, cowardly, well-to-do life. All inequality, I say, unless we are consciously striving to extinguish it, must in the end result in this last degree of inequality. The classes in a society can be 'moderately' unequal when a man can be 'moderately' honest and a woman 'moderately' chaste.

The Immigration Bill before the Congress of the United States has suddenly flashed on the capitalist press as a kind of morning star of hope. To build a brazen wall of perpetual peace round the fools and snobs of the civilisation of a Continent, so that no soul should inhabit it except the said fools and snobs and their miserable slaves, is indeed an invention worthy of the Nation of Inventors. It is no wonder that the *Telegraph* is so enthusiastic about it. A reasonable man, however, is likely to ask, 'Will it work or burst?'

Commonweal, Volume 5, Number 159,
26 January 1889, p. 25.

NOTES ON NEWS

Mr. O'Brien has got another four months, which no doubt is as little as could be expected 'under the circumstances.' But the circumstances are curious. A citizen is summoned before a court, and with his counsel has to fight his way *into* it; when in it, he finds that his judges are going practically to try him with closed doors, and being naturally indignant at this proceeding, takes the far more reasonable course of fighting his way *out* of it amidst the applause of everyone except the said judges. Here are strange proceedings against the respectability of a Court of law-and-order! Such things have been the immediate preface to open rebellion.

Robespierre in his time was accused of 'demoralising' the guillotine by too indiscriminating use. Mr. Balfour, in his career of pasteboard-Tory-Robespierre, will have to beware of this trap of the demoralisation of punishment; or rather he has already fallen into it, and thereby won the sincere thanks of all Socialists; for, though it may be said that the Balfourian persecution in Ireland is but a game being played between two bodies of politicians, yet it must be remembered that the tortures of the prison-cell are a very palpable reality, and also that they have not been inflicted only on 'gentlemen,' who have duly counted the cost and accept it as part of the political game, but also on poor people who will receive but a very moderate amount of glory as a reward. The felon's punishment has been 'demoralised' in Ireland, and bears with it no least shadow of disgrace, but honour rather; and the reflection of this demoralisation is spreading even to respectable England.

The *Star* and the *Pall Mall*, the two Radical prints of London, are at daggers drawn just now, and perhaps for the rest of their natural lives. This may well be thought a mere battle of the kites with the crows; though apart from the blind and obvious partyism of the *Star*, and the amusingly blatant jingoism of the *Pall Mall*, both papers have been of some service to us. But to a bystander the whole controversy anent the aldermen is a curious commentary on electioneering in general. 'Fight hard,' says the *Star*, 'get in your Liberals while you can, you may not have another chance.' 'Fight soft,' says the *Pall Mall*, 'perhaps our opponents will remember our generosity when their turn comes, and fight soft also.'

I must say that from a party point of view the *Star* seems to me to have the best of the argument; for if you go into the game, you must take the advantages of the game as they turn up, or lose them. On the other hand, that you should be obviously afraid to put up for re-election your men who have just won does not say much for the wisdom of the ballot-box. Our two contemporaries illustrate neatly the two quagmires in which politicians wade, and become so loathsome thereby. For the *Star*, reforms are means toward that great end the success of the Gladstonian Liberals, which by some unexplained magical process will at once both destroy poverty and sustain riches and make us all happy, – or if not, it isn't our business. For the *Pall Mall*, Radicalism is an enterprise for the discovery or manufacture of a moralized Toryism (under the name of democracy) whereby the British Empire, having reduced the rest of the world to starvation, shall reign supreme, with the ten Commandments of an exclusive ancient eastern tribe (glossed by modern hypocrisy) our rule of life, and a high court for the trial and punishment of amatory excesses; – or, indeed, is this also only another and less honest form of the great political maxim, 'We in, you out, and the rest to the Devil'?

The *Daily News*, in an article on the O'Brien incident, says, 'We disapprove of boycotting, whether it is practised by the Primrose or National League.' O holy simplicity! Of the journal, too, which the other day was praising the proposal of the United States Congress for the wholesale boycotting of Socialists from the soil of America. But *Nulle fides cum hereticis servanda* – no faith need be kept with heretics.

We have had another anniversary lately; that of the fall of Khartoum and the death of the general of the Christian commercialists – Gordon, to wit. It is to be supposed that as long as it is convenient to remember him and his virtues we shall have them dinned into our ears. But whatever they may have been, or however amiable they may have made him to his friends, do not let us forget that he *was* the general of these pests of the world; and that he had to carry on war as war – that is to say by means of slaughter and destruction – and that slaughter and destruction carried on wholesale in a bad cause is murder of the worst kind: murder, the evil consequences of which are hard to foresee or measure. The Fall of Khartoum was a victory of the oppressed; and whatever Gordon might have been had he been fighting for the good of the world, as it was he fell not as a martyr to a great cause, but as an instrument of oppression whom fate at last thrust aside.

The acceptance of Boulanger's triumph as a victory for monarchism can only come of ignorance or impudence: of course the various openly reactionary factions would vote for their champion, but it is now notorious even to our middle-class press that their votes would never have returned the General; and that a great mass of Socialists have voted for him simply to be used as a stick wherewith to beat the opportunist dog, and the worse the man is the properer for that purpose, for the easier he will be to throw away when he is done with. That is their view, but undoubtedly it is a dangerous game to play; surely they had better have voted for

Boulé, and thus have registered themselves definitely as revolutionists along with men like Vaillant. It is strange, too, that they should have forgotten the extra-ferocious part which Boulanger's regiment played amidst those who massacred the Commune.

Commonweal, Volume 5, Number 160,
2 February 1889, p. 33.

NOTES ON NEWS

The usual game is being played with Mr. O'Brien in Clonmel Jail as to prison clothes and the like. I suppose, since he has begun in this fashion, and has once considered himself bound to protest against 'degradation,' he must go on with it. We have over and over again in these columns expressed the commonsense view that it is the inflictor, rather than the endurer of prison brutalities, who is 'degraded' by them; and also that we do not see why there should be classes in prison any more than in the outside world. At the same time, no one can refuse admiration to O'Brien's staunchness; he accepts the rules of the game and is determined to play it out to the end, and if he sticks to it he must win.

Balfour and his mates are certainly piling it on. The sentences on Mr. Sheehy carry the matter on a step further; six months and four, not to run concurrently as I understand, is good measure according to modern views of political criminality. However, Mr. Sheehy and his friends must remember that worse things have been done within the last two years. In America they hang people outright for the same crime as Mr. Sheehy has committed, and the Balfourian revenge for which the Gladstonians very rightly consider so monstrous; and, indeed, we may say of Ireland. 'If they do these things in the green tree, what shall they do in the dry?'

The suicide of the Crown Prince of Austria is tragic enough – granted. Granted also that the contrast between his position, so high above the many agonies of ordinary struggling people, and the pain that slew him is dramatic. But not less tragic, surely far more so, is many a death that has taken place in London within the last few months that has had but a few disregarded lines in a daily paper for its epic. Even a day or two ago a poor man was charged before some magistrate with jumping into the Thames – with the crime of being able to bear it no more, since there was no chance for him on any side. I thought the piteous reasons he gave for committing this crime could hardly have been stronger; I am sure his case demanded considerably more pity than that of the late Prince; and, besides the pity, abundance of shame on our part; and between the pity and the shame longer newspaper articles might have been written, perhaps with profit, that have been concocted concerning the late tragedy in high life.

Mr. Goschen, in addressing a big Tory gathering at Stratford, took upon himself the pleasing and easy task of taunting Mr. Morley and Mr. Gladstone for not having done anything towards bettering the condition of the workers in spite of their democratic pretensions. This is a fair taunt coming from a Socialist, and even coming from a Tory cannot be satisfactorily answered by a Liberal; but a Socialist can answer with a clear conscience. 'Goschen, two wrongs don't make a right; you have done no more than the others, and you only plume yourself on doing no less because your principles bid you do less – which makes your boasts absurd. You can only get any credit for some little thing you may have been forced into doing, by putting your position in this way: "I am the enemy of the human race, and yet I have actually done something for the good of the human race." Goschen, with all your usurer's cleverness, you are a fool!'

By the way, what between Lord Wolseley on conscription, Mr. Goschen on the national defences, and Mr. Stanhope's promise of a rapidly approaching European war, it is pretty clear that we are going to have a pull at the guinea-tree next Session on behalf of the army and navy, and that some glorious jobs will be set on foot. Some of the papers, even the

Jingo *Pall Mall*, seemed to think that Mr. Stanhope had been overdoing it. That's quite a mistake; this kind of mustard-plaster should always be laid on with a trowel, and the *Pall Mall* shows by its practice that it understands that well.

The Balfourian banquet at Dublin with its 'great laughter,' and 'shouts of laughter' over a man in prison, may turn out rather more serious than Mr. Balfour thinks: people are often more moved by the way in which a thing is done than by the thing itself; and I should think that there could be few stomachs strong enough outside the purely party camp to stand this last strong meat (or strong drink perhaps) of Mr. Balfour. As to the man himself what can be said? The refined Cambridge gentleman, the superior person, the representative of culture, turning out such an unmitigated snob! Truly one doesn't want to scratch a middle-class tyrant very deep to find the low ruffian in him.

And after all, this hero, who boasts himself as having courage enough for anything, has funked and bolted, and Mr. O'Brien has had his clothes given back to him. Once again we fail to see that O'Brien has escaped a 'degradation'; but, on the other hand, it is pretty clear that Balfour has tumbled into one.

The *Star*, the manager of the London Council election on the Liberal side, has had a roughish shake; but is pretty much quit for the fright, since it has got its 'Progressive' list in as Aldermen with the single exception of the Earl of Meath, once Lord Brabazon (who the devil voted for him?)

But when you have looked at the list you won't find very much in it to frighten a Tory. The one distinguished person in it is Mr. Frederick Harrison, he has at least the advantage of not being a politician; but he himself would indignantly repudiate the name of Radical or Democrat, and he has on many occasions attacked Socialism directly. But certainly he is the best man on the list.

I am afraid that the *Star* having got rid of its fear, and having triumphed in this matter of the Aldermen, will not take warning by the incidents of the too obvious tendency of its machine politicians to rat when convenient.

We wish the *Star* well in virtue of some really useful articles it has from time to time; like the notes on our prison system which we quoted lately; or its excellent article on the Boulanger affair, which will clear the mind of many persons of misunderstandings on that point. But we wish it so well that its 'unprecedented success' does not make us specially happy. Rather we wish it could understand the advantages of being in a definite and even narrow majority; the honour, the pleasure, the *freedom* of that position. No longer then need we puff Lord Rosebery or even Sir J. Lubbock and Mr. Edis a little; no longer need we have with sinking hearts to put in a daily column of Jeames-ery for the benefit of the democracy, or dangle before the delighted eyes of the dwellers in very small houses in the suburbs visions of the laces and diamonds of Society – h'm, well! – ladies. No longer need we in the same breath curse Warren and bless Bonfield, or look upon O'Brien's cell with horror while we are mildly satisfied with Parsons' gallows. We might be free, though our circulation decreased.

A Radical as a Radical in these days, when Socialism has already been well preached, must be a half-informed and somewhat blundering person, but he need not be an opportunist, or a machine-politician: he may be honestly struggling towards the light, and may have a genuine indignation at the unmerited suffering of the poor, though he has not yet thoroughly learned what causes them and does not know a remedy for them. Such men we may quarrel with at times, but they are not enemies, and they mostly will become our comrades. Let the *Star* be the organ of these men, and it will find a real function to fulfil, and be the intermediary between honest democratic enquirers and those who have been happy enough to learn what the real current of events is. This will be better than collecting a kennel full of curs that they may turn round and snap at its heels on the first opportunity.

Meantime, the fact that a really popular paper must of necessity, in order to sell, be such a very 'mixed lot,' shows what a prodigious amount of work has to be done, even among those who are beginning to understand their degrading position of dependence on the rich – their masters.

Commonweal, Volume 5, Number 161, 9 February 1889, p. 41.

ON NEWS

At the meeting for considering the housing of the poor, Mr. Rowlands said that the present movement in that direction was not 'political bird-lime.' We may thank Mr. Rowlands for teaching us that word, and go on to say that it would be indeed disgusting if it were; a quite horrible thing to think of, that it should be possible for any set of men to make a false pretence of raising an agitation to house those like men who are now housed worse than dogs! To pretend that you are going to take trouble to make a man happier, when in fact you are only taking trouble to get his vote!

———————————

Yet 'he who excuses himself accuses himself,' says the proverb; and it is clear that Mr. Rowlands thinks that there may be people who would bring this accusation with some show of reason; for 'politics' have waded through such seas of mud and blood, that it has become impossible to clean them.

———————————

However, though we are forced to allow that there are probably some of those who are setting on foot this matter who are really on the bird-liming business, it would be unfair to assume that of all of them. After all, politics must have hardened a man's heart to stone, if he (being otherwise than a malicious fool) is not disturbed by the thought of a London slum, and would not do something to amend it. Besides, the fact that the political bird-lime is spread on this twig shows that the workers are beginning to think something of their own condition; and that is the first step to their changing it altogether.

———————————

It is certainly an indication of the direction in which things are moving that our friend the *Star*, which, once for all, whatever may be its merits or demerits, is the London Radical paper, has this sentence in its leader on the St. James's Hall meeting: *'There is no scheme which the wit of man can devise by which the poor can be made less poor without making the rich less rich.'* This is not Radicalism of ten years ago; not even the five years ago 'Socialism plus the Ten Commandments' – which latter some people think were made in the interests of the 'property' of the nineteenth century – *i.e.*, to control the poor and leave the rich free. On the contrary, it is a direct attack on private property.

When, however, we get to looking into what it is proposed to do, we Socialists cannot help seeing that the measures proposed are not only timid, but are insufficient also. Sir C. Russell said in his speech that the model (ugh!) lodgings of the Peabody and Waterlow companies were not inhabited by the poor of the working classes, but by those earning large wages (considerably less than Sir Charles 'earns,' however!), and were let at prices that could not be paid by the ordinary working-man. If that is the case – and I have not seen it denied – then this means that the ordinary working-man cannot pay the market price for tolerably (or not quite tolerable) decent lodgings: so that the least the municipality can do is to see that no lodgings are below that standard of decency, the price for which the ordinary working-man cannot pay: for if any such lower lodgings exist, he will infallibly be driven into them by the force of the action of the market.

But if all lodgings come up to this standard of decency, and the ordinary working-man is able, owing to the action of the municipality, to occupy them, that will mean just this, that the house-rent of the worker will be lowered. 'Well,' some will say, 'a very good thing too.' Doubtless, in itself; but please, my friends, note the weight of the chain which binds you. If your house-rent were lowered, you would with your present wages have more to spend on your clothes and food. Therefore, since though there would be a law keeping lodging up to a certain standard of decency, there would be none for keeping *wages* up to a certain point, your wages would fall under the influence of competition. Paying lower rent you would not need so much wages to buy your food and clothes, and consequently would not get as much; since the pinch of hunger would always force the poorest to undersell the others in the labour-market. This would happen unless you brought some form of compulsion to bear upon your masters, and *forced* them to pay you the same wages as before your rents were lowered; and even then they would find some means of evading any agreement you might come to.

For you must understand that you workmen are not paid in proportion to the work you do, but are paid just as little above mere subsistence (or starvation) wages as you will take without rebelling in some way. The natural operation of the labour-market forces you to accept subsistence such as a stingy slave-owner provides for slaves, whose labour can be done by almost any one, and whose places as beasts of burden can be readily supplied when they drop. Whatever any of you have got more than this, you have got, as the *Star* hints to you, by forcing your masters to give back to you some of the plunder they have stolen from you; stolen by means of the very poverty of you, which some of them are even now, hypocritically or ignorantly, deploring.

Some of the plunder you have forced them to give back to you, but how little! And even that little you get from them on the terms that you shall allow a vast number of the workers to be not in the least above that lowest standard of the over-driven underfed horse; to live a life as miserable as that of any slave that the world has yet seen. A life that would be but mere torture to any one who had not been compelled by the habit of his slavery to renounce the hopes and feelings of a man.

It is little indeed that you have forced your masters to yield to you; but you see you can force them to give up something. Put your hands to the task and force them to leave off plundering you altogether! That also can be done when you are determined to do it.

It is good indeed that London slums should be abolished – perhaps on any terms. But if only they could be abolished at the expense of those whose robbery has bred them! These half-measures if they succeed in abolishing them, which they will not, mean abolishing them at the expense of the poor who have suffered and do suffer by them. If this is all democracy can do, let it make haste to melt into Socialism, which alone can destroy poverty and riches, and all the grist of misery which these two mill-stones have ground between them.

Commonweal, Volume 5, Number 163, 23 February 1889, p. 57.

NOTES ON NEWS

The *Star* has been warlike of late, in view of the opening of Parliament, and has been urging on its leaders the duty of fighting hard so as to bring on a dissolution. The *Star* hints not obscurely at organised obstruction under the leadership of Mr. Gladstone. But Radicals may set their minds at rest, they will have no such excitement as this. Mr. Gladstone is no rebel, but a decent respectable party parliamentary leader; and to do him justice he has never pretended to be anything else. The gilded idol has not pretended to be alive itself, it has been its worshippers only who have seen life in the inert mass. Don't call the poor thing names if it won't get up and put out the fire – or, call it names if you like; but it will be all the same, it won't move.

If the Radicals who sympathise with Home Rule want to do anything at this juncture, they must not wait for their leaders but must do it for themselves. The time is not yet past when they might make the stroke (recommended in these columns before) of withdrawing from the House of Commons in a mass, and allowing the Tories and Whigs to govern them under protest. But, unfortunately, the Radicals are so wedded to a wretched little war of outposts, that they now scarcely perceive that there is a main battle. To exhaust your energies in attacking mere accidental effects of the evil, and wear out the patience of your adherents in winning victories that lead nowhere, and suffering defeats in which there is no dignity; these are the Radical tactics in England, and it is ten thousand pities that Socialists can be found to imitate them.

Under the name of 'Australian Working-class Vagaries,' the *Daily News* lately has had an article which may be worth a word or two. The writer rates the Australian workmen soundly for their folly in striking, when they already have such enormous wages. Of course, he assumes that he knows their business better than they know it themselves, and very naturally assumes that their business is to keep trade humming for the benefit of the capitalists. Of course he does not tell us what the purchasing power of the high Australian wages is, how much food and clothes and amusement (if any of the latter) they will buy; and we should like to have some information from our friend the *Australian Radical* on this head.

But even granted that the workmen in Australia are well supplied with necessaries comparatively with their British brethren, does not this wise-acre understand that workmen who are thrust into such a beastly corner of the earth, must be paid extra for living there, away from any chance of participation in the intellectual pleasures of the Old World, and that they will only be got to go there on those terms, unless, indeed, they are shipped off by obvious violent means?

This latter plan seems to be in the writer's mind. He says: 'The moral of the story is this, the supreme task of governments is the adjustment of the labour-markets. It is sheer folly to allow enterprise to slacken, and commercial ruin to spread, because men here or there make unreasonable demands. If the patient and frugal Chinaman is refused work that needs be done, then a much larger proportion of the 350,000 annual increase of the population of the United Kingdom must be emigrated to these shores.'

'*Must*'? Mr. Emigration Agent; and how, pray? On the whole, I think you will have to give up the idea of a press-gang for the purpose. And you need not grumble at that; there is plenty of compulsion at work to procure you[r] land-thieves in Australia the 'plenty of honest and moderately inexpensive labour' for which you say there is but one cry. Screw down the wages at home till people are rather past the verge of starvation and the streets are thronged with the unemployed; strengthen the chain of police and soldiery round them, so as to safeguard yourselves from anything more dangerous than an occasional unorganised bread-riot, which is always more serviceable to the masters than the slaves; and for aught I can see you will have for a little time 'moderately inexpensive labour' to enable you to go on living on other people's toil.

But here comes a hitch for you; and therein I see another moral to your tale which has escaped your eye. When you have deported your British starvelings to Queensland and other colonies, and they begin to be a little less starved, and have leisure and spirits to consider their position, you will find that they are not such fools as you thought. They will begin to say: Well, we are better off than we were; why should we not be as well off as we can be? Here are the recourses (*sic*) of nature, and here *we* are, the workmen; what else do we want to produce all the wealth we need? Why should we pay the greater part of all that we produce to people who do nothing but work hard at keeping up their position of being our masters? Dimly when we were worse off we knew *That the wit of man can devise no scheme by which the poor can become less poor without the rich becoming less rich.* And now that we are better off we see it clearer still, and we also see that we now have a chance of acting on our insight.

In short, 'the moral of the tale is this'; and it is a very encouraging one if the 'tale' is true: This is the moral, that the Australian workmen, having before their eyes all that wealth, actual and potential, refused to be bribed by somewhat higher wages than they would have at home into acquiescence with their position of inferiority to the useless classes!

The *Daily News'* Emigration Agent, on the contrary, clearly and very naturally looks upon the workmen in the colonies and at home as so much marketable goods and nothing else. What he is really aiming at is to transport the whole of the evils of our civilized life in England in the lump to our colonies, in order that by means of it he may make those evils more lasting in the old world. All honour to the workmen who consciously or instinctively resist such a vile scheme.

Commonweal, Volume 5, Number 164,
2 March 1889, p. 65.

NOTES ON NEWS

It is difficult indeed to say a word about the 'Great Case' which has not already been said dozens of times. Socialists must of course join in the general rejoicing. If things had gone the other way the reactionaries would have been encouraged to more and more acts of oppression, and the *Times* newspaper would have been our master till we could have mustered strength to upset the whole concern. As things go the *Times* has been hit hard indeed; and although it is true that by taking things quietly and letting the days pass, it will in a few months regain something of the appearance of its old *prestige*, yet at all events its *forward* movement to take us all by the throat has been checked.

As to Mr. Parnell, he is not of us, and probably, in time to come, will be very much against us; but it would be ungenerous indeed not to rejoice in his triumph over such a vile crew as the *Times* and the Tory Government. On the other hand, we think no better of him for being cleared of the *crime* of being art and part with the revolutionary party in Ireland; and as to the famous or infamous letter, when the fac-simile first appeared in the columns of the Friend of Informers, I remember rubbing my eyes and saying to myself, 'Why, what the devil has bit the *Times* now, where's the harm in that letter?'

For the Government of course the blow is serious; but the hopes of a speedy dissolution in which the *Star* and other Radicals are indulging are surely delusive. The Government majority on the amendment to the Address shows pretty clearly that though there may be some of the Tory party who are ashamed of the tactics of their leaders (now they have failed), yet they have no choice but to vote straight on a division.   Indeed, as to the shame, I doubt it; for politics make blackguards of us all.

However, when the general election does come, no doubt this defeat will go some way to overthrow the Tory party, and unless the unexpected weighs down the scales on the other side once more, we may look for a Gladstonian Parliament next time. Well, what then? As to Ireland compromise, and shelving the matter until it reappears, one may well hope, with a far more revolutionary aspect. As to the country in general? Well, what we may reasonably expect is, that the New Gladstonian Parliament will think that they have done enough for the popular side in conceding some crippled Home Rule to Ireland, and will set their face against any serious change in England. And on the whole I think that this which is likely to happen is the best thing that could happen. For there are many Radicals, and perhaps some Socialists, who expect *much* from a new Liberal Parliament, and if they get *nothing* perhaps they will bestir *themselves* a little, and try to push things forward.

For just think, while all these fine ladies and gentlemen, these miracles of refinement and cultivation, were crowding into the Court as into a theatre, to enjoy themselves over this judicial drama, the point of which was to find out, whether a certain Parliamentary leader was more or less mixed up with an enthusiastic and generous attack (though made on grounds that we should not agree with) on that great reactionary power, the British Empire – while all this was going on, and the corruption of well-to-do society was day by day being exposed, all around them thousands of poor people were (and are) dying of starvation and living in torment, without a hand being held out to help them.   Anything is good enough to obscure the thought of *that* and what will come of it – though nothing worse than itself *can* come of it.

And there is no wonder in that, for all this suffering is the foundation of 'Society.' Touch it, attempt seriously to remedy it, and down topples that false Society itself – and there is the remedy, and there is no other.

Commonweal, Volume 5, Number 165,
9 March 1889, p. 73.

NOTES ON NEWS

The London Liberal and Radical Union has played a kind of return-match to the meeting commented on by us last week. That respectable body is obviously somewhat shocked at M.P.'s being treated like common clay, and has proceeded to clap a plaster on their wounds, although not without a certain amount of protest from the other side, but of course Mr. Howell and Mr. Cremer took care that the due resolution should be passed. Mr. Howell thought it disgraceful for Radicals to attack the M.P.'s who had been doing their best for the right of public meeting. Dear me, Mr. Howell! if everybody did his *best* what a different world we should have! And as for these gentlemen, if they had done their half-best or their quarter-best, we should all have praised them as men quite up to the mark. But to speak plainly, what they did was – nothing: though it must be admitted that they rather regret it now.

Poor fellows! They had been investing largely in Irish 'political bird-lime,' and didn't see the point of making an experiment in English ditto at the time; besides, they thought that they had got their dicky-birds already, and need not catch them over again. Let us hope that they were mistaken. The extreme Radicals may yet take a leaf out of the book of a man who is much praised now – Mr. Parnell, to wit. How did he convert Mr. Gladstone to Home Rule? By organising his followers to vote Tory. It is an old story now; but perhaps the Radicals remember it yet.

After all, probably Mr. Howell was joking: his solemn condemnation of Sunday meetings, which followed this, gives one that impression; and more particularly his professing to think that anyone present wanted him at any meeting except a due proper official Whig one: for the joker who cried out that he would have to go to Sunday meetings was quite obviously a joker.

The fact is, to Mr. Howell a meeting is not an assemblage of citizens, gathered together to give genuine expression to a sense of their grievances; or to educate themselves into understanding their haplessly servile condition and its only remedy: to him a meeting in the open-air is a necessary though seldom-to-be-resorted-to piece of the machinery of the machine-politics of which he is a votary. Such a meeting as this does not need a Sunday or general holiday for its success; it is simply a matter of wire-pulling and money-spending, and the thing is done, whatever it may be worth; and that is not much, I fancy, even to its projectors. Meantime, do not forget, working-men, that this M.P. who so despises Sunday meetings is your special representative.

Mr. Matthews' humbug about the Square is exactly what we might have expected of him; but it is rather surprising that the *Star* should still talk the stale nonsense of trying the matter legally: surely all those poor fellows who were so shamefully treated by the police and other courts for *not* rioting have had enough of law. The law courts will take very good care to confirm the police and its generals in all they have done. As far as these matters are concerned, they are there for that purpose. When juries begin to refuse to follow the direction of the judge when persons accused of defending their rights are before them, that will be a sign that the well-to-do are beginning to sympathise with revolution – and when will that be?

Meantime, those Radicals who really take to heart this trampling down of what they conceive to be their rights, should turn themselves seriously to the duty of making the whole democratic party throughout the country, look at this affair of the Square from the same point of view that some (only some, I fear) of the London Radicals do. It is not and cannot be a mere London question, but concerns all strugglers for freedom throughout the length and breadth of the land.

Commonweal, Volume 5, Number 166,
16 March 1889, p. 81.

NOTES ON NEWS

The Liberal victory at Kennington is being received with a flood of self-gratulation by the organs of that side of the game of politics, which is a little trying to the feelings of Socialists, whose victories are yet to come; or to speak more correctly, as well as more hopefully, are still below the surface. Nevertheless, do not let us forget in the first place that it is a protest against open, brutal, undisguised coercion in Ireland, against which we Socialists have protested over and over again whenever we have had an opportunity, as indeed our principles compelled us to do.

In the second place, although it might be possible for the Tories to dish the Gladstonians by themselves bringing in an Irish Compromise, it is not very *probable* that they would make the compromise go far enough to shelve the Home Rule Question for the present; and, in fact, we shall be hampered with this question until the Gladstonians have come in pledged to definite Home Rule. Undoubtedly the Irish agitation has been of service to the cause of Revolution; but it has for the present done about all it can for us, especially since Mr. Parnell has been whitewashed into a very angel of respectability by the proceedings of the Commission.

Besides all this, a brutally Tory government in power, although it brings the Radicals and the Socialists into occasional alliance, and therefore seems to push forward Socialism, has this disadvantage – that it obscures the fact that Socialism is the *only* hope of the workers. Get together some three years hence some of those enthusiastic Radicals who have returned Mr. Beaufoy for Kennington, and ask

them how much better off they are for having a Liberal
Government in power, and you will have your answer short
enough I'll warrant.   By all means let the Tories go; they
proclaim themselves the enemies of the people, and
undoubtedly we must attack them.   Now then, let the
Liberals, the friends of the people, come in, and let us see
what they will do – in all essentials exactly the same as the
Tories.   Well, then we know where we are, and may expect
some of our democratic friends to come to the same
knowledge.

The great anti-Coercion meeting at St. James's Hall was
doubtless a success, and very enthusiastic; it was, I am told by
a friend who was present, wholly a middle-class meeting, as
might have been expected.   The lesson to be drawn from
these facts is encouraging, for they show us how suddenly the
public opinion may change about a measure which, to the
ordinary public at least, seems revolutionary.   I daresay Mr.
Morley's speech was more than all that was expected of him,
but how much more effective the following speech would
have been.

'Ladies and gentlemen, why waste time in going over for the
hundredth time what you all know about this matter? I prefer
rather to bring a blush of honest pleasure to your cheeks and
my own by recalling to you an incident which happened to
me about eight years ago, which will show you how much I
(and I believe you) have improved since that time. I was
standing as candidate for Westminster at the time, and was
addressing the electors summoned specially to hear me.   I
gave them my views on various political matters (for the
most part of no importance now), and then followed the
heckling; and I answered many questions to the complete
satisfaction of the audience.   At last a troublesome Irishman
in the gallery (I ask your pardon, Mr. Parnell) put me the
question, "How about Home Rule?"   I wish I could
remember the exact words of my answer, but they have

escaped me amongst all the other phrases I have been compelled to concoct and utter since. I can only say that logically, neatly, succinctly, I repudiated Home Rule as an impossibility, a danger, and a disgrace' – (signs of dissent amongst the audience) – 'and you cheered me to the echo.'

'Now, ladies and gentlemen,' he might have gone on to say, 'is not this cheering, in view of all the blessings of Home Rule which you now know by heart? In a very few years we have been, so to say, brought out of a barren wilderness of negation and coercion, into a paradise of goodwill and friendliness with our neighbours' – (great cheers) – 'and have found out that they were only asking for that self-government which we claim (but don't get) for ourselves. Now if there were no other countries in the world but Ireland and England (the latter entirely inhabited by happy middle-class people, producing nothing and living on each other, as you probably suppose is the case), I might ask you to disperse at once after having given three cheers for Mr. Parnell,' – (enormous cheering) – 'and – those who once put him in prison. But I have recently acquired information, which may perhaps reach you before long, and I wish to say a word or two to you about it.'

'I am now (with some reluctance, I must confess) prepared to admit that Home Rule for Ireland is not likely to be the only new and revolutionary measure which we may have to consider in our lifetime. It seems that the happy view of the composition of society in England which I have mentioned just now is not as strictly accurate as we once thought it. In fact it seems probable that we cannot include factory hands at 24s. a-week and farm labourers at 10s. in the middle classes, and that there are a great many of such persons, and also that they are getting it into their heads that as they *make* all, they ought to *have* all' – (groans and hooting) – 'Well, well, of course we know how idiotic that is now, just as we knew Home Rule to be idiotic nine years ago: but we may as well make up our minds that ten years hence we shall probably be meeting as we are now, to protest against coercion in England, and to pass resolutions in favour of the communization of the means of production' – (great uproar, amidst which Mr. Morley sat down, after having been heard by one reporter to say, 'Well, after all, it sounds as well as the other').

If the *Pall Mall* interviewer is to be believed, Mr. Beaufoy, M.P. has already stripped of his lion's skin. Questioned about Trafalgar Square, he answers: 'I do not think the electors had any more sympathy than I had with the extreme view which is prepared to defend the abuse as well as the use of the right.' Well, you may ask Mr. Beaufoy what that means. In the next sentence he explains: 'All our shopkeepers, at any rate, had a good deal of fellow-feeling with their West-end brethren, who objected very naturally to seeing Trafalgar Square turned into a place of public meeting in permanent session.' What our electioneering snob means is clearly that a 'respectable' meeting, one held for backing up some form or other of our capitalistic government, shall be allowed; but an unrespectable one, held by men with a real grievance, shall be bludgeoned. Exactly; that is just what we have always expected from the Liberals: 'Yes, you may speak if we are quite sure you will say nothing we don't like to hear.' Otherwise – well, here *is* one of those Radical M.P.'s for London whom Sir C. Russell advised the delegates the other day to elect in order to get them back the Square. These be your gods, O Israel!

Commonweal, Volume 5, Number 167,
23 March 1889, p. 89.

FROM WILLIAM MORRIS

Hammersmith, March 16th, 1889, 3 p.m.

To the Chairman of the Meeting, Commune Celebration.

'Dear Comrade, – I find, to my extreme vexation and disappointment, tha[t] I am unable to leave the house this afternoon, being still lame with rheumatism and gout. I should be obliged if you would excuse me to the assembled comrades.

'I need hardly say that I wish the greatest success to the meeting. The efforts of Socialist propaganda during the last few years have had their effect, which is obvious not only in the organisations of men and women definitely professing Socialism, but also on the whole of society: so that it cannot be doubted that there are vast numbers of persons who are preparing for Socialism, and who at the next crisis will be forced into our ranks. Meantime, in this country at least the masters of society are showing their uneasiness in other ways than the familiar one of mere brutal repression, though they are ready for as much of that as they may think necessary. Many schemes are on foot for removing the discontent which our masters are beginning to feel as a burden on them and a threat also; between the preaching of thrift to day-labourers, and the making the world happy by the aggregation of all fiscal burdens into the single tax; from the Charity Organisation Society to Mr. Henry George, – there are many and many idiotic evasions on foot; all of which have for their basis *the improvement of the condition of the poor, at their own expense, for the peace and happiness of their masters.*

'While the middle classes are beginning to admit the horror of the miserable life of poverty, they refuse to admit the idiocy of the system that causes it. Make the working classes happy – well and good! But are *we* to pay for it? Now it seems to me that the Commune of Paris was prepared to answer this question with a simple *Yes*, and that that is the reason why to-day we once more celebrate their defeat as the herald of the victory which is to be, and as a preparation for it. If there were any amongst the defenders of the Commune who did not understand that its ultimate aim, its reason for existence, was the abolition of class society, its enemies at least understood it well – and wrote their endorsement in the blood of 30,000 men slain after their foul and useless victory.

'I say this is why we celebrate year by year the heroic attempt of the Commune of Paris to lay the foundations of a new society. It is because we are engaged in the same struggle; and it is our special business amidst all the clatter and self-gratulation caused by the kind of schemes I have mentioned, to point out to the workers now awakening to a consciousness of their position that masters and slaves cannot be friends, that of necessity what one gains the other loses; that the only ground on which the workers can meet their masters is that on which the latter shall cast down their privilege of mastership; and that no master-class can be persuaded into this, but must be forced into it, either by the threat of force, or, if it must be, by its action; finally, that the workers must prepare this force by learning to understand their position, and by organising themselves into an irresistible power. This every Socialist must do his utmost to forward conscientiously, or he need hardly call himself a Socialist, since he really falls back into the ranks of those who have not learned the principles of action as he has, and who, being ignorant, can only wait for the impulsion of that *force*, which it is the Socialists' business to help to fashion for the realisation of the Society of Equality.

'With fraternal greetings to all comrades, and with expression of satisfaction that the S.D.F. and the S.L. are again holding this important celebration in common, I am yours,

WILLIAM MORRIS.'

Commonweal, Volume 5, Number 167,
23 March 1889, p. 91.

TO MANCHESTER FRIENDS

All comrades in and around Manchester desiring to see the cause of Socialism pushed forward, and willing to help in spreading the *Commonweal*, leaflets, pamphlets, and other revolutionary literature, or assisting in a paste-pot brigade, are asked to meet comrade W. Wess on Thursday night, at the International Working-men's Club, 122, Corporation Street, corner of Hanover Street; or to communicate with him at 31, Brompton Street, Cheetham, Manchester. Those sympathisers who cannot take the risk of doing active work, can greatly assist by subscribing, through the secretary of the Socialist League, towards [the] leaflet distribution fund, of which there is a great lack here.

Commonweal, Volume 5, Number 167,
23 March 1889, p. 93.

NOTES ON NEWS

If Socialists retain any illusion as to the apparent defeat of
Matthews and Warren (which was so loudly crowed over by
a part of the Radical press) having any influence over the
conduct of the police to the people, the brutality on 16th inst.
will surely have swept such illusion away. It is not easy to
imagine a worse case of arbitrary and cowardly violence than
that which was perpetrated on our comrades of Berner Street,
reproducing some of the worst features of Bloody Sunday,
such as the beating of prisoners in the police-cell.
Furthermore, is it probable that such things are done by the
police out of the pure cussed-ness of the individual? That
would be absurd to suppose; the authorities expect their men
to behave in this manner, such deeds are practically, not
condoned, but approved of. It is assumed that every poor
man must be treated as an enemy of that society which is
undoubtedly his enemy. And if he adds revolutionary ideas
to his poverty – well!!

I can imagine a smug orderly well-fed military-looking higher
officer of the police talking to some *refined* gentleman, and
saying to him, 'Well, my dear sir, you don't know the
London rough; you can do nothing with him unless you
knock him about; and as to who are roughs, why in such
places as Berner Street the whole population are roughs. You
must just let us act, my dear sir, and don't pay any attention
to any outcry that a parcel of poor Jews may make. They
can't do you any harm; the native roughs are quite inclined to
fall upon them, and some day it will have to be done.' And
the refined gentleman would go away thinking it was all
right, slumming being now out of fashion again. But if he
could only bring his mind to bear upon so dull a subject, he

might see that it is somewhat dangerous that it should have become an understood thing amongst the poor that the police are their natural enemies. 'Those whom the gods will destroy they blind,' says the ancient proverb.

The London County Council has made a very false step in closing the doors of its committee rooms on the public. This is going the way of the Board of Works. Why, it is exactly these committees that it is important for the public to know all about, that they may detect the first germs of corruption, criticise short-comings, discover incompetency, and encourage administrative qualities where they exist. It is very little use the public being admitted to the mere parade-days of the Council if it is to be excluded from its business meetings. The hole-and-corner resolution passed owing to the laziness of the Progressives on the Council, who, one would have thought, might at least have been present on such an occasion. Or what explanation have they to offer?

The government have not been leading a happy life lately. The opposition have been working their victory in the Parnell Commission for all it is worth, and it has proved rather remunerative. However, one need neither affect to feel special moral reprobation, and still less surprise. Morally they are in a bad position, because they have been found out; that is all. For the rest, though they are cornered as to matters of detail, they have a good defence to put forward in the lump which should be accepted by the other side if *they* were not so steeped in hypocrisy.

For, after all, what is their business? The defence of property; the defence of the brigandage of the classes. We must at once get out of our heads that they have *anything* else to do. So what these Tory robber-chiefs or thief-syndicate have to say to their Liberal attackers is simply: 'You know the interests which we have to defend, and how paramount they are; *you* in the enthusiasm of playing the party game have made a false step, and (no doubt without intending it) have attacked the rights of property, and have let loose upon us a crowd of ignorant Irish peasants, who don't know what they want, though they know that we (and you) keep them poor. They are headed by an ambitious, astute, and satisfactorily short-sighted politician, Mr. Parnell. So now it is our business to try and cure your blunder, if it be not incurable; and the only way to do that, as you yourselves will one day find out, is to use all our resources of force and fraud, and set ourselves stiffly to say "No" to any claims that could be brought against us, whatever humanity or justice there might be in them.'

'And as to all this pother you are making about our using our advantages in the shape of prisons and spies and rapscallion magistrates, really it is very unconstitutional of you, when you *know* that any and every government would use the same instruments whenever it thought it necessary. Why didn't we have a State prosecution against Parnell and his gang? Why, because we thought it would be such a breakdown if we failed, as we feared we might; and we thought that if we carried it on under cover of the *Times*, that at all events some of the dirt might stick, and that we might have gone about bragging that we *could* have prosecuted had we pleased. However, you will see, the time will come when a Liberal Government will have to do just the same sort of thing, when these damned Socialists begin to make a little head, perhaps. And how ill *you* like it then? No, my friends, remember that passage of holy writ, and do as you would be done by.'

But if the Government are rather hard set on by their declared enemies, they can't be said to help themselves much. Just as there is a fate on the Liberals to push on questions which they had much better have left alone, like the agrarian question in Ireland, so there is a fate on the Tories to discredit

their party by saying the very worst that they possibly can for
themselves. Lord Salisbury, *e.g.*, made a most unaccountable
blunder in his hint that perhaps after all the forged letters
were not so very much forged. Real generosity is not to be
expected from politicians on any occasion, but a little
simulation of it would help them wonderfully sometimes,
and on this occasion a little 'frankness' of this sort might
almost have retrieved the position for the Tories. It is lucky
that reactionaries are such fools.

Neither should a man in his position have begun by using the
words 'calumnies and falsehoods.' Says the proverb, 'Don't
speak of a rope in the house of a man whose father was
hanged.' And the parliamentary history of the last few days
has done something towards putting some of the said
'calumnies and falsehoods' into a different category, that of
facts.

As to the rest of his speech, it was in the main, if properly
read, an eloquent plea for revolution, under cover of a
defence of law and order; for what is practically said was
this: 'Granted that the Irish have grievances against us, that
the prison system is bad, that men are being put in prison for
making political speeches of a certain tenour (*sic*); yet is it not
all law? Did not you, the English democracy, allow these
laws to be made? If you want them altered go to parliament
and get them altered.' Behind all which there was a kind of
gleeful chuckle, Don't you wish you may! For of course Lord
Salisbury's true complaint is that his opponents have used the
really effective weapons of boycotting and the Plan in the
teeth of constitutionalism, and he very naturally 'says you
haven't played fair.'

All this may be damaging argument for a debate, in which
pure constitutionalism is to be assumed. But we may almost
hope that pure constitutionalism is getting played out, and

that the democracy will have the wits to see that if a change is good, it is good against the law, and that those who try to uphold the law against it are simply the enemies of the human race. Meantime it is encouraging to think that the great Liberal party, with Mr. Gladstone at its head, are accused of egging on people in Ireland to break the law wholesale, and that as a matter of fact it cannot rebut the accusation.

But we must not be too sanguine; it is only in Ireland that the Liberals like law-breaking as an instrument for law-mending. Doubtless the time will come when they will have to face the same trouble in England. The Irish question once shelved, the question of labour and capital which is involved in many side issues in the Irish matter will lie bare and obvious before them, and what will they do then? How, for instance, will a Liberal Government treat a no-rent manifesto in London? And why should a labourer be fined for wanting to sleep under a roof in London any more than in Tipperary? Will you say, the Irish cottar has laboured on his land, and has got just enough to keep himself and can pay no rent. True, but has not the English labourer done the same? Yet Lord! What a set of evasions the politicians will have to use to point out the essential difference between the two! And how easy it will be to clap Socialists into jail for doing the sort of thing that O'Brien has been doing and over whose fate the Liberals have been so indignant.

Commonweal, Volume 5, Number 168,
30 March 1889, pp. 97–8.

NOTES ON NEWS

A Sunday Closing Bill (second reading) has been passed by a House of Commons which is very susceptible to the voting power of any solid body of the public. M.P.'s know not only that the teetotallers are a large and well-organised set of people, but also that they will go to the poll at election time. Meantime, the said members do not trouble themselves in the least about the real wants and hopes of the mass of the people, and so between carelessness as to the *lives* of the people and anxiety about their *votes*, if these can only be gathered together in formidable proportions, they pass measures like this bill of Mr. Stevenson's, a gross and abominable piece of oppression, a measure fit only for a set of helots, while they allow the public to be poisoned by any and every commercial rascal who finds that in the competitive race for position, water and chemicals are more for his purpose (selling for profit) than the result of properly fermented malt and hops.

John Bright is dead, and the newspapers have been busy heaping up a dung-head of rotten nonsense over his dead body. The first thing that must strike any thoughtful and dispassionate observer, is that for any public purpose 'the Great Tribune' has been dead several years. For the rest, it is fair to say that the man was personally honest always; but so essentially blood, bone and soul a middle-class person, that he could not escape from the conventionalities of that class, *i.e.*, from its innate hypocrisy. He was utterly incapable of imagining himself in the position of any one outside the great commercial middle-class; to him that class included all the human reality of society. The upper class was a mere perverse obstruction to the progress of Podsnap; the lower, mere machinery to enable Podsnap to carry on his business. Business and the kind of family affection, and the kind of religion suitable to it, were the whole duty of man, and anything which came in its way was to be sternly swept aside.

In this view of life John Bright was singularly consistent. Some Home Rule Radicals wondered that he should turn anti-Gladstonian in his last days; it would have been wonderful if he had not. For in these later days the Irish Question has begun to look towards revolution, and against that Bright always set his face most determinedly.

It would have argued genius and quickness of wit in Bright, neither of which qualities he ever had, if he could at any time of his life have perceived that he himself was engaged in a war continuous and implacable, the war of commerce. But what he *could* see as war he did genuinely hate; nor did he favour a war, as more dishonest persons of his way of thinking have done, because it was a war of the market, a crime necessary to commerce.

No one who was not in this respect a man of principle, could have assumed the attitude which he did at the time of the Crimean War. Though he was hated bitterly at that time by the Whigs and Tories, he was very popular with the advanced Liberals, and, to do Bright justice, he was no man to seek the popularity from his enemies. Well, this popularity he threw away at the bidding of principle, as he saw it, coolly and deliberately, and became the very outcast of politics. I remember well the fury of hatred against him, which could not have been surpassed if he had proposed to meddle with the property of the rich. The sacramental phrase was, 'I should like to hang John Bright.'

A middle-class, repentant of having so mauled their true and steady champion, is now heaping fulsome flattery on his unconscious head; and one enthusiast was especially anxious that he should be buried with all the honours in Westminster Abbey. Truly a solace for the dead worth having! To form one of the gang of fools, rogues, and ruffians, whose capacity for pushing themselves into notoriety is expressed in a series of undertaker's lies, whose outward hideousness pollutes the most beautiful building ever raised in England by the hands and hearts of the people. Whatever wrongs we may have against John Bright, we would not revenge ourselves by thus ticketting him fool and dunce.

Commonweal, Volume 5, Number 169,
6 April 1889, p. 105.

NOTES ON NEWS

'Civilisation' is happy again, for Stanley is alive and successful and is 'coming home.' Meantime, since there have been several persons hanged for murder during the last few months, we may well ask whether when he comes home Stanley will be put upon his trial for the capital offence? Or if not, wherein his hanging men because they refused to serve him at the risk of their lives differs from murder? This is, indeed, a short way with breach of contract, which no doubt many rich people at home would like to take if they durst.

As some of our readers may not have seen former notes and articles in the *Commonweal* on this subject, we may as well explain to them in a few words how it is that Stanley is the enemy of workmen in Great Britain as well as of the natives in Africa. His mission is 'to open up Africa;' that is, to establish regular trade with the people of the interior of that vast continent. Now this trade the natives do *not want*, and resist as much as they can. They do not want trousers, rum, bibles (printed by scab labour), or cotton cloth scientifically weighted with sulphate of barytes; and, in point of fact, the bargain in our trade with them would be, that we should take from them what we want and give them what they do not; which they understand and consequently will only admit the trade if it is *forced* on them. This as we see, Mr. Stanley (and the whole British nation, which clearly approves of his hanging his hirelings for refusing to go on with him) is quite prepared to do. Therefore, he is clearly the enemy of the natives of Africa.

But is he the friend of the natives of England? Will he not render a service to them by 'opening up Africa,' by getting fresh trade whereby to employ the workmen here? Some workmen uninstructed in the truths of Socialism may believe this, but we Socialists *know* that it is false. If the position of the labourers in England is a good one, it *may* be a good thing to supplant African barbarians by English labourers; if it is not, it only spreads the evils which we are suffering from here, and by that process helps to perpetuate it. And this is *all* the good which this piracy can get for the English workman. There will be gains indeed from the plunder of Africa, but those gains will fall to the capitalists and their middlemen and led captains; they will be called 'profits,' and will be sweated out of the workmen, English and African, who will be enslaved by this march of civilisation.

English workmen, therefore, should know that this man is the friend of their enemies and the enemy of their friends. The friend of the capitalist who lives by robbing the workman of the results of his toil, and therefore by that very act is his enemy; the enemy of the barbarian who lives by the labour of his hands, and is therefore the brother of the English *workman*. It is to be hoped then that if, unfortunately, Stanley reaches England safely, the workmen of this country will make some demonstration against him, and so clear themselves of participation in his crimes.

As there is some probability that during the current year the trustees of the British Museum may be induced to throw their institution open on Sundays, the Parliamentary friends of Sunday opening think it better not to raise the question by means of a direct motion, but have, it is said, decided to bring it forward on the Estimates. – *Pall Mall.*

This is a curious instance of the kind of hold that the people has upon its own property and over its servants. We are to sneak behind the possible goodwill of the trustees, instead of claiming our rights straightforwardly. '*Their* institution' too!!! O yes, it is but too clear that it isn't *ours*. Britons never never never *will* be slaves! Won't they?

Last week the House of Commons managed to spare a little time from the consideration of the difference between tweedle-dum and tweedle-dee, to the consideration of the position of the poor in our big towns. Mr. Broadhurst, who was once poor and is now rich, was the initiator of the discussion, which to say the truth might just as well, for all the good it could do, have been held in a middle-class discussion-forum. For, indeed, the habitual discussion of tweedle-dum and tweedle-dee does not educate men to consider the great tragedy of life in the lower classes. Besides, from the nature of their position, the loyal members of that House *must* shut their eyes to the causes of the misery which now and again in the course of years they deem it politic to talk about.

For truly what *is* the disease, the mere symptoms of which Mr. Broadhurst (who was poor and is now rich) called their attention to? What is the disease, but these very gentlemen themselves and the life that they live of sweating the poor for their own aggrandisement? When that proprietary class, which (and which only) they represent, is got rid of, the symptoms will no longer be there for us to deal with. When the rich are gone there will no longer be any poor. That is the one truth that our rulers have got to learn. But can they learn it? That is more than doubtful. The rich class exists, it is a living and active organism, and it is difficult or perhaps impossible for that which exists to realise non-existence.

Also, of course, it is the business of these gentlemen to insist on the necessity for their existence, nay the impossibility of their extinction. Their song chanted in various tones is always, 'As it was in the beginning, is now, and ever shall be, world without end. Amen.' – or hurrah!

Under these circumstances it is not wonderful that the debate was languid to the last degree, and that the pretence of having anything to say about such a subject was not even decently kept up, and that none of the party leaders had a word to say on the subject, so that even as 'political birdlime' it was but a failure.

But consider what a condemnation of the whole of our political system! The condition of the poor (*i.e.*, of almost the whole of the working-classes) in our big towns. What a subject! Surely a six nights debate on it is not too much to consider it in; surely all the big bucks of both parties will be in their places eager to claim their share in dealing with the most, nay, the only important matter of the day. The Irish will forget Home Rule, for they also have big towns in Ireland; the Tories will try to show the advantages of a benevolent demi-semi despotism; the Liberals that the franchise will educate even a sweated tailor to claim his rights; the Radicals will make a sudden leap towards Socialism, and the whole country will hang breathless on their deliberations.

Alas! none of that happened. The condition of the poor is not 'practical politics.' Their votes, when they have any, can be got at even when they are left to starve. So what does it matter? Indeed, what everybody in this wretched fag end of a debate, or conversation, really said was, '*Who cares?*' Yes indeed, who, if the workers themselves do not?

This is an old and hackneyed pass-word of Cobbett's, but is always good and necessarily true: 'House of Commons – Den of Thieves.'

Commonweal, Volume 5, Number 170,
13 April 1889, p. 113.

NOTES ON NEWS

There has been a sharp discussion going on in the columns of the *Star* as to whether the Socialists or Social Democrats (which on the whole is the properer name for those really implicated) ought to respond to the invitation of the *Star* Radicals to form some sort of alliance with them. Mr. Hyndman began the discussion in a very able letter, in which he pointed out the indisputable fact, that in whatever the present day Radicals differ from the Liberals they owe the distinction to the adoption of Socialist views; and in which he asserted that though it was natural for the Radicals to seek for the alliance it would be wise for the Socialists to refrain from it.

This discussion must clearly have to do with the position of Radicals and Socialists as *parties*, for already on many occasions Socialists have not hesitated to ally themselves with the Radicals for a purpose which seemed clear to both. For example, the League as well as the S.D.F. has shown itself at almost all the anti-Coercion meetings where they thought they could be of service in pushing forward what appeared to them a revolutionary movement. We cannot declare against a proposition merely because Radicals (or for the matter of that Tories) agree to it.

But as to parties? It is quite true, as Mr. Hyndman implies, that in all alliances between parties the stronger uses the weaker and throws it off when it finds it convenient to do so: running the risk, however, meantime of finding that the weaker party has, as it were, eaten its way into the skin of the stronger and so destroyed it. It is equally true also that the stronger or respectable party must make its programme from the programme of the weaker, spoiling it as much as it dares to do in the process.

And then what is a party? Our old acquaintance, Mr. Mahon, in a letter to the *Star*, says that there is no Socialist party, but only a propaganda; his view being, I suppose, that for the sake of gaining the advantages of 'a party' the Socialists should merge themselves in the Radical party. But, after all, is there a Radical party? There are plenty of Radicals, doubtless; but how can they be called a party when they themselves are now declaring for what they at least believe to be a modified Socialism, and yet they must feel or simulate enthusiasm for their leader, Mr. Gladstone, who has never heard of Socialism, and for their other leader, Mr. Morley, who knows just enough about it to be able to use phrases which repudiate it? Their policy is to attach themselves to the Liberals and work them to further their semi-Socialism, just as some of our Social Democratic friends want to work the Radicals to further their Socialism. They have no party leaders and no party representatives.

And what is a Radical? I mean, of course, a Radical of to-day. The *Star* in its answer to Mr. Hyndman really answers this question quite ingeniously, and shows us that a Radical of the new type is a man who would believe in Socialism if he could only find out what it is, and who would cast Whiggery aside if he could only convince himself of its being possible to carry on without it. The *Star*, which we have been taking all along as the representative of this view, often prints sheer Socialism, which we have been glad to quote at times; but also often exhibits the most commonplace Whiggery. Therefore, without imputing any bad faith to its disclaimer of using Socialism as 'political birdlime,' I say it is being so used, and I don't agree with its prophecy that when Home Rule is got it will still advocate this semi-Socialist Radicalism. On the contrary, we may be sure that the Gladstonian success will produce a fresh cleavage; the Whig element in Radicalism will declare itself Whig (or Tory, it does not matter which), and the Socialist element will declare itself Socialist.

At the same time I think we must accept with cheerfulness this fact of Radicalism permeated by Socialism. Six years ago the attitude of the Radicals, even the furthest advanced of them, was Mr. Morley's 'I don't know you.' And now what are these words in the leader of a Radical paper about contract? 'It' (the new Radicalism) 'does not recognise that free contract exists between the workers and the capitalists, the landlord and the tenant.' My Radical friends, that is an attack on the very palladium of Radicalism; on the recognition of that free contract between the monopolist and his 'dependent' our present holy society rests. What middle course can there be between that 'Free Contract' and the abolition of monopoly?

But the *Star* wavers through its terror of the might of Whiggery: 'It does recognise that if such contracts are made, they should be subject to the constant revision in the interests of the weaker party.' O impotent conclusion! For it means the robber shall still be allowed to rob, but that some of his stealings shall be taken away from him. How much? 'A great deal if I can manage it,' says the Radical. 'None at all, if I can help it,' says the Monopolist, 'I and my armed executive.' What can come of these two differences of opinion in the long run? Abolition of monopoly in the teeth of the monopolist – nothing else.

Meantime, while the Radicals are drifting towards Socialism, let Socialists be contented to be a propaganda and not a party. A propaganda can afford to have principles genuinely believed in by its members; a party in order to constitute itself must give up some principle, or make a semblance of doing so, which semblance is very likely to grow into a reality; and when it has got as far as that, this mere piece of opportunism is likely to become a shibboleth which all members of the party must utter or be boycotted. The Socialist propaganda has done perhaps already more than we who have been living amongst it know. If ever there should be a Socialist party, at least let there be a Socialist propaganda of principle existing beside it and not tied to it. I am sure that we cannot do without that, whichever way politics may turn.

Commonweal, Volume 5, Number 171,
20 April 1889, p. 121.

NOTES ON NEWS

The rich are getting so extremely kind to the poor, that, if they don't take care, they (the rich) will expend all their time in performing these kindnesses, and will have no time left for performing the absolutely necessary duty of finding means of wasting the wealth which they have sweated from the poor; and a pretty mess we shall be in then! For since the 'poor' are only employed by the sweating process, and depend for their subsistence on the sweaters, if the sweaters don't sweat we shall be all undone together – unless the workers have come to the conclusion that they will employ themselves for their own benefit.

Here is a queer example of this rash philanthropy, this killing people with kindness. The National Home Reading Circles Union, which resolved the other day 'that it was advisable to organise in a large and effective manner a plan by which to direct and encourage home-reading among all classes of the people,' etc., etc.

'All classes.' Yes, but they mean one class. You bet they won't come to me – I wish they would. At the meeting in question the stream of twaddle flowed on very steadily. Said the Bishop of London: 'It would not be difficult to make home-reading a very living thing, though not quite so powerful as the voice of the teacher.' 'The voice of the teacher,' that means the Bishop, I suppose; 'the voice of the teacher' is good, very good.

The Venerable Archdeacon Farrar thought, 'That it would do much to counteract the flood of wicked, malicious, and frivolous literature with which England was inundated.' I say, which of the three are we of the *Commonweal*? Not 'frivolous,' I think; 'wicked and malicious,' I fear. O parson, parson, what tall words you use; but taller follow. 'They might find in them (books) fruits which are fruits of Nepenthé, and flowers that are flowers of Amaranthe.' Yes, only I fear that the cases are not uncommon where beefsteak and porter would be more welcome than Nepenthé and Amaranthe; nay, would enable us to find those 'articles' in our books – if we have any.

In short, what the devil is it all about? Are there not books enough written year by year in this country drowned in 'culture'? Are they not cheap enough, as cheap as worthless paper and scab labour can make them? What is needed, O benevolent rich gentlemen, to further 'home-reading'? I think you know, though you don't choose to confess it. Leisure, freedom from anxiety about livelihood, pleasant roomy clean dwellings, access to pretty places and the rest; in short, reasonable ease of life, and above all unanxious leisure. When people have this they will read such books as they will, such as suit them, and, *pace* Mr G. Howell, amuse them. Can a man have this when he is a trembling dependent for his livelihood on the caprice of another man, who is himself a slave to a system of cut-throat competition? We all know he cannot.

In short, O benevolent persons and parsons, your kindness to the working-classes will be welcome to them when it is no longer used as an excuse for your continued robbing of them. Is it 'malicious,' I wonder to quote Scripture and say, 'Let him that stole steal no more.' Meantime, it is not a little ridiculous to see the efforts of these worthy folk to wag the dog's tail for him since he declines to wag it himself.

Commonweal, Volume 5, Number 172,
27 April 1889, p. 129.

STATEMENT OF PRINCIPLES

The Socialist League advocates International Revolutionary Socialism. That is to say the destruction of the present class society, which consists of a class of men who live by owning property and therefore *need not work*, and a class that has no property and therefore *must work* in order that they may live to keep the idlers by their labour. Revolutionary Socialism insists that this system of society, which is the modern form of slavery, should be changed to a system of Society which would give every man an opportunity of doing useful work, and not allow any man to live without doing useful work. The result of this would be that livelihood would not be precarious nor labour burdensome. Labour would be employed in co-operation, and the struggle of man with man for bare subsistence would be supplanted by harmonious combination for the production of common wealth without the waste of labour or material.

Every man's needs would be satisfied from this common stock, but no man would be allowed to own anything which he could not *use*, and which consequently he must *abuse* by employing it as an instrument for forcing others to labour for him unpaid. Thus the land, the capital, the machinery, and means of transit would cease to be private property, since they can only be *used* by the combination of labour to produce wealth.

Thus men would be *free* because they would no longer be dependent on idle property owners for subsistence; thus they would be *brothers*, for the cause of strife, the struggle for subsistence at other people's expense, would have come to an end. Thus they would be *equal*, for if all men were doing useful work no man's labour could be dispensed with. Thus the motto of Liberty, Fraternity, and Equality, which is but an empty boast in a society that upholds the monopoly of the means of production, would at last be realised.

This Revolutionary Socialism must be International. The change which would put an end to the struggle between man and man, would destroy it also between nation and nation. One harmonious system throughout the whole of civilisation would take the place of the old destructive rivalries. There would be no great centres breeding race hatred and commercial jealousy, but people would manage their own affairs in communities not too large to prevent all citizens from taking a part in the administration necessary for the conduct of life.

Thus, while we abide by the old motto

LIBERTY, FRATERNITY, EQUALITY,

we say that the existence of private property destroys Equality, and therefore under it there can be neither Liberty nor Fraternity.

We add to the first motto then this other one –

FROM EACH ACCORDING TO HIS CAPACITY, TO EACH ACCORDING TO HIS NEEDS.

When this is realised there will be a genuine Society; until it is realised, Society is nothing but a band of robbers.

Commonweal, Volume 5, Number 173,
4 May 1889, p. 137.

[UNTITLED PARAGRAPH]

The sentence on the Zulu chiefs for the crime of having the hardihood to defend their country against land-thieves, is worthy of the very worst days of the Roman Empire; amongst all the records of tyranny nothing worse has been recorded than this last piece of cruelty of 'civilisation.' It seems hardly possible that the sentence can be carried out, bad as we are.

Commonweal, Volume 5, Number 173,
4 May 1889, p. 137.

NOTES ON NEWS

Few people who have watched the course of what is called 'justice' in the present day, and especially Sir Peter Edlin's administration of it, will have expected anything like what justice is poetically supposed to be from the Clerkenwell Sessions House when presided over by that legal luminary; but even those who have read of the case in the ordinary reports of the daily papers, will be a little startled at the disgraceful sentence passed by Edlin on our comrades of Berner Street.

It seems that Edlin is so pleased with himself, that he is going to ask the County Council to raise his salary by £500. The *Star* suggests very appropriately that they might so far take his request into consideration as to lower it by that amount. For, after all, *is* Sir Peter really earning his salary? from his employer's point of view I mean. The 'law' or 'administration of justice,' or whatever else you call it, is *at its best* such a cruel instrument of oppression against the poor, that those servants of it, the judges, would best serve the interests of the ruling classes that employ them, who should carry on their vile office with an affectation at least of moderation and fairness. The game of the masters of Society at present is to get people to say, 'Well, the system has its blemishes, but you see it doesn't work so ill. Let it alone!'

But men like Edlin are resolved, it seems, to prove that the system is *all* blemishes; to make it clear to poor people that the law *is* their enemy. He seems determined to carry on the tradition of the police-courts after Bloody Sunday, and to show those that are discontented with their share of the wealth of the country (all kicks and no half-pence), that to be accused by a policeman is to be condemned by the Court, and that the boasted liberty of Englishmen is only meant to apply to those who have property to back it.

In fact, 'too much zeal' is surely injuring the usefulness, to their employers the upper classes, of some of our judges. The other day Sir Peter Edlin pointed out to the public the abuses of our law courts in the matter of judge-directed verdicts, by an unsuccessful attempt to bully a jury into accepting his view of the evidence instead of carrying out the spirit of their oath by insisting on their view. This again was a very poor service to render to the votaries of law-'n'-order.

In short, if the County Council do raise Sir Peter Edlin's salary, they will surely do so in virtue of their sympathies with Revolution, and consider him as a revolutionary agent to be encouraged in his present course; so that at last people will find that the whole thing is *unbearable*, that the very air they breathe is so corrupted by tyranny and oppression that it stifles them.

Mr. John Morley took some pains at Newcastle the other day to pronounce against the eight hour's movement. Whatever our views as Socialists may be as to the value of this movement (and I amongst others think it will prove illusory), Mr. Morley means by pronouncing against it to pronounce against Socialism, and against the Socialist-Radical movement as led by the *Star*. That paper considers Mr. Morley's disclaimer as courageous on his part; but I don't know. All it means is that he has cast up the pros and cons as to the effect to be produced on his election on the one hand, and his position as a claimant for Mr. Gladstone's shoes on the other, and has come to the conclusion that it will be better for him to run the small risk of the Socialist vote at Newcastle, rather than involve himself in an alliance with the Progressive Radicals, and be suspected of Socialist tendencies. The time is not yet come when a *statesman* can get beyond Whiggery. Will it ever come?

———————————

The *Pall Mall Gazette* has taken up the cause of the Primrose Ladies with such fervour, that one may hope it is so blinded with enthusiasm as not to perceive that at the best that valuable institution is furthering the emancipation of *Ladies*, not of *women*. For otherwise, judging by this and other articles (notably a long-winded essay by that very hard-shell Radical, Admiral Maxse), one must say of it that it is becoming almost too fair for journalistic war, and shows signs of being on the verge of conversion by Balfour's heroism and Salisbury's 'sweet reasonableness.'

Commonweal, Volume 5, Number 173, 4 May 1889, p. 140.

NOTES ON NEWS

One could hardly have a better specimen of the inefficiency, stupidity, and humbug of Parliament, than the debate on the Leasehold Enfranchisement Bill. In the first place, the measure, whatever its merits or demerits, might be, purported to be a bill in the interests of the working-classes. This was enough to thin the House down to the number which are usually got together when anything of any interest to the public has to be discussed, for nothing of that kind of course interests the House at all.

Then consider the ignorance of these legislators! Both sides approached this bill as though it were a terribly Socialistic and revolutionary affair; its promoters thought they were making a great concession to the growing feeling for Socialism, and that the working-classes would almost have a new life given them by it. The professed reactionaries attacked it on the same grounds, the useful Mr. Matthews saying that he looked at it as blank Communism, and that it attacked the principles of private property directly.

What an exhibition of ignorance! The truth is that it is really a definitely Conservative and reactionary measure, and the booby Matthews with the whole of his colleagues ought to have supported it, carried it, and put it into working order. Here is the point, stated over and over again by Socialists. Landlordism is bad; landlords are bad; *therefore*, says this sham Socialistic measure, let us break these few landlords up that now exist into many pieces, and so have more and more landlords; each one of these landlords will be a 'kind of a man' with an interest in the monopoly in which he shares, and which he will do his utmost to defend. What can possibly result except the strengthening of the monopoly which it is the business of Mr. Matthews and his crew to defend, and which it is the business of every Socialist to attack?[1]

The Vigilance Committee who are so watchful over our morals are making another attack on Zola, this time through *expurgated* English editions. Apart from the blatant hypocrisy which attacks the symptoms and lets the causes alone, this is a gross piece of stupidity. What do they object to? The coarseness? This is a matter of art; it must be admitted that there are works which sin against art in this direction. But what then? Is bad taste to be made a matter for a criminal court? In that case I think the prisons might be filled to overflowing with criminals taken from the 'culti-vated' and 'refined' classes. Besides, there are many sinners among the English classics in this respect; in a breath – Fielding, Chaucer, Shakespeare, and our translation of the Bible must be condemned and expurgated.

Or is the demoralising effect on people to be the matter to be considered in the extremely 'moral' air of a Court of justice? And how pray? I hold that there are dozens of most respectable works which the Vigilance Society wouldn't think of attacking, which are far more demoralising and corrupting than Zola. Henry James' novels for instance; or even in their feeble way, Mr. Besant's imitations of Charles Reade, whose

---

[1] It may be worth preserving for future reference the following particulars:-
The second reading of the Leaseholders Enfranchisement Bill in the House of Commons on Wednesday, May 1, was supported by 124 Gladstonian Liberals, including Mr. Gladstone, Sir William Harcourt, Mr. Mundella, and Sir George Trevelyan; 13 Irish Nationalists; 11 Conservatives: Sir George Elliot, Sir E. Lechmere, Sir John Puleston, Admiral Mayne, Colonel Hughes, Messrs. Holloway, Kelly, Mallock, B. Robinson, Seton-Karr, and Whitmore, and eleven Liberal Unionists, including Mr. Chamberlain and Mr. Caine. The majority which rejected the bill was composed of 172 Conservatives and 15 Liberal Unionists.

books, though very amusing, are not specially 'moral' (small blame to them) according to the standard of the Vigilance Society.

Commonweal, Volume 5, Number 174,
11 May 1889, p. 145.

NOTES ON NEWS

No one will wonder that the second reading of the new flogging bill has passed the House of Commons with a large majority. It was a matter of course that the present house would not lose an opportunity of showing how reactionary it is. But after all this was not, and was not likely to be, a matter of party; the Quaker Pease being as hearty in voting for it as any of the older kind of oppressor of the people. The vote was essentially the vote of the unthinking middle classes, and the debate was thoroughly in accordance with it.

It would be mere waste of time to take in hand the various forms which the ferocity and folly of these Philistines of Philistines took; but one may say that there were two lines taken up by the defenders of the measure. No. 1 was the effectiveness of brutality as a deterrent of brutality, and No. 2 was the exaltation of the moral duty of making the enemy whom you have caught pay for the enemy whom you cannot catch. On the one hand rank cowardice, on the other stupid revenge are the motives of such legislation.

With such cowards and ruffians as the reactionists of the House of Commons it would be loss of time to argue; and it would, of course, be no less a waste of time to prove to Socialists that while the gigantic wrong of class robbery supported by violence is overshadowing us like the deadly upas-tree, individual theft of any kind cannot excite much moral indignation in us; but since this paper will, it is hoped, fall into the hands of open-minded persons who have not yet learned what Socialism is, we may as well point out first that severity of punishment does not deter persons from committing offences which they are forced into by their surrounding circumstances; and next, that if it did, it might be possible to buy this benefit too dear; and that the price which these severe moralists and benefactors of their kind are prepared to pay for a diminished list of violent burglaries, is the degradation of the whole public.

Furthermore, these wiseacres might if they had read a little history (but fancy an M.P. reading history!) have noted that however pleasant revenge may be, it is an expensive pleasure, and that cowards should not meddle with it. And it is not easy to believe that the shopkeepers who want to add new tortures to our criminal law would venture on doing so if they really understood the necessary consequences of driving violent and brutal men (men *made* violent and brutal) to despair, and that what their precious bill will do will not be to deter the 'criminal class' for burglary, but to egg them on to murder. It will probably, if it becomes law, prove the death-warrant of many a quiet householder, who might otherwise have gone on sanding the sugar and calling to prayers for many years.

But really it is a sickening job arguing about a set of cowardly and hypocritical pirates who have got just one idea into their heads on the subject of theft, which is that they alone amongst all the world should be allowed to rob with violence and then escape the consequences of robbery by violence.

Commonweal, Volume 5, Number 175, 18 May 1889, p. 153.

NOTES ON NEWS

The Royal Duke and the policeman have escaped all possibility of fine or imprisonment for assaulting Mr. Simms. We know by experience that the policeman at least had nothing to fear from a magistrate, even if he had gone to much greater lengths than the collaring of an innocent citizen for the crime of being hustled by a member of the royal family. Yet it was, no doubt, an advantage to him to be in the company of an 'August Personage.'

Imagination *will* run away with one in picturing the fun that a person might have, who had a turn for a spree without disagreeable consequences, if he could only secure the co-operation at one and the same time of a member of the royal family and a member of the metropolitan police force. They might have adventures which would quite throw into the shade those of the famous trio – the Caliph Haroun Alraschid, Giaffar the Vizier, and Mesrour the executioner. Indeed, those worthies sometimes got into awkward corners in the course of their sprees; whereas the modern lot would only have to declare themselves in order to walk off with honour and dignity. We get on fast, don't we, in these days of absolute equality before the law?

It is difficult to treat such a matter seriously, and Mr. Simms has only been treated rudely, instead of being wounded first and sent to prison as a plaster for the wound, as many of our friends have been; and yet we cannot help feeling a sense of fresh degradation at such an exhibition of servility to a testy old martinet as the police-courts have given us, in the teeth of all the lying bluster about our freedom and our equality before the law. A Socialist indeed may say that it is not worth while considering such a trifling nuisance as a monarch and a royal family, when we have the real practical whip of capitalism flourished daily over our heads; but we must not forget that this gilded sham of a relic of feudalism, which was once powerful for good and evil, does now represent nothing but that very tyranny of the commercial master and slave-driver, and the executive power which keeps him in his place. It is a significant symbol of our false society that the Duke of Cambridge, the policeman, and the magistrate have been yokefellows in this shabby business.

A vice-consul in Servia has been telling us that the very simple method of competition which consists of pirating trademarks, has been damaging British trade in that country. Hats made of brown paper, knifes that wouldn't cut, shirtings half made of starch which disappeared on the first washing, etc., have been sold as British goods. Well, well, Servia is an out-of-the-way place, and possibly traditions of the excellence and honesty of British manufactures linger there, and so we may suppose that this legitimate means of competition, as John Bright would have considered it, may be effective there; but we who live in this great centre of civilisation would be inclined to think that the pirate had thrown away his industry; for in some branches at least it would be difficult to surpass British skill in adulteration; as, for example, in the weighting of cotton cloths with that useful creature, sulphates of barytes – not starch, my consular friend, – a glorious invention of England within the last few years; and there are many such-like inventions.

The correspondence between Mr. Henry George and our friend Cunninghame Graham in the *Star*, has settled down on the pros and cons concerning competition. Mr. George need hardly have told us that he is in favour of competition, indeed we know that he is prepared to hang people who are engaged in trying to abolish it. Cunninghame Graham, on the other hand, says that Socialists are trying to abolish it; and surely he is right in saying so. Competition will be impossible under genuine Socialism – or let us call it Communism, since all Socialists who know what their aim is know that they are aiming at that. Let us, however, see what we are to understand what we mean by the word competition, since I think the word is used vaguely very often.

Man must live in society of some kind: that society must be either a society of classes or of equals. Now, competition implies the struggle for thriving at other people's expense. In the class society this struggle must go on, and it is threefold: First there is the struggle between the classes, one of which is privileged, the other unprivileged. The privileged class strives to enhance its privilege, the unprivileged strives to reduce it; or in other words is driven by its inferior position to strive to destroy that privilege. Secondly, there is the competition for subsistence amongst the members of the unprivileged class, which is forced upon them by their dependent position. 'Don't feed him, master, feed ME; I am the best man,' is what each of them is forced to cry out and act on. Thirdly, there is the competition amongst the members of the privileged class each for his own share of privilege. This competition for privilege is what is usually meant by persons who use the word competition, and I must assert it is what Mr. George means when he uses it.

Change the picture, and let us look at a society of equality. How can competition exist in it? There will be no classes, privileged and unprivileged, to tug against one another. *That* war will be over. There will be no privilege for a robber class to squabble over the partition of. *That* war will be over. And lastly, as a blessed consequence, since freedom and mutual help will have taken the place of dependence on a master (*i.e.*, slavery), the hideous 'competition' or war amongst the unprivileged will have come to an end.

In short, the issue on this matter is clear between Mr. George and the Socialists: he is championing the condition of ceaseless war which is inherent in the present form of society, – the society of the master who has slaves without paying for them; of the slave who is forced to *give himself* to a master instead of being sold to him by somebody else. This war and the society of which it is an essential part is abhorrent to Socialists. It is by no means inconsistent in Mr. George to champion this competition for privilege. But it would be a mistake to suppose that he is anything else than an enemy of Socialism.

Lord Dufferin is now the hero of the jingo *Pall Mall*, which has lately outdone itself in an article of magniloquent jingoism; and considering the many benefits which the capitalist class reap from that unlucky country, India, the milch-cow of tyrants for so many ages, it is not wonderful that he should feel himself bound to make the best of the British tyranny there, the latest and worst of all, because it is an economical tyranny. But a curious commentary on this blowing of the British trumpet, as to the beneficence of our rule there, was given me the other day by a friend (a Socialist) who has been many years in India, and who told me when he first went out he tried to get intimate with the natives, but had long ago been forced to give up the attempt. And he is by no means the first person who has told me the like. We are a hated garrison in India, and hold it by means of force and fraud for the advantage of the robber class in England. That is what the heroics of the *Pall Mall* must be reduced to.

Commonweal, Volume 5, Number 178,
8 June 1889, p. 177.

NOTES ON NEWS

The dam above what was once Johnstown in Pennsylvania
turns out to have been the crowning triumph of what we call
in England jerry-building – *i.e.*, building not for the *use* of the
public but for the *profit* of the speculator. The crowd of
unfortunate people who were lost in that stupendous tragedy
have in fact been sacrificed to the demon of profit-mongering
to which hundreds and thousands of the disinherited classes
are sacrificed every day, whether the kind of sacrifice be the
actual death caused by privation, or the living death of
hopeless poverty.

To the demon of profit they were sacrificed, and also to the
demon of waste: for it seems that that huge mass of water,
held temporarily in check by its jerry-built dam, was in fact
a pleasure lake, the property of a fishing-club; so that this
gigantic threat of sudden death to thousands was simply one
of the means of wasting the riches which the idle class wring
by force from the workers, and which they cannot *use* but
can only waste.

I do not wonder at the anger of the survivors from this
artificial deluge, this subsidised terror, against the owners or
holders of the pleasure-lake; but if there be any members of
the class which lives on the enforced labour of the workers
amongst these angry men, their anger is illogical; because
they themselves are doing the same kind of thing (unconsciously maybe) every day. Let Keats speak to it:

For them alone did seethe
A thousand men in troubles wide and dark:

Half-ignorant, they turned an easy wheel
That set sharp racks at work to pinch and peel.

On the other hand, those of the disinherited classes who have shown their anger are abundantly justified in being angry; but if they understood their position better, their anger would seek wider afield, for they would know that the profit and pleasure of the masters of slaves does not produce mere spasmodic accidents only of death and misery, but is and must be the constant and necessary cause of continuous death and misery.

Will you say, 'How do I know that there was a slave class in and about Johnstown?' If I did not know it otherwise, I should be sure of it by the token that after the catastrophe there were people found so miserable and brutalised that they used the occasion to rob the dead bodies – and were shot for doing it by others (doubtless maddened by the terror that surrounded the place) who did not, and we will say could not, remember the words of a great teacher, 'Let him who is without sin amongst you lift up the first stone against her!' O shooters of the robbers of the rich dead, is it not a worse crime to rob the living poor, and that not now and again, but constantly, systematically, and legally?

The 'large employers of labour in the printing trade,' who have just lately published a circular to prove that they are the true friends of labour, 'protest too much.' We don't need to be told that they will do what they think best to bring them in a profit; but surely workmen don't need to be told that this *must* mean their paying the lowest wages they can safely pay. We shall have more on this subject.

Advanced Radicals boycotting Socialists is a sight which would please Tories more than any other party. *Reynolds* please take note of this, and do not refuse to publish our lecture-lists. *Star* please take note also, since you seem to be beginning that game. The *Dispatch* has not the same terror of us as other Radical papers have, but publishes our places and times of meeting regularly.

A poor little boy was run over and killed the other day in getting out of the way of a tram-car. The driver of the said car was arrested and brought before Mr. De Rutzen. But the evidence that the man was not in the least responsible was so clear, that the magistrate remarked that 'no doubt what had been done by the police was in accordance with police regulations, but why the person before him should be taken into custody he was utterly at a loss to understand.' The reason, I think, is rather clearer to us; it is in accordance with police regulations to badger and bully poor men on every possible occasion, and even on what would seem to ordinary persons *impossible* occasions.

Commonweal, Volume 5, Number 179,
15 June 1889, p. 185.

NOTES ON NEWS

On this side of the Atlantic we have had an 'accident' of the kind the responsibility for which it is impossible for us not to take on our own shoulders; nature or ill-luck or what not, must be accused after us and not before us. As a matter of course, we have nothing to say about the men who have been arrested: even if they should be proved guilty of carelessness, yet after all it is not they who would be the real criminals, but rather ourselves, who allow monopolist companies to work our railways for profit, with the necessary consequence of low wages and long hours and short-handedness amongst the underlings out of whose pay and leisure the monopolists have to scape up a dividend. What *can* come of such a system but misery and disaster on all hands?

I see the Rev. Mr Viner, in presiding over a meeting of the Plumstead tram-car men, said that the object of the movement was not to make war on the company, but to get for the men a fair day's wages for a fair day's work. Well, the words are pretty, but unmeaning; the men *are* at war with the company, and must be so as long as they don't get a fair day's wage for their work; that is, until *they* are employed by the public and get what the public pays for riding in the cars instead of their do-nothing, dividend-drawing masters. The masters are showing that if the men don't learn to understand their position, and fight as hard as they can, they will soon be taught by their masters the meaning of one of the maxims of war: 'Woe to the vanquished.'

In point of fact, they are at the lesson now: the companies are acting in a quite straightforward commercial manner, and see the necessity of crushing the movement at once: they know their enemies, and put them *hors de combat* by giving them the sack without quarter. The public, however, are beginning to be a little uneasy at such straight 'application of economical principles,' as the bourgeois slang goes, and it is not so certain that the dividend-drawers will win.

Here is what a non-Socialists friend told me last night. Asking why a certain tram was late, one of the men told him that the company had extended their dinner time ('hour,' I was going to write) from eight minutes to fifteen; and that in consequence they had to put on the extra minutes' work at the end of the day. How is that for shabbiness in this world where nature is so superabundant? I call it the very sublime of shabbiness: the true antithesis to the Widow's Mite.

The respectable critics have been very much down on Ibsen's play of 'A Doll's House,' now being acted at the Novelty Theatre, and profess to be shocked: Mr. Buchanan, *e.g.*, reiterating the phrase a 'young woman of criminal proclivities' *apropos* of the heroine, whose crime one may say in passing is merely a technical one. How is this to be explained, linked as it is with the fact that the Socialists obviously look on the play as making for Socialism, and are enthusiastic about it? It is not difficult of explanation: whatever may be the demerits of 'A Doll's House' as an acting play (by the way, if it is *different* from an ordinary modern play it must be better, just as any day different from last Whit-Monday must be better than it) – I say in any case it is a piece of the *truth* about modern society clearly and forcibly put. Therefore clearly it doesn't suit the critics, who are parasites of the band of robbers called modern society. Great is Diana of the Ephesians! But if my memory serves me, her rites were not distinguished for purity.

I note that the critics say that Ibsen's plays are pessimistic; so they are – to pessimists; and all intelligent persons who are not Socialists are pessimists. But the representation of the corruption of society carries with it in Ibsen's works aspirations for a better state of things, and that is not pessimism. Therefore Socialists recognise in them another token of the new dawn.

Commonweal, Volume 5, Number 180,
22 June 1889, p. 193.

NOTES ON NEWS

The right of asylum is threatened in Switzerland; nay it seems pretty much as if it had come to an end, since Switzerland is so completely between the pincers of the great absolutist tyrannies. 'Grief in your neighbours' garth is grief at your own door,' says an old proverb of the North; so we may well look at home to see what is likely to happen here in case any spy-supported absolutist government finds it convenient to pick a quarrel with Great Britain. Truth to say, it seems improbable that there will be a recurrence of the indignation which the Bonapartist colonels stirred up here which cost the popular Palmerston his place. There is no doubt as to what the Tories and Liberals would say and do, judging by the reactionary *Standard* and shabby-respectable *Daily News*. Let us hope the *Star* really represents the opinions of the Radicals in this matter, and that they will remember their old traditions.

To make the world not only a prison, but an utterly hopeless prison is the great ambition of these tyrants. After all, they are not likely to advance their ends by attacking what even political Radicals must think the very elements of liberty. They will find that the sweep of their net is too wide, and that their miraculous draught of fishes will make a hole in it.

A citizen complained of a nuisance, in the form of a stink, in a police-court the other day, and the whole subject was thought to be very funny, the magistrate (Mr. Plowden) leading off the laughter. We cannot tell from the report what the merits of this particular case might be; but we do know that a neighbourhood may be stunk out without a legal nuisance being established, which is indeed ridiculous enough, though not more ridiculous than most of our law. Perhaps the magistrate and his audience were laughing at English law in general. Or perhaps they thought it a preposterous joke that a well-to-do citizen should make a fuss about commerce annoying him with a mere stink when it murders so many poor people day by day. No doubt this is a joke, but I can't laugh at it. There is another explanation, which is that these laughers were such dullards that they had no conception that people might possibly restrain commerce so as to allow people to live decent lives. *That* also is no laughing matter.

Commonweal, Volume 5, Number 181,
29 June 1889, p. 201.

NOTES ON NEWS

The police have been playing the usual game, and in all probability with the usual impunity to them and the usual punishment to the 'rioters,' so called. We shall not be suspected of agreement with the doctrines of the Salvation Army; but on this occasion the processionists must be looked on as citizens going about on their lawful errands and suddenly attacked by a band of organised and armed ruffians without any cause whatever.

Here is again an opportunity for testing the genuineness of the protestations of both parties in the State. Even the Tories might be expected to take up the matter on behalf of persons with no taint of revolutionism in them; and as for the Liberals! – Well, I must say that they are fast qualifying themselves for the name which they used to bestow on their Tory opponents – the Stupid Party. In fact their stupidity is a deep well – to fathom. They haven't even the wits to pick up a safe opportunity like this, but are determined to play into the hands of the 'advanced' party, which is advancing in no doubtful way towards Socialism.

Our friend Mr. Cunninghame Graham was probably not particularly disappointed at the adverse vote against him about the instructions to the British delegate to the Berne Conference. To be invited to a Conference and to understand perfectly well what would be the only important subject discussed there, and then to say Yes, we will send delegates, but those delegates shall not take part in the discussion of the real subject which the Conference has been called together to discuss – this would undoubtedly seem to the dispassionate observer from another planet a piece of absurdity impossible to men claiming to hold a dignified and responsible position; but to us living on the Earth under a bureaucratic government, it is a quite familiar incident.

In short, it is *the* position of the Whig-Tory or Tory-Whig governments that we are such fools as to put up with. How could it be otherwise? What would happen if they were to allow the discussion of subjects affecting the welfare of the mass of the population? Clearly the preliminary to the useful discussion of these subjects would be that such governments should take themselves off; and, as it is the business of their lives *not* to go off, from this point of view Mr. Morley was right in declaring the question unpractical, although, as he knows well enough, all thinking workmen throughout civilisation are (rightly or wrongly) crying out for *practical* discussion of this subject of the limitation of the hours of labour.

Yet the position of Lord Salisbury's Government is more logical than Mr. Morley's, who blames them for refusing to discuss the question and then points out that it cannot be discussed; and his arguments against the limitation of labour are of the stale kind which would be quite as effective against the limitation of the working day of women and children as of adult males. In fact in this matter Mr. Morley is not really considering the position of the workers in their factories and workshops, but his own position as a politician in the House of Commons: that is why he is so anxious to ticket himself as a Whig. If the Whigs should be driven at any time to legislate about the working day, we shall find him naively assuming that all liberal-minded men were always in favour of the eight-hour day: just as he assumes that they were always in favour of Home Rule.

Mr. Cunninghame Graham must be thanked for giving the House of Commons and the Liberal party, including their organ the *Daily News*, another opportunity for showing the people how little they have to hope from them; and moreover the question is one that must be discussed, and I repeat will be, in spite of the attempt of the so-called leaders of the trades unions to burk the discussion. For my part I think that 'unpractical' as the question is, legislation limiting the working hours of adult males will be forced on the Government, and that before very long.

If that legislation were effective, it would certainly give more leisure to the workers, which of itself would be a great gain whatever came with it, and lower wages for the mass of the workers, the unskilled, could not accompany it, because they are already working for mere subsistence wages. Also the struggle between the masters and the men would be embittered by it, because the masters would try to force down the wages of the skilled or half-skilled workmen, and to give less wages for the eight hours than they now give for the nine, ten, or twelve hours. Competition for profits would force them to do this, and the men of course would be obliged to resist this, so that there would be fresh strikes and fresh discontent throughout the world of labour, which would further our Cause.

On the other hand, the masters would be driven to meet the comparative scarcity of labour by carrying still further and faster the development of machinery and the organisation of labour, which is such a great feature of these days, of the last ten years especially; so that if less labour hours were available, less would be needed. And the improvement in machinery would increase the intensity of labour, so that the amount done in each hour and the consequent wear and tear to the workman would be greater than under the longer working-day. All these would disappoint the hope of those who think that the eight hours day would give more employment to the mass of workers. The system of wage-slavery and the profit-market necessitates 'a reserve army of labour,' *i.e.*, of a starvation army waiting for the short crisis when it suits the capitalist slave-holders to take on all the hands whom they can sweep up from the workhouse and the street corners; and no shortening of the hours of labour will do away with this wretched state of things that does not bring with it obvious revolution, that is to say a change in the basis of society.

The workers must settle for themselves whether the gain of leisure, which it may be assumed would be the result of a limitation of the day's labour, would so far outweigh these drawbacks as to make it worth their while to carry on the agitation for it vigorously. But they must certainly *settle it for themselves*; if they allow the gentlemen of the House of Commons to settle it for them, they will find as usual that they will have something given them with the right hand to be taken back with the left.

In any case I beg them not to expect too much from the success of such an agitation, and above all not to think that it would relieve them of one scruple's-weight of their duty to struggle for the destruction of our present class-society. Mr. Graham, unconsciously perhaps, gave us a warning on this matter in his speech the other night. He reminded the House that for 24 years the eight hours' day had obtained in Victoria, and said that no harm had come of it. We know from the definite information of our comrades in the antipodes that a revolution is just as necessary there as here; and so it is, and will be all over the world as long as there are privileged classes living on the disinherited classes.

Tennyson's northern farmer heard his cantering horses' hoofs play the tune of 'Proputty, Proputty, Proputty!' No wonder; it is the one thought in the mind of all respectable people. Some luckless persons the other day at St. Bees ate a poisoned joint of beef, and one (a lady) died of it, and the others were made very ill. Says the daily press anent this luckless business: 'The occurrence is a most unfortunate one, as St. Bees is so popular and Mr. Scott is a new tenant of the hotel.' The poor lady's epitaph then must be a moan over the lost 'Proputty, proputty, proputty!'

Commonweal, Volume 5, Number 182,
6 July 1889, p. 209.

NOTES ON NEWS

The Royal Grants! We shall be expected to have a word or two to say about them. I hope what follows will not be considered too irreverent either towards the sovereignty of the sovereign or the sovereignty of the people; but it cannot be helped; it is impossible to treat the matter wholly seriously, though there is food for serious reflection in it. Let us put before our readers various views on the subject.

No. 1. The gracious Monarch of this land, the Empress of this beneficent Empire of Great Britain (on which the sun never sets), is pleased to inform her loyal and loving subjects that, owing to circumstances over which she has no control, she has grandchildren (who cannot *work* but are *not* ashamed to beg) who require pensioning, and that she is well aware how pleased all her l. and l. subjects will be to hear of this opportunity of showing their love and loyalty, and of expressing their sense of gratitude for the privilege which they enjoy of being so kindly allowed to live (if they can) under the shadow of the glory of the said empire. All this notwithstanding the fact that there are certain apes and demons in human form living amongst us, who have a dim idea that to pay a great deal for nothing at all is not their ideal of doing business in an ordinary way.

That is the official view of the matter, held as an article of faith by the greater part of the flunkey and ignorant middle-class population, and that part of the working classes who would be middle-class if they could. It is not meant to state facts; it is an article of faith, like the Athanasian Creed.

No. 2. England is practically a democratic republic, and as good a country as need be for an active and well-to-do middle class man to live in: but there are anomalies in it which are troublesome to the logic of a commonsense man. Amongst these is a survival from the feudalism of the Middle Ages in the form of a sovereign who is usually of no great harm and never of much use. But even we commercial progressive people think it worth while to keep this sham going as a sort of symbol that we don't want to go too fast: still, having this gilt figure-head, as business men we don't want to pay too much for it, and of course we will take every opportunity of curbing its extravagancies.

That is the ordinary Radical view, and considers itself very superior and knowing. It is after all only a translation of No. 1 into a language understanded of the people, and still leaves room for other views.

No. 3, for instance. 'Well, what's the use of all this talk? Of course the old lady tries to get as much as she can from us and to do as little as possible for it; and since she is queen, she can easily best us: so we had better stump up, and say no more about it.'

That is the ordinary commonsense working-man's view of it, looking at it from the outside. It is not very far from the fact as times go. But there is still room for the Socialist point of view: call it[.]

No. 4. We are governed by a bureaucracy – *i.e.*, a government of professional officials governing in their own interests as representatives of the proprietary classes. This Bureaucracy thinks it necessary to have a head ornamental official and to call it king or queen, though it has nothing whatever to do with the old feudal king, who had definite duties to perform. The present demand for more money is not made to the people in any form, but to the Bureaucracy, by its head official. That Bureaucracy, knowing well that its safety depends on its being as reactionary as possible, replies, 'More money? certainly: only don't overdo it,' and then proceeds to work the oracle by the usual parliamentary means; and the whole business of semi-opposition, and down-right opposition, is all a solemn farce. The bureaucracy does not object. Let anyone else object if he pleases; he can't *do* anything.

After, all, working-men needn't lament the vote too much: if the Queen were not to have the money, they wouldn't. It will go just where it would have gone in any case – to the association for wasting the labour of the workers – *i.e.*, the privileged classes. Cast your eyes over the list of the rubbish offered to our gilt gibbie-stick of royalty on this very occasion, and reflect on the toil and skill of ingenious and laborious men which has been cast away into the gutter in producing things that nobody wants, and how that toil and skill might have been employed in producing what everybody wants, and you will think that our head official with the sham mediæval cloak cast about it, is but a very natural expression of the great fraud and folly of our age.

Here is a sham Society, a real band of robbers, that steals and steals from all men who do anything, till it makes life hard and miserable for the great majority of men, and yet it can do no better for itself than waste its stolen resources in ugly and ridiculous toys, that those who are cumbered with them can do nothing with but bury or forget. For such a Society the crowned toy is good enough, and I can only wish it had to pay for it really instead of seemingly.

Yet, mind you, for the serious Radicals who voted against this natural and necessary insult to the community on principle and not for cheese-paring reasons, we cannot help feeling sympathy. But, poor souls, what are they to do if they have tacked themselves on to the skirts of such leaders as they are bound to put up with? All amateurs of oratory agree that Mr. Gladstone has at last made a speech worthy of his best period. What has he spent that rhetoric upon? Home Rule? Freedom of speech? Surely at least the independence and dignity of the House of Commons? Not at all, it was made in favour of the grant to save the Queen's pocket. What is to be said after that?

Also will anyone explain why the Irish members voted for the Government on Mr. Labouchere's amendment? Is that part of the whitewashing into respectability of Mr. Parnell? or is it part of some Parliamentary tactics, a dodge that 'almost no feller' can understand?

In any case the Irish members ought to consider whether the support of the 'thoroughly respectable' is worth more to them than that of the democratic working men who have honestly taken up the cause of the poor in Ireland without any thought of their own self-interest.

As to Mr. Chamberlain, what need be said but that if one's enemy likes to roll himself in filth, it is not our business to warn him that he will stink afterwards.

Commonweal, Volume 5, Number 186,
3 August 1889, p. 241.

NOTES ON NEWS

The *Daily News*, after a considerable amount of shilly-shally in the matter of the Maybrick case, has set itself to publishing a lot of meaningless politeness towards Mr. Matthews and the white-washing of Mr. Justice Stephen's 'conscientiousness.' This is all very well, and we don't want to go into people's 'motives' like some judicial persons do; deeds that we *do* see must be taken as interpreting motives that we *don't* see; and the sentence on Harrison is the measure for us of Mr. Justice Stephen's 'carefulness and conscientiousness.' Nor can we forget that he was one of the first to set a-going the modern doctrine of the 'superior pusson,' and that in his published writings he has practically declared himself an enemy of the people. It is frightful to think of such a man wielding that abuse of our criminal procedure, the judge's summing-up.

The dock labourers' strike is one of the signs of the times, so fruitful of strikes of late, and at last of strikes among the unskilled. It must not be forgotten, however, that this kind of strike if successful (and, of course, every honest man must wish these poor fellows success) owes its success to the fact that public opinion is powerful in great centres of population, and that public opinion cannot help being on the side of these poor men, whose oppression touches even the sluggish imagination of the ordinary middle-class man. In places or under circumstances where overwhelming public opinion cannot be brought to bear, such strikes are doomed to certain failure; as, indeed, are most strikes.

Since then we are amidst such a period of strikes, and since whatever may be the effect of such strikes it is clear that they are inevitable, is it not the time to press on the workers general combination in this matter of the regulation of wages? Strikes, once more, are generally defeated now because the strikers are only acting in a scattered and skirmishing way, and can be crushed in detail. But suppose the inert and languishing body of trades' unionism revivified by a 'plan of campaign,' which would mean the whole mass standing shoulder to shoulder in all strikes (and much increased in numbers as it certainly would be), surely that would be worth a heap of parliamentary legislation, and armies of paid and lukewarm inspectors! Every strike, I say, should have the whole weight of the organised workers at the back of it.

Again, if we have found strikes useful towards the revolutionary propaganda, it has been because in these days of widespread Socialist agitation they tend to enlighten the workers on their real relation to the masters, and to show them that the position of antagonism between the two taken up at a time of strike, is not an accident to the system of capital and labour, but an essential of it; that the masters as a body, and whatever may be the good will of any individual, are at enmity to the men; and that that enmity must take an obvious and practical form as soon as any group of the workers attempt to be anything more than mere passive tools in the hands of the employers.

Now surely, if the labour struggle were carried on by the workers organised in combination, this fact of the necessary opposition of the interests of master and men would no longer be hidden from the slowest capacity; and it would be understood that whatever gains the workers made could only be made at the expense of the masters, and when *that* was understood surely the step would not be long to the clear understanding that the masters are (at best) a mere useless clog on the workers, to be got rid of as soon as possible; and under these circumstances it would very soon be possible to get rid of them.

Commonweal, Volume 5, Number 189,
24 August 1889, p. 265.

NOTES ON NEWS

If the non-Socialist middle-class sympathisers with the strikers could grasp one side of the situation, I think it ought to stagger their complacency with the present arrangement of society. Let us take their own view of that situation, which is pretty much this: A body of workmen very much oppressed by the operation of the wages and capital system have demanded a slight increase of wages, and a revision of an iniquitous system of sweating; the public generally have admitted the justice and moderation of the men's claim; but their employers have simply buttoned up their pockets and said 'We can't and shan't,' and the public have absolutely *no* means of compelling them to yield.

Could anything condemn our present society more clearly and completely than this deadlock? Here is the whole of humanity and morality crying out loudly on the shabby employers to give way to the men's demands, and the shabby employers in fact replying to that cry: Humanity and morality may go to H(eaven) for us; we have to create a dividend; we stand on our legal right to starve as many people as may be convenient to us. And the public morality and humanity is helpless before them; for their legal right is undoubted: their legal right to put citizens to death by starvation.

Yes, in spite of its prisons and ropes and hangmen for those whom it calls specially 'criminals,' the law is the Great Murderer!

Here, then, at last is the *reductio ad absurdum* of *laissez faire*; which of course means, let the privileged alone to make the most of their privilege of driving the weakest to the wall. For clearly if you attack privilege you at once abjure *laissez faire*; you are not letting alone, you are becoming revolutionary.

Once more, we must not suppose, however, that this sympathy of the well-to-do for the strikers is universal; I believe that if you polled the well-to-do generally they would give you a handsome majority for Norwood. The *Daily News* the other day gave a specimen of a conversation with a man of business, who proposed to remedy the strike by locking up four of the ringleaders, and taking advantage of the rioting, which would be sure to follow, for putting down the whole agitation by means of a little murder in the streets.

I really believe that this conversation was genuine; for, happening to be in a Conservative club last week (I don't habitually frequent such places), I listened with much amusement to the 'natives' (I must say, a rather gruesome-looking set of savages) putting the other view to that which has been generally put in the papers; and, as a matter of course, it was all on the lines of the *Daily News'* interlocutor; and Burns (I am happy to say) was by no means flattered by these worthies, a long term of imprisonment being the best wish for him. It is true that some pity was expressed for the 'poor men' for their ill-luck in being led astray by such scoundrels, and their ruin (the deprivation of 6s. a-week) abundantly prophesied.

This may seem a kind of a joke to us: but do not let us forget that the theories of these ruffians would have been put into practice if they could have been. These strikes are not less dangerous to the supremacy of the landlords and their abettors than the Trafalgar Square incidents, but more dangerous. There is only one reason why Burns is not going to Pentonville this time, and why the streets are not cleared by the bludgeon, and if necessary by the bayonet, and that is because the rulers of this happy land are afraid to do it. The men are too many and too desperate, and their miserable condition has really impressed itself on a large part of the non-political middle classes; and lastly and above all, their brother-workers are really in active sympathy with the strikers.

The rejection by the men of the so-called compromise on Monday was a certain thing, for less than this they cannot get. The promise of the extra penny at some future date is seen by everybody to be a delusion; as who can say what may happen between now and then to serve the directors as an excuse for breaking their promise? they have shown themselves very fond of using the well-known formula of moneyed men, 'We cannot,' and will not be slow to do so in the future we may be sure.

It has seemed as though the provinces have not shown that enthusiasm for the strikes, or that understanding of them, that might have been expected; but, at least, the conduct of the 15 Dundee labourers who set out to tramp back when they found that they would interfere with the strike here, is a bright spot in the dullness. All honour to the brave men! As to the conduct of Mr. Christopher Peacock, it was what might have been expected from a Nupkins. We can only be glad that the men met in the end with a little better reward of loyalty than seven day's hard [labour], though that is a type of such rewards too. Let us echo the cheers of the Lincoln folk who saw them off to Dundee again.

This last Trades-Union Congress has turned out thoroughly reactionary, and there has been plenty of bowing down to Gessler Broadhurst's hat, both by the men and in the press. It is to be feared that the explanation of this is simply that the influential men in the respectable trades-unions are fossil Whigs, and of course need a fossil Whig for a leader (and have got him). This at first seems discouraging to those who have had any hope of socialising the trades-unions, and I don't know that the hope was ever worth much.

It must not be forgotten, however, that not only has revolt begun amongst the older trades-unions, but that what is now going on is a threat of their final disappearance into a far wider and more generous association of the workers, which will be inspired with socialistic feeling. The unions of the so-called unskilled labourers, which are part of the consequences of the present strikes, very much reduce the importance of Mr. Broadhurst and his brother officials who pretend to represent the workers of the country. There is a curious analogy, ominous of good, between the position of these two groups and that of the struggle of the Trade Guilds of the Middle Ages against the exclusive and aristocratic Merchant Guilds. That struggle ended in victory for the true workmen, and it is hardly indulging in prophesy to say that a similar victory may be looked forward too once more. Mr. Broadhurst's triumph and the solidifying of the Whig element in the official trades-unions does nothing but widen the gap (always a pretty wide one) between him and the workmen of the country.

Commonweal, Volume 5, Number 192,
14 September 1889, p. 289.

NOTES ON NEWS

The dockers have won their victory; for with all drawbacks it must be called a victory. They have shown qualities of unselfishness and power of combination which we may well hope will appear again before long. For one thing, they have knocked on the head the old slander against the lower ranks of labour, and shown that the mere 'fringe of labour,' the 'roughs,' the 'vagabonds' – in short, the men named by the insults of the real criminal class, who have thrust them into their terrible position, – that these men can organise themselves at least as well, and be at least as true to their class, as the aristocracy of labour. No result of the strike is more important than the effect it will have as a blow against class jealousy amongst the workers themselves. Henceforth any working-man attempting to make distinctions between skilled and unskilled will be obvious to his fellows as a traitor and reactionary.

The *Daily News*, which, like several other definitely capitalist papers, espoused the cause of the strikers, was nevertheless very anxious to show that the strike had nothing to do with Socialism. Now if that means that it was no artificial agitation, but was caused by dire necessity, we can all agree with that. If it means anything else it is nonsense. For in the first place, although mere combination amongst the men, with no satisfactory ulterior aim, is not itself Socialism, yet it is both a necessary education for the workers, and it is an instrument which Socialism cannot dispense with. Furthermore, the attitude of the *Daily News* itself and of the well-to-do sympathisers with the strikers (including, doubtless, a large part of the lower middle class), remains, when all deductions have been made, a remarkable fact; and a fact, moreover, quite impossible to be explained except by admitting that the preaching of Socialism has frightened some and, at least partly, convinced others of the respectable classes. They are becoming at once terrified and shocked by the horrible poverty of London. Is that the result of the efforts of the Charity Organisation to make poverty respectable? of the efforts of the philanthropists to make it dumb? of the parsons of all sects to make it religious? No. It is the result of the efforts of the Socialists to make poverty actively discontented.

Let us go on with those efforts then, encouraged by the step that combination amongst the workers has taken, but remembering that the new epoch of combination is only just beginning. Let us make it clear to the middle-class sympathisers with labour, that very little has been done even to palliate the most obvious evils of the system which makes them a middle-class, *i.e.*, a class of sweaters. The dockers are to have their 'tanner' (if the companies keep faith with them, which is very doubtful), but what will be their position when they reap the result of their hard won victory? Let us be plain on this matter. They will receive precarious mere-subsistence wages for the hardest of hard work. They will be lodged in hideous and foul slums; they will have no reasonable pleasure, no taste of the comforts and the luxuries which their labour helps to win for others. In a word, they will still be slaves as far as their material condition is concerned, though they have shown that they are not the stuff of which it is safe to make slaves.

For us, it is our business to make them understand that they never can be anything else than slaves till they have swept away class domination and privilege; that in spite of all the soft words of the capitalist press, they and the capitalists are and must be irreconcilable enemies; that whatever either gains must be at the expense of the other. When they have learned that, their combination will both be infinitely improved as an instrument, and they will also be compelled to use it for its one real use, the realization of Socialism, to which undoubtedly this strike has been a step, as part of the labour struggle, as part of the attack on our enemy – Capitalism.

Commonweal, Volume 5, Number 193,
21 September 1889, p. 297.

NOTES ON NEWS

The events of the Great Strike, the pushing forward of the lower part of the 'lower orders,' coming as a sequel to the agitation of the last six years in England, have much impressed the minds of that part of the public which thinks at all. Socialism, once a mere word to them, then a foolish fad, then a bugbear, bearing with it confusion and violence and nothing else, is at last presenting itself to them as a possible change in society which their own eyes may see, and which will perhaps be bearable to them.

Good so far. But what do they mean by Socialism, these well-to-do people who are beginning to think that it is coming and that it will suit them pretty well (as indeed it will, but scarcely in the way they think)? Doubtless if questioned on the point as to what they expect from Socialism, they will answer with a phrase or two like this from the *Pall Mall Gazette*: 'From the point of view of political economy, Socialism means the collective instead of the individual administration of capital, rent, and interest.'

Yes, yes; but what does the 'collective administration of capital, rent, and interest' mean? I suspect to the *Pall Mall* writer, nothing at all; and that when he comes to find out that it means the abolition of private property, he will cry off his Socialism – if he can.

In fact, his jubilant satisfaction, shared no doubt by many of the cultured classes, at the aspect of things at present, rather shows what a very limited idea he has of the coming new society. He echoes Sir William Harcourt's humbug, 'We are all Socialists now!' Are we indeed? Well, I must say in that case we need not have taken the trouble to become Socialists; since the days are still so hard on the workers that it is considered a great victory for them when the hardest worked people in London can screw a very minute gain out of their masters, who are still living in luxury earned by the employment of doing nothing; while the slums in all our big cities are just as bad as they were ten years ago, and there is no prospect of their being bettered perceptibly by our present masters in the next ten years. We may be preparing the kingdom of heaven on earth, but I think I can bring many credible witnesses to prove to the most sanguine that it has not reached them yet.

Again, if we are all Socialists now, how does it come that we of the well-off are not holding mass meetings, and appointing committees to look into the best method of relinquishing our privilege in favour of the disinherited? Surely if we have acknowledged the tremendous truths which modern Socialism has laid open to us, we ought to be busy acting on them, unless we are prepared to brand ourselves as the feeblest curs yet told of in history.

Our *Pall Mall* friend quotes Sidney Webb to show that we are all Socialists in his well-known platitude about the individualist City Counsellor enjoying the advantages of Socialism without knowing it, and miscalling Socialism all the time. Of course our Fabian friend knew very well what a piece of claptrap he was putting forward, and that what the City Counsellor was really saying went rather in this way: 'Ha, ha! So these damned fools think that all this municipal business is Socialism – what fun! And they wonder that I am pretty well satisfied with such Socialism, as I really think I ought to be, when they work to provide me with these fine things, and I enjoy them without working. Hurrah for

Socialism of this kind, say I; so long as the *word* contents them!'

What is the real gate which will pull up these soft Socialists, who so long as they are allowed to steal the goose will not object to give the giblets to the poor? This is the barrier which they will not be able to pass, so long as they are in their present minds, *the acknowledgement of the class war*. The 'Socialists' of this kind are blind as to the essence of modern society. They hope for a revolution, which is not *the* Revolution, but a revolution which is to ignore the facts that have led up to it and will bring it about.

It is strange that they are so blind! Granted, as they must grant, the existence of a class which consumes without producing, and which, instead of being treated as a criminal class that has forfeited its rights of citizenship, is the master of the producing class, and has arranged all its law, religion, and morality to fit in with the theory of the beneficent eternity of privilege, – granted all this, how far can the class which supports these criminals, these violent robbers, go, without knocking up against the laws, the religion, the morality of robbery? Surely not a step. 'Let us rob you a little less,' say these Constitutionalists, 'and then be contented. Or, at least, you who are most discontented, let us shuffle off some of your burdens on to another group of the disinherited, and then at least *you* can be contented.'

It won't do! When one man employs another, and as a consequence of the 'employment' takes from him a large part of what he produces, what is the use of telling him to go to a third person to recover the wealth he has been diddled out of? His resource is obvious and at hand in the form of the robber's purse, and nothing else can compensate him.

It is most important that young Socialists should have this fact of the class-war always before them. It explains past history, and in the present gives us the only solid hope for the future. And it must be understood that it is only by the due working out of this class-war to its end, *the abolition of classes*, that Socialism can come about. Suppose the whole of the middle-classes agreed on the necessity of Socialism, how are they going to realise it unless it is demanded by the workers?

Give up their privilege, as above said, you may say. Yes, but they live on that privilege, and if they attempt to give it up without the world of labour being prepared to receive them as workers, they simply throw everything into confusion by competing with the workers for the employment of the world-market, which exists only as a machine for keeping capitalism going. It is the workers only, enlightened as to the class-war, and therefore no longer carrying it on blindly, as they have hitherto done, who must make the machinery of free labour and mutual exchange, which will supplant the machinery of capitalist commerce, and at one stroke both *compel* the resignation of privilege and make it possible.

Deduction: the worker cannot better himself at his own expense but only at the expense of his master, who for his part, driven by competition, cannot help striving against the attempts of the worker to better himself. These two, therefore, are necessarily enemies, and to blink that fact does not render them less so, but only gives a little longer day to the enemy of the workman. *Therefore* it is that the middle-class semi-Socialists, driven by class instinct, preach revolution without the class struggle; which is an absurdity and an impossibility.

Commonweal, Volume 5, Number 194, 28 September 1889, p. 305.

NOTES ON NEWS

There seems to be a risk of the London County Council making a huge blunder, which it certainly will do if it approves the report of its Licensing Committee. That committee proposes in the first place that the Council shall act as a censor of morals as to the matter of what is said or sung in the Music Halls, and it is impossible for them to fulfil this function except on the old reactionary lines. Granted that the songs provided by the music halls are often coarse and often nasty, who is to gauge the degree of coarseness and nastiness which shall be enough to deprive a hall of its licence? Whose standard is to be applied? That of a Scotch goody-goody, a fanatical Salvationist editor of a commercial sensational journal, or that of a sensible man?

But no sensible man will have anything to do with such nonsense as trying to make people moral by Act, either of Parliament or of County Council. The standard, therefore, will be the standard of 'purity' fanatics, who will be backed up by politicians anxious to catch the votes of the very powerful Nonconformist Liberals.

And all the time they will let alone the nastiness and *double entendre* of the respectable theatres, which are every bit as bad as the coarseness of the music halls.

It won't do. As a people is, so are its entertainments, and both the music halls and the theatres are but a reflex of the life of the slums. To that must you play down, gentlemen and ladies of the stage, or your managers will not be able to fill their houses, and your salaries will tumble down. Given a society corrupted by the existence of general misery, and founded on sheer robbery of the disinherited, and what are its theatrical entertainments likely to be? At the best, corruption whitewashed with respectability; at the worst? – but can there be anything worse than that?

As to the other side of this moral outburst of the over-righteous of the London County Council, the shutting up of a place of entertainment because it shelters prostitutes; that is worse still. You want to turn these poor women out into the streets, and when they are in the streets you want to run them in for being there. And all the while you know perfectly well that they are just as necessary an institution of modern Society as the banker who looks after the money that pays them, or the policeman who runs them in.

In short, this is an attack on the public by the Puritans, and it will be a thousand pities if the London County Council allows them to jump into the saddle and so injure its possible usefulness. And it is grievous to think how much power this Puritanism still has. Although it has sunk from a destructive fanaticism into a slimy superstition, it is still a dangerous ally of the gigantic robbery of capitalism, which first gave it birth. Such a body of voters as it can bring to the polling places!

The Bishop of London in the chair of the St James's Hall meeting, gave a clear expression of its arbitrariness in refusing to allow our friend Headlam to move an amendment or to speak. His conception of a public meeting as a place where only one side is to be heard is refreshingly naïve, and really beats Bradlaugh.

Certainly it would be a preposterous blunder of the London County Council to jump at the office of a subsidiary Lord

Chamberlain, and carry out his antiquated rules with extra zeal, even to the shutting up of the unprivileged small dramatic entertainments with (naturally) the full concurrence of Mr. Augustus Harris.

The 'Turkish Atrocities' in Crete and Armenia are such an obviously good card for the Liberal party to play, that one cannot help feeling some suspicion on the subject. Such things, however, are the natural outcome of a dominant race with a population of workers under them, whether they be peasants or what not. We shall be less likely to question the substantial truth of these reports when we remember English 'atrocities' in Ireland, India, Jamaica, Egypt, and other places where that blameless, religious, and practical race has been dominant.

Certainly two wrongs do not make a right, and we should be heartily glad to hear of the Cretans and Armenians rising against their tyrants, especially if that could be done without furnishing them with a fresh set of tyrants in the form of westernised stock-jobbers subservient to the world-market, as I fear it could not. But we must not forget meanwhile that these 'atrocities' are nothing more than the form which exploitation takes in rough societies; and that our own workers *forced* to live (?) in slums, to work in the factory hell, to have to *enjoy* bad beer and a low music hall as *their* share of the comforts and luxuries of civilisation, can show 'atrocities' in competition with Crete, Armenia – or Hell, and that their case is a pretty considerable 'disgrace to Europe,' as the newspaper posters were phrasing it the other day.

For again let us remember that while the 'atrocities' in Crete are spasmodic, the atrocities in England are chronic: *they* are always going on day after day, though we sometimes sprinkle a little rose-water on them in the hope (?) of a

remedy. The very fact that the Cretan peasants can raise such
a clamour over their sufferings shows that they have a well-
grounded hope of their ceasing. What hope can our slum-
dwellers have of curing their sufferings? Only those of them
can have formed a hope who, dimly it may be, see the Social
Revolution advancing.

———————————

To think that there are people in England by the hundred
thousand who *cannot* hope for happiness because they have
had no opportunity of forming an idea of what happiness is!
Yet this is the foundation on which our modern society rests.

Commonweal, Volume 5, Number 197,
19 October 1889, p. 329.

NOTES ON NEWS

The last few elections, though they prove little in themselves, yet taken with other symptoms seem to show that, unless something very startlingly unexpected happens, the Gladstonites will have a majority in the next Parliament, and even make it probable that there will be a dissolution before long. The fact is that the swing of the pendulum is operating; the promise of performance of the old government has died out; they have pretty much exhausted their powers of pretentious do-nothing plus coercion, and people are beginning to think, 'Now let us have a general election, and give the other fellows a turn.'

Well, so be it! We shall weep dry-eyed for the Tories; who, to speak shortly, are always and everywhere our declared and deadly enemies, and who include no section that can be of any use to us except as stimulating revolt by their stupid reactionism. Let us hope that no single Socialist and no group of workers will be taken in by the game of the Tory Democrats and their coquetting with one side of Social Democracy, or State Socialism, whichever you may please to call it. The Irish prisons show us pretty well what the meaning of Tory State Socialism really is. Let us remember that it can never go further than this – the bettering of one or more groups of workmen at the expense of other groups, the whole to be paid for by votes at the next election; which votes will, of course, be used for coercion in some form or other.

At the same time I don't see how we can throw up our hats very high for the advent of the Liberals to power. All we can hope of them is that they will be forced to clear away the Irish matter for awhile: though no doubt they, as well as the Tories, would be glad enough if they could keep on lugging it backwards and forwards as a convenient red herring across the trail of the welfare of the workers.

———————

But when they have done that, what next? Will they even be near adopting the programme of the Socialist Radicals? which itself means nothing unless it is at once going to become real Socialism. It is pretty clear that they cannot turn themselves into incipient Socialists. It will be the old story: a few more Radicals more advanced than earlier Radicals were, but quite powerless in Parliament; a great accession to the strength of the Whigs, who as soon as the crisis is over will turn their minds to becoming more Tory than the Tories themselves.

———————

This is the regular history of party government in England. A Tory government with a Whig opposition, backed by a Radical revolt according to the ideas of Radicalism current at the time. The Radicals (as notably now the Socialist Radicals) make a great stir, and begin to move popular public opinion. They get the Whigs in, and these, when in, kick the Radicals to the devil, where they may do what they can.

———————

This is quite sure to happen once more. Let us hope that it will be a dangerous game for the Whigs this time, and that *after* the kick, since they won't do it before, the Socialist Radicals will drop the latter end of their name, which means nothing, and become real Socialists looking forward to revolution as the only possible true change, and relegating the phrase 'Parliamentary reform' to Mr. Murray's new dictionary of the English language.

Commonweal, Volume 5, Number 198,
26 October 1889, p. 337.

NOTES ON NEWS

Mr. Gladstone's speech to the working-men of Saltney last week, though as long as need be, and doubtless as attractive to the platitude-lover in its oratory as his utterances usually are, scarcely needs much comment in detail; it plays the same wearisome tune which we have been used to hear played from the period of 'leaps and bounds' onward. It is called optimistic, but really and truly is in the depths of pessimism; for this is the meaning of it.

'Friends, *we* are very comfortable, and we should be glad if *you* also could be so, always so long as your comfort takes away nothing from us. To say the truth we fear that you are *not* living in comfort, but since it is for *our* good that you should go on living as you do, pray endure your misery, and don't try to alter matters. Meantime, we will do you this service, if no other; we will pretend that you are getting better and better as the days go on, and that really compared with what you were half a century ago (when you were all but in universal open revolt against us), you are quite happy, or at least ought to be. So be contented, thrifty, and hopeful – of *our* continued prosperity.'

This sort of poisonous and lying twaddle was what was *always* said by Liberal politicians when addressing the workers twenty, nay, ten years ago; it now needs a G.O.M. to say it in its completeness. Does the dim old man believe it, I wonder? Perhaps he does, as much as a hardened old politician can be said to believe anything. But just fancy this preacher of contentment, this old Conservative gentleman, being the dangerous revolutionary person who used to terrify the Tories so! He has undergone the usual fate of political heroes, and is now a stationary mile-stone on the road, marking the rate of progress which live men are making.

The Art Congress just over at Edinburgh was on the whole but a dull affair, and would have been very dull indeed but that to a Socialist its humours showed some signs of the times. It goes without saying, that though there were people present who were intent on playing the part of the art-philanthropists, all the paper-readers, except the declared Socialists, showed an absurd ignorance of the very elements of economics; and also, of course, that the general feeling was an ignoring of the existence of the working-class except as instruments to be played on.

Education was much talked of; but it was not understood that if you have condemned a man to be a slave, his education *must* be that of a slave. Art for the working-classes was talked of by men who chose to ignore the fact that men anxiously facing starvation, or wearily bearing it, are not free to receive pleasure from a work of art; although at the Congress meetings the clock-hands pointing to lunch-time at once emptied the room of the well-fed audience. Socialist artists and craftsmen (since there were none but Socialists capable of taking up the job) were set to lecture audiences of Edinburgh workmen on the due methods of work for producing popular art, though both lecturers and workmen audience knew but too well that such art was impossible for wage-slaves either to make or enjoy.

However, the said lecturers did not hide this fact under a bushel: and since a reactionist Edinburgh evening paper angrily declared that the Socialists had ruined the Congress, it is probable that their plain speaking had some effect. It must also be said that the working-men audiences received any allusion to Socialism, or any teaching founded on it, with more than assent, with enthusiasm rather. The definitely Socialist meetings, held under the auspices of our Edinburgh friends, were very successful, and the local Socialists are well satisfied with the result of the week.

Commonweal, Volume 5, Number 200, 9 November 1889, p. 356.

NOTES ON NEWS

A curious article in the *Pall Mall Gazette* is a good example of how far the force of conventional ignorance can go. It is in praise of advertisements, and its writer actually says, and I suppose really does think, that advertisements cheapen wares! Says he, 'The morning cup of cocoa pays for the morning newspaper,' thinking apparently that the said cocoa is cheapened by its having to bear its share of the advertising-rag, differentiated by this that or the other political humbug, which we are pleased to call a newspaper.

Did it ever occur to this very droll writer that the said advertising sheet cost *labour*, and that that labour might have been employed in producing things useful to the citizens, instead of puffing the private adventure of some capitalist which has for its object the robbing of anyone who will allow himself to be robbed?

An advertisement is, in short, an act of war, and cheapens wares just as much as a battery trampling down a wheatfield cheapens bread. If the *Pall Mall Gazette* in its enthusiasm for advertisement, and the rotten rags called newspapers, would give us the statistics of advertising of all kinds, say in the form of the 'Puffer's Almanack,' it would earn my eternal gratitude.

Another *Pall Mall* writer (or perhaps the same) has a rapturous article on the subject of the Eiffel Tower, and hopes we shall have several in London. Now as to its beauty (?) tastes differ, but I shall not allow myself to be bullied by

Philistia into silence even on that point; so I say that it appeared to me a hellish piece of ugliness; but let that pass. But what is the meaning or use of it? Its use is simply to catch francs. All the labour of the thousands of workmen employed on it has been devoted to the erection of a franc-catching trap; a piece of brigandage on the public.

That teacher of the public, the *Pall Mall Gazette*, ought to be able to see that these Eiffel Towers, advertisements, and the rest of it, are on one side of them mere acts of war of the predatory classes, the capitalists; and on the other bonfires wherewith to burn up the energies of the working-men, to waste their labour as much as if it had never been; to have fed, clothed, and housed the men who built the Eiffel Tower without providing them with 'employment' would have been comparatively an act of wisdom. This is the kind of folly, to pay for which the lives of the workers are worn away in shame without their ever having had a day's real pleasure. Do not let us tolerate for a single moment any act of the accursed thing – Capitalism.

Commonweal, Volume 5, Number 201, 16 November 1889, p. 361.

NOTES ON NEWS

The success of the bakers' strike is producing the usual crop of advice from the capitalistic press. They are told, for instance, that now would be the time to form a union between the masters and men, a kind of court of conciliation between the two bodies whose interests are opposed to each other by the very nature of the arrangement between masters and men. Fancy a court of conciliation between a Roman landowner, of the time of the great revolt of the slaves, and the unskilled labourers of *his* factory-farm! And then remember that the modern employee and the above-said landowner are essentially in the same position, except that the ancient slave-owner had to *buy* his slave while the modern one has his slave gratis.

Meanwhile, our baker friends no doubt think that they are lucky, and that ten hours is a short days work. I do not; neither will they in a year's time. Besides, of one thing they may be sure, that their masters are even now engaged in considering how and in what form they shall take back the advantages (real ones this time, I admit) which have been gained by the men. As for them, their attitude must be a fighting one, until their fighting has abolished masters and they set themselves to work like men, and are no longer set to work like machines.

Baron Huddlestone's zeal for his employers, the governing classes, has probably not done them much good; he has a little overdone it, and made it somewhat clearer than it was before that the impartiality of the law, when it is a question of freedom *versus* respectability, is a transparent fiction. If that pretence were to be maintained, would not a judge, even as a matter of decency, be *expected* to give his charge on some such principles as these? – 'I am a Tory, a reactionist, and as such I look on Mrs. Besant's views with the greatest horror; if the jury are to be left free in their verdict, and both sides have fair play, I must all the more not express my personal and party views; so I will just tell them what the law is and not say a word more.'

That is what the baron *might have been* expected to say if the governing classes (largely manned by lawyers) cared to keep up even the pretence of fairness in the law courts. But, as it is, no one expected him to do anything but what he did do, that is act as an advocate for the defence. Clearly, therefore, no one expects the law courts to be fair in cases *where any public interest is involved.* And other cases – what business have they to be tried at all at the expense of the public? Our whole system of civil and criminal law is as regards the upper classes, whose instrument it is, a mere muddle of incongruities, and as regards the workers a mere instrument of oppression. And the fact is that the upper classes put up with those preposterous incongruities, *because* in spite of their absurdity they do not injure the system much *as* an instrument for the oppression of the poor, which is its primary purpose.

Imperial Federation is on its dunghill again, but not crowing very loud in the person of Lord Rosebury, who, though he began with some Jingo sentences of the usual type and ended with conventional rubbish about the Anglo-Saxon race and the Amphictyonic Council, employed the greater part of his time in pointing out with some skill that Imperial Federation is impossible, and that it is a mere party cry to catch votes.

In case any of our readers should be caught by the sound of the word 'Federation,' I must remind them that this 'Imperial

628   Journalism

Federation' means in the first place, a Jingo competitive scheme for doing as much injury as possible to all peoples and countries outside the British Empire; and in the second place, a plot for setting schemes a-foot for bolstering up the tottering capitalist *régime* by finding new markets for it; that is to say, new commercial fields for the exercise of the 'sword of cheapness.' It is, in short, one of the dams which the middle-classes are building against the rising flood of Socialism. Happily, it is a dam built of paper and big words.

Mr. Goschen on the stump at Cardiff said some rather smart things about the Liberal party, and amongst others, in answer to cheers for Gladstone, wished that in the new Liberal Government the G.O.M. could have the real ordering of affairs, quoting (naturally with approbation) G.O.M.'s servility about the Royal Grants, and then going on to say that Gladstone would be controlled by Parnell, and his lieutenants by various politicians supposed to be progressive. This is amusing, but couldn't Goschen have carried it further and told us who were to control the controllers? I am afraid that the said controllers, Parnell, Tim Healy, Labouchere, and the rest, are at once too stupid and too political (*i.e.*, false) to allow the people and common sense to control them. They will just stand with staring eyes and gasping mouth, not knowing what to do – but to stick to office.

For the rest, Mr. Goschen was somewhat too optimistic. 'The system of limited liability and a wider diffusion of wealth had made working-men capitalists in a small way, and given them not only profits on their wages [what *does* that mean?] but on the capital they invested. Did not this result prove [?!!] the fact that capital was not antagonistic to labour, but was really the accumulated earnings of labour? Capital was no longer regarded as a kind of vampire, for workmen had a large share in the increased prosperity of the country, and they were entitled to it.'

Mr. Goschen must have a strong belief in the gullibility of working-men to deliver himself before them of such a mass of lies and twaddle. But he appears to have been justified by the ignorance of the Cardiff workmen, who hooted him for his political views and cheered him for his economics (?). But really, I repeat, he is too optimistic. Things have got a little further than that, thanks to the Socialist propaganda: working-men who are 'capitalists' know that their 'small way' is a very small way; that their wages are even in times of 'prosperity' none too large to be eaten, worn, and paid to the rent-collector. They are at this moment showing all over the country that capital *is* antagonistic to labour by *forcing* capitalists to pay them more.

It is true that some of them know that 'capital is the accumulated earnings of labour'; but more still know that they are robbed of their earnings, and the number of these is increasing every day, and more and more workmen are becoming alive to the fact that (individualist) capital is a kind of vampire – and the worst kind – and that in spite of the large share they have in the 'prosperity' of the country, they have no share in *its land*, but must swelter in slums summer and winter, enjoying no beauty or pleasure of the 'land they live in,' with leave when they come out of their slums to 'move on' on the highway and nothing else, under penalties of fine and imprisonment.

'At present,' says this trickster, this battener on other men's labour, 'things are prosperous, and prosperity does not give rise to violent political changes.' Letting alone the baseness of the cowardice which thus hugs itself on the supposed sloth and apathy of the oppressed, we might ask this person how long this prosperity will last, and what kind of changes the next depression following on inflation will give rise to? Let us meanwhile go on steadily with our propaganda, in the hope that not *all* men are curs who will be 'contented' with a little more dogs' wages than they have been having of late; that not *all* men are so stupid as to be humbugged by politicians of the Goschen type.

Commonweal, Volume 5, Number 202,
23 November 1889, p. 369.

NOTES ON NEWS

There is an exhibition on show, it seems, for 'Garments for the Poor.' It is a difficult thing to see how such an exhibition can be made a novelty, considering the many exhibitions in which the triumphs of cheap labour and shoddy are set forth, and which are open to all and several (who have any money in their pockets) under various glowing titles, which, however, do not conceal the fact that they are the markets of the miserable; shops where wares are sold which no one would buy if he had not been forced to labour for nothing by a robber. Really, I don't see how this new exhibition can compete with Petticoat Lane, as a remarkable object – as a sign of our civilisation.

But if I might give a hint to the promoters of this exhibition, here it is. I suppose that those to whom they give the new garments adapted to their condition of life, when they take the new will strip off the old. Well, suppose these were collected and an exhibition made of them, the garments *of* the poor, instead of *for* them. If the gift of garments were done on a large enough scale, the cast-off clothes might make an exhibition of some interest for us of the well-to-do class, and might prepare us for that Exhibition of the Poor themselves, which will take place one day, and will be an imposing ceremony for those of the rich who may chance to survive it.

In fact, if I had dropped down from the moon into a London reading-room and had got hold of a newspaper, I should have said to myself, 'The Poor, who are they? They seem to be a very lucky set of people; here are folk always doing something for them, which they wouldn't do for anybody else! Why, amongst other things, here's a man given them £250,000, whatever that means!'

However, not having come into England by way of the moon, I am rather puzzled about this 'magnificent gift to the London Poor,' and am principally sure of one thing, that if I were a member of that much-cared-for body, I would willingly speculate on my share of the said £250,000, and take, say, a pound of sausages in exchange for my chance; and meantime, I should like to ask a question or two.

---

1. How is the donor going to get at the poor so that they may receive the 'gift'?
2. He will build houses with it, will he? Well, when built, who is to inhabit them? and on what terms?

   (a) Are the 'poor' to live rent free in them?
   (b) Or to pay rent below the market value of them?
   (c) If so, who amongst the poor are to be thus favoured?
   (d) And where are the rest going to live?

3. Or is this, after all, another building company to whom the Guinness is going to lend his money?

When all these questions are answered quite satisfactorily, and I am so far assured that a gift has been given, I have still another question to ask, namely, *Where did the money come from?*

The Brazilian revolution would appear to be, as Mr. Cunninghame Graham hints, a revolution of the ordinary political type which does not touch the workers at all, but it *may* turn out otherwise. If so we shall soon see. It will not be a matter of 'freeing' the slaves in the bourgeois sense of the word; that may be done, as we in England know too well,

without making one stroke at the slavery of poverty. If the
Brazilian revolution is to be a real one, Capitalism, the root
of all evil, must be attacked definitely; then we shall believe
in it. 'By their fruits ye shall know them.'

We have lost by death an energetic worker in the Cause,
William Sharman, who, although he was addressed by the
title of 'reverend,' had long shaken off any priestly
assumption of dogmatism or special holiness. William
Sharman was one of those Unitarian preachers who have
become entirely convinced of the truth of Socialism, and see
no reason for keeping their light under a bushel; he was a
centre of Socialism in a very unsocialistic neighbourhood,
and quietly and steadily did much good; a genial, unselfish
man, his personal friends will miss him sorely.

Commonweal, Volume 5, Number 203,
30 November 1889, p. 377.

NOTES ON NEWS

Clothes again! This time it is an advertisement in a pushing draper's catalogue of 'Charity clothes, as supplied to her Majesty.' At first sight this appears to emanate from a 'boiling-over' Radical Republican, annoyed by the fact that he and his like are paying rather heavily for the pension of royalty which has ceased to earn its money but not ceased to draw it; for surely all 'her Majesty's' outfit is 'charity.' The other interpretation is that the advertiser supposes that the Queen follows the fashion of which an example was mentioned last week of kindly considering the position of the 'poor' by taking care not to give them clothes which would compromise them and cause them to be mistaken for persons above them. Is not this over-anxiety? The poor wear a livery of their own not easy to mistake.

Well, well, the poor go on with the strain of luck mentioned in our issue of last week! Here are people again who want to teach them how to cook. If once they learn that, they will so far be ahead of their fellow-countrymen or women. Perhaps the next thing after teaching them how to cook will be to allow them to get hold of something which can be cooked – and eaten.

Lord Salisbury's Nottingham manifesto will be a disappointment to those opportunist semi (of demi-semi) Socialists who look upon the Tories as possible allies in the enterprise for the abolition of Toryism. His admissions came to no more than this, that the Irish Question had been played out in its function of football to the two 'great' parties who are playing the game of political jobbery, and that some other football must be found. For the rest, his speech on 'Social Questions' was the usual string of platitudes, contradictions, and falsities which make up the big lie political.

So remarkably stupid it was, that one is tempted at first sight to think that the Marquis was restraining his wisdom and knowledge for the sake of talking down to the comprehension of his Tory audience; but a moment's reflection shows one that whatever intelligence the man once possessed has long ago been drowned in the muddy sea of political dishonesty: he was no whit better than his audience.

For after all, what was the real meaning of his stale sham-economics? It is very simple, and should read thus: 'My friends, we are living in ticklish times, in which Socialism (about which we know nothing) is advancing on us rapidly. Some of our party are in favour of recognising the fact and tossing some considerable tub to the whale; I don't see my way to that, for we have no tub to toss that we don't want ourselves; so I am in favour of ignoring the advance of Socialism altogether. So you had better go about and say that the working-man will be no better off for having less work and more pay, and that since the land of England is only half-cultivated he had better emigrate at once to countries which produce less wealth at the expense of more labour. And look here! you had better say, also, that the question as to whether the workman is to have more than a bare subsistence (*i.e.*, starvation) wage is a matter of 'philanthropy.'

Thus much Lord Salisbury, who, it must be said, makes a very halting advance towards the progressive side. But the other party, will they come any further? That seems more than doubtful. The Whig Rag, for instance, in commenting on the marquis's speech, while attacking his political views, is highly satisfied with his social and (save the mark!)

economical utterances. The workers had better not trouble
themselves in the least as to what such worn-out nullities as
Salisbury and Gladstone may say, but look to it not to wait
to have things given them, but take them for themselves.
The gifts will mean nothing; they will be like the fairy gold in
the old tale which turns into dry leaves in the morning light.

Commonweal, Volume 5, Number 204,
7 December 1889, p. 385.

NOTES ON NEWS

At first sight the programme put forward by the Gladstonians at Manchester seems like an advance towards the Socialist-Radical position, and as if they were determined to avoid being dished by the Tories. However, the Radicals had better not halloo till they are out of the wood; for they must remember that there is a very wide distance between what a caucus meeting of the Outs will put forward as a promise, and what a party in office will attempt to carry.

Let the Radicals who think that they have a chance of being something more than the tail of the Liberal party, note the significant difference between the reception of such startling revolutionary novelties (?) as the giving of some real powers to the County Councils, the taxing of ground-rents, etc., and a bit of the regular old caucus programme, the Disestablishment of the Scotch and Welsh Churches. The assembled delegates had received the announcement of the former with decent signs of approbation, but they roared with delight at the announcement of the latter.

Now, certainly, we must all admit that it is a good thing that all churches should be disestablished; but to express such unbounded enthusiasm for a subject so stale, such a foregone conclusion, is ominous of the Gladstonian future, and shows that the Liberal party might almost as well be called the Nonconformist party, and that we may look forward after the tremendous birth-pangs of the political mountain to see a small Whig mouse (or rat rather) creep forth on to the surface of things, and the Radicals with their mongrel and impossible demi-semi-Socialist programme as hopelessly excluded from any Parliamentary political power as ever.

Whatever power the Radicals may have now, they have in virtue of their making some approach toward Socialism amongst a population who is beginning to have an inkling of Socialism; but that very power with the people makes them weak in Parliament, which is a mere drag on popular aspirations. And in any case they (the Radicals) only have any reason for existence as a party because the mass of the people is only *beginning* to turn towards Socialism. When the people understand the matter better, the Radicals of to-day, who are anything better than political tricksters, will have become Socialists, and the rest of them will be declared reactionists.

There never will nor can be a Radical party in Parliament; that belongs to the days when Radicalism saw nothing ahead of itself in progress. It has now become quite conscious of some form of Socialism being its necessary development. It is accepting its transitional position, and is waiting for the transformation to take place. Such a body must necessarily be too nebulous to form a political party, for it is of the essence of a political party to consider its position as a final one; that is to say, that a political party is the outcome of opinions which have been superseded in the minds of all thoughtful persons by new developments of thought. It is no longer the growing fruit-tree, but the dead log; useful – for burning.

The Radicals, therefore, are to be congratulated for their powerlessness as a political party; it is a sign of life and growth in them. As for Mr. Gladstone's Manchester audiences, it is clear that they were, as aforesaid, Nonconformist Whigs; and they were engaged in devising the best form of giving the people stones for bread.

The strikes which are now taking place have a tendency which is noteworthy, and surely, amidst all shortcomings, encouraging. They are not merely strikes for a rise of wages, but show a desire for independence on the part of the men; strikes against blacklegs, or against the imposition of conditions under the guise of a gift. This, we may well hope, shows that the workers are gradually becoming conscious that their existence as workers means that they are engaged in a class war. That whatever gains they make, whatever improvements in their condition they conquer, must be at the expense of the master-class.

They will be aided in this new acquirement of knowledge by the attitude of the middle class, which a month or two ago was so 'sympathetic.' For in the struggle against blackleg treachery and the dictation of conditions by the masters they need look for no 'sympathy' from the master-class. Expressions of sorrow at their having made such a mistake as to take the step absolutely necessary to true combination they will get in plenty, if that is any good to them; but, for the rest, it will be the kind masters who are so generously offering to share profits with their men who will receive the 'sympathy of the public.'

A word about this profit-sharing. What is it but a feeding of the dog with his own tail? It means on the one hand a writing down in the account-books of wages as profits shared by the men; while on the other hand its gets more work out of the men than the obvious wage-paying for the same money paid, and is, of course, praised by its advocates for that very reason. For the rest, the men are quite right in seeing in it a dodge to break up their organisation; an instrument for detaching some of the men from furthering the interests of their class by deluding them into thinking that their interests are one with those of their masters, who, if only they had eyes to see, are visibly living on their labour. Whether the gas-stokers' strike fails or not, the mere fact that the men

have gained this much of insight into the capitalist trickery is
very encouraging.

A curmudgeon (name of no importance) is determined to
put the pretty river Mole, or certain reaches of it, into his
own pocket, and the public is naturally angry at the
proceeding, to the extent of forming a society for the
protection of the said river; but as their only means of
'protection' seems to be going to law with its owner, it is
certain that the Mole will remain pocketed till 'when the
revolution comes.'

For my part, I sympathise heartily with the sorrow of those
who have been locked out of the Mole; for I should like to
live on a river three quarters of the year; and the Mole is an
exceedingly pretty little meadow-stream. But on the other
hand it is no bad thing that the middle class – even the lower
at that – should have a reminder of their position in relation
to the landowners. I must say to them, 'You *would* have it
so, my friends! *Now* perhaps you begin to understand the
meaning of the "sacred rights of property," the right of using
and *abusing* wealth, which is so dear to the souls of the
Liberty and Property Defence League. Turn Socialists my
friends, and one day you shall have the Mole again.'

Commonweal, Volume 5, Number 205,
14 December 1889, p. 393.

NOTES ON NEWS

The 'intelligent and sympathetic' middle-classes do not seem to have had the strike-fever in a very severe form. After having contributed to the victory of the dockers (whatever that amounted to), they seem to have thought that they had exhausted all the claims that could be made on their 'intelligent sympathy,' and allowed the poor folk at Silvertown to be slowly crushed down by capitalist tyranny, without showing any signs that they were conscious of that terrible struggle against starvation with or without employment.

Of course, I except Stopford Brooke's eloquent appeal for justice to these poor people; but it fell upon the ears of a class who were not going to accept two such bothers in one year as *two* strikes that shocked their sensibility.

As to the gas-stokers' strike, that is quite another matter. For are they not in the receipt of quite splendid wages? Don't they get as much in a week as a very small gentleman of the proprietary class, or the parasitical class, gets in a day? What on earth can they want more? They want to be free to strike, forsooth, in case their employer thinks fit to put on the screw! What next? They will get ideas of independence into their heads, and what becomes of us, then, the pensioners, of us the parasites? No, no, this is no case for sympathy; these men are our *enemies*, and, what is more, are beginning to know it. Instead of subscribing *for* them, let us use brute force *against* them, and show them that *they* shall not be allowed to argue with their fellow-workmen.

Well, gentlemen! there is much truth in this view of your period of convalescence from the strike fever. These men are indeed your enemies, for their interests are opposed to yours; and as a class, gentlemen, whatever you may think in your more maudlin moments, when your hypocrisy gets so much the better of your tyrannical greed that it even deceives yourselves, you will not and cannot give up anything to the workers beyond the mere subsistence wage according to the standard of the day, unless you are compelled to do so by force; *i.e.*, by the fear of material injury to your purse or persons.

And that standard of the day, gentlemen, do you really trouble yourselves as to the lowness of it? the horror and disgrace of such a mass of semi-starvation? Silvertown did not move you. And indeed why should it have done so, when such a livelihood is so common? When you know, or could know by asking a very few questions, what the standard of livelihood is for our field-labourers! When you know, and cannot help knowing, that you have made the beautiful garden-like country-side of England into a mere hell of barrenness for the people who feed you! A hell from which the country people flee to that other hell of the city slums, to make for you fresh entanglements of that 'social problem' that you gabble about continuously – with no real intention of trying to solve it.

Who can wonder, so sweet as life is for rich people in our civilisation? Nothing short of the fear of imminent break-up, of a break-up of the 'status and lives' of those now living at least, can really fix their attention on the fate of the 'nation of the poor' amongst whom they dwell; and, for the rest, the strikes do not seem to them threatening enough for them to trouble much about them. As for the field-labourers, they know how weak they are; perhaps they think them weaker than they really are; and the cry of 'the land for the people' frightens them so little, that some of them will even coquette with it in the game of politics, which is the top amusement of the proprietary classes. Let us hope that we may live to see the day when they will learn what it really means – to wit, the abolition of the class of compulsory pensioners.

I wonder whether these strike-cured gentlemen noted, as I did, a little incident of civilisation which took place the other day about the Solomon Islands, where one of our war-ships was used for the safe amusement of 'punishing' the islanders for cannibalism? Did it in that case occur to them, as it did to me, that while the poor devils of Solomon Islanders were engaged in eating their enemies, the 'superior persons' of British Islanders were eating the people whom they call their friends and fellow-countrymen; their equals before the law, and before God, as the cant phrase goes?

Cannibalism for cannibalism, it seems to me, that that of the poor ignorant poverty-stricken Solomon Islanders is less deserving of punishment than that of the British Islanders; and that the word 'punishment' ought to make the latter shake in their shoes, if ever they think, as I fear few of them do, of the natural results of artificial compulsory poverty in a land which nature and the traditions of labour would make so wealthy for all people if the non-producers did not eat up the lives of the producers after the manner of civilised cannibalism.

Commonweal, Volume 5, Number 207, 28 December 1889, p. 409.

CONTRIBUTIONS TO *COMMONWEAL*

1890

NOTES ON NEWS

The *Labour Elector* appeals to the mass of the trades' union workmen, and is supposed to do something toward teaching them; but one of its last efforts in this direction is not a happy one. English people are fond of boasting that they do not hit a man when he is down; but here is the *Labour Elector* attacking Mr. Parke in a way that it is difficult to characterise, although he is in prison for doing what most people believe he thought to be his duty.

Mr. Parke has made a mistake, and is paying a frightful penalty for it. Twelve month's persistent and intentional torture, administered by a pedantic system that does not recognise humanity except as an inconvenient something to be repressed, one would think sufficient 'punishment' for any 'crime' in the calendar, let alone the crime of a mere mistake, which any generous-minded man would at once forgive. But this is not enough for the '*Newest* Journalism'; which out-herods Herod, out-*Saturdays* the *Saturday*, in calling for pit, gallows and rack in defence of an injured society. Really, the *Labour Elector* has learned its lesson from its coercionists friends only too well. It seems bent on reducing political persecution to an absurdity.

The bourgeois papers are congratulating the German Socialists on their victory over Bismark, but to a Socialist onlooker it does not seem so tremendous, or at least must be read by the light of the extra-coercionist state of things in Germany. For the only doubts that the respectable parties had was as to the best method of damaging Socialism; and all the Liberals wanted to do apparently was to get a coercionist bill which should have a certain amount of respectability about it, so that it might last the longer and be put in force the more rigorously.

The Tory gentleman, Prince Zu Carolath, who spoke against the Bill and so astonished his colleagues, appears to be rather a Simple Simon. To us, at any rate, the crushing of Socialism by intellectual argument seems rather like a joke; since by this time nobody but Professor Huxley or the regular debating-club bore ventures to argue against Socialism in front; let alone that it seems rather late in the day for the countrymen of Karl Marx and Lassalle to *begin* to talk of intellectual opposition. But no doubt there is something in the argument that brutal coercion consolidates a forward movement.

An article in the *Star* the other day carried the 'We are all Socialists now' about as far as that stale piece of cant could be carried. 'We have had municipal Socialism for fifty years,' said its writer. Have we indeed? It must be a valuable article, then, considering how it has abolished all the evils of which Labour has to complain! Let alone the London slums, I could show our *Star* friends a biggish population in the fields of merry (?) England to whom Socialism of any kind would be of some advantage if it were real. Whereabouts is this municipal Socialism? I should like to find out. I think it must be Socialism for the rich; that is the reason why we cannot find it out; they keep it to themselves, I suppose, like they do all the rest of their stealings.

Commonweal, Volume 6, Number 212, 1 February 1890, p. 33.

NOTES ON NEWS

The *Daily News*, in giving a glowing account of the Gladstonian meeting, of which William O'Brien and John Morley were the bosses, says that it would be a great mistake to suppose that the country is tired of the Irish question; that this feeling of weariness does not exist outside the London clubs, etc. Perhaps a Tory would answer with the proverb, 'He who excuses himself accuses himself.' Why should the *Daily News* suppose that people are tired of the Irish question? To speak plainly there is no doubt that everybody that is not a professional politician is heartily tired of the Irish question *as it has been presented to us*. In other words, it has about served the business for which it was taken up by the politicians, *i.e.*, a game over which people could get desperately angry so that they might forget the real matters of importance – matters of life and death that are crying out to us.

The Irish are beaten then? All this excitement has been for nothing? No, surely not. On the contrary the English democrat has made up his mind, and for him the Anglo-Irish tyranny is a thing of the past. I suspect also that the intelligent Tory (if there be such a thing) has made up *his* mind also, and is preparing for a climb down by means of the inevitable ladder of compromise.

The real point to be noticed in the lull on the subject of Home Rule is this, it has lost its *relative* importance because of the advance of opinion within these last years. It is no longer the Great Wrong to be righted by the Great Redresser of Wrongs, the Great Liberal Party under the leadership of the G.O.M.   Many Radicals, I think, honestly believed in this once, and thought that they, the freemen, could set this nation of slaves free.

All that is gone indeed! How fast the 'wide-roaring loom of time' goes! How the web is changing! The Irish peasant oppressed by his landlord is not the only figure that the English workman sees on whom to exercise his political heroism, for he sees himself also in pretty much the same condition as his Irish brother, and for him to give freedom to any one before he has got it for himself is beginning to seem to him a dull job.   The Irish question is getting to be swallowed up in the one question of classes.   As a political football it has been pretty much kicked to pieces.   But the Irish working-man, under whatever name, need not trouble himself about that.   That he could be freed from *his* exploiter while other workmen were groaning under theirs, was a mere delusion of his, and the only hope for his freedom lies in the awakening of his English brethren.

In commenting on the proceedings of the Society for the Preservation of Footpaths, the *Daily News* says of the stealers of footpaths: 'Generally the attempt is made more from want of thought than from any desire to rob the public.'   H'm, well; I don't think landowners do these things in their sleep. I remember a country lawyer telling me that the chief part of his business came from his devising means for the shutting up of rights of way.   I asked him what he thought of his career set beside that of Jack Sheppard, and he replied that he must live.   He seemed rather hurt by my views on *that* question.

Commonweal, Volume 6, Number 213,
8 February 1890, p. 41.

NOTES ON NEWS

The Kaiser has quite fluttered the capitalistic doves by his rescripts. Of course we get the irrepressible article in the *Pall Mall Gazette,* assuring us once more that we are indeed all Socialists now, and praising heaven for the House of Hohenzollern and this last development of Monarchism. Of course, on the other hand, we get the general 'Pooh! pooh!' of the orthodox capitalistic press, both Liberal and Tory.

Most of them say, 'Ah! Kaiser, here's an opportunity for you! If you would only be good like us English, and have free trade, *then* we would go to your Congress; *then*, at last, and not before, would be the time to consider whether our working population should starve or thrive – or, at all events, to pretend to consider it. For, of course, you will understand, that while free trade is a practical question *to us*, the questions you are suggesting of the duration of the day's labour, the conditions of factories, and so forth, have ceased to be practical questions to us since we passed the consolidation of the Factory Acts in order to make the Factory Hell respectable. And as to *our* working-classes, we assure you we are not at all afraid of them; they are sheep and like to be shorn, and if they baa a bit under the operation, our nerves are strong enough to bear it. Liberty of the press! Free competition! Unrestricted march of economic laws! Free Trade! Imitate us and keep on bawling out these phrases, which cost nothing, and you will live peacefully and die happy.'

Well, perhaps! And yet, on the surface of things, it scarcely seems likely that the Kaiser should set out on his enterprise of dishing the Socialists without some reason behind him, even if his step be only an electioneering dodge, as seems likely. It is not unreasonable to suppose that he is impressed, not to say alarmed, by the spread of Socialism, and feels that it would be no bad stroke if he could detach a considerable body of working-men from the Socialist party: a thing which he may consider possible in Germany, where the superstition of loyalty is yet strong. At any rate, if the workers refuse to bite at his phantom minnow, his 'intentions' will help to respectablise his position amongst the respectables of all Europe, and in no case will they cost him much. For who knows if the quarrel with Bismark is anything else than a bit of stage effect?

Commonweal, Volume 6, Number 214, 15 February 1890, p. 49.

NOTES ON NEWS

The labouring mountain of the Parnell Commission has at last produced its mouse; which is in fact the final acceptance of Mr. Parnell into decent political society. If this was the aim of the *Times* in its 'Parnellism and Crime,' that renowned paper has been eminently successful. But in view of its own comments on the Report we can hardly accept that theory. We must admit that the *Times* has been heavily thrown; and the *Times* was, or perhaps *is*, one of the chief bulwarks of respectability.

———————————

Yet, it *is* breaking up, this respectable 'Society' of oppression, which it is the business of Socialists to attack. It is shaken in its policy of bluster, and the carrying of everything by means of the high hand. The mere political business of Home Rule will not last much longer as a pretext for our political tricksters. They will be face to face presently with the necessities of the working people, not only of Ireland, but of England and Scotland also; and in that position they will be absolutely helpless.

Commonweal, Volume 6, Number 215,
22 February 1890, p. 57.

NOTES ON NEWS

It seems that Bismark really has resigned, and yet the world hangs together and has not been dispersed into space. Exultation at the disappearance from active life of this most prosaic of all tyrants, this tyrant of a commercial age, is checked by the doubt as to whether it is not merely a theatrical stroke; as to whether he may not, after all, govern safely and irresponsibly under the veil of resignation. On the other hand, if circumstances have driven him to resign, it is once more a clear enough token of the advance which Socialism is making. Let us hope that it is so.

Commonweal, Volume 6, Number 219,
22 March 1890, p. 89.

NOTES

In commenting on the terrible tragedy at Crewe, which is indeed quite a typical example of the results of the conventional authority misnamed Society, the *Star* says, 'Whatever these boys are, they were made by the man whom they murdered,' and goes on to say that on these grounds apart from others the capital sentence should not be carried out. With both the conclusion and the reason for it we must most heartily agree. We would go further and say that if these lads are hanged, this second and judicial murder will quite throw the first homicide into the shade; further still we will go, and say that the fact that such a sentence should be given at all, amidst a sobbing court by a judge 'deeply affected,' is a good example of the horror of the tyranny of that false Society that enthralls us; especially when we know that the life or death of these two poor creatures now hangs on the mood of one not very wise man – the Home Secretary, to wit.

'Whatever these boys are, they were made by the man whom they murdered.' Just so; and is not that sentence, little altered, true also of by far the greater part of all the 'criminals' whom 'Society' slays and tortures so coolly, passing by on the other side like the priest and the Levite in the gospel? It has been said over and over again in these columns, but let us say it again as *the* moral of the Crewe murders: 'Society' first makes its enemies and then, dastard as it is, revenges itself upon them.

Commonweal, Volume 6, Number 220, 29 March 1890, p. 100.

NOTES ON NEWS

The great excitement of these last days, to wit, Mr. Balfour's Land Bill, will not excite Socialists, nor need they trouble their heads about the matter. On the face of it, it is a bill for raising the value of landlord's rents; but its real aim is to try to make the long-talked-out Irish question last a little longer as a piece of occupation for our 'representatives' in the House of Commons, which may delude the people into thinking that the said representatives are doing something. It is hoped, in fact, that the nearly used-up football will still hold wind enough to bear a little more kicking.

All honest men, whether they call themselves Socialists or not, will applaud the jury at the Leeds Assizes who had the courage of their opinions, and refused to hand over our comrade Bingham to the tender mercies of Justice Grantham, who was quite prepared to show the world that it is a dangerous thing for even a well-to-do man to have any aspirations towards better conditions of life than the present; dangerous, that is to say, if he expresses those aspirations openly; and if he keeps them to himself – well, it is an old saying of the philosophers, that there is no difference between that which is not, and that which is not visible.

It may be too much to hope that this verdict is the token of the beginning of a new epoch in jury-work, in which juries will give verdicts according to their consciences (and according to their oaths, too, if that matters) in spite of the judge's summing-up. But it is a significant fact that the verdict in this case was loudly applauded in Court by the general public.

It seems unlikely that the Crewe lads will be executed. But if they are not to be hanged, which, as Wilkes said, is the worst use to which you can put a man, why should they be treated to the second worst way of using a man, to wit, putting him in prison? To give a long term of imprisonment to these unfortunate young men would be a mere cruel piece of subservience to the letter of the law. Our friend, Mr. Grant Allen, acting on this view, has been circulating a petition to the Home Secretary asking for a free pardon or at least a short term of imprisonment. Surely all those people, from the judge upwards, who were so 'touched' in Court the other day, will agree to this.

Commonweal, Volume 6, Number 221,
5 April 1890, p. 105.

NOTES ON NEWS

Murder at Knutsford! dreadful murder! Dreadful enough
this time, certainly; only it has been committed practically by
the British nation, and therefore does not shock the moral
sense of comfortable easy-going people, who think, probably,
that it does not much matter to them, since they are never
likely to come into the clutches of the Judge and the Home
Secretary. But to those who have learned to feel the burden
of collective responsibility, these legal murders are far worse
than any of those homicides caused by passion or misery,
which our lawyer-rulers put side by side with the calculated
commercial slayings of such men as Palmer. The peculiar
baseness of Matthew's 'compromise' in this case is in fact
swallowed up by the shame which a person, not absolutely
stupefied by the cowardly convention of a 'society' founded
on wrong-doing, feels at such murders as those authorised by
law at Knutsford and Worcester. The only immediate
practical remedy for such horrors is that the juries should in
such cases return no more than a verdict of manslaughter.

Commonweal, Volume 6, Number 222,
12 April 1890, p. 116.

NOTES ON NEWS

In Mr. Morley's speech the other day, while talking about the subject of labour legislation, he said that though State Socialism was a bad thing yet it had this advantage, that it might save us from Revolutionary Socialism, which was a worse one. Political men are so sloppy in their public talk, that they probably seldom recognise the meaning which their words bear to the ordinary intelligent person; and probably all Mr. Morley meant by this phrase was to temporise with the tendency toward labour legislation while at the same time he declared himself opposed to Socialism. But what he has actually done is to ticket himself a reactionary before the world, and a stupid one at that.

For the plain meaning of his phrase is this, 'These measures you ask for will do you workmen more harm than good, that *I know*; but in order to amuse you, and prevent your looking into your own affairs too closely, I will yield with a good grace to your injuring yourselves; it will at least help in keeping things as they are.' Isn't this politics all over? That is, the completest development of charlatanry.

In the same spirit the House of Commons and the Liberal press have been dealing with the question of profit-sharing; the *Star* especially publishing an article on the subject, which is simply reactionary, and also very nonsensical and shilly-shally; with one hand putting forward *laissez faire*, with the other State Socialism, and always working the practical-politics wire, the shut-your-eyes-to-anything-that-is-not-before-Parliament platitude, which one would think too stale for even a daily paper by this time.

The *Star* says, 'We dismiss from our consideration all proposals which look to the twenty-first century for their realisation.' This is nothing but the usual platitudinary sneer of the debating-club bore; in the mouth of a writer in the *Star* it is either a dishonest evasion of the point at issue, or it is the result of the 'inevitable ignorance' of a reactionist masquerading as a Progressive Radical. I can only say that those who will not look to the essential principles of a serious subject are (I speak gravely) triflers and fools, and very dangerous fools too. Those who with all opportunity of learning what the true claims of labour are, do not learn to understand them, and who do not state them openly and simply when they have understood them, are doing their best to prepare for us a period of violence and misery in the twentieth century, or not improbably in what is left of the nineteenth.

The real question for all people not professed reactionaries is how can we speediest make an end of the disinheritance of the useful classes? How can we the speediest take the resources of nature out of the hands of the monopolists? And I assert that this profit-sharing business is not even an advance, however small, towards the answering of this question.

Here is a plain question or two on profit-sharing which every workman can understand. Will the workers who share in the profits have to pay rent to an individual for the land on which the factories stand? Will they have to pay interest to an individual for the capital which they use? Or, to put it in other words, will the factories which *they* have built, standing on the land which *their* labour has made valuable be *their* property, or the property of their masters who looked on while they were toiling?

Or, shall we say, What shall be the workers' share of profit? Will his employer claim extra shares, – first, because he is a manager; secondly, because he is a gambler in the world-market; and thirdly, because he is the owner of land or the instruments of labour?

Again, how many workers are to share in the profits? The dockers, the brickmakers, the navvies, the tram-men, the railway-men, the field labourers, the women and children whom the curse of commercialism has driven from their homes (when they have any) into the Factory Hell? Is the fringe of labour (*i.e.*, nine-tenths of it) to be left out in the cold then?

There's the rub; for, in short, my practical friends, the meaning of these schemes is an attempt to avoid the consequences of the class-war which commercialism is fast bringing to a point where it will break up 'modern society;' an attempt to manufacture a new class of privileged persons (though their privilege will be but a little one) in order to keep those wicked lower orders in order. My practical friends, the present strike-war, though it *is* wasteful and laden with misery, has two advantages over this twaddle. In the first place, it is the *only* way of compelling the master class to share any of the profits with the men; and in the second, it will lead to the sweeping away of profits, masters, and all – and that long before the twenty-first century.

By the way what is the matter with the *Star*? Amongst other smaller sins, mostly of omission, it indulged in a sin of commission in publishing a morceau of twaddle far out-doing the debating-club-bore of two or three years ago, for that obnoxious creature is being educated into silence now. This strange production, which was as dull as *Punch* and as fatuous as the *Times*, was called a 'translation from the

German.' Hey-day! is Berlin down to that standard then? Did the Kaiser send it to Mr. T. P. O'Connor? Or, is it perhaps a joke (a very bad one in that case) of our usually brilliant friend G. B. Shaw? Or, lastly, is the 'German' that branch of the Teutonic tongue which is current in Dublin?

On the other hand, the *Star* has had the grace to give the public some of the facts about the Hero of the Day, the Rifle-and-bible newspaper correspondent Stanley; in guarded language certainly, but still so that it cannot be misunderstood; as thus, Stanley is (perhaps) a hero; but he has done no good; killed a great many people for nothing; rescued a man who was in no danger, and didn't want to be rescued; and the reason why we are so fond of him is that we hope and believe that he is helping us Britons (who are fond of keeping curates to do the rough work) in the 'scramble for Africa,' which is disgracing the nations of Europe at present. All this is good as far as it goes, and we must congratulate the *Star* on saying it.

Commonweal, Volume 6, Number 225,
3 May 1890, p. 140.

NOTES

The Commission on the ill-treatment of the so-called dynamiters in Chatham prison has reported on the subject in the way that might have been expected from a Commission sitting on a very bad case; that is to say, that while practically admitting the charges, it said – 'Well, it doesn't matter.' The case seems to have been so plain that even the respectable *Daily News* has had its stomach turned by it, and a man of sense and humanity writing in its columns has condemned the finding of the Commission in cautious words, but very clearly. Let us say a few plain words on the subject.

The prison system of this country is, and is meant to be, a system of torture applied by Society to those whom it considers its enemies; but this fact is kept in the dark as much as possible, lest ordinary good-natured people, who do not want to torture persons unless fear drives them to it, should be shocked, and the system should be swept away – or at least altered. The ordinary middle-class man, till within the last few years, had no idea of what went on in a prison; and even now, after some light has been thrown on it by the imprisonment of 'gentlemen' both in Ireland and England, he shuts his eyes to it as much as he can. Keeping things dark is the necessary rule in a prison.

Now it is clear that no one could accept the office of habitually torturing his fellow-creatures unless he were a specially callous and degraded man, and were probably also driven to it by hard need; it follows as a matter of course that the officials of a prison must be chosen from the off-scourings of the earth. Surely the evidence of such people should be taken with great reserve by men not interested in suppressing anything.

But the ruling classes are, as we have seen, deeply interested in proving that our prison-system is reasonable and humane; and any knowledge of the real facts will dispel that idea, and show that it is a system of hideous and wanton cruelty. Can we expect, therefore, that any enquiry into the treatment of men considered as the special enemies of Society will be a fair one? It is clearly impossible that it should be, as that highly respectable paper, the *Daily News*, has found out.

I appeal to all honest and generous-minded men, whatever their opinions may be, to consider what this extra torment and insult means applied to men already tortured by the mere cast-iron system up to the limits of endurance. Surely the insulting or tormenting of a prisoner so over-burdened with misery already, so helpless as he is, is such a dastardly and abominable crime, that any crime committed by the prisoners in a jail sinks by comparison into insignificance. You men of the comfortable middle-classes, so kind and unselfish in family life, so scrupulous in business – so respectable, in a word – think of what you are doing vicariously by means of the dreadful tools you have made necessary to you! Think of it – if you dare!

Amongst this Commission of Evasion we read the names of Mr. Drummond and Mr. George Shipton. These gentlemen were, no doubt, put there because our rulers thought, or pretended to think, that they represent the working-classes. I appeal, not to Socialists, but to the working-men in general to say whether it is not about time to let the said rulers understand clearly that this humbug can be stood no longer, and that these gentlemen and others like them do not represent the working-classes, or any section of them.

Commonweal, Volume 6, Number 227,
17 May 1890, p. 157.

NOTES ON NEWS

The *Daily News* the other day had an elaborate congratu-latory article on the progress of Italy, which was once nothing at all, and is now a great nation courted and flattered by all the great powers. I do not know nor care how much the Italian bourgeois patriot likes this 'condescension' of the English ditto, but I cannot help feeling that all this glorifi-cation of the progress of the commercial class in the country (for that is what it comes to) is little better than an insult to the general humanity of Italy.

All this glory of the nation to which he has the honour to belong, what will it do for the Italian peasant, the Italian labourer, the Italian town-workman? The Lombard field-labourer driven to his toil in a gang, dying by inches of *pellagra* (in English, starvation) in the very garden of Europe, I wonder what touch of national vanity (which is what people mean by 'patriotism') his master's grinding has left in him. The town workman in whom even trades' unionism is a crime, I wonder whether he thinks that his nation has done all they can for him in driving out the Germans and leaving the capitalists to fatten on his labour?

Italy is like other 'civilised' nations, she keeps her successes, her progress, her civilisation for a class of masters. Who could venture to say that Italy has 'progressed' who thinks of the condition of those that alone make Italy, the workers, the useful part of the country? Those who write flattering articles about Italy's progress, do in truth think of nothing human in Italy except the middle-class; to them the rest are not men and women, but parts of the huge machine which grinds the masters sweet idle life. But how if the machine should one day *burst*?

Commonweal, Volume 6, Number 232,
21 June 1890, p. 192.

NOTES ON NEWS

There is, as everybody can see who wastes his time in reading the capitalist papers, a great pother going on about our bargain with Germany, as to what we, each of the two countries, consider our property. Just so, two highwaymen armed and masked (*we* are the most careful about the mask), finding themselves on the same 'lay,' look sourly on each other for a while, and then see the necessity of coming to some sort of agreement as to their action; and having come to the agreement each regrets that he has not bested his brother robber a little more; and each has friends to twit him with his folly, and enemies to inform the world in which he moves that he is a dunder-head and a dastard.

———————————

I think I have heard, or seen it written, that nations were got together and grew in order to afford mutual protection to their members. If so, it was a long time ago, and perhaps a long way off. For clearly the object for their existence now is organised robbery of the weak both within and without their own bounds; and surely this African business gives us as good an instance of the game as easily can be read of in history.

———————————

Then also, we must have Stanley's opinion of the said bargain, and, indeed, wait with trembling anxiety till he has pronounced before we go for the Salisbury government neck or nothing. The sense of relief shown by the *Daily News*, for instance, when it finds that that great and sympathetic soul does not actually condemn the transaction, is delicious to witness. Stanley has spoken and we can be happy.

———————————

Well, well! we have had several 'uncrowned kings' in my time, and Stanley, it seems, is the last of them, and may be said almost to have thrust Gladstone from his throne. One thing must be said, that his filibustering majesty keeps up the traditions of kingship pretty well. The African massacres and the hanging of unwilling 'soldiers of civilisation,' are quite in the style of the best performers in the trade. And surely the adoration of this last 'uncrowned one' shows us pretty well what would be the fate reserved for persons at home inconvenient to the commercial aristocracy, if only the latter dared. Black men in Africa were not killed because they were black, but because they were weak.

Mr. Gladstone has been spinning one of his yarns to the railway men, and began by buttering them all over, and told them how happy they were to be a part of the machinery of commerce (if they only knew their happiness); what a blessing it was for them that it was a necessity of their occupation that they were compelled to form habits of regularity and order; and how much better they were in all respects than the old servants of the mail-coach days, – which latter is probably true enough, for if ever there was a black-guardly system of travelling, surely that was the most black-guardly in all respects.

So far so good: but what reward does Mr. Gladstone propose for these treasures that he praises so much? Well, chiefly that they shall be allowed to exercise that noble virtue, *thrift*. That is, that they, by compulsion (for that is what it comes to) shall half-starve themselves and their families in order to get a very small account at a savings-bank, so that they may provide against their wholly starving. In short, these admirable public servants, as Mr. Gladstone, surely not without warrant, considers them, are to be kindly allowed to pay the poor-rate which the shareholders would otherwise have to pay.

Please to observe, meantime, that *thrift* is the art of *thriving*. If that be so, I cannot call the saving railway men thrifty, for they are but poor professors of the 'art of thriving.' They might be so much more thrifty that they could compel the shareholders, who contribute no iota toward the business of carrying passengers and goods, to hand over to them their ill-gotten gains, wrung out of the labour of these poor useful men. That would be thriving. Their present thrift, which Mr. Gladstone praises so, is not thriving, but starving; and no one starves except a madman or a slave.

Mr. Gladstone talks about the eloquence of figures. A hundred and ten hours a-week, at fifteen shillings a-week are, it seems, the wages paid to the 'cleaners.' Is there no eloquence in *those* figures then? To think that half the United Kingdom should bow down before *this* uncrowned king, Gladstone! What shall we call him? Mere invective is meaningless. Perhaps he was once a man: what he really is now is an official, whose public life is simply a constant conventional masking of facts in order to make them presentable to the office. Carlyle calls him an unconscious hypocrite. I do not know that the description can be bettered.

Commonweal, Volume 6, Number 233,
28 June 1890, p. 204.

NOTES ON NEWS

'Signor Arrigo has given particulars of his detention by the brigands. He declares that nothing can be more horrible and infamous.' Yes; quite so. What happened to the signor apart from the anxiety about his life, and his loss of liberty, was that he was ill-fed (as one is in *English* prisons at least). In other words he shared the short commons of his captors, and has at least gained this advantage from his captivity, that he has found out how the poor live. It is to be hoped he will use his knowledge in doing his best to get rid of that condition of poverty which he found to be so 'horrible and infamous.'

It is a curious thing, by the way, that even acknowledged brigandage is duly exploited, and gives a profit to the enterprising capitalist. For it seems the industrious working brigands are in the employ of gentlemen, who live on their somewhat ill-paid labour. Signor Arrigo's guard, who seems to have been a very good-natured friendly fellow, was one of these journeyman brigands, and found it as difficult 'to better himself' as most journeymen do. So commercial is the present age! So bent upon using up all waste in the process of making money! Even when that waste is no better than the lives of a few poor men.

Commonweal, Volume 6, Number, 234,
5 July 1890, p. 212.

NOTES ON NEWS

The Peace Congress has been sitting in London of late, amply reported by the capitalist press; and certainly if it were certain that it could have any influence in bringing about PEACE no one but a fool could have anything to say against it. But there are some forms of ignorance of a subject, some methods of ignoring the gist of it, that are so damaging to the cause which it is professed to further, or, which one may say, do so entirely hamper any possible action towards furthering the said cause, that is this case, as in some others, a word or two may be said as to the good intentions of the Peace Congress and its members.

War (of the bullet and bayonet kind, I mean) is a horrible thing – if you please, an insane thing; and it is good to try to get the peaceable bourgeois to realise its horrors, so that the report of battles and slaughters may mean something more to him (who, as he thinks, will never come into *that* danger) than the amusement of his breakfast table. But the good people of the Peace Congress must be told that even this violent war of modern times, and the preparation for it, is just as much a part of the present capitalist system as banking is, and can no more be dispensed with than that.

Supposing arbitration taking the place of standing armies, and those armies disbanded, what is the first obvious result? Why, the dismissal from their bread-earning occupation, however miserable and wasteful it may be, of millions of civilised men. A good thing, too, some peace-society man may say. Yes, so it would be, if society were free to accept their capacity for labour and turn it into useful channels.

But as things now are, with labour hampered by the masters of labour, who will only allow it to act when it acts for their profit, we all very well know what a disaster it would be to our present society. Not that we Socialists need fear it: for in all probability the shock to society, so-called, would be so great that it would force on the advent of real society – which is one reason, amongst others, why the disarmament will not take place.

But, indeed, does any reasonable man, thinking of the matter coolly, suppose that the capitalists, the real masters of society, will disband their army? It does not, indeed, seem to need many soldiers for the first stage of, *e.g.*, the opening up of Africa; but how about the inevitable sequel? Africa (and other *barbarous* lands) opened, can the capitalists – *i.e.*, the ruling and managing powers of that tremendous thing modern Europe – help rushing forward at any cost for the markets so opened? No more than the Huns could help overrunning the fertile lands of the Roman Empire. It would have been an errand as fruitful to have preached peace to the Huns, as to the modern capitalist. For the latter *must* have national competition as a part of his machinery; and war is the grist which that mill grinds.

But suppose for a moment that the nations of Europe agree to arbitration and disarming – and keep to the agreement, will the Governments of Europe need no soldiers then? Shall we be free to beat our Gatlings into reaping machines, and our magazine rifles into telescopes to search the moon for fools, since they will have left the earth? Alas! no. Nobody, however, little he knows of the present state of society and of the movements of labour, even dreams of a modern government, however free it may be from fear of foreign war, dispensing with an army; be that army big or little, or by whatever name it may be called.

This is strange! The Peace Society triumphant; no more wars, either for a dynasty, or an idea, or a market, and yet an army necessary? For what in the name of patience can an army be wanted in a time of deep peace? Press your innocent bourgeois a little, and he will have to answer, *To keep down the People*!

Yes, that is the blind alley which the Peace Society is aiming at. To make peace and find war going on all around them, only prevented from breaking out into its crudest form by means of the old threat – an army of most elaborately armed and carefully trained men. How can there be peace so long as the great mass of the population are *forced* into positions of misery and inferiority by a privileged few? That is the real question, and the Peace Society does no good service to the cause of peace by ignoring it. Those only are really seeking *peace* who are seeking *equality* first.

Commonweal, Volume 6, Number 237,
26 July 1890, p. 235.